CENTENNIAL BIOGRAPHY.

MEN OF MARK

OF

CUMBERLAND VALLEY, PA.

1776—1876.

ALFRED NEVIN, D. D., LL. D.

Greenville
South Carolina

This volume was repropuced from
a personal copy located in the
Publisher's private library
Greenville, South Carolina

All rights reserved. No part of this publication may be reproduced, stored in a retieval system, Transmitted in any form, posted on to the web in any form or by any means without the prior permission of the publisher.

Please direct ALL correspondence and book orders to:
www.southernhistoricalpress.com
or
**Southern Historical Press, Inc.
PO Box 1267
Greenville, SC 29602-1267**
southernhistoricalpress@gmail.com

Originally published: Philadelphia, PA 1876
ISBN #978-1-63914-040-4
All Rights Reserved
Printed in the United States of America

INDEX.

	PAGE
HISTORICAL SKETCH	1-52

AGNEW, COLONEL JAMES	241
AGNEW, REV. DR. JOHN HOLMES	353
AGNEW, SAMUEL, M. D.	270
ALLEN, WILLIAM HENRY, M. D., LL. D.	394
ALLISON, REV. DR. PATRICK	312
ARMSTRONG, GEN. JOHN, SR.	75
ARMSTRONG, GEN. JOHN, JR.	84
ARMSTRONG, JAMES, M. D.	103
AUDENREID, COL. JOSEPH CRAIN, U. S. A.	397
BOGGS, JOHN, M. D.	215
BROWNSON, REV. DR. JAMES I.	391
BUCHANAN, HON. JAMES	231
BUCHANAN, REV. JAMES	300
CATHCART, REV. DR. ROBERT	98
CRAIGHEAD, REV. THOMAS	59
CRAIGHEAD, REV. JOHN	67
CRAIN, COL. RICHARD M.	96
CRAWFORD, EDWARD	239
CRAWFORD, MAJOR GENERAL SAMUEL WYLIE	436
CRAWFORD, REV. DR. SAMUEL WYLIE	160
CRAWFORD, WILLIAM, M. D.	107
CHAMBERS, GEORGE, LL. D.	139
CHAMBERS, BENJAMIN	53
CREIGH, REV. DR. THOMAS	281
CULBERTSON, SAMUEL DUNCAN, M. D.	288
CULBERTSON, REV. MATTHEW SIMPSON	371
DAVIDSON, REV. DR. ROBERT, SR.	112
DAVIDSON, REV. DR. ROBERT, JR.	341
DENNY, REV. DAVID	133
DENNY, MAJOR EBENEZER	92
DUFFIELD, REV. DR. GEORGE	87
DUNCAN, HON. THOMAS	204
DUNLOP, JAMES	373
ELLIOTT, DAVID, D. D., LL. D.	180
ELLIOTT, COM. JESSE DUNCAN, U. S. N.	219
ELLIOTT, MAJOR GENERAL WASHINGTON L., U. S. A.	408
FINDLAY, HON. WILLIAM	151
FINLEY, GENERAL CLEMENT A.	447
FISHER, REV. DR. SAMUEL R.	350
FOSTER, ALFRED, M. D.	257
FULLERTON, HON. DAVID	217
GIBSON, HON. JOHN BANNISTER, LL. D.	135
GRAHAM, HON. JAMES HUTCHINSON	327
GRIER, HON. ROBERT COOPER	325
GUSTINE, LEMUEL, M. D.	251
HAMILTON, HON. JAMES	213
HARBAUGH, REV. DR. HENRY	383
HERRON, REV. DR. FRANCIS	114
JOHNSTON, ROBERT, M. D.	177
JUNKIN, CAPTAIN JOHN	192
JUNKIN, JOSEPH	186
JUNKIN, GEORGE, D. D., LL. D.	195
KAUFMAN, HON. DAVID SPANGLER	402
KENNEDY, REV. ROBERT	167

(iii)

INDEX.

	PAGE
KENNEDY, REV. JOHN H.	361
KENNEDY, THOMAS B.	446
KING, JOHN	178
KNOX, REV. DR. JOHN	254
KREBS, REV. DR. JOHN MICHAEL	358
LAIRD, REV. DR. FRANCIS	280
LANE, N. B., M. D.	297
LINN, REV. JOHN	276
McCARRELL, REV. DR JOSEPH	235
McCLELLAND, HON. R. M.	328
McCLURE, COLONEL ALEXANDER KELLY	410
McCONAUGHY, D., D. D., LL. D.	120
McCOSKRY, RT. REV. SAMUEL A.	451
McCULLOH, HON. THOMAS GRUBB	310
McCULLOUGH, REV. DR. JOHN W.	320
McELROY, REV. DR. JOSEPH	209
McGILL, ALEXANDER TAGGART, D. D., LL. D	345
McGINLEY, REV. DR. AMOS A.	205
McKIBBIN, GENERAL D. B.	443
McKINLEY, REV. DR. DANIEL	330
McKNIGHT, REV. DR. JOHN	274
McLANAHAN, HON. JAMES X.	386
McPHERSON, HON. EDWARD	380
MOODEY, REV. JOHN	131
MOORE, REV. DR. THOMAS VERNER	375
NEVIN, MAJOR DAVID	284
NEVIN, JOHN WILLIAMSON, D. D., LL. D.	293
NISBET, REV. DR. CHARLES	108
PENROSE, HON. CHARLES BINGHAM	323
PENROSE, RICHARD ALEXANDER F., M. D., LL. D.	413
PENROSE, COL. WILLIAM McFUNN	449
POMEROY, JOSEPH	314
POMEROY, MAJOR JOHN M	418
RANKIN, WILLIAM, M. D.	333
RANKIN, DAVID NEVIN, M. D.	378
RAUCH, REV. DR. FREDERICK AUGUSTUS	338
REED, HON. JOHN, LL. D.	268
RICHARDS, JOHN CUSTIS, M. D.	404
RITNER, HON. JOSEPH	155
SANDERSON, HON. GEORGE	389
SCHNECK, REV. DR. BENJAMIN SHRODER	343
SCOTT, COLONEL THOMAS A.	369
SENSENY, A. H., M. D.	420
STEWART, JOHN	401
SHARP, REV. DR. ALEXANDER	229
SMITH, FREDERICK	278
SNODGRASS, WILLIAM T.	452
SNOWDEN, ISAAC WAYNE, M. D.	441
SNOWDEN, JAMES ROSS, LL. D.	356
SPEER, REV. WILLIAM	202
STEEL, REV. JOHN	71
STEVENS, HON. THADDEUS	302
THOMPSON, REV. SAMUEL	62
THOMSON, HON. ALEXANDER, LL. D.	422
THOMSON, WILLIAM, M. D.	428
THOMSON, FRANK	432
WATTS, DAVID	94
WATTS, HON. FREDERICK	307
WATTS, HON. HENRY M.	315
WEIR, JAMES WALLACE	347
WILKINS, HON. WILLIAM	106
WILLIAMS, REV. DR JOSHUA	136
WILSON, REV. DR. HENRY R.	164
WILLIAMSON, HUGH, M. D, F. R. S.	80
WING, REV. DR. CONWAY PHELPS	366
WHITEHILL, ROBERT	65
WOODS, REV. DR. JAMES S.	261
WOODS, RICHARD	335
WOODS, DAVID FLAVEL, M. D	416
YOUNG, REV. DR. JOHN CLARKE	206

PREFACE.

IN placing this work before the public, the author needs not to be told of its imperfections. Any one, however, attempting the same task, would in all probability find equal reason for confession of defectiveness. Much of the volume consists of material drawn from the distant and unwritten past, and there are few things of more difficult and delicate execution, than to get access to such material in its floating shape, and present it in an accurate and attractive form. All that can reasonably be expected is, that he who enters upon such an undertaking, will do the best he can in the circumstances, and this the author is quite sure can be affirmed of *his* effort.

His inability to embrace in the book a much larger number of biographical sketches has occasioned him sincere regret. No district of our broad, beautiful, and blessed country has furnished more representative men—men distinguished for their ability, integrity and influence—than Cumberland Valley. Such, and such only, has he aimed, or been willing, to put on record, and it would have been a real gratification to include many more of them than are embraced in this work, had not the limited space precluded such possibility, and made a necessity even for laying aside some sketches that had been prepared, and were justly entitled to publication. And the disappointment growing out of this desired gratification is intensified by the fact that some, eminently worthy of notice, and whom he would gladly have welcomed to these pages, would not consent to occupy a place in them either for themselves or friends, from motives of indifference or delicacy, which, though of course entitled to respect, are none the less to be deplored in the result to which they have led.

It was the author's design to have the sketches inserted, if possible, in chronological order, but this could not be done on account of the irregularity with which they came into his possession. Their length was not in every case under his control, and where brevity was observed, a compensation in directness and comprehensiveness was aimed at. In view of the ancient boundaries of the region, and its connection with contiguous districts by ecclesiastical and political arrangements, several persons are sketched who were not, or are not, citizens of the valley. Special acknowledgment of aid in preparing the book, is gratefully made to S. G. Lane, M. D., A. Brady Sharp, Esq., S. R. Fisher, D. D., C. P. Wing, D. D., J. R. Snowden, LL. D., and Hon. Edward McPherson. The "Historical Sketch" was written with much care, and will, it is hoped, in correctness and completeness, be found convenient for reference. Should the present edition of fifteen hundred copies of the work prove insufficient for the demand, a second may possibly be issued.

The author has felt compelled to decline the complimentary request of several distinguished, but too partial friends, that a sketch of himself, which they would prepare, should have a place in his book. As, however, most persons wish to know something of one who stands thus related to the volume which they read, the following brief statement may be admissible: He was born in Shippensburg, of a parentage elsewhere noticed in this work. At a very early age he graduated at Jefferson College. In 1837, he received the degree of L. B. from the Law School of Dickinson College, and was admitted to the bar of Carlisle. After three years' study at the Western Theological Seminary, he was licensed by the Presbytery of Carlisle, in 1840, to preach the Gospel. His first charge was "The Grove Church," Lancaster county. During this pastorate, (in 1841,) he married Sarah, youngest daughter of the Hon. Robert Jenkins, of Windsor Place, in the county just named, eminent as an iron master, and for a term or two Representative of his district in Congress. Subsequently he preached in Chambersburg for seven years, in Lancaster city for five years, and then removed to Philadelphia, where he established the Alexander Presbyterian Church, which he served for several years. Retiring from this pulpit, he entered upon the career of editing and authorship. He originated, and, until impaired health demanded temporary respite from labour, edited the "Presbyterian Standard," and, afterward, the "Presbyterian Weekly." The principal books from his pen are, "The Christian's Rest," "Spiritual Progression," "Churches of the Valley," "Guide to the Oracles," "Words of Comfort," "Notes on Exodus," "The Age Question; or, a Plea for Christian Union," "The Voice of God," and "Popular Commentary on the Gospels and Acts."

In the preparation of the work now sent forth at the close of an eventful century, the author has found great delight, as historiographer, in dealing with the honored living and the lamented dead of his native valley, to which he is attached by so many strong and tender ties. And he now yields the book to the friends of those whose names it has drawn from the past, or shall transmit to the future, with an earnest desire that it may impart corresponding interest to *them*, as well as stimulate the coming generations of Old Cumberland to an emulation of the sterling virtues of those who have so worthily preceded them in the grand and solemn march of life.

PHILADELPHIA, *January 1st*, 1876.

HISTORICAL SKETCH.

THE Province of Pennsylvania owes its name to an honourable recognition of official merit. It was so called by Charles II, in honour of *Sir William Penn*, an eminent Admiral of the English Navy, who, at his death, left claims of considerable amount against the Crown for his services. The following letter, in reference to this event, from William Penn, son of the distinguished naval officer to whom this high compliment was paid, and founder of the Province, is not without historic interest. We give it in its original form, with the exception of a few orthographical corrections.

5th of 1st Mo., 1681.

To Robert Turner.

DEAR FRIEND :

My true love in the Lord salutes thee, and dear friends that love the Lord's precious truth in those parts. Thine I have, and for my business here, know that after many waitings, watchings, solicitings and disputes in council, this day my country has confirmed to me under the great seal of England, with large powers and privileges, by the name of PENNSYLVANIA, *a name the king would give it in honour of my father. I chose* NEW WALES, *being, as this, a pretty hilly country, but* PENN *being Welsh for a* HEAD, *as* PENMANMOIRE *in Wales, and* PENRITH *in Cumberland, and* PENN *in* BUCKINGHAMSHIRE, *the highest land in England, called this* PENNSYLVANIA, *which is the high or head woodlands, for I proposed when the Secretary—a Welshman—refused to have it called New Wales, Sylvania, and they added* PENN *to it, and though I much opposed it, and went to the king to have it struck out and altered, he said 'twas past, and would take it upon him, nor could twenty guineas move the under secretaries to vary the name, for I feared lest it should be looked on as a vanity in me, and not as a respect in the king, as it truly was to my father, whom he often mentioned with praise. Thou mayest communicate my grant to friends, and expect shortly my proposals : 'tis a clear and just thing, and my God that has given it me through many difficulties will, I believe, bless and make it the seed of a nation. I shall have a tender care to the government, that it will be well laid at first: no more now, but dear love in truth.*

Thy true friend,

W. PENN.

CHARTER CONFIRMED.

The charter of the grant here mentioned, was in due time confirmed by the royal proclamation. The assent of the Duke of York, then the proprietor of all "New Netherlands," (as the lower part of the Province had been called,) and that of Lord Baltimore, whose possessions joined on the south, had been obtained to the provisions of the charter, and Lord North, then Lord Chief Justice, was careful to add several clauses in favor of the king's prerogative, and the parliament's right of taxation. The extent of the Province was three degrees of latitude in breadth, by five degrees of longitude in length, the eastern boundary being the Delaware river, the northern "the beginning of the three and fortieth degree of northern latitude, and on the south a circle drawn at twelve miles distance from New Castle, northward and westward unto the beginning of the fortieth degree of northern latitude, and then by a straight line westward to the limits of longitude above mentioned." Emanuel Bowman, who was Geographer to his Majesty, King of England, says in his "Geography," which was printed at London, 1747,—" The Province contained all that tract of land in America, with all the islands belonging to it, from the beginning of the fortieth to the forty-third degree of north latitude, whose eastern bounds, from twelve miles above New Castle, otherwise Delaware town, run all along upon the side of the Delaware river—these bounds and extent were set down in the original grant, but Mr. Penn having afterwards obtained part of *Nova Belgia* from the Duke of York, it was added to the country given in the *first* grant, so that it extends now to the thirty-eighth degree and fifty-five minutes north latitude." Penn at once saw the importance of having the title and jurisdiction of the three lower counties (Delaware), which constituted, as it were, a vestibule to his Province, and hence the wisdom of his policy in obtaining a grant of them from the Duke, "together with all the royalties and jurisdictions thereunto belonging."

Soon after the charter was obtained for the tract of land in the new world, the proprietor published "certain conditions or concessions" to adventurers, drew up a form of government, and a code of laws, all bearing the stamp of his benevolent mind, and sent forward his kinsman, William Markham, with three ships and a number of planters, to take possession of the country, and prepare for the reception of a larger number of colonists. Many persons, principally Quakers, were induced to emigrate. An association was formed at London and Bristol, the "Free Society of Traders," who purchased lands, with a view both to agricultural settlement and for the establishment of manufactories, and for carrying on the lumber trade and whale fisheries.

Arrival of Penn.

Having carefully adjusted his preliminary plans, Penn took an affectionate leave of his family and friends, and sailed for Pennsylvania, in the ship Welcome, on the 30th August, 1682. Near a hundred colonists accompanied him, many of whom died of small-pox during the voyage. At length, after a long passage, the gallant ship anchored at New Castle, and the eager colonists, of every nation, tongue and people—English, Dutch, Swedes—hastened to welcome the beloved proprietor. He addressed the magistrates and people, setting forth his designs, and assured them of his intentions to maintain their spiritual and temporal rights, liberty of conscience, and civil freedom. At Upland, (now Chester,) he convened the Assembly, and made known his plans and benevolent designs. The Assembly tendered their grateful acknowledgments. The Swedes deputed Lacy Cock to inform him that "they would love, serve and obey him, with all they had," declaring "it was the best day they ever saw." At this Assembly, which continued only three days, an Act of Union was passed, annexing the three lower counties to the Province. The frame of government, with some alterations, was accepted and confirmed, the laws agreed upon in England, with some changes, were passed in form, and the Dutch, Swedes and other foreigners, were received to the privileges of citizenship. Penn had been careful, on sending out his deputy, Markham, to enjoin upon him and his colonists to deal amicably with the Indians, and soon after his own arrival he held the memorable interview with the native chiefs under the great elm at Shackamaxon, now Kensington. No authentic record has been preserved of this treaty, yet there is every reason to believe that its object was not the purchase of lands, but the establishment of a lasting covenant of love and friendship between the aborigines and Penn. "Under the shelter of the forest," says Bancroft, "now leafless by the frosts of Autumn, Penn proclaimed to the men of the Algonquin race, from both banks of the Delaware, from the borders of the Schuylkill, and, it may have been, even from the Susquehanna, the same simple message of peace and love which George Fox had professed before Cromwell, and Mary Fisher had borne to the Grand Turk. The English and the Indian should respect the same moral law, should be alike secure in their pursuits and possessions, and adjust every difference by a peaceful tribunal, composed of an equal number of men from each race." The intercourse of Penn with the Indians was ever, indeed, marked by the strictest justice, and by a most commendable generosity. He *might*, on the world's maxim that "might makes right," have asserted a claim to the soil granted him by the charter he had received. Nor would it then have much damaged his character if he had done so, for a principle had obtained in Europe, that a newly discovered country belonged to the nation whose people first discovered it. Eugene IV, and Alexander VI, successively granted to Portugal and Spain all the countries possessed by infidels, which should be occupied by the industry of their subjects, and subdued by the force of their arms. But the noble Quaker was influenced by "the higher law." As has been remarked, with an eloquence equal to that of the author just quoted, "he was influenced by a purer morality, and sounder policy, than that *prevailing principle* which actuated the more sordid. His religious principle did not permit him to wrest the soil of Pennsylvania by force from the people to whom God and nature gave it, nor to establish his title in blood, but under the shade of the lofty trees of the forest, his right was fixed by treaties with the natives, and sanctified, as it were, by smoking from the calumet of peace."*

IMMIGRATION INCREASING.

As the advantages offered to settlers by the Province of Pennsylvania became more and more known, emigrants from other countries in ever growing numbers were attracted. "It was recommended by its free and constitutional government—by the character of its fundamental laws, adopted and established by the first emigrants to its territory—its fertile soil, salubrious and temperate climate—its adaptation to a large and rural population, with advantages for trade, commerce and manufactures. The dissatisfaction prevailing with large classes of intelligent, industrious and enterprising men, under several of the European governments, directed their attention to the American colonies, and by men of this character Pennsylvania was more generally preferred for their abode, after the organization of its government."†

It does not admit of question, however, that the speedy and large increase of population within the limits of the Province, is mainly to be attributed to the religious toleration which was secured to the colony, by its charter and fundamental enactments.

> "What sought they thus afar?
> Bright jewels of the mine?
> The wealth of seas, the spoils of war?
> They sought a faith's pure shrine
> Ay, call it holy ground,
> The soil where first they trod!
> They have left unstained what there they found—
> Freedom to worship God."

---

* Smith's Laws of Pennsylvania, ii, 105.
† "A Tribute to the Principles, Virtues, Habits and Public Usefulness of the Irish and Scotch Early Settlers of Pennsylvania; by the Hon. George Chambers," from which we have derived important aid in writing this article.

The persecution of the Quakers and other religious denominations, during the reign of Charles II, and especially during that of his successor, the intolerance exercised by the Papists over the Protestants of Europe, and the overbearing or persecuting spirit, on religious accounts, in many of the other colonies, as contrasted with the liberality of the Quakers of Pennsylvania, who were disposed to open their arms to all denominations of professing Christians who might be inclined to settle among them, induced the flocking of men by tens, by hundreds, and by thousands, to a place where man pretended not to assume the prerogatives of Deity, nor judge, condemn, and punish in His stead.

Scotch Irish.

Of those who migrated hither from the north of Ireland, the greater number, or their ancestors, had formerly removed from Scotland. But they were treated, after a short residence in Ireland, with much ingratitude and neglect, and hence they sought refuge in America. The Earls of Tyrone and Tyrconnel, in the Province of Ulster, having conspired against the government in the reign of James the First, fled from the kingdom to escape punishment. Some of their accomplices were arrested, condemned and executed, but the two Earls were attainted by a process of outlawry, upon which their vast estates, about five hundred thousand acres of land, escheated to the crown. King James resolved, if possible, to improve a country that was covered by woods, desolated by war, infested by robbers, or inhabited by ignorant adherents to the Romish Church. For this purpose he divided the escheated lands into small tracts, and those he gave to adventurers, who were to settle them within four years, with a certain number of sub-tenants. According to his advice, the preference was given, in distributing the lands, to adventurers from the west of Scotland. They were Protestants from his own country. They were industrious people, and the passage being very short, they might, with the greater ease, settle the lands according to their contracts. The establishment of prelacy in Scotland, in the year 1637, and afterwards in the year 1661, among people who had adopted the more simple form of Presbyterian worship, became the additional cause of numerous emigrations from that kingdom to the North of Ireland.

The superior knowledge, industry, and temperance of the Scotch farmers, in a short time enabled them to supplant the natives among whom they lived, and six of the northern counties, by the end of the seventeenth century, were chiefly inhabited by the descendants of Scottish emigrants, or the remains of Cromwell's army. That Protestant colony has been the chief support of government against all attempts to establish a Catholic prince, by treason, insurrection, or murder. Those men have been the steady and active supporters of the Hanover succession. Their faithful services, and uniform attachment to government, had placed them in the rank of good and faithful subjects, and their unshaken loyalty had entitled them to confidence and public favour. But they were treated like aliens and strangers, with marks of distrust in their civil capacity, and they were depressed in their religious capacity, by the spirit of intolerance, because they were not of the established church of Ireland. Men who were thus degraded and vexed by incapacities and burdens, migrated in thousands to Pennsylvania, in which they knew the principles of civil and religious liberty had their full operation. Their first settlements were in Bucks county, but chiefly in the territory which, in 1729, was organized into the county of Lancaster. Settlements were made in it about 1717, on Octorara creek, and about the same time, or earlier, in Pequea, and in 1722 in Donegal and Paxton. About 1737, quite a number of these emigrants located themselves in the northwestern part of York county, on the water of Tom's and Marsh creek, (now Adams county.)

ENGLISH.

"In England, ever since the memorable St. Bartholomew's day, all eyes had been anxiously directed to the Trans-Atlantic settlements, notwithstanding they were as yet a wilderness, and while some fled to Holland, a great number, together with many of the ejected ministers, betook themselves to New England, Pennsylvania, and other American plantations. In Scotland, fines, imprisonments, and whippings, were abundant from 1662, when the Act of Conformity was passed, until 1688, when the Act of Toleration gave relief under the Presbyterian Prince of Orange. The Western and Southern counties, which, according to Hume, were the most populous and thriving, were the most obnoxious, and the severity of the persecutions surpassed, in the judgment of Bishop Burnet, the merciless rigours of the Duke of Alva. Many sold their estates and crossed over to the Scots of Ulster, where, for a time, unrestricted liberty was allowed. But the arm of intolerance soon followed them to this retreat, and the hunted-down non-conformists felt that they had no resource short of absolute expatriation. In order that the fury of the prelates might have full sweep, the Presbyterians and their ejected ministers were forbidden to fly into Scotland to avoid it. Of these ejected ministers, both in Scotland and Ireland, Wodrow gives a catalogue amounting to four hundred."*

CLASSES OF IMMIGRANTS.

In consequence of the persecutions of 1679, 1682 and 1685, crowds of voluntary exiles sought an asylum in East New Jersey, Pennsylvania, Carolina and Maryland.

Prominent among those who fled to this land for conscience's sake, were the Huguenots, or French Protestants. The persecutions to which they were exposed during the reign of Louis XIV, consummated by the revocation of the edict of Nantes, in 1685, drove hundreds of thousands of those unhappy people from their native country. Though the frontiers were vigilantly guarded, upwards of five hundred thousand of them made their escape. They fled to Switzerland, Germany, Holland and England, and large numbers of them came to this country, many of whom settled in Pennsylvania, chiefly on Pequea Creek, near Paradise, Lancaster county.

The Welsh, also, from their numbers, deserve particular notice. The principal settlement of them at an early period, was upon the left bank of the Schuylkill. They there occupied three townships, and in a few years their numbers so increased that they obtained three additional townships. Subsequently many of them settled in various parts of the Province. They were characterized by energy, integrity and perseverance.

Nor must the German settlers in Pennsylvania, by any means be overlooked in this enumeration. Their immigration commenced as early as 1682 or 1683, and very rapidly increased. The Mennonists or German Baptists, a sect which adhered to the principle of non-resistance, persecuted in Europe, and driven from one country to another, sought the toleration of Penn's colony, and immigrated between the years 1698 and 1717, settling in Lancaster, Berks, and the upper parts of Chester county. The Dunkards, also a non-resistant sect, began to immigrate about the year 1718, and subsequently established a sort of monastery and convent at Ephrata, in Lancaster county.

In 1719, Jonathan Dickinson, who held the important offices of Chief Justice of the Province, Speaker of the Assembly, and Member of Council, remarks: "We are daily expecting ships from London which bring over Palatines, in number about six or seven thousand. We had a parcel who came out about five years ago, who purchased land about sixty miles west of Philadelphia, and prove quiet and industrious."

---

*History of the Presbyterian Church in the State of Kentucky, by the Rev. Robert Davidson, D.D.

From 1730 to 1740, about sixty-five vessels, well filled with Germans, arrived at Philadelphia, bringing with them ministers of the Gospel and schoolmasters to instruct their children. A large number of these remained in Philadelphia, others went seventy to eighty miles from that city—some settled in the neighbourhood of Lebanon, others west of the Susquehanna, in York county. From 1740 to 1755, upwards of one hundred vessels arrived, which were filled with emigrants of the same nation, and in some of which, though small, there were between five and six hundred passengers. With regard to the Germans in Pennsylvania, Mr. Andrews, in a letter dated October 14, 1730, says: "There is, besides, in this Province a vast number of Palatines, and they come in still every year. Those that have come of late are mostly Presbyterian, or, as they call themselves, Reformed, the Palatinate being about three-fifths of that sort of people." "There are many Lutherans and some Reformed mixed among them. In other parts of the country, they are chiefly Reformed, so that I suppose the Presbyterian party are as numerous as the Quakers, or near it."

Such, then, were the materials out of which the original population of the Province of Pennsylvania was constituted. As our necessarily brief sketch indicates, they were not homogeneous, but were diversified by their origin, religious principles, habits, and language. Yet notwithstanding these divergences, they were one in spirit, actuated by a common impulse, and controlled by a similar ambition. They were united in devotion to the principles of the Reformation, and in favour of civil and religious liberty. Equality of rights, and the liberty of worship according to the dictates of conscience, were standard principles which had won their steadfast adherence, and which they were not willing any party or power should dare to assail. That they were not free from faults, is not to be denied. This was to be expected. The circumstances in which they were thrown together in a new world, the difference of the reigning spirit of the several localities from which they migrated, the influence of early education, the necessity for combating the untried exigencies of pioneer life, and the difficulties always incident to the mutual adjustment of masses of people in a new territory, as well as to the framing of wise and just laws for self-government,—all these considerations made an antecedent probability that the new social and civil systems would not be inaugurated and established without a development of some of the errors and evils which it is so difficult for lapsed human nature to avert or avoid. But, over and above these imperfections, those men had in general, a character challenging our highest admiration, who first took possession of our noble territory, when it was a vast, dense and solitary wilderness—the hut of the savage and the dwelling of the beasts of prey—felled its forests, cleared its streams, fenced its plains, decorated its hill-tops with humble yet happy homes, churches and school-houses, framed its salutary legislation, and proclaimed the principles which have made it the abode of civilization and the home of an intelligent, enterprising, moral and religious community. They were, as a body, men of independence and integrity of character, exemplary morals and a deep reverence for the institutions of religion.

Character of Immigrants.

The author of the work already referred to, thus alludes to the three classes—the English, the Scots and Irish, and the Germans, into which the first settlers of Pennsylvania by reason of their diversity were divided, a division which was maintained for some generations, and is not even yet effaced :

"The associates and followers of Penn, who were amongst the first to establish the government of the Province, were an honest, intelligent, virtuous, peaceful and benevo-

lent population, known in England and the colonies by the name of Friends or Quakers."
.... "The Germans were a hardy, frugal and industrious people, and in many districts have preserved their foreign manners and language. They have established in every part of the State, communities much respected for religious and moral character, many of them emigrated for conscience's sake, and others to improve their condition and circumstances. Their industry and frugality have enabled them to add greatly to their own wealth and resources, whilst they were increasing that of the Province and State. With most of this class, education has been promoted, and their descendants, in acquirements and intelligence, are in advance of their ancestors, and many are amongst the most respectable and useful citizens of the Commonwealth, whilst they have, by branches of their families, contributed greatly to the industrious and useful population of several of the Western States.' ...... "From their conscientious scruples against bearing arms, the Mennonists did not enter the army to fight the battles of the country but when Independence was acknowledged, and a new government organized and established, they were obedient in all things to its requisitions. They have ever been in Pennsylvania a peaceable, industrious and moral community, paying their taxes regularly; avoiding strife, and living in peace with all men with whom they had intercourse. They never allow the poor members of their society to be a public charge, but support them in the society." ...... "The Scotch and Irish settlers of Pennsylvania are men who laid broad and deep the foundations of a great Province, and who, with a master's hand, erected a structure of government that was stable, capacious and elevated, whose prosperity and greatness command admiration, and which, by public accord, constitutes the great keystone of the political arch of the American Union. The men who were instrumental in this structure of government, with its free institutions of religious and civil liberty, were more than ordinary men, to hold the plough and handle the axe, or ply the shuttle. They had other qualities, we would infer from their works, than enterprise, energy, bravery and patriotism, and they were not surpassed, for lofty virtue and consistent piety."

Penn's Purchase of Lands.

Soon after William Penn's arrival in the Province, the date of which has been already noticed, and before his return to England, in 1684, he resolved "to purchase the lands on the Susquehanna from the Five Nations, who pretended a right to them, having conquered the people formerly settled there." For this purpose, being too busy to give his personal attention to the matter, he engaged Governor Dongan, of New York, where the Five Nations chiefly quartered, to buy from them, "all that tract of land lying on both sides of the river Susquehanna, and the lakes adjacent in or near the Province of Pennsylvania." Dongan effected a purchase, and conveyed the property to Penn, January 13th, 1696, "in consideration of one hundred pounds sterling."

How careful the wise Quaker was to have this purchase well confirmed, appears from the following document which stands among the early records of the Province:—

"September 13th, 1700, *Widagh* and *Andaggy-junk-quagh*, Kings or Sachems of the Susquehannagh Indians, and of the river under that name, and lands lying on both sides thereof. Deed to W. Penn for all the said river Susquehannagh, and all the islands therein, and all the lands situate, lying and being upon both sides of the said river, and *next adjoining the same*, to the utmost confines of the lands *which are*, or formerly *were*, the right of the people or nation called the Susquehannagh Indians, or *by what name soever they were called*, as fully and amply as we or any of our ancestors have, could, might or ought to have had, held or enjoyed, and also *confirm* the bargain and sale of the said lands, made unto Colonel Thomas Dongan, now Earl of Limerick, and formerly Governor of New York, *whose deed of sale* to said Governor Penn we have seen."

Penn in Council with the Five Nations.

In April, 1701, Penn met in council the chiefs of the Five Nations with those from the Susquehanna and the Potomac, and the Shawnese chiefs, and after going through the solemn forms of Indian diplomacy, covenanted that there should be "forever a firm and lasting peace continued between William Penn, his heirs and successors, and all the English and other Christian inhabitants of the province, and the said kings and chiefs, &c., and that they shall forever hereafter be as one head and one heart, and live in true friendship and amity as one people.' At this treaty, regulations were adopted to govern their trade, and mutual enforcement of penal laws, and former purchases of land were confirmed. Especially was there a necessity for a confirmation of the sale just referred to as having been made in September of the preceding year. The Conestoga Indians, it seems, would not recognize the validity of this sale, believing that the Five Nations had no proper authority to transfer their possessions. In consequence of this difficulty, Penn entered into articles of agreement with the Susquehanna, Potomac and Conestoga Indians, by which they ratified and confirmed both Governor Dongan's deed of 1696, and the deed by *Widagh* and *Andaggy-junk-quagh*, of 1700.

In October, 1736, a purchase was made by the Proprietaries, from the Six Nations, calling themselves Aquanuschioni, *i. e.* the United People, of all the lands west of the Susquehanna " to the setting sun," and south of the *Tayamentasachta* hills, as the Kittochtinny or Blue Mountain was called by the Six Nations. " Their Sachems or chiefs," says Mr. Rupp,* "were appointed with plenary powers to repair to Philadelphia, and there, among other things, settle and adjust all demands and claims connected with the Susquehanna and the adjoining lands. On their arrival at that city, they renewed old treaties of friendship, and on the 11th of the month just mentioned, made a deed to John Penn, Thomas Penn and Richard Penn, their heirs, successors, and assigns. The deed was signed by twenty-three Indian chiefs of the *Onondaga, Seneca, Oneida* and *Tuscarora* nations, and granted to the Penns "all the said river Susquehanna, with the lands lying on both sides thereof, to extend eastward as far as the heads of the branches or springs which run into the said Susquehanna, and all the lands lying on the west side of the said river to the setting sun, and to extend from the mouth of the said river, northward, up the same to the hills or mountains called in the language of said nations *Tayamentasachta*, and by the Delaware Indians the *Kekachtannin* hills." In July, 1754, at Albany, the proprietors purchased of the Six Nations all the land within the State, not previously purchased, lying southwest of a line beginning one mile above the mouth of Penn's creek, and running northwest by west "to the western boundary of the State."

Emigration Westward.

As the eastern part of Pennsylvania gradually increased in population, the tide of migration rolled westward. In 1729, the upper parts of Chester county were constituted a separate county called "Lancaster county," which then, and till 1749, embraced York, Cumberland, part of Berks, and all the contiguous counties, as it did also Dauphin till March 4th, 1785. The first permanent and extensive settlement made near the

---

* *History and Topography of Dauphin, Cumberland, Franklin, Bedford, Adams and Perry Counties, by I. D. Rupp,*—to which we here make a general acknowledgment of obligation for assistance in the preparation of this sketch.

Susquehanna, was commenced by some Swiss immigrants. They were persecuted Mennonists, who had fled from the Cantons of Zurich, Bern, Schaffhausen in Switzerland, to Alsace, above Strasburg, where they had remained some time before they immigrated to America. This they did in 1707 or 1708, choosing for their location the western part of Chester, now Lancaster county, near Pequea creek. Before 1720, settlements had been extended northward beyond the Chickasalunga creek. Donegal township, organized in 1722, had been principally settled by Irish, or Scotch immigrants.

JOHN HARRIS.

Settlements were now made northward, and along the Susquehanna river. John Harris, a native of Yorkshire, England, had made an attempt, prior to 1725, to settle near the mouth of Conoy creek, not far from the present site of Bainbridge, but it seems he preferred to settle higher up the Susquehanna, near an Indian village called Peixtan, at or near the present site of Harrisburg. Harris was in a few years followed by others, principally emigrants direct from the north of Ireland. "About the time of the settlement of this pioneer at (Peixtan) Harrisburg," says his great-grand-son, George Washington Harris, Esq., "Indian towns were existing near to Squire Wills' stone house, (in Cumberland county,) opposite Harrisburg, and at the mouth of the Conodoguinett and Yellow Breeches creeks. There had been one on the low ground on the river, about the lower line of Harrisburg, and another at the mouth of Paxton creek. These two are supposed to have been abandoned at the time of making his settlement. The Indians, who resided in this neighborhood, were of the *Six Nations*, and, it said, that at one time, by firing a gun, six or seven hundred warriors could be assembled at the present site of Harrisburg."*

KITTOCHTINNY VALLEY.

The valley of the Susquehanna, opposite Harris' Ferry, was called by the Indians Kittochtinny valley, from the extensive mountain range constituting its western boundary, "Kittochtinny" signifying "endless mountains." That part of the valley west of the Susquehanna, embraced what now constitutes the county of Cumberland, and almost all the county of Franklin. For fertility of soil, abundance of copious springs, clear running streams, variety of forest timber, luxuriance of vegetation and salubrity of climate, presenting as a boundary on two sides mountain ranges, with a wide valley, made up of hills, plains and dales, it was not surpassed by any of the American colonies. Yet, attractive as it was, its settlement was retarded from being a frontier remote from the eastern settlement, the Indian claim to which was not purchased by the Proprietary of Pennsylvania, until October, 1736. A great part of it was in controversy with the Proprietary of Maryland, who claimed the same as belonging to that Province. The purchase just mentioned, being made; and the Maryland controversy being at the same time suspended, by agreement of the Proprietaries of the two Provinces, the Land Office of Pennsylvania was opened in January, 1737, for the sale and appro-

---

* Article in "Napey's Harrisburg Business Directory." In the same article the following interesting incident is related: "On one occasion, a band of Indians, who had been down the river, or, as is said, to the East, on a trading excursion, came to the house of John Harris. Some, or most of them, were intoxicated. They asked for *lum*, meaning West India Rum, as the modern whiskey was not then manufactured in Pennsylvania. Seeing they were already intoxicated, he feared mischief if he gave them more, and he refused. They became enraged and seized and tied him to the mulberry tree to burn him. Whilst they were proceeding to execute their purpose he was released, after a struggle, by other Indians of the neighborhood, who generally came across the river. How the alarm was given to them, whether by firing a gun or otherwise, or by whom, is not now certainly known. In remembrance of this event, he afterwards directed that, on his death, he should be buried under the mulberry tree which had been the scene of this adventure. He died about the year 1748, and was buried where he had directed—under the shade of his own memorable tree, and there his remains still repose, with those of some of his children."

priation of lands *west* of the Susquehanna on the usual terms. The applications for warrants, and the influx of settlers, were now great into this valley. As early as 1730-31, some resolute and enterprising citizens were induced by the Proprietary Agents of Pennsylvania to make settlements in this district, under the authority of the State, in order to assert and maintain its claims and jurisdiction, but only at and after the opening of the Land Office for the sale of lands in the Kittochtinny valley did settlers rush into it. Their number in 1740 reached several thousands; in 1749 the number of taxables was 807, and in 1751 it had increased to 1134.

Organization and Settlement of Cumberland County.

Before the organization of the county of Cumberland, this part of the Kittochtinny Valley was called by the whites "the North Valley," to distinguish it, as is supposed, from the extension of the same valley in Virginia, south of the Potomac River. Afterwards, it very generally received the name of the "Cumberland Valley," taking its name from the county, of which it was a small part. Cumberland county was organized January 27th, 1750. Up to this date it belonged to Lancaster county, which was established in 1729, and then included the whole country west of the boundary of the State. The inhabitants of the North Valley, by a petition to the Assembly, represented the great hardships they endured by reason of their remoteness from Lancaster, where the courts were held and the public offices kept, how difficult it was for the "sober and quiet part" of the valley to protect themselves from theft and other abuses, frequently committed by idle and dissolute persons, who, to escape punishment, resorted to the more remote parts of the Province, and owing to the great distance from the place of trial and imprisonment, frequently escaped, and the result of this application was an enactment,—"That all and singular the lands lying within the Province of Pennsylvania to the westward of Susquehanna, and northward and westward of the county of York, be erected into a county to be called *Cumberland*, bounded northward and westward with the line of the Province, eastward partly with the river Susquehanna, and partly with the said county of York, and southward in part by the line dividing the said Province from that of Maryland. Cumberland county was named after a maritime county of England, on the borders of Scotland. It is scarcely necessary to say, that its extensive limits have been gradually reduced by the formation of other counties.

The Valley Divided.

In 1735, by the order and appointment of the Court, the valley was divided into two townships, by a line crossing the valley at the "Great Spring," now Newville, the eastern one called "Pennsborough," and the western one, "Hopewell," and a Justice of the Peace and a Constable were appointed for each. In 1741, the township of Antrim was established, embracing the Conococheague settlement and what now constitutes the county of Franklin, with a Justice of the Peace and Constable for it.

When Cumberland county was erected, Robert McCoy, Benjamin Chambers, David Magaw, James McIntire and John McCormick were appointed commissioners to select the site for a court-house. Shippensburg was selected as a temporary seat of justice. After Carlisle had been laid out, *it* was chosen permanently in 1751 for this purpose.*

---

* Mr. Conynham says—"Messrs. Lyon and Armstrong were elected by the proprietaries to lay out a town on the road from Harris' Ferry, leading through the rich valley of Cumberland, including the old stockade and blockhouse, and extending over the big spring called Le Tort, (now Letort,) after James Le Tort, a French Swiss, who acted as Indian interpreter and messenger to government, and who had erected a cabin at its source as early as the year 1735. Carlisle was laid out in pursuance of their directions in 1750." This stream rises in South Middleton township, from a large fountain as its source, gives motion to several mills, passes through the borough of Carlisle, and empties into the Conodoguinett two miles northeast of the borough.

The Orphans' Court, during the years 1750 and 1751, seems to have followed the judges. At one time it was held at "William Anderson's," another time at "Antrim," sometimes at "Shippensburg," and then again at "Peterstown," ("Peters Township.") The removal of the Court of Common Pleas and the Criminal Court from Shippensburg to Carlisle, produced great dissatisfaction among the people of Conococheague, which was then quite a populous settlement, and complaint was made to the Assembly. In their petition for a redress of their grievances, they affirmed their full persuasion that the continuance of Shippensburg would have quieted the whole county, though it was *northeast* of the centre. They also alleged that it would always impoverish them to carry and expend their money at the extremity of the county, whence it would never circulate back again, that neither the interest of the proprietaries nor the prosperity of the town of Carlisle would be advanced by changing the seat of justice, and that no good wagon road could be made across the North Mountain "until beyond Shippensburg, up the valley." The citizens of the eastern end denied the statements of the Conococheague men, and the courts remained at Letort's Spring, where it was for the proprietary interest that they should be.

Interesting Letters.

Gov. Hamilton, in his letter of instructions, April 1, 1751, "to Nicholas Scull, Surveyor-General, which will serve likewise for Mr. Cookson," states that he had been led to select the site of Carlisle on account of there being, among other advantages "about it, a wholesome dry limestone soil, good air, and abundance of vacant land, well covered with a variety of wood." He also charged his agents, in selecting the site, "to take into consideration the following matters, viz:—the health of the citizens, the goodness and plenty of water, with the easiest method of coming at it; its commodiousness to the great road leading from Harris' Ferry to the Potowmac,* and to other necessary roads, as well into the neighbouring county as over the passes in the Blue Mountains."

In May, 1753, John O'Neal, who had been sent to Carlisle by Governor Hamilton, for the purpose of repairing the fortifications, thus wrote:

"The garrison here consists only of twelve men. The stockade originally occupied two acres of ground square, with a blockhouse in each corner; these buildings are now in ruin. Carlisle has been recently laid out, and is the established seat of justice. It is the general opinion that a number of log cabins will be erected during the ensuing Summer on speculation, in which some accommodation can be had for the new levies. The number of dwelling houses is five. The court is at present held in a temporary log building, on the northeast corner of the centre square. If the lots were clear of the brushwood, it would give a different aspect to the town. The situation, however, is handsome, in the centre of a valley, with a mountain bounding it on the north and south at a distance of seven miles. The wood consists principally of oak and hickory. The limestone will be of great advantage to the future settlers, being in abundance. A limekiln stands on the centre square, near what is called the deep quarry, from which is obtained good building stone. A large stream of water runs about two miles from the village, which may at a future period be rendered navigable. . . . . The Indian wigwams, in the vicinity of the Great Beaver Pond, are to me an object of particular curiosity."

Curious Stockade.

In the same year, 1753, another stockade of very curious construction was erected, whose western gate was in High street, between Hanover and Pitt streets, opposite lot

---
* Laid out by order of the court at Lancaster, in 1736.

100. This fortification was thus constructed: Oak logs about seventeen feet in length were set upright in a ditch dug to the depth of four feet. Each log was about twelve inches in diameter. In the interior were platforms made of clapboards, and raised four or five feet from the ground. Upon these the men stood and fired through loopholes. At each corner was a swivel gun, which was occasionally fired " to let the Indians know that such kind of guns were within."* Three wells were sunk within the line of the fortress, one of which was on lot 125, another on the line between lots 109 and 117, and the third on the line between lots 124 and 116. This last was for many years known as the "King's Well." Within this fort, called "Fort Louther," women and children from Green Spring and the country around often sought protection from the tomahawk of the savage. Its force, in 1755, consisted of fifty men, and that of Fort Franklin, at Shippensburg, of the same number. At a somewhat later day, or perhaps about the same time, breastworks were erected a little northeast of the town—as it was then limited—by Col. Stanwix, some remains of which existed until within a comparatively recent date.†

BARBAROUS MURDER AT CARLISLE.

The town of Carlisle, in 1760, says Mr. Day, was made the scene of a barbarous murder. Doctor John, a friendly Indian of the Delaware tribe, was massacred, together with his wife and two children. Capt. Callender, who was one of the inquest, was sent for by the Assembly, and, after interrogating him on the subject, they offered a reward of one hundred pounds for the apprehension of each person concerned in the murder. The excitement occasioned by the assassination of Dr. John's family was immense, for it was feared that the Indians might seek to avenge the murder on the settlers. About noonday, on the 4th of July, 1763, one of a party of horsemen, who were seen rapidly riding through the town, stopped a moment to quench his thirst, and communicated the information that Presqu'isle, Le Beuf, and Venango had been captured by the French and Indians. The greatest alarm spread among the citizens of the town and neighboring country. The roads were crowded in a little while with women and children hastening to Lancaster for safety. The pastor of the Episcopal church headed his congregation, encouraging them on the way. Some retired to the breastworks. Col. Bouquet, in a letter addressed to the Governor, dated the day previous, at Carlisle, urged the propriety of the people of York assisting in building the posts here, and "sowing the harvest," as *their* county was protected by Cumberland.

CONDITIONS OF PEACE.

The terror of the citizens subsided but little, until Col. Bouquet conquered the Indians in the following year, 1764, and compelled them to sue for peace. One of the conditions on which peace was granted was, that the Indians should deliver up all the women and children whom they had taken into captivity. Among them were many who had been seized when very young, and had grown up to womanhood in the wigwam of the savage. They had contracted the wild habits of their captors, learned their language and forgotten their own, and were bound to them by ties of the strongest affection. Many a mother found a lost child; many were unable to designate their children. The separation between the Indians and their prisoners was heart-rending. The hardy son of the forest shed torrents of tears, and every captive left the wigwam with reluctance. Some afterwards made their escape and returned to the Indians. Many had intermarried with the natives, but all were left to freedom of choice, and

---

* Haz. Reg. iv, 390. † Char., &c., of Carlisle.

CARLISLE.

those who remained unmarried had been treated with delicacy. One female, who had been captured at the age of fourteen, had become the wife of an Indian and the mother of several children. When informed that she was about to be delivered to her parents, her grief could not be alleviated. "Can I," said she, "enter my parents' dwelling? Will they be kind to my children? Will my old companions associate with the wife of an Indian chief? And my husband, who has been so kind—I will not desert him!" That night she fled from the camp to her husband and children.

THRILLING INCIDENT.

A great number of the restored prisoners were brought to Carlisle, and Col. Bouquet advertised for those who had lost children to come there and look for them. Among those that came was an old woman, whose child, a little girl, had been taken from her several years before, but she was unable to designate her daughter or converse with the released captives. With breaking heart the old woman lamented to Col. Bouquet her hapless lot, telling him how she used many years ago to sing to her little daughter a hymn of which the child was so fond. She was requested by the Colonel to sing it then, which she did in these words:

> "Alone, yet not alone am I,
> Though in this solitude so drear;
> I feel my Saviour always nigh,
> He comes my every hour to cheer,"

and the long-lost daughter rushed into the arms of her mother.

CARLISLE A RENDEZVOUS.

Quietude being secured to the citizens by the termination of the Indian war, they directed their attention to the improvement of their village and the cultivation of the soil. No important public event disturbed them in their peaceful occupations, until the disputes which preceded the war of the Revolution arose between the colonies and the mother country. During this war Carlisle was made an important place of rendezvous for the American troops, and, in consequence of being located at a distance from the theatre of war, British prisoners were frequently sent thither for secure confinement.* Of these were two officers, Major Andre and Lieutenant Despard, who had been taken by Montgomery near Lake Champlain. While here, in 1776, they occupied the stone house on lot number 161, at the corner of South Hanover street and Locust alley, and were on parole of honour of six miles, but were prohibited going out of the town except in military dress.

AN UNFLINCHING WHIG.

In the immediate neighborhood lived Mrs. Ramsey, an unflinching Whig, who detected two Tories in conversation with these officers, and immediately made known the circumstance to William Brown, Esq., one of the County Committee. The Tories, being pursued, were arrested somewhere between the town and South Mountain, brought back, tried *instanter*, and imprisoned. Upon their persons were discovered letters written in French, but no one could be found to interpret them, and their contents were never known.

After this occurrence, Andre and Despard were not allowed to leave the town. They had in their possession fowling pieces of superior workmanship, with which they had been in the habit of pursuing game within the limits of their parole, but now, being

---

* The *United States Barracks*, located about half a mile from the town, but within the borough limits, were built in 1777. The workmen employed were Hessians captured at Trenton.

unable to use them, they broke them to pieces, declaring that "no d———d rebel should ever burn powder in them." During their confinement here, a man by the name of Thompson enlisted a company of militia in what is now Perry county, and marched them to Carlisle. Eager to make a display of his own bravery and that of his recruits, he drew up his soldiers at night in front of the house of Andre and his companion, and swore lustily that he would have their lives, because, as he alleged, the Americans who were prisoners of war in the hands of the British, were dying by starvation. Through the importance, however, of Mrs. Ramsey, *Captain* Thompson, who had formerly been an apprentice to her husband, was made to desist, and, as he countermarched his company, with a menacing nod of the head he bellowed to the objects of his wrath, "You may thank my old mistress for your lives."

Bribe Refused.

On the following morning, Mrs. Ramsey received from the British officers a very polite note, expressing their gratitude to her for saving them from the hacking sword of the redoubtable Captain Thompson. They were afterwards removed to York, and before their departure, sent to Mrs. Ramsey a box of spermaceti candles, with a note requesting her acceptance of the donation, as an acknowledgment of her many acts of kindness. The present was declined, Mrs. Ramsey averring that she was too staunch a Whig to accept a gratuity from a British officer. Despard was executed at London in 1803, for high treason. With the fate of the unfortunate Andre every one is familiar.

Relief for the Distressed.

In 1763 there were many refugees, from the most western parts of the Province, in Carlisle, driven thither by distress arising from Indian hostilities. The Congregations of Christ's Church, and St. Peter's Church, Philadelphia, both Episcopal, raised the sum of £662 for the relief of these frontier inhabitants. The Rev. William Thompson, an itinerant Episcopal minister for the counties of York and Lancaster, in a letter from Carlisle, August 24th, acknowledging this generous act, wrote as follows:

"We find the number of the distressed to be seven hundred and fifty families, who have abandoned their plantations; many have lost their crops, and some their stock and furniture, and besides these we are informed that about two hundred women and children are coming down from Fort Pitt. The unhappy sufferers are dispersed through every part of this county, and many have passed into York. In this town and neighbourhood, there are upwards of two hundred families, and having the affliction of the small-pox and flux to a great degree."

The first tax upon the citizens of Carlisle, of which we have any account, as appears from the charter of the town, was laid in December, 1752, and amounted to £25 9s. 6d.

Col. John Armstrong.

Prominent among the citizens of Carlisle at this time, was Col. John Armstrong. He was of Irish nativity, and a man of intelligence, integrity, and high moral and religious character. He was resolute and brave, and, through living habitually in the fear of the Lord, he feared not the face of man. The corporation of Philadelphia thus testified their esteem for this valiant and brave soldier:

Col. John Armstrong.

Sir:—The Corporation of the City of Philadelphia greatly approve of your conduct and public spirit in the late expedition against the town of Kittanning, and are highly pleased with the signal proofs of courage and personal bravery given by you, and the officers under your command, in demolishing of that place

I am therefore ordered to return you and them the thanks of the Board for the eminent service you have thereby done your country. I am also ordered by the Corporation to present you, out of their small public stock, with a piece of plate and silver medal, and each of your officers with a medal and a small sum of money to be disposed of in the manner most agreeable to them; which the Board desire you will accept as a testimony of the regard they have for your merit.

Signed by order,

January 5th, 1757. ATWOOD SHUTE, *Mayor*.

Col. Armstrong was, in 1776, appointed by the American Congress, a General of its Revolutionary Army, on the recommendation of Washington, who had served with him in Forbes' Campaign in 1758, and knew his qualifications. He served his country with ability and fidelity in the trying struggle for American Independence.

CHURCHES.

About the year 1736, the Presbyterians erected a log church on the Conodoguinett creek, about two miles north of Carlisle, or West Pennsborough, as it was then called, at a place known ever since as the "Meeting-House Spring." No vestige of this building now remains, nor are there any of the oldest residents of the neighbourhood who are able to give anything like a satisfactory account of it. The first pastor of this Church—the Rev. Samuel Thompson, from Ireland—was ordained and installed November 14th, 1739. It seems probable, however, that for some time previously to Mr. Thompson's settlement, the Rev. Messrs. Craighead and Caven had laboured there in the character of stated supplies.

Shortly after Carlisle was laid out, a Presbyterian congregation was organized in it, and a church was built. In relation to this movement, Col. Armstrong, who was an Elder of the church, wrote to Richard Peters, as follows :—

"CARLISLE, *June 30th*, 1757.

"To-morrow we begin to haul stones for the building of a meeting-house, on the north side of the square;—there was no other convenient place. I have avoided the place you once pitched for a church. The stones are raised out of Col. Stanwix's entrenchments: we will want help in this political as well as religious work."

About the year 1760, a license was obtained from Governor Hamilton, authorizing the congregation to raise, by lottery, a small sum of money to enable them to build a decent house for the worship of God, and in 1766, the minister and others petitioned the Assembly, for the passage of an Act to compel the "managers to settle," and the "adventurers to pay," "the settlement of the lottery having been for a considerable time deferred," by reason of the "confusion occasioned by the Indian wars." The Act prayed for was passed. The method of raising money by lottery, for church purposes or any other, was not, of course, at that time regarded as it is now.

The Rev. Geo. Duffield, D. D., was installed Pastor of the church in Carlisle, in 1761. A short time afterward, the congregation in the country, then under the care of the Rev. Mr. Steele, constructed a two-story house of worship in town, and, some time before the Revolution, erected the present "First Presbyterian Church," on the northwest corner of the Centre Square,"* which, however, has since been several times

---

* It should here be stated, that the Presbyterian Church at Silvers' Spring, (so called from the fact that the land around the stream near which the church edifice stands, was originally owned by Mr. Silvers, one of the first settlers in that region of the county,) had an early existence. The congregation was first known as "the people over the Susquehanna." Afterwards (1736) as connected with the congregation at Carlisle, it was known as the "Lower Settlement of Conodoguinnett." Still later we find it designated "Lower Pennsborough." The Gospel was first preached here by Rev. Alexander Craighead, by appointment of Presbytery, in 1734. For several following years the church was supplied occasionally by the Rev. Messrs. Bartram,

remodeled and repaired. The two congregations differed somewhat in doctrinal views, and were called the "Old Lights," and "New Lights," in virtue of a division which then prevailed throughout the Synod. "The house in which Mr. Duffield's congregation worshipped," says Dr. Wing, "was situated on the east side of Hanover street, nearly opposite the place where the Second Presbyterian Church now stands. Soon after Mr. Duffield's removal to the Third Church of Philadelphia (1772,) this building took fire and was entirely consumed. During the confusion incident to the War of the American Revolution, neither congregation appears to have flourished, and soon after the death of Mr. Steele, (August, 1779,) both congregations worshipped alternately in the stone church, which had now been completed by Mr. Duffield's former people finishing off and occupying the gallery." After the removal of Dr. Duffield to Philadelphia, and the death of Mr. Steele, the two congregations united, and called, in 1785, the Rev. Robert Davidson, D. D., who was an eminent scholar and divine. The following year the congregation, thus united, was incorporated. Dr. Davidson was removed by death, December 13th, 1812. In connection with him, and as his colleague, the Rev. Henry R. Wilson, D. D., preached some time to the congregation, whilst Professor in Dickinson College. In 1816, the Rev. George Duffield, a licentiate of the Presbytery of Philadelphia, and grandson of Dr. Duffield above referred to, was called to the pastorate of this church. Dr. Duffield resigned the charge in 1835. The congregation was subsequently served by the Rev. Messrs. Granger and Burrowes, as supplies, and the Rev. Messrs. W. T. Sprole and E. J. Newlin as pastors, until the Rev. Dr. Wing assumed the pastorate, which he still continues to fill.

The "Second Presbyterian Church of Carlisle," was organized in the town hall in 1833. Rev. Daniel McKinley, D. D., was its pastor from 1833 till 1838, the Rev. Alexander T. McGill, D. D., from 1839 till 1841, the Rev. T. V. Moore, D. D., from 1842 till 1845. The succeeding pastors were the Rev. James Lillie, the Rev. Mervine E. Johnson, the Rev. Dr. Eells, and the Rev. John C. Bliss, who yielded the pulpit to the Rev. George Norcross, by whom it is still occupied.

EPISCOPALIANS.

In 1765, the Episcopalians of Carlisle also secured the passage of an Act by the Assembly, authorizing them to raise by lottery a sufficient sum to complete a church "in part erected," but whether they availed themselves of it, does not appear. The edifice then built stood near the same spot—the northeast corner of the public square—on which the present church, St. John's, is located. The itinerant missionary already referred to, in the interest of the Episcopal Church, for the counties of York and Cumberland, was maintained by the "Society for the Propagation of the Gospel in Foreign Parts," for several years after these counties were founded. This office was held by him as late as 1776.

GERMAN REFORMED AND LUTHERAN.

The German Reformed and Evangelical Lutheran churches, in Carlisle, both incorporated in 1811, were organized about 1765, the latter under the pastoral care of the Rev. Mr. Butler. They worshipped on alternate Sabbaths in the same church, which

---

Thomas Craighead, Golston, and Thompson, the last of whom became pastor in 1739. Mr. T. resigned on account of "bodily weakness" in 1745, and was succeeded in the pastorate, in the same year, by the Rev. Samuel Caven. In 1764 the Rev. John Steel served the congregation in connection with the church at Carlisle. In 1782 the Rev. Samuel Waugh was installed over the church. In 1808 the Rev. John Hayes became successor of Mr. Waugh. The church was subsequently under the pastoral care of Rev. Henry R. Wilson, D. D., the Rev. James Williamson, the Rev. George Morris, and others. The present church edifice was erected in 1783.

stood on the lot then used as the German Reformed burying ground, opposite to Dickinson College, until 1807, when each congregation erected a house of worship for its own use. This lot having been sold for a Preparatory School for the college, another German Reformed church was built in 1827, at the corner of High and Pitt streets, which was subsequently sold to the Methodists, and then, in 1835, the building was erected in Louther street which is now occupied. The Lutherans also erected a handsome structure.

METHODIST.

Soon after the Revolution Methodist ministers commenced their labours in Carlisle, worshiping first in the market-place, then in the Court House, and subsequently in a small frame building in Pomfret street, in which last place they formed a class of about twelve members, in 1792 or 1793. Their number, increasing, a few years afterwards they built a small stone house in Pitt street, in which they worshiped a short time, and then erected a brick edifice in Church alley. Having sold this in 1835, they purchased from the German Reformed congregation the stone church on the corner of Pitt and High streets.

ROMAN CATHOLIC.

The Catholic chapel was erected in 1807, and enlarged in 1823. The lot was at an early day owned by the Jesuits of Conewago, who had upon it a small log church, in which the Catholic congregation worshiped until the present one was built.

ASSOCIATE PRESBYTERIAN.

The Associate Presbyterian congregation of Carlisle was organized in 1798. The lot on West street, upon which the church is built, was conveyed, in consideration of £6, by the Messrs. Penn, in 1796, to "Wm. Blair, Wm. Moore, John Smith, and John McCoy, Trustees of the Associate Presbyterian congregation, adhering to the subordination of the Associate Presbytery of Pennsylvania, of which the Rev. John Marshall and James Clarkson" were then members. The building was put up in 1802, and the Rev. Francis Pringle, their first pastor, called the same year.

EVIDENCE OF PROGRESS.

The following extract from a letter written by Thomas S. Craighead, Junior, of White Hill, Cumberland county, and dated December 16th, 1845, will strike every one with interest, who is acquainted with the present prosperous condition of Cumberland valley, as indicating the vast progress which has marked the last thirty years of its development :

"I saw the first mail stage that passed through Carlisle to Pittsburg. It was a great wonder—the people said the proprietor was a great fool; I think his name was Slough. I happened a short time ago to visit a friend, Jacob Ritner, son of that great and good man, Ex-Gov. Ritner, who now owns Captain Denny's farm who was killed during the Revolutionary War. The house had been a tavern, and in repairing it Mr. Ritner found some books, &c., which are a curiosity. Charge,—breakfast, £20, dinner, horse feed, £30. Some charges still more extravagant, but we know it was paid with Congress money. The poor soldier on his return, had poor money, but the rich boon, liberty, was a price to him far more valuable. So late as 1808, I hauled some materials to Oliver Evans' saw mill at Pittsburg. I was astonished to see a mill going without water. Mr. Evans satisfied my curiosity, by showing and explaining everything he could to me. He looked earnestly at me and said, you may live to see your wagons coming out here by steam. The words were so impressed that I have always remembered them. I have lived to see them go through

Cumberland county, and it seems to me, that I may see them go through to Pittsburg, but I have seen Mr. Evans' prophecy fulfilled beyond what I thought possible at the time, but things have progressed at a rate much faster than the most gigantic minds imagined, and we are onward still."

Washington's Visit.

In 1794, several thousand troops were assembled in Carlisle, on their way to quell the "Whiskey Insurrection." On the first of October, the Governor of the State arrived at Carlisle, and in the evening delivered an animated address in the Presbyterian church. On Saturday, the fourth, George Washington, President of the United States, accompanied by Secretary Hamilton, and his private Secretary, Mr. Dandridge, and a large company of soldiers, besides a great mass of yeomanry and many members of the House of Representatives, arrived. A line was formed, composed of cavalry, with sixteen pieces of cannon, with the infantry from the various parts of Pennsylvania, amounting in the whole to near three thousand men. The Court House was illuminated in the evening, and a transparency exhibited with this inscription in front: "Washington is ever triumphant," on the one side, and on the other side, "The reign of the Laws—Woe to arnarchists."

The following letter was presented by a number of the principal citizens to the Father of his Country:

To George Washington, Esq., President of the United States.

Sir:—We, the subscribers, inhabitants of this borough, on behalf of ourselves and fellow citizens, friends to good order, government and the laws, approach you at this time, to express our sincere admiration of those virtues which have been uniformly exerted, with so much success, for the happiness of America; and which, at this critical period of impending foreign and domestic troubles, have been manifested with distinguished lustre.

Though we deplore the cause which has collected in this borough all classes of virtuous citizens, yet it affords us the most heartfelt satisfaction to meet the Father of our Country, and brethren in arms, distinguished for their patriotism, their love of order, and attachment to the constitution and laws; and while on the one hand we regret the occasion which has brought from their homes men of all situations who have made sacrifices, unequaled in any other country, of their private interests to the public good, yet we are consoled by the consideration, that the citizens of the United States have evinced to our enemies abroad and the foes of our happy constitution at home, that they not only have the will, but possess the power, to repel all foreign invaders, and to crush all domestic traitors.

The history of the world affords us too many instances of the destruction of free governments by factious and unprincipled men. Yet the present insurrection and opposition to government is exceeded by none, either for its causeless origin, or for the extreme malignity and wickedness with which it has been executed.

The unexampled clemency of our councils in their endeavours to bring to a sense of duty the western insurgents, and the ungrateful returns which have been made by that deluded people, have united all good men in one common effort to restore order and obedience to the laws, and to punish those who have neglected to avail themselves of, and have spurned at, the most tender and humane offers that have ever been made to rebels and traitors.

We have viewed with pain the great industry, art, and misrepresentations which have been practiced to delude our fellow citizens. We trust that the effort of the general government, the combination of the good and virtuous against the vicious and factious, will cover with confusion the malevolent disturbers of the public peace, and afford to the well disposed the certainty of protection to their persons and property.

The sword of justice, in the hands of our beloved President, can only be considered as an object of terror by the wicked, and will be looked up to by the good and virtuous as their safeguard and protection.

We bless that Providence which has preserved a life so valuable through so many important scenes—and we pray that He will continue to direct and prosper the measures adopted by you for the security of our internal peace and stability of our government; and that after a life of continued usefulness and glory, you may be rewarded with eternal felicity.

To this Gen. Washington thus replied:

GENTLEMEN:

I thank you sincerely for your affectionate address. I feel as I ought, what is personal to me, and I cannot but be particularly pleased with the enlightened and patriotic attachment which is manifested towards our happy constitution and the laws.

When we look around and behold the universally acknowledged prosperity which blesses every part of the United States, facts no less unequivocal than those which are the lamented occasion of our present meeting were necessary to persuade us that any portion of our fellow citizens could be so deficient in discernment or virtue, as to attempt to disturb a situation which, instead of murmurs and tumults, calls for our warmest gratitude to Heaven, and our earnest endeavours to preserve and prolong so favoured a lot.

Let us hope that the delusion cannot be lasting; that reason will speedily regain her empire, and the laws their just authority, where they have lost it. Let the wise and virtuous unite their efforts to reclaim the misguided, and to detect and defeat the arts of the factious. The union of good men is a basis on which the security of our internal peace and stability of our government may safely rest. It will always prove an adequate rampart against the vicious and disorderly.

If in any case in which it may be indispensable to raise the sword of justice against obstinate offenders, I shall deprecate the necessity of deviating from a favourite aim, to establish the authority of the laws in the affections of all, rather than in the fears of any.

GEORGE WASHINGTON.

DICKINSON COLLEGE.

The inhabitants of Cumberland county, immediately after the Revolutionary war, showing their appreciation of a high grade for the education of young men in science, literature and theology, turned their attention to the establishment of a college within their bounds. They did not wait to repair the losses and sacrifices to which they had subjected themselves, by a military service in distant places, during the protracted war for American Independence, before they would provide for elevated education. They were ready to act at once in the matter, and this at a time when the government of the state, as well as that of the Confederation, was embarrassed with war debts, want of financial resources, and a confederation of independent states that was deficient in effective provisions, and in strength was little better than a rope of sand. The people were also called upon to meet heavy taxation, for local, state and national purposes, with little or no currency of value, and with very limited resources. Yet the spirit that animated with energy and resolution the men who had encountered the wilderness, defended the frontiers of the colony against the savages and their French allies, and given themselves up to the defence of their country against royal despotism and parliamentary usurpation, induced them to give their energies and perseverance, recruited by a short period of peace, to provide for education by an institution that would be worthy of public confidence and respect. Measures were taken to collect funds for it, and in 1783, a charter was obtained from the Legislature, by which the Institution was located at Carlisle, and called Dickinson College, in commemoration of John Dickinson, President of the Supreme Executive Council of the State, who had been liberal in his donation to it. This Institution has graduated many young men of celebrity as lawyers, jurists, statesmen and divines, in this and other states. The Faculty was first organized in 1784, by the election of the Rev. Charles Nisbet, D. D., of Montrose, Scotland, as President, and the appointment of Mr. James Ross, as Professor of Languages, to whom were added in the following year, the Rev. Robert Davidson, D. D., as Professor of Belles-Lettres, and Mr. Robert Johnston, Instructor in Mathematics. In 1798, the spot now occupied by the college buildings, between High and Louther streets and west of West street, was selected, and the first edifice erected and ready for use in 1802. The edifice was destroyed by fire in 1804, but the trustees proceeded to erect another, which was completed in September, 1805, and is now known as the west college. Before the completion of this building, the college sustained a heavy loss in the death of Dr. Nisbet, which occurred on the 14th of February, 1804. The office of President was exercised *pro tempore* by Dr Davidson, until, in 1809, the Rev. Jeremiah Atwater, D. D , was elected to fill the vacancy. The Institution was prosperous under his direction, and the class of 1812 was the largest that had graduated for twenty years. In 1815, President Atwater resigned, and the following year the operations of the college were suspended, and were not renewed till 1821. In that year, the Rev. John M. Mason, D. D., was called to preside over the Institution, and during the first part of his adminstration there was a considerable influx of students ; but previously to his resignation, which took place May 1st, 1824, the college began to decline, and continued to languish, except for brief intervals, while under the presidency of Drs. Neill and Howe, until 1832, when the trustees determined that the operations of the Institution should cease. This result was, in a great measure, attributable to the want of attention and interest on the part of its trustees, and to dissensions prevailing with that portion of them living in the vicinity, to whom, as is usual with literary and religious institutions, its management was chiefly committed.

In 1833, the control of the college was transferred to the Baltimore, Philadelphia and New Jersey Annual Conferences of the Methodist Episcopal Church, by the resignation, from time to time, of some of the trustees, and by the election of others, named by the said Conferences, in their stead, until finally a complete change was effected in the management of the Institution. By this change the college took a fresh start, and the organization of the Faculty was commenced by the election of the Rev. John P. Durbin, D. D., as President, and the establishment of a Law Department under the charge of John Reed, LL. D., the President Judge of the District. The other members of the first Faculty were Merritt Caldwell, A. M., and Robert Emory, D. D.

NEWVILLE.

Newville was incorporated February 26th, 1817. About two miles from this borough, in 1830, Mr. William Denning, who is here entitled to special mention, departed this life at his residence, in the 94th year of his age. " The deceased," says *Hazard*,* " was an artificer in the army of the Revolution. He it was who, in the days of his country's need, made the *only successful attempt ever made in the world* to manufacture *wrought iron cannon,* two of which he completed at Middlesex in this county, and commenced another and larger one at Mount Holly, but could get no one to assist him who could stand the heat, which is said to have been so great as to *melt the buttons on his clothes.* This unfinished piece it is said, lies as he left it, at either Holly Forge or the Carlisle Barracks. One of those completed was taken by the British at the battle of Brandywine, and is now in the Tower of London. The British government offered a large sum, and a stated annuity, to the person who would instruct them in the manufacture of that article, but the patriotic blacksmith preferred obscurity and poverty in his own beloved country, to wealth and affluence in that of her oppressors, although that country for which he did so much kept her purse closed from the veteran soldier till near the close of his long life, and it often required the *whole weight* of his well-known character for honesty, to save him from the *severest* pangs of poverty. When such characters are neglected by a rich grovernment, it is no wonder that some folks think Republics ungrateful."

BIG SPRING CONGREGATION.

Of the Big Spring congregation, (Presbyterian,) or Hopewell, as it was then called,

---

* Register, Vol. 7.

SHIPPENSBURG

the Rev. Thomas Craighead was the first pastor. He was called in 1737, installed in October, 1738, and died in June of the ensuing year. In relation to him, one of his lineal descendants, Thomas Craighead, Jr., then living at White Hill, Cumberland county, thus wrote, under date of December 16th, 1845, to Mr. Rupp:

"At Big Spring, protracted meetings were held for public worship. So powerful, it is said, were the influences of the Spirit, that the worshipers felt loath, even after having exhausted their stores of provisions, to disperse. I have heard it from the lips of those present, when Thomas Craighead delivered one of the parting discourses, that his flow of eloquence seemed supernatural,—he continued in bursts of eloquence while his audience was melted to tears, himself, however, exhausted, hurried to pronounce the blessing, waving his hand, and as he pronounced the words, 'farewell, farewell!' he sank down, and expired without a groan or struggle. His remains rest where the church now stands, the only monument of his memory."

After Mr. Craighead's demise, Mr. James Lyon, of Ireland, supplied the pulpit at Hopewell for some months. After his term of service had expired, Big Spring was connected with Rocky Spring and Middle Spring, as a charge, under an arrangement "that the minister's labours be equally divided in a third part to each place, as being most for the glory of God and good of His people." The next point at which it is possible to write with any confidence of the regular occupancy of this pulpit is 1759. In that year the Rev. George Duffield was installed over Carlisle and Big Spring. The Rev. William Linn was Mr. Duffield's successor over the latter church when it became a separate charge. He resigned the pastorate in 1784. Mr. Linn was succeeded by the Rev. Samuel Wilson, who continued with the church until he was removed by death, in March, 1799. The call which he received to take charge of the church is still in the possession of his descendants, in which the congregation promises to Mr. Wilson "the sum of one hundred and fifty pounds, Pennsylvania currency, in specie, and to allow him the use of the dwelling-house, barn, and all the clear land on the glebe, possessed by their former minister, also plenty of timber for rails and fire-wood, likewise a sufficient security for the payment of the above mentioned sums during his incumbency." The Rev. Joshua Williams, D. D., was called to Big Spring church in 1802, and resigned the pastorate about 1829. His successors have been, the Rev. Robert McCachren, who was pastor until 1851, the Rev. Mr. Henderson, the Rev. Mr. Maury, and the Rev. E. Erskine, D. D. The earliest elders of Big Spring, now known, were John Carson, John McKeehan, John Bell, David Ralston, Sr., Thomas Jacobs, Alexander Thompson, William Lindsay, and Atcheson Laughlin.

Progress of the Place.

It is with Newville now, as with other localities in Cumberland valley—in gazing upon it the mind is filled with amazement at the mighty change which has taken place. The time is almost within the memory of some who live, when the dark shadows of the gloomy forest fell upon all that region, and the savage Indian roamed over the surrounding hills and valleys, but now the eye is there called to survey a large and prosperous town, with admirable schools and handsome churches, the circumjacent country highly cultivated, and densely inhabited with a moral and religious population, the whistle of the rushing rail-car having taken the place of the war-whoop,* as travelers are borne along with rapid speed, and the quiet magnetic wires annihilating both time and space with the electric celerity of their communications.

Middle Spring.

The Presbyterian church at Middle Spring, about two miles north of Shippensburg,

---

* The Cumberland Valley Railroad was incorporated in 1834.

came into existence about the year 1740. In 1738, a place of worship was erected, which was a log building, near the gate of the "Lower Graveyard," about thirty-five feet square. Soon this edifice, in which, for a while there was preaching only four or five times a year, was found to be too small to accommodate the people, and it was demolished, and another of the same material erected on the same spot. This was considerably larger, being about fifty-eight feet long and forty-eight feet wide. In a little while it became necessary again that the house of worship should have its capacity extended, and this desideratum was effected by removing three sides of the building then in use, and embracing a little more space on either side, which was covered with a roof, something in the form of a shed. Up the sides of these additions to the main edifice, and over the roofs, were fixed wooden steps, by which access was gained into the gallery. This arrangement was made for want of room in the interior of the building for the construction of a stairway. About the year 1781, the old stone church was erected, whose site, as many yet living well remember, was beside that of the present building. This was still larger than its predecessor (being fifty-eight by sixty-eight feet), and was necessarily so, by reason of the rapid increase of population. About the same time that this church was built, and which, for its day, was one of more than ordinary elegance, the graveyard, immediately in its rear, was located. The present building at Middle Spring was erected in 1848.

Trials before Session.

The subjoined extracts from the Session-Book of this church, will serve to show the spirit of the times :

"1744. The Session condemn D. S.'s manner of expressing himself, as being very untender to his neighbour's character, and appoint the Moderator to occasion to warn their people against speaking abroad slanderous reports upon neighbours, either privately, or more publicly in company, and more especially when they have no solid grounds for, or knowledge of them, as being very inconscientious, discovering a willingness or disposition to take up an ill report, a breach of the ninth commandment, in backbiting their neighbour, wounding to religion, having a tendency to fill the minds of people with jealousies, and thereby exposing church judicatories oftentimes to reflections, as tho' they covered sin, when upon tryal they can't find guilt."

"1746. J. P. was cited to the Session for taking venison from an Indian, and giving him meal and butter for it on the Sabbath day. J. P. appeared and acknowledged that being at home one Sabbath day, he heard a gun go off twice quickly after each other, and said he would go out and see what it was, his wife dissuading him, he said he would go and see if he could hear the Horse-bell: having gone a little way he saw an Indian, who had just killed a fawn and dressed it: the Indian coming towards the house with him to get some victuals, having, he said, eat nothing that morning, he saw a deer, and shot it, and charged and shot again at another, which ran away. Said P. stood by the Indian until he skin'd the deer; when he had done he told said P. he might take it in if he wou'd, for he would take no more with him; upon which said P. and W. K., who then had come to them, took it up, and carry'd it in; when he had given the Indian his breakfast, said Indian ask'd if he had any meal, he said he had, and gave him some; then the Indian ask'd for butter, and asking his wife about it, he gave the Indian some; but he denies that he gave these things as a reward for the venison, inasmuch as they had made no bargain about it.

"The Session judge that J. P. do acknowledge his breach of Sabbath in this matter, and be rebuk'd before the Session for his sin."

The Rev. Mr. Calls, of Ireland, and the Rev. Mr. Clarke, of Scotland, served the congregation of Middle Spring, each of them about six months or a year. They were succeeded by the Rev. Mr. Blair, of the duration of whose pastorate we are not able to write. Nothing definite is known of the supply of the pulpit until 1765, when the Rev. Robert Cooper was chosen overseer of the flock. Dr. Cooper continued in the pastoral relation until 1797. The Rev. John Moodey succeeded Dr. Cooper in 1803 and continued in office about fifty years. The pastors of the church, since his resignation, have been the Rev. Messrs. Hays, Richardson, and Wylie.

SHIPPENSBURG.

This borough, called after its original proprietor, Edward Shippen, and the oldest town, except York, in Pennsylvania, was incorporated January 21st, 1819. During the French and Indian wars, two forts, Fort Morris and Fort Franklin, were erected there, the remains of one of which were, until within a few years, still to be seen. Some idea of the size and condition of the place, about a century and a quarter since, may be derived from the subjoined extracts from a letter dated June 14th, 1755, to Governor Morris, from Charles Swaine, who was then on a visit to the place on public business:

"I judge there are sufficient buildings for storing the provisions without erecting any."

"I find not above two pastures here, those but mean as to grass, from drought, but there is a fine range of forage for upwards of four miles in the woods, quite to the foot of the South mountain."

The present prosperous condition of the town contrasts pleasantly with its feeble beginning. In it, in its early history, many of the frontier settlers in their flight for life from the Indians, took refuge. "In July, 1763," says *Gordon*,* "there were here, one thousand three hundred and eighty-four of these poor, distressed inhabitants. Of these, three hundred and one were male adults, three hundred and forty-five women, and seven hundred and thirty-eight children, many of whom were obliged to lie in stables, barns, cellars, and under old leaky sheds, the dwelling houses being all crowded. The inhabitants were kept in constant alarm for eight or ten years, not knowing at what moment they would be surprised by a blood-thirsty enemy." The same author says: "The 17th of March, 1764, the Indians carried off five people from within nine miles of Shippensburg, and shot one man through the body. The enemy, supposed to be eleven in number, were pursued successfully by about one hundred provincials. The houses of John Stewart, Adam Simms, James McCamman, William Baird, James Kelly, Stephen Caldwell and John Boyd were burnt. These people lost all their grain, which they had threshed out, with the intention to send it, for safety, further down among the inhabitants."

CHURCHES.

One of the earliest churches in Shippensburg was the *Associate Reformed Presbyterian*. Until this organization was effected the Episcopal element was, perhaps, dominant in the borough, through the influence of Mr. Shippen, the proprietor, who was connected with that denomination. This church was under the care of the Second Presbytery of Philadelphia, in connection with the Associate Reformed Synod. Its first pastor was the Rev. James Walker, who resigned the charge in 1820. The pulpit was then filled by the Rev. Thomas M. Strong. In 1823, the Rev. Henry R. Wilson was called, with the permission of the Presbytery, to take charge of the congregation, and continued in connection with that body until 1825, when it was dissolved, and he was received by the Presbytery of Carlisle. Dr. Wilson continued to be pastor of the church until 1839. The Rev. James Harper, D. D., was the successor of Dr. Wilson, assuming the pastorate in 1840, and withdrawing from it in 1872. The Rev. W. W. Taylor, of Philadelphia, then took charge of the congregation, serving them for two years.

The first elders of this church, of whom there is any record, were John Means and

---

* History of Pennsylvania.

William Bard. The following persons have since successively constituted the session: George McGinniss, John Reside, Daniel Henderson, Stephen Culbertson, Benjamin Reynolds, Alexander P. Kelso, William Rankin, M. D., Robert Mateer, Benjamin Snodgrass, John Mateer, John Craig, John Bridges, and Robert C. Hays, M. D.

The old white church, in which the congregation worshiped for many years, was a short time after Dr. Harper's settlement, claimed by a few Associate Reformed members still resident in the place, and their claim was confirmed by an appeal to the civil law. The Presbyterian congregation then erected a neat edifice for worship in another part of the town, which, after standing some years, gave place to the present beautiful and commodious structure, so creditable to the taste and liberality of the people.

Methodist, Lutheran and German Reformed congregations were organized in this place at an early day, and all of them now have handsome and convenient churches.

One of the principal ornaments of Shippensburg is the very large and handsome Cumberland Valley State Normal School, of which we here furnish a picture. The charter of this institution was secured in April, 1870, its corner-stone was laid with Masonic rites May 31st, 1871, it was accepted by the State authorities as a State Normal School for the Seventh Normal District July 22d, 1873, and it was inaugurated April 15th, 1873, the school opening with three hundred students in attendance. The ground owned by it embraces ten acres which are admirably adapted for ornamentation and use, and the cost of which inclusive of that of the buildings, was about $135,000. Of this amount the state paid $40,000, and $60,000 have been raised by private subscription to the stock of the Institution. Its present Principal is George P. Beard. Its Board of Trustees consists of Hon. A. G. Miller, Hon. Lemuel Todd, John A. Craig, E. J. McCune, George R. Dykeman, Hon. Geo. W. Skinner, H. G. Skiles, J. A. C. McCune, John Grabill, Samuel M. Wherry, William Mell, N. L. Dykeman, C. L. Shade, and J. H. McCullough.

A Tradition of Conococheague Valley.

Before Franklin county was established, September 9th, 1784, it constituted the southwestern part of Cumberland county, and was designated "The Conoeocheague settlement," from its principal stream, the Conococheague creek. It is a tradition that a great part of the best lands in the Conococheague Valley were, at the first settlement of the county, what is now called in the Western states *prairie*. The land was without timber, covered with a rich luxuriant grass, with some scattered trees, hazel-bushes, wild plums, and crab apples. It was then called generally "the barrens." The timber was to be found on or near the water-courses, and on the slate soil. This accounts for the preference given by the early Scotch-Irish settlers to the slate lands, before the limestone lands were surveyed or located. The slate had the attractions of wood, water-courses and meadows, and was free from rock at the surface. Before the introduction of clover, artificial grasses, and the improved system of agriculture, the hilly limestone land had its soil washed off, was disfigured with great gullies, and was sold as unprofitable, for a trifle, by the proprietors, who sought other lands in Western Pennsylvania.

Early Settlers at Chambersburg.

Among the first to explore and settle the Kittochtinny valley, were four adventurous brothers, James, Robert, Joseph and Benjamin Chambers, who emigrated from the county of Antrim, in Ireland, to the province of Pennsylvania, between the years 1726 and 1730. Benjamin, the youngest brother, settled permanently at the confluence of Falling Spring and Conococheague creeks, where Chambersburg is situated. He was

CUMBERLAND VALLEY STATE NORMAL SCHOOL, SHIPPENSBURG, PA.

the first white settler in what is known as Franklin county. The interesting incidents which marked the early history of Col. Chambers, are presented in his sketch in the body of this volume, to which the reader is respectfully referred. His career as a pioneer was characterized by a remarkable degree of energy, courage, decision, self-denial, sound judgment and practical tact, under which the wilderness and the solitary place blossomed with the indications of the march of civilization and the power of religious influence. He maintained a friendly intercourse with the Indians in his vicinity, who were attached to him; with them he traded and had so much of their confidence and respect that they did not injure him or offer to molest him.

When, however, the western Indians, after Braddock's defeat, in 1775, became troublesome, and made incursions east of the mountains, killing and making prisoners of many of the white inhabitants, Col. Chambers, for the security of his family and neighbours, found it necessary to erect, where the borough of Chambersburg now is, a large stone dwelling-house, surrounded by the water from Falling Spring, and situated where the straw paper-mill now is. The dwelling-house, for greater security against the attempts of the Indians to fire it, was roofed with lead. The dwellings and the mills were surrounded by a stockade fort. This fort, with the aid of fire-arms, a blunderbuss, and swivel, was so formidable to the Indian parties who passed the country, that it was but seldom assailed, and no one sheltered by it was killed or wounded, although in the country around, at different times, those who ventured out on their farms were surprised and either slaughtered or carried off prisoners, with all the horrors and aggravations of savage warfare. A man by the name of McKinney, who had sought shelter with his family in the fort about 1756, ventured out in company with his son to visit his dwelling and plantation, where the Hollywell paper-mill is, on the creek below Chambersburg. They were discovered, however, by the Indians, and both killed and scalped, and their dead bodies brought to the fort and buried.

Chambersburg Laid Out.

: In 1764 Col. Chambers laid out the town of Chambersburg, adjoining his mills. The intercourse with the western country being at that time very limited, and most of the trade and travel along the valley to the south, he was induced to lay his lots in that direction, and the town did not extend beyond the creek to the west. The increasing trade with the western country, after the Revolution, produced an extension of the town on the west side of the creek, which was located by Capt. Benjamin Chambers, son of the Colonel, about 1791. The first stone house erected in the town is still standing at the northwest corner of the Diamond, built by J. Jack, about 1770, and now owned by Mrs. Lewis Denig. The first courts holden in the county were in this house, up stairs, and on one occasion, the crowd was so great as to strain the beams, and fracture the walls, causing great confusion and alarm to the court and bar.* The first tavern in the place was kept by Robert Jack, in a little log-house which stood where the bank now is. Chambersburg remained but a small village until after the erection of Franklin into a separate county in 1784, since which period it has progressively improved, until it has become one of the most beautiful and flourishing inland towns of the State.

Col. Chambers had appropriated to the use of the public for a burial-ground a romantic cedar grove on the banks of the creek. This spot still retains some of the

---

*The first court was held September 15th, 1784, before Humphrey Fullerton, Esq., Thomas Johnson, Esq., and James Finley, Esq. Edward Crawford, clerk. The second court was held December 2d, before William McDowell, Esq., Humphrey Fullerton, Esq., and James Finley, Esq. Jeremiah Talbot, sheriff. The Grand Jury consisted of James Poe, Henry Poweling, William Allison, William McDowell, Robert Wiklins, John McConnell, John McCarny, John Ray, John Jack, Jr., John Dickson, D. McClintick, Joseph Chambers and Joseph Long.—*Rupp.*

beauties of nature and rural scenery. This, with some additional grounds, he conveyed by deed of gift to P. Varen and others, as trustees, on the 1st of January, 1768, "in trust for the Presbyterian congregation of the Falling Spring, now professing and adhering to, and that shall hereafter adhere to and profess, the Westminster profession of faith and the mode of church government therein contained, and to and for the use of a meeting-house or Presbyterian church, session house, school house, graveyard, and such religious purposes." Of this congregation he was an efficient, active and attentive member. He also continued a member of the board of trustees until 1787, when on account of his advanced age and infirmities, he asked leave to resign. His death occurred Feb. 17th of the ensuing year.*

Church at Chambersburg.

In the cedar grove, already referred to, and near the spot where the present church edifice stands, there was erected a small log building, in 1739, for the double purpose of a school house and place of worship. It was entered by a door on the eastern side and another on the southern, and lighted by long, narrow windows, which were of the width of two small panes of glass, and reached from one end to the other of the building. When this house, as was frequently the case, proved too small to accommodate all who wished to worship in it, the congregation abandoned it for the time in favour of Col. Chambers' saw-mill, which stood on the bank of the creek, on what is now known as "The Island," and which was surrounded by a lovely green plot. On that grassy space, when it was at all proper, they gathered around, seated themselves, and listened with interest and eagerness to the messages of God from his commissioned ambassador.

In 1767, this rude log structure was demolished, and another edifice for sacred services erected, which was considerably larger than its predecessor, being about thirty-five by seventy feet, and was of better finished material. It stood where the present church does, though its position was somewhat different, as it presented a side view to the street.

The present church edifice of Falling Spring, which was erected in 1803, and had been several times remodeled since, is at once simple, neat, and beautiful. Its elevated site, also, is a most desirable one, calling as it does for those who worship within the sanctuary, to leave the pursuits and associations of a bustling yet fading world, and come up to the service of the Lord. The shadows which fall around it, likewise, from trees which were standing when the footstep of the white man first broke the silence of the wilderness, are not without their deep significance, neither is the ivy which covers its walls, as if to bear constant testimony to the truth, that, with a steadiness and tenacity which neither sunshine nor storm nor revolving seasons can impair, man's affections should rise above the earth, clear to the risen Saviour, and cluster around the church which He hath purchased with His precious blood.

The first pastor of Falling Spring church—Rev. Mr Caven, resigned his relation in 1741. His successor, in 1767, was the Rev. James Lang, or Long. After Mr. Lang, 1794, came the Rev. William Speer, whose pastoral relation was dissolved in 1797. The Rev. David Denny then took charge of the congregation, and continued to labour among them until 1838. Mr. Denny was followed in the pastorate, by the Rev. William Adam, the Rev. Daniel McKinley, D. D., the Rev. Joseph Clarke, the Rev. Mr. Fine, the Rev. S. J. Niccolls, D. D., and the present incumbent, the Rev. J. A. Crawford, D. D.

---

* From a manuscript sketch written by the Hon. George Chambers in 1839.

WILSON FEMALE COLLEGE.

Early in the history of Chambersburg, German Reformed, Lutheran, and Methodist churches were organized, which, until now, have had a flourishing existence. There is also a Catholic church in the place.

Chambersburg is one of the handsomest towns in the interior of Pennsylvania, and has always had an intelligent, orderly and cultivated population. It was well worthy of being selected as the site of that excellent institution, "Wilson Female College," of which we are able to give our readers a correct representation.

Rocky Spring.

As the population of Franklin county increased, new churches were needed for the convenience of the people, and gradually sprang into existence. Prominent among these was the church at Rocky Spring, about four miles from Chambersburg, on the tortuous road which runs over the Slate hills, towards Strasburg. The original edifice, which was built about the time the ancient congregation was organized, stood between the present building and the graveyard. It stood pretty much in the relation to the points of the compass which the new church sustains, the front being towards the south, and smaller ends facing the east and west. It was erected about one hundred and thirty-two years ago, and was a rough log building, a story and a half high, and was built in the rude style of architecture peculiar to that early day. It had one row of windows on the lower story, the lights of which were small and few in number. It was entered by two doors, which were placed in the eastern and western ends of the house. The doors were small and single; they were made of plain boards without any panel work.

The present building, an ancient and time-worn structure, was built in 1794, by Mr. Walter Beatty. The old building having in the course of years become incapable of accommodating the growing congregation, an addition to the house was built by constructing a small square building, which was attached to the south side of the church, and which extended only one-half the length of the main structure. The roof was then continued over it from the original edifice. When completed the wall between it and the church was sawn away. There were no windows in this addition, and it was consequently poorly supplied with light. In a few years after this alteration the increasing size of the congregation demanded still more room, and another similar addition was built by its side. These alterations gave the house a singular, slanting appearance towards the south end.

About the time the original church was erected there was also built a small, rough log structure, about fifteen feet square, with a wide fire-place, and a large wooden chimney covered with mortar, and extending nearly along the whole end of the house. This structure stood close by the church at the northeastern end, and was called the "Study House." Tradition says it was originally built as a receptacle for the saddles of the members in rainy weather, as in those early days they generally came to church on horseback, carriages and other vehicles being rarely used. In later years, the minister was accustomed to use it in preparing for the services, when he chanced to arrive before the hour at which they began. The church Session also met here and arranged the business of the church and examined candidates for admission to membership. After the first service, the minister would resort to it to prepare for any afternoon service which was to be held. The "Study House" stood for nearly a century, and not very many years have elapsed since its removal.

The first pastor of Rocky Spring church was the Rev. Mr. Craighead. In the graveyard, on broken pieces of stone slab, may be read the following inscription:

"In memory of the Rev. John Craighead, who departed this life the 20th day of April, A. D., 1799, aged 57 years. Ordained to preach the gospel and installed pastor of the congregation of Rocky Spring, on the 13th of April, A. D., 1768. He was a faithful and zealous servant of Jesus Christ."

Mr. Craighead's successor was the Rev. Francis Herron, D. D., who after ten years of service among the congregation was chosen pastor of the First Presbyterian church of Pittsburg. After Dr. Herron's removal the Rev. John McKnight, D. D., ministered to the people for several years, when his pastoral relation was interrupted by an invitation to preside over Dickinson college. The vacancy thus occasioned was supplied by his son, the Rev. Dr. John McKnight, who, after preaching several years, removed to Philadelphia. In 1840 a call from "Campbellstown and Rocky Spring" to Rev. A. K. Nelson, with the understanding that the half of his time was to be given to each of these congregations, was accepted by him, and Mr. Nelson continues to be the pastor to this writing.

More Indian Hostilities.

Further proof of the annoyance to which the inhabitants of Cumberland valley were subjected by the inroads of the Indians, who murdered the people, burned their houses and barns, destroyed their crops and committed the usual atrocities characteristic of savage warfare, is furnished by the operations of the savages in the neighbourhood of Strasburg and Roxbury, from which and their vicinage the congregation of Rocky Spring was largely drawn. On one occasion the Indians captured a number of persons in the neighbourhood of and not far from Rocky Spring, and proceeded with their prisoners toward Bedford. About the same time another party burned the fort (which then stood near Bossart's mill,) after shooting the only man who happened to be in at the time, and then followed in the same direction taken by the preceding gang. A company of the inhabitants of the neighbourhood, under the command of Captain Alexander Culbertson, went in pursuit of the Indians and overtook them near Sideling Hill. A desperate fight ensued in which the company of Capt. C. was defeated and himself killed. A number of the men were made prisoners and carried off by the Indians. The stream known as "Bloody Run" is supposed by some to have derived its name from this battle, which is represented to have occurred in its vicinity.

Major McCalmont.

Just at this point special notice is due of James McCalmont, Esq., who lived near Strasburg, who was a Major in the Revolutionary war, and who became distinguished as a brave and accomplished soldier. This gentleman,* was generally selected as the leader of the parties sent in pursuit of the savages after the perpetration of their numerous hostile acts, and from his success in discovering their haunts and inflicting summary vengeance upon them for their atrocities, he became quite celebrated as an Indian hunter, and was considered by the savages as a daring and formidable foe. As a bush-fighter he was quite equal to the most wily Indian. One day he met unexpectedly a tall, desperate-looking savage, while alone in the woods near his residence. Both happening to see each other simultaneously, took to trees, and each endeavored to get a shot at his antagonist. After evading each other for some time the savage incautiously peeped from behind the tree, and instantly received a ball from the rifle of his dexterous enemy. Upon another occasion, while returning home from Chambersburg,

---

*Sketch of Rocky Spring church, by William C. Lane, M. D.

HISTORICAL SKETCH.

he was pursued by a party of Indians who were bent on securing the scalp of their old and hated enemy. After running for a considerable distance, he darted into a barn which stood near by, and escaped out of the other side, and secreted himself in a thicket unobserved by his pursuers. The savages supposing he was yet in the barn set it on fire, and stood around it yelling in exultation at their supposed success in capturing their foe. When they discovered that they were baffled they commenced the search after the Major, and soon found his trail and again joined hotly in the pursuit. The Major was remarkable for his swiftness of foot, and succeeded in outrunning the Indians, who pursued him to the fort at Shippensburg. They often chased him to this fort, it is said, and on several occasions he selected men from the garrison and in turn pursued the Indians and avenged himself by returning with their scalps. During the war the Major was working one day in the field with several other persons at harvest-time. The guns of the party were in a distant part of the field. A gang of several prowling savages suddenly sprang from the thicket, and one, more bold than the rest, ran for the guns. McCalmont also started off on the same errand, and, although the Indian had the advantage of the ground, reached the guns first, one of which he snatched from the stack, and with it shot the savage dead. The settlers coming up soon after the Major, the Indians retreated. He was considered by the Indians as quite as swift a runner as they, and fully equal to themselves in all the wiles and strategy of their peculiar warfare. In consequence of his extraordinary fleetness and agility, they bestowed on him the appellation of "Supple McCalmont." On the southwestern side of the town of Strasburg there is a cave called "McCalmont's Cave," in which he was accustomed to hide when closely pursued by the Indians. It was in the midst of a thicket, and so covered with thick vines and bushes that it afforded an admirable retreat in times of danger.

The major was a tall, muscular man, of modest and unpretending manners. In private life, his quiet, diffident deportment, gave no indication of the dauntless spirit of the man, of which he presented so many evidences in his encounters with the Indians, as well as with the British army during his campaign under General Washington. After the conclusion of the war, he was appointed one of the Associate Judges of Franklin county, soon after its formation. He died at Strasburg, in 1809, and his remains are interred in the graveyard of Rocky Spring.

COMPANIES FORMED FOR DEFENCE.

During the eight years and more in which the Kittochtinny valley was harassed with the ravages and cruelties of savage warfare, the defence of it being cast almost entirely on the inhabitants by the remissness of the Royal and Provincial Governments to provide for the public defence, men frequently organized themselves into military companies, under the command of some selected leader. Among the first companies organized in West Conococheague, on the bloody outbreak of the Delaware Indians, in 1755, was one which chose for its captain, the Rev. John Steele, their Presbyterian pastor. This command was accepted by Mr. Steele, and executed with so much skill, bravery and judgment, as to commend him to the Provincial Government, which appointed him a captain of the Provincial troops. This appointment he held for many years, to the benefit of the public service, and the satisfaction of the Government.[*]

---

[*] Mr. Steele was reputed a sound divine, of piety and learning, and did not relinquish the ministry for arms. Such was the state of the country, that he often exercised his ministry with his gun at his side, addressing his congregation, the men of which had their weapons within reach.

Aid Solicited.

In 1763, a petition was presented to the Assembly by the inhabitants of Great Cove, and Conococheague, setting forth, that the petitioners, by recent depredations and ravages of the Indians, committed on their neighbours, being in very imminent danger, were under the necessity of taking into pay a number of men, amounting to thirty, accustomed to hunting, endured to hardships, and well acquainted with the country, for the protection of themselves and families, and "humbly praying the house would take the premises into consideration, and enable them to continue the aforesaid body of men, in such manner, and subject to such directions, as they should judge most proper and advantageous."

Green Castle.

The town of Green Castle was laid out by Colonel John Allison in the year 1782, and incorporated by an Act of Assembly, March 25th, 1805. Among the first settlers here were Crawfords, Statlers, Nighs, McCulloughs, Carsons, Clarks, Watsons, Davisons, Grubbs, Lawrences, McClellands.

Murder by the Indians.

The neighbourhood of Green Castle is memorable for a cruel murder, committed by the Indians in 1764. John McCullough, in his narrative, thus refers to the massacre:

"Some time in the summer, whilst we were living at *Kid-ho-ling*, a great number of Indians collected at the forks of *Moos-hing-oong*. Perhaps there were about three hundred or upwards. Their intention was to come to the settlement and make a general massacre of the whole people, without any regard to age or sex. They were out about ten days, when most of them returned. Having held a council, they concluded that it was not safe for them to leave their towns destitute of defence. However, several small parties went to different parts of the settlements; it happened that three of them, whom I was well acquainted with, came to the neighbourhood of where I was taken from—they were young fellows, perhaps none of them more than twenty years of age; they came to a school house, where they murdered and scalped the master and all the scholars, except one, who survived after he was scalped; a boy about ten years old, a full cousin of mine. I saw the Indians when they returned home with the scalps, some of the old Indians were very much displeased at them for killing so many children, especially *Neep-paugh-whese*, or Night Walker, an old chief, or half king. He attributed it to cowardice, which was the greatest affront he could offer them."*

Richard Bard, also, in his narrative, makes the following allusions to this memorable and melancholy event:

"According to the best accounts of the time, my father and his family, from fear of the Indians, having moved to my grandfather's, Thomas Poe's, about three miles from his own place, took a black girl with him to his own place to make some hay, and being there at work, a dog which he had with him began to bark and run towards and from a thicket of bushes. Observing these circumstances, he became alarmed, and taking up his gun, told the girl to run to the house, for he believed there were Indians near. So they made towards the house, and had not been there more than an hour, when from the left of the house they saw a party, commanded by Captain Potter, late General Potter, in pursuit of a party of Indians who had that morning (July 26th, 1764,) murdered a schoolmaster of the name of Brown, with ten small children, and scalped and left for dead one by the name of Archibald McCullough, who recovered, and was living not long since. It was remarkable that with but few exceptions the scholars were much averse to going to school that morning. And the account given by McCullough is, that when the master and the scholars met at the school, two of the scholars informed him that on their way they had seen Indians; but the information was not attended to by the master, who ordered them to their books. Soon afterwards two old Indians and a boy rushed up to the door. The master, seeing them, prayed them only to take his life, and spare the children; but, unfeelingly, the two old Indians stood at the door, whilst the boy entered the house and, with a piece of wood made in the form of an Indian maul, killed the master and scholars, after which the whole of them were scalped." †

---

* Loudon's Narratives, I, 334.   † Incidents of Border Life, p. 122.

The schoolhouse, to which reference is made in these extracts, stood on a farm about three miles from Green Castle. Some of the remains of it existed as late as 1845, and marked the place of its location. "It was," says a citizen of that borough, in a letter written in the year just mentioned, "truly a solitary one, and would be considered so at this day. It was situated on the brow of a hill. In the front of it there is a ravine, deep and dismal. On the north and west the surrounding hills are covered with a thick growth of underwood."

Conococheague Settlement.

The "Conococheague Settlement" having many natural advantages, and being fed from the older counties as well as from the old world, was of rapid growth, and the nucleus of the settlement from the beginning was a Presbyterian church. It appears that the whole Conococheague settlement, including Chambersburg and the portions of the valley lying farther west and south, was at first under the supervision of the Presbytery of Donegal, in the care of a single minister, and that Divine service was held at different points for the better accommodation of all the people. In 1736 we find this Presbytery refusing to sanction the employment of a Mr. Williams, from England, who was then preaching in the settlement, and the people allowed to make application to the Presbytery of New Castle. In November, 1837, Mr Samuel Cavin, a licentiate under the care of the Donegal Presbytery, was ordered to the Conococheague to labour as a supply. During the ensuing year another licentiate, Mr. Samuel Thompson, seems to have spent part of his time, by invitation, among the people of Conococheague. It soon became apparent, however, that the territory of the settlement was too extensive to be embraced within the limits of a single organization. Accordingly, in 1738, the people of the settlement agreed in an amicable way to separate and form two congregations, the one to be called "East Conococheague," and the other to be called "West Conococheague." In that agreement it was stipulated that the boundary line between them should be "west from Alexander Dunlap's to the fork of the creek, and thence the creek to be the line until it came to the line of the Province."

East Conococheague.

At the time the settlement agreed to divide into two congregations, the people of East Conococheague made out a call for the pastoral services of the Rev. Mr. Cavin, which was accepted. At this time, this congregation and that of Falling Spring were united as one charge. The probability is that Mr. Cavin continued to be pastor of East Conococheague until 1774. His place was supplied in 1754 and 1755 by the Rev. John Steele,* who had charge of the congregation for this length of time in connection with the congregation of West Conococheague, but was obliged, by the Indian disturbances, which increased after Braddock's defeat, to abandon his post This last mentioned congregation was without a settled pastor for a number of years, the long vacancy being attributable partly to the Indian troubles, and perhaps also in part to the well-known division in the Presbyterian church, arising out of the revivals in 1732. In the year 1769, the union between the congregations of East Conococheague and Falling Spring, which had previously been dissolved, was re-formed, and the Rev. James Lang was called as pastor of the charge, and, it seems, continued so until 1802. In October

---

* On one occasion, as Mr. Steele was preaching in a barn on the farm since owned by Mr. Adam B. Wingerd, and while engaged in the service, a messenger came bringing the intelligence that a party of Indians had appeared in the neighbourhood of McCullough's, now Rankins' mill, killing a man named Walter, and firing several houses. Instantly the services were discontinued, the women and children were sent to the block-house, situated near to the subsequent residence of Mr. William Allison, and the man of God, ready for any warfare to which he might be called, closed the Bible, and called upon the men of the congregation to follow him in defence of their homes.

of the same year, the Rev. Robert Kennedy accepted a call to "the united congregations of East and Lower West Conococheague," or Welsh Run, and continued to be their pastor until 1816, when his relation to them, by his own request, was dissolved. Mr. Kennedy's successor was the Rev. James Buchanan, who served the church until 1840. The pulpit has subsequently been supplied by the following pastors: Rev. J. T. Marshall Davie, Rev. T. V. Moore, D. D., Rev. Edwin Emerson, Rev. W. M. Paxton, D. D., Rev. W. Beatty, Rev. J. W. Wightman, and the present incumbent, Rev. Mr. Richardson.

Associate Reformed Church.

At the time of the settlement of Mr. Buchanan in Green Castle, there was a congregation worshiping in what is known as the White Church, holding ecclesiastical connection with the Associate Reformed Presbyterian church. Its relations had formerly been with the Reformed Presbyterian church, having for its first pastor the Rev. Matthew Lind, who came to this country from Ireland, 1774, and organized the church there, probably soon after his arrival. In 1782, when the partial union was effected between the Reformed and the Associate churches, Mr. Lind, taking his people with him, entered into that reunion, and from that date the church of which he was pastor became an "Associate Reformed church."

Their building, near town, was erected probably in 1792. The indenture was made by Messrs. James McLanahan and John Allison jointly, transferring the ground on which the building was located, and bears date May 5th, A. D. 1791. The trustees to whom the transfer was made were John Gebby, George Clarke, Andrew Reed, John Coughran, and James Crooks. The building stood in the graveyard on East Baltimore street. It was originally built of logs, the timber of which was cut on the property of John Coughran, Esq. Afterwards it was weather-boarded and painted white. There, in that building, we may say, was the birth-place of the Associate Reformed church. There their Constitution and Standards were formally issued May 31st, 1799. There, in May, 1804, was held the first meeting of their General Synod, at which time they formally inaugurated the movement for the establishment of the first Theological Seminary in the United States. There, too, at a later date, (or rather in the grove at the head of Bierly's Spring, for the want of room in the building,) was held one of the warmest and most protracted discussions on the close communion question, in which the cause of liberty and charity was plead in person by its greatest champion, Dr. John M. Mason.

These frequent meetings of so important a body in Green Castle would indicate that the Associate Reformed congregation there was at that time large and flourishing. There are, however, no records of the church proper from which we can draw authentic information. Tradition tells us that the following were members of Session: James McClanahan, William Gebby, Andrew Reed, David Fullerton, George Clarke, and Joseph Gebby.*

Church at Green Castle.

The congregation at Green Castle had a house of worship as early as 1738. The character of that building, and even the certain location of it, are lost sight of. It probably stood, however, on or near the site of its successor, the old Red Church, at the Moss Spring. The Red Church, it is thought, was built in the first years of the pastorate of Mr. Lang. The date is not certainly known, but there are traces of it

---

* Rev. J. W. Wightman's His. Dis.

extending back about that far. It was a frame building twenty-eight and a half by forty-two and a half feet, the pulpit of the old half-octagon style, perched upon a pedestal, was placed at the side, crossing immediately in front of it was the main aisle leading to a door in either end of the building. At right angles with this were two other aisles, leading each to a door in the side of the church, opposite the pulpit. This arrangement was odd, and the building unpretending.

The first Session of the church, of which we have any knowledge, included the following: Mr. Joseph Smith, Colonel John Allison, Elias Davidson, Sr., Andrew Robinson, Sr., and James McLain. Their successors in office were Robert Crunkelton, Robert Robinson, John M. Davidson, John Watson, and Mr. Kellar.

STUDY HOUSE.

Near it stood, for many years, what was called the "Study House," used in part as a Session room, but more particularly as a sort of resort for the minister in the interval between the first and second service—a place where he might be alone, and prepare himself for his further duties. It was the custom then to have two sermons, with an intermission of half an hour, and the theory was, that the minister should spend this in the "Study House," while the people, lunch in hand, would gather to the spring-head and drink of its limpid waters, or stroll away at will among the rocks and trees of the surrounding grove.

In that same old "Study House," says Mr. Wightman, there was, during the pastorate of Mr. Kennedy, a classical school, in which a number of young men received their training, who afterwards attained eminence in their several walks of life. Among these were John X. Clarke, Matthew St Clair Clarke, Esq., Clerk of the House of Representatives, Thomas G. McCullough, Esq., Dr. John Boggs, and Rev. John Lind.

It is an interesting fact that the institutions of learning all over the country have grown up from just such schools as this, established in the beginning in connection with the church, and nurtured by the prayers and devotion of some godly minister. It is thus made apparent that the gospel of Christ is the germinating seed of the world's intellectual progress, and that the real fostering mother of these educational privileges of which we now boast so loudly, is not the form of government under which we live, but the faith which has been bequeathed to us by our fathers.

LUTHERAN CHURCH.

The corner-stone of the venerable Lutheran church, which now stands in Green Castle, was laid September 13th, 1792, and the building was completed in 1795, when the Rev. John Ruthrauff became pastor, and served the congregation for forty years. The successive pastors have been Revs. John Reck, Jeremiah Hanful, Jacob Martin, Peter Sahen, Michael Eyster, James M. Harkey, Edward Breidenbaugh, William F. Eyster, Thomas F. Everett.

GERMAN REFORMED CHURCH.

The first German Reformed church in Green Castle was a log building. In 1805, this was torn down, and a new church erected on South Carlisle street. The successive pastors have been Revs. Frederick Rauhauser, Frederick Schull, Hamilton Vandyke, Jacob Mayer, John Rebaugh, J. S. Foulke (during whose pastorate, from 1850 to 1858, a new church was built on East Church street), T. G. Apple, D.D., S. N. Callender, D.D., Moses Kieffer, D.D., and Stephen K. Kramer.

Interesting Incident.

Before we pass from Green Castle, there is an incident of a patriotic character which should not fail of record. Here W. H. Riels, of Philadelphia, the first soldier that was shot on "free soil" during the late rebellion, fell within its corporate limits, on the 20th of July, 1863, in a skirmish with the Confederate army, when on its way to Chambersburg. He lies buried in the southern church yard, and the citizens, it is said, propose to erect a suitable monument to his memory.

Lower West Conococheague.

In consequence of the division in the Presbyterian church, previously mentioned, a church, then known as "Lower West Conococheague," and originally a part of "Upper West Conococheague," or what is now called Mercersburg, was organized at Welsh Run, so called because the original settlers principally came from Wales. This organization was effected in 1741. Though it sprang mainly from the cause mentioned, it was required by the convenience of the congregation, the territory covered by the mother church being too extensive to allow the people to meet weekly in the same place of worship, and it was done with so much good feeling that both churches still adhered to the same Presbytery.

The first house erected for their worship, (probably in 1741,) of which we give a representation, was built of logs and located near Mr. Elliott's. It was burned by the Indians about 1772. There seems to have been no other church erected until the close of the Indian war in 1774, when one was built on the same spot where the present edifice stands.

The ground now held and occupied by the church, was originally given to it by Robert Smith, in 1774, or about that time. The building erected on this ground in 1774, originally log, afterwards weather boarded, having undergone various repairs, served its day and three generations, or a century of years. It was of the ancient model, with high pulpit, elaborately ornamented sounding-board, and seats having backs high as the tops of the shoulders.

The congregations assembled at this second building on sacramental occasions were so numerous that, the church being insufficient to accommodate them, it was not an unusual thing for two ministers to be preaching at the same time, the one in the church, and the other in a temporary building near at hand called the Tent. From this circumstance this place of worship was sometimes called the "Tent Meeting House."

The Presbyterian Historical Society, at Philadelphia, has in its possession one of the communion tables used in the old church at Welsh Run. It is made of unpainted yellow pine, and is 12 feet 7 inches long, 14 inches wide and 30 inches high. When used it was placed in the centre of the aisle, with a white linen cover on it. Around this plain table God's people gathered, and having given to the elders the "token" which they had received previously as an evidence of their right to partake of the holy supper, renewed their covenant engagements to be the Lord's. Certainly there was much deeper solemnity in such an observance of the sacrament than accompanies the modern method of observing it. The society already mentioned has one of the tokens just referred to, with the inscription on it: *C. C.*; designating the name of the church at that date—"Conococheague Church."

The present noble and tasteful church edifice at Welsh Run, erected upon the foundations of the preceding building, by Elias Davidson Kennedy, of Philadelphia, only surviving son of Rev. Robert Kennedy, as an expression of his appreciation of the

OLD WELSH RUN CHURCH.—(BURNT 1772.)

character and usefulness of his deceased father, was dedicated to the worship of Almighty God, September 30th, 1871. Most appropriately did the Trustees, by an unanimous vote, resolve, in testimony of their gratitude to Mr. Kennedy, that the name of the church should be changed from " Welsh Run Presbyterian Church " to " The Robert Kennedy Memorial Church," and to have a marble corner-stone placed in the foundation, with this inscription on it.

Pastors of Welsh Run.

The first pastor of this church was Rev. James Campbell, from Scotland, who seems to have laboured with them fifteen years or more, or till the Indian war broke out, in 1756. After the expiration of Mr. Campbell's pastorate, the Rev. Mr. Dunlap seems to have supplied them with preaching till their first house of worship was burned by the Indians, about 1760, or a few years later. Just before the close of the Indian war, the Rev. Thomas McPherrin became pastor of the church (1774), and continued so for twenty-five years. The church then became connected with the Green Castle Church, and was supplied with the pastoral services of the Rev. Robert Kennedy. In the early period of its history, it was a large and numerous congregation, the entire population of the surrounding country being Scotch-Irish, all of whom were connected with it. Now the great mass of the people are Germans, and belong to the Dunkers and River Brethren Still, the church continues to prosper, as is indicated by the fact that, under the ministrations of its present pastor, the Rev. J. H. Fleming, thirty-six persons were added to it at their last communion, twenty-eight by profession, and eight by letter.

Mercersburg.

Where the town of Mercersburg now stands, a mill was built by James Black, about the year 1729 or 1730. William Smith purchased this property, and his son laid out the town, about the year 1786. The place was named in honour of General Mercer, of the Revolutionary army,* who had shown great kindness to the proprietor, or his father, while the army was encamped near New Brunswick, in New Jersey. Governor William Findlay, who filled the executive chair of Pennsylvania in 1817, and of whom our book gives a sketch, was born in this place about the year 1770.

"Mercersburg, in early days," says Mr. Day,† "was an important point for trade with Indians and settlers on the western frontier. It was no uncommon event to see there 50 or 100 pack-horses in a row taking on their loads of salt, iron and other commodities for the Monongahela country. About three miles west of Mercersburg there is a wild gorge in Cove mountain, and within the gorge an ancient road leads up through a narrow, secluded cave or glen, encircled on every side by high and rugged mountains. Here, at the foot of a toilsome ascent in the road, which the old traders designated as 'The Stony Batter,' are now a decayed orchard and the ruins of two log-cabins. Some fifty years since a Scotch trader dwelt in one of these cabins, and had a store in

---

* Dr. Hugh Mercer, a Scotchman of talent and education, had taken up his residence in the southern part of this valley, near the Maryland line, a short time before Braddock's defeat. Having enjoyed some military training and experience in Europe, and having a taste for military life, he was, early in 1756, appointed a captain in the provincial service, in which he was continued for some years, being promoted to the rank of colonel. Colonel Mercer was appointed by the American Congress a general in the Revolutionary army, on the recommendation of Washington, by whom he was well known and highly esteemed. General Mercer, who had the confidence of the army and the country, fell mortally wounded and mangled by the British soldiery, at the battle of Princeton, in January, 1777, whilst gallantly and bravely leading his division against the royal army.

† Writing in 1843.

the other, where he drove a small but profitable traffic with the Indians and frontier-men who came down the mountain-pass, exchanging with them powder, fire-arms, salt, sugar, iron, blankets, and cloths, for their 'old Monongahela,' and the furs and skins of the trappers and Indians. The Scotchman had a son born here, and James Buchanan was cradled amid these wild scenes of nature and the rude din of frontier life. The father, thriving in trade, moved into Mercersburg, after a few years assumed a higher rank in business, and was able to send his son James to Dickinson College, where he graduated in 1809. Passing over the intermediate scenes of his life, we find him, in his future history, one of the most accomplished, eloquent and distinguished members of the Senate of the United States," and we can add, Secretary of the State under President Polk's administration, Minister to Russia, Minister to England, and finally President of the United States.

EARLY SETTLEMENTS.

This part of the country began to be settled about the year 1736. The land being taken from the proprietors by those only who designed to settle on it, the settlements soon became numerous. About the year 1738 the Presbyterians formed themselves into a congregation and enjoyed supplies of preaching from that time. About the year 1740 the congregation, for a reason already assigned, divided. The "Upper Congregation" called the Rev. John Steele, previously of West Nottingham congregation. He was installed in 1754, holding also the charge of "East Conococheague."

In the next year the settlement was greatly disturbed by the irruption of Indians, in consequence of Braddock's defeat. This continued for two years, until the settlement was for a time entirely broken up, and Mr. Steele accepted an invitation to the church at Carlisle. After the people returned to their desolated habitations they adopted their old form of a congregation, and engaged supplies from the Presbytery of Donegal for several years, being in the years 1762 and 1763 again disturbed and greatly harassed by the Indian war.* They, after this, made some attempts to obtain a settled ministry.

REV. DR. KING.

Their efforts were unsuccessful till the year 1768, when they called Mr John King, then a candidate under the care of the Presbytery of Philadelphia Mr. King was installed August 30th, 1769, and continued to discharge the pastoral duties for more than forty years. He died in 1813, about two years after retiring from his ministry, having been so afflicted with rheumatism that, while he continued his ministrations, for several years he was obliged to sit in the pulpit during service.

Dr. King was a man of good natural parts, which he lost no opportunity to cultivate. During the intervals of his pastoral avocations he continued to increase his stores both of theological and miscellaneous knowledge. He was proficient in the Latin, Greek, Hebrew and French languages, and had attentively studied the several branches of natural science. In 1792 he was honoured with the degree of D. D. from Dickinson College. As a pastor, he was sound in doctrine, kind, sociable, cheerful and instructive, and steady in attention to his duties. He left behind him a character without a

---

* The original place of meeting is two and a half miles from Mercersburg. The Church edifice in the town was erected in 1794, and for a number of years was without a ceiling, floor, pews or pulpit. The ground on which it stands, and that which surrounds it, was given to the congregation by the Hon. Robert Smith. The following persons composed the Session, in succession, from 1767 till 1800: William Maxwell, William Smith, John McDowell, William McDowell, John Welsh, Alexander White, John McClelland, Jonathan Smith, William Campbell, Robert Fleming, Samuel Templeton, Patrick Maxwell, Joseph VanLear, Mathew Wilson, William Lowery, James McFarland, Henry Helm, William Waddell, Archibald Irwin, James Crawford, John Holiday, John McMullin, John Johnston, Edward Welsh, William Reynolds, Robert McFarland, John McCullough, John Scott, Robert McDowell, James Dickey.

blot. He was the author of a doctrinal catechism, especially calculated to fortify the young against the spirit of skepticism and infidelity which threatened at that time the morals of youth; of some pieces in the Assembly's Magazine, on the subject of a man's marrying his former wife's sister; and of a dissertation on the prophecies, referring to the present times, &c. There were about one hundred and thirty families in the settlement at the commencement of his ministry. He has left a little book containing a list of all the heads of families, with their children, residing within the limits of his congregation. The names are almost universally Scotch—Campbells, Wilsons, McClellands, McDowells, Barrs, Findlays, Welshs, Smiths, &c.

In 1812, Mr. David Elliott (afterwards D. D., and of whom also our volume has a biographical notice,) was called to the charge of the congregation, in which he continued about seventeen years. In 1831, Mr. Thomas Creigh (now D. D.,) of Carlisle, was installed over the church, and up to this time continues in charge of it. The Session was composed of the following members in 1767: William Maxwell, William Smith, John McDowell, William McDowell, John Welsh, Alexander White, John McClelland, Jonathan Smith, William Campbell, Robert Fleming, Samuel Templeton—names probably of some of the most respectable and worthy families in the neighbourhood in that day.*

Theological Seminary.

* For a long time the Theological Seminary of the German Reformed church was located in Mercersburg. It was transferred there from York, about the year 1834. This removal was followed, in the course of a short time, by the resignation of the Professor of Theology, the Rev. Dr. Lewis Mayer, whose name had been identified with all the fortunes of the institution from the beginning. Dr. Frederick A. Rauch was assistant of Dr. Mayer. The vacancy thus created was filled, in 1840, by the unanimous and earnest choice by the Synod of the church, of John Williamson Nevin, D. D., LL.D., who was at the time Professor in the Western Theological Seminary at Pittsburg. Dr. Rauch, to whom had been committed the Department of Biblical Literature, died in 1841, and was buried in a secluded corner of the tract of ground set apart as a place of burial for the use particularly of the institution. For a time all the duties of the seminary devolved upon Dr. Nevin. In 1844, the Rev. Dr. Philip Schaff was elected to the Professorship of Church History and Sacred Literature.

Marshall College.

Marshall College, which was also founded by the Reformed church, was transferred to Mercersburg from York, a few years after the removal of the Theological Seminary. It sprang from the High School which had been established in connection with the Theological Seminary at the last mentioned place in 1832. The Institution was chartered by the Legislature of Pennsylvania, in the year 1835. The Presidency at the beginning fell, by the election of the Board of Trustees, on Dr. Rauch, by whom the original Grammar School had been established in York. On the decease of Dr. Rauch, Dr. Nevin was chosen President of the College. About the year 1855 it was removed to Lancaster, where it assumed the name of Franklin and Marshall College, and has ever since been in successful operation, Dr. Nevin still continuing to act as President. Not long afterwards the Seminary, which for some years was under the instruction of Bernard C. Wolff, D. D., followed the College to the same city, where it

---

* From an Historical Sketch by Dr. Creigh.

still exists and prospers, its chairs being occupied by E. V. Gerhart, D. D., and Thomas G. Appel, D. D. From these institutions many men have gone forth who have reached literary, political, and theological distinction.

PATRIOTISM.

Patriotism was a predominant trait among the early settlers of the Kittochtinny valley. They were conspicuous among the Provincial troops in the old French war, and throughout all the Indian wars they sustained nearly the whole burden of defending the frontier. When a new purchase was made, they were the first to make an opening in the wilderness beyond the mountains, and when the alarm of the American Revolution echoed along the rocky walls of the Blue mountain, it awakened a congenial thrill among the inhabitants of the valley which it bounded, especially in the blood of that race which years before, in Ireland and Scotland, had resisted the arbitrary power of England.

MEETING AT CARLISLE.

At a meeting of freeholders and freemen from several townships of Cumberland county, held at Carlisle, July 12th, 1774, in view of the first vials of displeasure which were being poured out by Great Britain upon citizens of Boston by way of forcing the colonies to servile submission, the following action was taken:

Resolved, 1. That the late act of the Parliament of Great Britain, by which the port of Boston is shut up, is oppressive to that town, and subversive of the rights and liberties of the colony of Massachusetts Bay; that the principle upon which the act is founded is not more subversive of the rights and liberties of that colony than it is of all other British colonies in North America, and therefore the inhabitants of Boston are suffering in the common cause of all these colonies.

2. That every vigorous and prudent measure ought speedily and unanimously to be adopted by these colonies for obtaining redress of the grievances under which the inhabitants of Boston are now labouring, and security from grievance of the same or of a still more severe nature, under which they and the other inhabitants of the colonies may, by a further operation of the same principle, hereafter labour.

3. That a Congress of Deputies from all the colonies will be one proper method for obtaining these purposes.

4. That the same purposes will, in the opinion of this meeting, be promoted by an agreement of all the colonies not to import any merchandise from nor export any merchandise to Great Britain, Ireland or the British West Indies, nor to use any such merchandise so imported, nor tea imported from any place whatever, till these purposes shall be obtained, but that the inhabitants of this county will join any restriction of that agreement which the General Congress may think it necessary for the colonies to confine themselves to.

5. That the inhabitants of this county will contribute to the relief of their suffering brethren in Boston at any time when they shall receive intimation that such relief will be most seasonable.

6. That a committee be immediately appointed for this county to correspond with the committee of this Province, or of the other Provinces, upon the great objects of the public attention, and to co-operate in every measure conducing to the general welfare of British America.

7. That the committee consist of the following persons, viz: James Wilson, John Armstrong, John Montgomery, William Irvine, Robert Callender, William Thompson, John Calhoun, Jonathan Hoge, Robert Magaw, Ephraim Blane, John Allison, John Harris and Robert Miller, or any five of them.

8. That James Wilson, Robert Magaw and William Irvine be the deputies appointed to meet the deputies from other counties of this Province at Philadelphia, on Friday next, in order to concert measures preparatory to the General Congress.

LETTERS FROM THE COMMITTEE.

In a letter from the committee of Cumberland county to the President of Congress, dated at Carlisle, July 14th, 1776, ten days after the Declaration of Independence was proclaimed, it is stated: "By the intelligence we have already received, we think ourselves warranted to say, that we shall be able to send *five* companies, viz.: one from each battalion, to compose part of the flying camp, provided so many good arms can be had, and three companies of militia for the present emergency, some of whom will march this week. With pleasure we assure you that a noble spirit appears amongst the inhabitants here. The spirit of marching to the defence of our country is so prevalent in this town that we shall not have men left sufficient to mount guard, which we think absolutely necessary for the safety of the inhabitants and ammunition, and as a watch over the ten *English* officers, with their ten servants, to keep their parole of honour, especially as their brethren, lately, at Lebanon, in Lancaster county, lost it; and as there will not be more left in town for the above purpose, we shall be obliged to hire a guard of twelve men from the county."*

In a letter from the same committee to Congress, dated at Carlisle, July 31st, 1776, it is said: "The inhabitants have voluntarily and very generally offered their services, and by the answers which we have received from the officers, it appears to us that *eleven* companies will be sufficiently armed and accoutred, and the last of them marched from this place in about a week from this time. Three companies more are preparing, if they can get arms, and many more declared themselves willing to march; but we are well assured arms are not to be got in this country. If arms and accoutrements are to be had at Philadelphia, we can send *more men*."†

At the time these volunteers from the Cumberland valley were pressing forward in surprising numbers, it is to be recollected that from this district there were then in the Continental army a number of officers as well as rank and file, who, the year preceding, had entered the army and were still absent in the military service of their country. Among those officers were Generals Armstrong and Irwin, Colonels Magaw, Chambers, Watts, Blair, Smith, Wilson, Montgomery, Buchanan, and Majors, Captains and subalterns in numbers too great to be enumerated here.

In a letter from the same committee to Congress, dated August 16th, 1776, it is stated that "The *twelfth* company of our militia are marched to-day, which companies contain, in the whole, eight hundred and thirty-three privates—with officers, nearly nine hundred men. Six companies more are collecting arms, and are preparing to march."‡ §

WAR OF 1812.

On the breaking out of the war of 1812, the citizens of Carlisle manifested an equally commendable zeal in volunteering for the defence of our common country. Four fine companies were soon raised, viz: the "Carlisle Infantry," under Captain William Alexander, and a "rifle company," under Captain George Hendel, which served a term of six months on the northern frontier, the "Carlisle Guards," under Captain Joseph Halbert, who marched to Philadelphia, and the "Patriotic Blues," under Captain Jacob Squier, who were for some time in the entrenchments at Baltimore.

CAPTAIN CRAIGHEAD.

The same spirit of patriotism prevailed in Franklin county. The Rev. Mr. Craighead, of Rocky Spring, in eloquent strains, exhorted from the pulpit the youth of his congre-

---

* Amer. Arch., 5th Ser., 1 vol., p. 328.
† Ib. 619.
‡ Ib. 994.
§ The companies marching from Cumberland county, in August, 1776, were commanded by Captains John Steel, Samuel Postlethwaite, Andrew Galbreath, Samuel McCune, Thomas Turbott, James McConnel, William Huston, Thomas Clark, John Hutton, Robert Culbertson, Charles Lecher, Conrad Schnider, Lieutenant Colonel Frederick Watts. Other Captains were preparing to march.—*Amer. Arch. 5th Ser., 1 vol., p.* 619.

gation to rise up and join the noble band then engaged under the immortal Washington in struggling for the freedom of our country. On one occasion, it is said, the patriotic preacher declaimed in such burning and powerful terms against the wrongs we were then suffering, that, after one glowing description of the duty of the men, the whole congregation rose from their seats and declared their willingness to march to the conflict. There was but one, tradition says, in the entire assembly, who was not overcome by the stirring appeal that was made, and that was an aged female, in whom maternal affection, recently caused to bleed, completely mastered both a sense of propriety and the love of liberty. "Stop, Mr. Craighead," she exclaimed, "I jist want to tell ye, agin' you loss such a purty boy as I have, in the war, ye will na be sa keen for fighting. Quit talking, and gang yersel' to the war. Ye're always preaching to the boys about it; but I dinna think ye'd be very likely to gang yersel'. Jist ga and try it."

Graphic Description.

A graphic writer thus describes the display of patriotic spirit which was made at the Rocky Spring church:

"As we walk reverentially over the hill, we feel as if we were treading upon sacred ground dedicated to God and American Liberty. We can almost fancy we see the man of God standing where we now stand, telling to the assembled multitude the story of their country's wrongs, and urging them to hesitate no longer which to choose, cowardly inactivity or the noble part of brave defenders of their country's rights. We hear him call on them, as he stands before his old church, and request those who desire to march with him to battle, to hesitate no longer, but place themselves by his side, and acknowledge him their commander, who will lead them to the field of battle, where they will save America or perish in the cause of Freedom. One by one they approach their pastor, and soon a long line of dauntless spirits stretches across the green to the neighbouring road. The wives, mothers and sisters, stand gazing on the exciting scene, and with sweet, encouraging words urge them to stand by their pastor and captain, and trust in the arm of the Lord of Hosts for the result. At length the line is completed, and they are dismissed to meet on the following Monday. Soon after the dawn of day, might be seen the sturdy husbandman with grey hairs scattered over his brow, and the youth of few years, reaching down their old fire-arms, hitherto used only for beasts of prey, or the wild game, but now to be used for other purposes. They fling around their necks their rude powder horns and bullet-pouches, and shouldering their guns march to the place of rendezvous. As the eye wanders over the neighbourhood, in the distance they may be seen, one by one, drawing near the hill. Soon they are all assembled and their company is organized, and after an eloquent appeal to the Almighty, the Reverend Captain places himself at their head, and the noble band marches off to battle. As they march away over the hills, ever and anon they cast a lingering look back upon their beloved friends, who stand weeping upon the hill, and upon their old and loved place of worship, which many of them will never enter again. The company joined the army of Washington, and gave undoubted evidence that their courage was of no mean order but was based upon the hallowed principles of Christianity, which, although discountenancing bloodshed and war, does not forbid the oppressed to make an effort to throw off the yoke of the oppressor."*

---

* Captain Craighead, during the hours spent in camp, habitually acted as Chaplain to his soldiers. After the war was over he returned to his charge and faithfully watched over his congregation until the period of his death, which occured in 1799. Of his valour there can be no question. "He fought and preached alternately," says a friend, in noticing his character, "breasted

Patriotism of West Conococheague.

We find the citizens of West Conococheague animated by the same self-sacrificing patriotism which marked the other sections of the valley during the Revolution. Dr. King, who was installed pastor of the church at Mercersburg, in 1769, not only volunteered his services, and went as chaplain to the battalion which marched from that part of the country, but many were the addresses which he delivered in behalf of the liberties of his country.

In an address delivered to Captain Huston's company, as they were about to leave their homes for the battle field, Dr. King said:

"The case is plain, life must be hazarded, or all is gone. You must go and fight, or send your humble submission, and bow as a beast to its burden, or as an ox to the slaughter. The king of Great Britain has declared us rebels—a capital crime. Submission, therefore, consents to the rope or the axe. Liberty is doubtless gone: none could imagine a tyrant king should be more favourable to conquered rebels than he was to loyal, humble, petitioning subjects. No! no! If ever a people lay in chains, we must, if our enemies carry their point against us, and oblige us to unconditional submission. This is not all. Our tory neighbours will be our proud and tormenting enemies."

In a sermon preached by this patriotic preacher, he spoke in these animating words to his congregation:

"My dear brethren: Since God, in the course of his providence, has so ordered matters as to require every true-hearted American to appear in defence of his liberties, it affords me great pleasure to see you stand forth, with others, in the glorious cause. We have heard your declarations on the point, we have seen your diligence in preparing, and now we see that these were not the efforts of cowardice, boasting at a distance, but that in real earnestness your hearts have been engaged in the matter. After observing in you this heroic and laudable disposition, I apprehend there need not much be said to animate you in the grand object of your present attention, and more especially as you enter upon this warfare, not from the low and sordid views which are the main object of ignorant mercenaries, but with a proper knowledge of the reasons of the contest, and I hope, too, with a consciousness of duty.

"You see an open field before you, wherein you may acquire reputation and honour to yourselves, and do a most beneficial service to your country. The cause of American independence and liberty, which has now called you to go forth to the scene of action, is indeed a cause in which it will be glorious to conquer and honourable to die. The victory, however dearly bought, will be but a cheap purchase, for what of all worldly goods can be of equal value to freedom from slavery, the free and lawful enjoyment and use of our own property, and the free possession of our own lives and consciences? This is an object worthy of our vigorous exertions, a price worthy of a Christian soldiery, a price we are commanded to strive for by the voice of nature and the voice of God. We have now assumed the independent rank we ought to have among the nations of the earth, and we are resolved to be free. Our enemies, with all their own and foreign force they could obtain, are attempting their utmost to make us slaves, and this appears to be the main time of

---

all danger, relying on his God, and the justice of his cause for protection." His company was present at the battle on Long Island and acquitted themselves with much gallantry. Mr. C. was also with the army when Fort Washington was evacuated. There was also present on this occasion, the Rev. Robert Cooper, D. D., pastor of the Presbyterian church at Middle Spring, "a man of sound and strong mind, as well as a divine of great judiciousness and piety," whose congregation were part of the force of volunteers that marched from Carlisle in August, 1776, accompanied by their brave, patriotic, and pious minister. He and Mr. C. were very intimate, and were in the same mess, as they were congenial spirits. Mr. Craighead was somewhat celebrated as a humourist. One day, it is said, going into battle a cannon-ball struck a tree near him, a splinter of which nearly knocked him down. "God bless me!" exclaimed Cooper, "you were nearly knocked to staves." "Oh, yes," was his reply, "and though you are a Cooper you could not have set me up."

the trial—the very turning point which will decide the question, and determine either for freedom or bondage. If their designs can be baffled for this campaign, it is most probable they will despair of success, and give up the cause. At least it will be a powerfully animating motive for Americans to proceed on that course, which they must at all events go through, having nothing before them but success or the most ignominious and shameful alternative."

Such was the patriotic spirit that prevailed in Cumberland valley in Revolutionary times. The application of the word Tory, which designated a person opposed to the war and in favour of British claims, was rare if to be found at all. Not to be zealous in the cause of American Independence was a reproach that not only subjected the suspected individual to public disfavour, but in some instances brought down upon him the notice or discipline of the church. A well authenticated case is related in which a charge was presented to the Session of the church at Falling Spring against a member as a ground for exercising discipline towards him, that "*he is strongly suspected of not being sincere in his professions of attachment to the cause of the Revolution.*"

SACRIFICES.

In contemplating the spirit and action of the men of those times, and of this territory, their descendants have just reason to be proud. Their devotion to their country was signal and emphatic. " Nowhere in the colonies was there more patriotism, resolution and bravery than was evinced on a call to arms, by the hardy, intelligent citizen soldiers of this Scotch-Irish settlement. Their territory and dwellings were in no danger of invasion, or of being trodden by a hostile army. Distance, intervening forests, rugged roads and large water courses were obstacles not to be encountered by an enemy who were dependent on their ships for their supplies and their safe retreat in case of reverses. The freemen of this extensive valley did not at this crisis hold back their movements, either in time or numbers, for forced requisitions, in retaliation for the indifference manifested by the citizens of the eastern border of the province of Pennsylvania, for sufferings and privations of the inhabitants of their valley, when for years, they were exposed to the merciless cruelties of savage enemies aided and instigated by French power, though they could not forget that their repeated supplications to the Provincial government for measures of defence and protection during the Indian wars that were laying waste their settlements with fire and the blood of women and children, were either disregarded or met by tardy and inefficient provision by a government, whose legislation was under the control then of the Representatives of Philadelphia, Chester and Bucks. The brave and hardy men of the Cumberland valley, who had for ten years been exercising their strength and vigour to repair the waste and desolation of their homes and property, from which many had been driven, and for years compelled to seek for their families safety in the counties of Lancaster and York, did not allow themselves to think of resentment or retaliation when the enemy of their country was menacing their State. These patriotic men were too magnanimous and generous in the hour of danger and public necessity to speak or think of old wrongs, committed against them by their fellow-citizens or their late government. But a few days were required to arrange their affairs, collect their arms and plain accoutrements, when they marched forth with drawn swords and shouldered arms, to meet the public enemy, wherever commanded, either on Pennsylvania soil, on the plains of New Jersey, or elsewhere.

Such is a succinct and imperfect history of the settlers and settlement of Cumberland valley. In it we have given somewhat of a prominence to the Scotch-Irish element, but there was a necessity for so doing, which we are sure all will acknowledge, inas-

CHAMBERSBURG IN RUINS.

much as the early population that flocked into this beautiful territory was so largely composed of this class of people. Never need their descendants feel ashamed of so noble an ancestry. Never, either, can they over-estimate the sacrifices which they made in taking possession of the lovely valley in which their spirit yet lingers. No privation seemed to depress them, no exposure to intimidate them, no toil to discourage them. As true as graphic was Rev. Dr. Thomas Creigh's description of them, in his address at the memorable Presbyterian Re-union on the camp ground near Oakville, September 24th, 1871, when he said :

"They were a *hardy* people. They were enured to hardships from the beginning— not only in felling the forests and in preparing the land for cultivation, and so on— but in consequence, also, of their contests and warfare with the Indians. It would require a volume to tell of all these trials and troubles. They were plain in their habits, and were contented with their style of living, which was of the plainest kind. They knew nothing about the extravagances and follies of the present age. With their log cabins of 20 feet by 25 feet, built of logs, with clap-board roof and puncheon floor, they were perfectly contented. It was their parlor, their family room, their chamber, nursery and kitchen all in one. The ordinary wear of the *men* was a loose waumus or hunting shirt, with trousers made of the same material, and moccasins made of deer skin. The ordinary dress of the *women* was a short gown and petticoat made of linsey woolsey, with a sun-bonnet or hood.

"This was their ordinary wear. But still they had something better, *i. e.* those who could afford it. The male attire was a coat of homespun and a waistcoat, with breeches often made of buckskin, with knee buckles, long stockings, shoe buckles, and a cocked hat. The ladies' attire was a dress of silk, or of some other material equally costly, a bonnet made of material to correspond, a kerchief of white around the neck, and covering the upper part of the breast. Their food was equally simple and plain. Hog and hominy and potatoes, with mush and milk, were their standing fare. And as for coffee and tea, if the old folks could have them once a week, and this on the Sabbath day, they were more than satisfied with the privilege. Nor must we forget to mention the little shelf on which rested the family Bible, the Confession of Faith, Psalm Book, Pilgrim's Progress, Boston's Fourfold State, Saint's Rest, and volumes of a kindred character."

Thus was it that the daring pioneers laid the foundations of the intelligent and upright community which has succeeded them, and were able to bequeath the rich legacy their children enjoy.

THE BURNING OF CHAMBERSBURG.

We feel that our sketch would be incomplete without some account of the destruction of Chambersburg by the rebel force under General Early, July 30th, 1864. However familiar to those now living this event may be, it is in every sense desirable that the history of it should be found in our volume, for the sake of the generations to follow. This we shall give, confining ourselves strictly to the calamity itself, with its accompanying incidents, and we are happy to be able to do so from statements prepared by citizens of the place, who were witnesses of the occasion.

ENTRANCE OF THE REBELS.

"The rebels, having been interrupted in their entrance into the town until daylight, they employed their time in planting two batteries in commanding positions, and getting up their whole column, fully three thousand strong. About 4 o'clock on

Saturday morning they opened with their batteries and fired some half a dozen shots into the town, but they did no damage. Immediately thereafter their skirmishers entered by almost every street and alley running out west and southwest, and finding their way clear, their cavalry, to the number of eight hundred and thirty-one, came in under the immediate command of General McCausland. General Bradley Johnson was with him, and also the notorious Major Harry Gilmore.

Plundering Promptly Commenced.

"While McCausland and Gilmore were reconnoitering around to get a deal with the citizens for tribute, their soldiers exhibited the proficiency of their training by immediate and almost indiscriminate robbery. Hats, caps, boots, watches, silverware, and everything of value, were appropriated from individuals on the street without ceremony, and when a man was met whose appearance indicated a plethoric purse, a pistol would be presented to his head with the order to 'deliver,' with a dexterity that would have done credit to the freebooting accomplishments of an Italian brigand.

Tribute Demanded.

"General McCausland rode up to a number of citizens, and gave notice that unless five hundred thousand dollars in greenbacks, or one hundred thousand dollars in gold, were paid in half an hour, the town would be burned; but no one responded to his call. He was promptly answered that Chambersburg could not and would not pay any ransom. He had the Court House bell rung to convene the citizens, hoping to frighten them into the payment of a large sum of money, but no one attended. Infuriated at the determination of the people, Major Gilmore rode up to a group of citizens, consisting of Thomas B. Kennedy, William McClellan, J. McDowell Sharpe, Dr. J. C. Richards, William H. McDowell, W. S. Everett, Edward G. Etter, and M. A. Foltz, and ordered them under arrest. He said that they would be held for the payment of the money, and if not paid, he would take them to Richmond as hostages, and also burn every house in town. While he was endeavouring to force them into an effort to raise him money, his men commenced the work of firing, and they were discharged when it was found that intimidation would effect nothing.

Town in Flames.

"The main part of the town was enveloped in flames in ten minutes. No time was given to remove women or children, the sick, or even the dead. No notice of the kind was communicated to any one, but the work of destruction was at once commenced. They divided into squads, and fired every other house, and often every house, if there was any prospect of plunder. They would beat in the door with iron bars or heavy plank, smash up furniture with an axe, throw fluid or oil upon it, and ply the match. They almost invariably entered every room of each house, rifled the drawers of every bureau, appropriated money, jewelry, watches, and any other valuables, and often would present pistols to the heads of inmates, men and women, and demand money or their lives. In nearly half the instances they demanded owners to ransom their property, and in a few cases it was done, and the property burned. Although a number of persons, mostly widows, paid them sums from twenty-five to two hundred dollars, there were but few cases where the property was saved thereby. Few houses escaped rifling; nearly all were plundered of everything that could be carried away. In most cases houses were entered in the rudest manner, and no time whatever was allowed for the families to escape, much less to save anything. Many families had the utmost difficulty to get themselves and children out in time, and not one-half had so much as a change of clothing with them. They would rush from story to story to rob, and always fire the building at once, in order to keep the family from detecting their robberies. Feeble and helpless women and children were treated like brutes—told insolently to get out or burn; and even the sick were not spared. Several invalids had to be carried out as the red flames licked their couches. Thus the work of desolation continued for two hours, more than half the town on fire at once; and the wild glare of the flames, the shrieks of women and children, and, often louder than all, the terrible blasphemy of the rebels, conspired to present such a scene of horror as has never been witnessed by the present generation. No one was spared, save by accident. The widow and the the fatherless cried and plead in vain that they would be homeless and helpless. A rude oath would close all hope of mercy, and they would fly to save their lives. The old and infirm, who tottered before them, were thrust aside, and the torch applied in their presence to hasten their departure. In a few hours the major portion of Chambersburg, its chief wealth and business, its capital and elegance, were devoured by a barbarous foe—three millions of property sacrificed—three thousand human beings homeless, and many penniless, and all without so much as a pretence that the citizens of the doomed town, or any of them, had violated any accepted rule of civilized warfare. Such is the deliberate, voluntary record made by General Early, a corps commander in the insurgent army."*

Description of the Scene.

"As to the scene itself," says the Rev. Joseph Clark, "it beggars description. My own residence being in the outskirts, and feeling it the call of duty to be with my family, I could only look on from without. The day was sultry and calm, not a breath stirring, and each column of smoke rose black, straight and single, first one and then another, and another and another, until the columns blended and commingled; and then one vast and lurid column of smoke and flame rose perpendicularly to the sky, and spread out into a vast crown like a cloud of sackcloth hanging over the doomed city, whilst the roar and the surging, the crackling and the crash of falling timbers and walls broke upon the still air with a fearful dissonance, and the screams and sounds of agony of burning animals, hogs, and cows, and horses, made the welkin horrid with sounds of woe. It was a scene to be witnessed and heard once in a life time."†

"The aged, the sick, the dying, and the dead were carried out from their burning homes; mothers with babes in their arms, and surrounded by their frightened little ones, fled through the streets jeered and taunted by the brutal soldiery. Indeed, their escape seemed almost a miracle, as the streets were in a blaze from one end to the other, and they were compelled to flee through a long road of fire. Had not the day been perfectly calm, many must have perished in the flames. The conflagration in its height was a scene of surpassing grandeur and terror. A tall black column of smoke rose up to the very skies, around it were wrapped long streamers of flames, writhing and twisting themselves into a thousand fantastic shapes, while through it, as though they were prayers carried heavenward by the incense of some great altar sacrifice, there went up on the smoky flame-riven clouds the cries and shrieks of the women and children. But the moment of greatest alarm was not reached until some of the more humane of the rebel officers warned the women to flee, if they wished to escape violence to their persons. We cannot in this letter describe the scenes of the sad flight which followed."‡

---

* Colonel A. K. McClure's article in the "Franklin Repository," August 24th, 1864.
† Article in the "Presbyterian" of August 6th, 1864.
‡ Rev. S. J. Niccolls, in the "Pittsburgh Evening Chronicle."

"For miles around, the frightened inhabitants fled, they knew not whither, some continuing their flight until they dropped to the ground with exhaustion. Pocket-books and watches were taken by wholesale, bundles, shawls and valises were snatched out of women's and children's hands to be thrown away. Cows and dogs and cats were burned to death, and the death-cries of the poor dumb brutes sounded like the groans of human beings. It is a picture that may be misrepresented but cannot be heightened."*

INCIDENTS OF THE BURNING.

One scoundrel accepted five dollars from a frightened female to carry her trunk to a place of safety, where he coolly broke it open and helped himself to the most valuable part of the contents. A little dead child was enclosed in a chest and buried by the terrified parents in their garden for fear it would be burned in their house. A lady in delicate health was watched by one of the robbers, and allowed to drag her trunk outside of the town, after which he searched it, and appropriated the valuables it contained. She asked, whether that was southern chivalry and received for reply, "Take that back or I'll blow your brains out." She did *not* retract, and did *not* have her brains blown out. An old and very estimable lady, who had not walked for three years, was told to run, as her house was on fire. She replied that she had not walked for three years. With horrid curses the wretch poured powder under her chair, declaring that he would teach her to walk, and while in the act of applying fire to his train some neighbours ran in and carried her away. A rebel soldier threatened a young man to "blow his brains out" if he would not let the fire burn. With a revolver in hand his sister rushed out of the adjoining room, her eyes flashing with a more terrible fire than that of rebel kindling: "Begone, thou brutal wretch!" said the heroine, as she aimed with precision at the rebel's head, who scampered away in a terrible fright. Three sides around a lady's house (Mrs. Denig's) were on fire. The fourth was enclosed with an iron fence. An attempt to cross the fence burned her palm into crisp. She sat down in the middle of her narrow lot. Around her she folded a few rags dipped in water, to shelter her person against the heat. An old negro crouched down by her side and helped to moisten the rags. Her face though covered was blistered by the intense heat. Now and then God sent a breath of wind to waft the hot air away and allowed her to take breath. Virtually it was a martyrdom at the stake, those two hours amid the flames. Only after she was rescued did the sight of her ruined home open the fountain of tears. "Don't cry, missus," said Peter, the old negro; "de Lord saved our lives from de fire." A squad of rebels seized a flag which a lady happened to have in her house. With some difficulty she wrested it from their grasp, folded it around her person and walked away from her burning house past the furious soldiery, determined that the flag should become her shroud ere it should fall into the hands of the foe. A mother of a large family of children was ordered to leave the house in five minutes as the house must be burned. She collected them all around her to obey the cruel summons. Preparations were at once made to fire the building, in the rooms above and below, and as the family group walked out of the large and beautiful mansion, the children burst into loud weeping. "I am ashamed of you," said the tenderly loving, yet heroic woman, "to let these men see you cry;" and every child straightened up, brushed away the falling tears, and bravely marched out of the doomed home. An elderly woman, of true Spartan grit, gave one of the house burners such a sound drubbing with a heavy broom, that the invader retreated, to leave the work of destruction to be performed by another party, after the woman had left to escape the flames of the

---

* J. K. Shryock, Esq., in "Lutheran and Missionary."

CHAMBERSBURG.—MAIN STREET, SOUTH FROM CENTRE SQUARE.

adjoining buildings. The house of Mr. James Watson, an old and feeble man of over eighty, was entered, and because his wife earnestly remonstrated against the burning, they fired the room, hurled her into it, and locked the door on the outside. Her daughters rescued her by bursting in the door before her clothing took fire. Mr. Jacob Wolfkill, a very old citizen, and prostrated by sickness so that he was utterly unable to be out of bed, plead in vain to be spared a horrible death in the flames of his own house, but they fired the building. Through the superhuman efforts of some friends, he was carried away safely. Mrs. Lindsay, a very feeble lady of nearly eighty, fainted when they fired her house, and was left to be devoured in the flames, but fortunately, a relative reached the house in time, lifted her in a buggy, and pulled her away while the flames were hissing each other over their heads on the street. Mrs. Kuss, wife of a jeweller on Main street, lay dead, and although they were shown the dead body, they plied the torch and burned the house Mrs. J. K. Shryock had Mrs. Kuss's sick babe in her arms, and plead for the sake of the dead mother and sick child to spare that house, but it was unavailing. The body of Mrs Kuss was hurriedly buried in the garden, and the work of destruction went on. When the flames drove Mrs. Shryock away with the child, she went to one of the men, and presenting the babe, said, "*Is this revenge sweet?*" A tender chord was touched, and without speaking he burst into tears. He afterwards followed Mrs. Shryock, and asked whether he could do anything for her, but it was too late. The houses of Messrs. McClellan, Sharpe, and Nixon, being located east of the Franklin Railroad, and out of the business part of the town, were not reached until the rest of the town was in flames, and the roads were streaming with homeless women and children. Mr. McClellan's residence was the first one entered, and he was notified that the house must be burned. Mrs. McClellan immediately stepped to the door, and laying one hand on the rebel officer, and pointing with the other to the frantic fugitive women and children passing by, said to him: "*Sir, is not your vengeance glutted? We have a home and can get another; but can you spare no homes for those poor, helpless people and their children? When you and I, and all of us, shall meet before the Great Judge, can you justify this act?*" He made no reply, but ordered his command away, and that part of the town was saved. Captain Smith, son of Governor Smith, of Virginia, with a squad of men, passing by all the intervening houses, entered the beautiful residence of Colonel McClure, one mile from the centre of the town, with the information to Mrs. McClure, then, and for some time before, an invalid, that the house must be burned by way of retaliation. Ten minutes were given her in which to leave the house, and in less than ten minutes the flames were doing the work of destruction, and Mrs. McClure and the other members of the family at home, started on foot, in the heat of the hottest of days, in order to escape the vengeance of the chivalry. Whilst the flames were progressing in the house, as well as the large and well-filled barn, the Captain helped himself to Mrs. McClure's gold watch, silver pitcher and other valuables. The gold watch and other articles were easily concealed, but the silver pitcher was rather unwieldy, and could not be secreted from profane eyes, as he rode back through the town from the scene of his triumph. He resolved, therefore, to give a public display of his generosity. He stopped at the house of the Rev. James F. Kennedy, and handed the pitcher to his wife, with the request, "Please deliver this to Mrs. Colonel McClure, with the compliments of Captain Smith." Among the principal sufferers was the Rev. Dr. Schneck, a distinguished minister of the German Reformed church, long a resident of the place. Vainly did he contend with the flames. His cosy, substantial house, with all that it contained—the costly relics borne home from two European tours, his valuable library, all his manuscripts, precious domestic keepsakes and furniture—all became a heap of undistinguishable ruins.

Retribution.

Several of the thieves who participated in burning Chambersburg were sent suddenly to their last account. An officer, whose papers identified him as Major Bowen, Eighth Virginia Cavalry, was conspicuous for his brutality and robberies. He got too far south of the firing parties to be covered by them, and in his desire to glut his thievish propensities, he was isolated. He was captured by several citizens in the midst of his brutal work, and was dispatched promptly. When he was fired at and slightly wounded, he took refuge in the burning cellar of one of the houses, and there, with the intense heat blistering him, he begged them to spare his life, but it was in vain. Half the town was still burning, and it was taxing humanity rather too much to save a man who had added the boldest robbery to atrocious arson. He was shot dead, and now sleeps near the Falling Spring, nearly opposite the depot.

Mr. Thomas H. Doyle, of Loudon, who had served in Easton's Battery, followed the retreating rebels towards Loudon, to capture stragglers. When beyond St. Thomas, he caught Captain Cochran, Quartermaster of the Eleventh Virginia Cavalry, and as he recognized him as one who had participated in the destruction of Chambersburg, he gave him just fifteen minutes to live. Cochran was armed with sword and pistols, but he was taken so suddenly by Mr. Doyle that he had no chance to use them. He begged piteously for his life, but Mr. Doyle was inexorable, the foe who burns and robs must die, and he so informed him peremptorily. At the very second he shot the thief dead, and found on his person $815 of greenbacks, all stolen from the citizens of Chambersburg, and $1,750 of rebel currency. His sword, belt and pistols were brought to Chambersburg by Mr. Doyle.*

Such was the burning of Chambersburg, with its accompanying acts of insolence, theft and violence. The dreadful deed was performed under a written order from General Jubal A. Early, in retaliation, as he alleged, for the burning of six houses in Virginia. Justice requires it, and we gladly make it a matter of record, that fiendish and relentless as were McCausland and most of his command, there were notable exceptions, who bravely maintained the humanities of war in the midst of the infuriated freebooters who were plying the torch and securing the plunder. One surgeon, when he saw the fire break out, wept like a child, and publicly denounced the atrocity of his commander. A captain, formerly of Baltimore, peremptorily refused to participate in the burning, but aided many people to get some clothing and other articles out of their houses, and asked a citizen to write to his friends in Baltimore and acquit him of the hellish work. Another surgeon, who gave his horse to a lady to get some articles out of the burning town, publicly deplored the sad work of McCausland, and when asked who his commanding officer was, answered, "Madam, I am ashamed to say that General McCausland is my commander." Another rebel officer, whom Mr. Jabob Hoke met in his house, as the enemy was about to fire it, said, "My friend, for God's sake, tell me what you value most, and I will take it to a place of safety. They are going to burn every house in town."

It is only necessary to add, that the people of Chambersburg, under their great calamity, did not yield to gloom or despondency, but maintained a noble equanimity and fortitude, and that out of the ruins which they were called to contemplate, have, through their energy and perseverance, risen fine structures, now making the place one of the handsomest towns in the State.

---

* From Rev. Dr. Schneck's work on "The Burning of Chambersburg," to which we make a general acknowledgment of indebtedness for facts here presented.

MEN OF MARK.

BIOGRAPHICAL SKETCHES.

BENJAMIN CHAMBERS.

BETWEEN the years 1726 and 1730, four brothers—James, Robert, Joseph and Benjamin Chambers, emigrated from the county of Antrim, in Ireland, to the province of Pennsylvania. They settled and built a mill shortly after, at the mouth of Fishing creek, now in Dauphin county, and purchased a tract of very fine land at that place from the Proprietaries of the Province.

These adventurous brothers, attracted by the fine country beyond the Susquehanna, were among the first to explore and settle in the Kittatinny, now Cumberland valley. James made a settlement at the head of Green Spring, near Newville; Robert at the head of Middle Spring, near Shippensburg; and Joseph and Benjamin at the confluence of Falling Spring and Conococheague creeks, where Chambersburg is situated, whither they were attracted by a description received from a hunter of the fine waterfall he had observed in one of his excursions through the valley. These settlements and locations were made about or before 1730. By an arrangement among the brothers, Joseph returned to their property at the mouth of Fishing creek, and Benjamin, the younger brother, then about twenty-one years of age, improved his settlement at the Falling Spring, thus becoming the first white settler in what is now Franklin county. Having procured a title to as much land as he desired, he proceeded to erect a log house, covered with lapped shingles and fastened by nails, a style of building out of the common mode of round logs and clapboard roofs secured by beams. Some time after, being induced to visit the east side of the Susquehanna, he left his house unoccupied for a short time, and on his return found it burned to ashes. This was afterwards ascertained to be the work of an unprincipled hunter, who was induced to do it for the sake of the *nails*, which at that day, in this wild region, were esteemed no ordinary prize.

Notwithstanding his reverses, the young pioneer prosecuted anew his improvements, building houses and clearing lands. Soon he built himself a saw mill at the mouth of Falling Spring. This was an important improvement to himself and others disposed to settle in the surrounding wilderness. In a few years after, he erected a flouring mill, an accommodation which contributed much to the comfort of the early settlers, and had considerable influence in inducing settlements in the vicinity.

Mr. Chambers maintained a friendly intercourse with the Indians in his region, traded with them, and had so much of their confidence and respect that they did not injure or molest him.

On one occasion, being engaged in hay making in his meadow below Chambersburg, he observed some Indians secretly stalking in the thickets around the meadow. Suspecting some mischievous design, he gave them a severe chase in the night, with some dogs, across the creek and through the woods, to the great alarm of the Indians, who afterwards acknowledged they had gone to the meadow for the purpose of taking from Benjamin his *watch*, and carrying off a negro woman whom he owned, and who, they thought, would be useful to raise corn for them; but they declared that they would not have hurt the colonel.

During the controversy between the Penns and Lord Baltimore, relative to the boundaries of their respective provinces, Mr. Chambers went to England to assist by his testimony in determining the issue involved. His evidence was of great value to the Penns, and had a decisive influence upon the settlement of the controversy. During his absence on that business, he revisited his native place and induced many persons to accompany him on his return, generously defraying the expenses of those who were poor and without means. His settlement steadily grew in numbers and in wealth. Although surrounded by Indians, his tact, upright dealing and rigid justice secured and commanded their respect and friendship. He spoke the language of the Delawares with fluency, and was on terms of intimacy with their chief men. A sacred truce was long maintained between them, and the tomahawk was buried deep. The influence of this just and pacific policy towards the aborigines was of necessity confined within a very narrow sphere. Untoward and sinister agencies were active elsewhere. French ambition, assisted by the baleful influence of French gold, poisoned the blood of the red men and fired their hearts with an intense and savage desire for vengeance. A war of extermination was proclaimed and waged against the English.

The life of the isolated and scattered settlements of the Kittatinny country was about to go out in blood. The dark war cloud came rolling in upon the infant settlement at Chambersburg. It was a time when the stoutest heart might well quail and the manly cheek might well blanch, for friend and foe were alike victims upon the altar of Moloch.

On the 3d of July, 1754, Colonel Washington was compelled to capitulate to a superior force of allied French and Indians, at Fort Necessity, Under the weight of this dire calamity the frontier settlements invoked the assistance and protection of the Provincial Government. The following petition will serve to illustrate the earnestness of the appeal and the imminency of the peril.

To the Honourable James Hamilton, Esq., Lieutenant Governor and Commander-in-Chief of the Province of Pennsylvania and Counties of New Castle, Kent, and Sussex, in Delaware.

The address of the subscribers, inhabitants of the county of Cumberland, humbly sheweth :

That we are now in the most imminent danger by a powerful army of cruel, merciless, and inhuman enemies, by whom our lives, liberties, and estates, and all that tends to promote our welfare, are in the utmost danger of dreadful destruction, and this lamentable truth is most evident from the late defeat of the Virginia forces; and now, as we are under your Honour's protection, we would beg your immediate notice, we living upon the frontiers of the Province, and our enemies so close upon us, nothing doubting but that these considerations will affect your Honour; and as you have our welfare at heart, that you defer nothing that may tend to hasten our relief, etc.

This petition was signed by Benjamin Chambers and seventy-four others, and dated Cumberland, July 15th, 1754.

The intelligence of the bloody drama which closed the march of Braddock's doomed army on the 9th of July, 1755, completed the dismay of the unprotected settlements. Many of the people fled, with what effects they could carry, to Shippensburg and Carlisle.

Mr. Chambers, ever upon the alert to save his infant colony from the destruction which seemed to be close at hand, wrote and forwarded the following letter:

Falling Spring, Sabbath Morning,
Nov. 2d, 1755.

To the Inhabitants of the Lower Part of the county of Cumberland.

Gentlemen :—If you intend to go to the assistance of your neighbours, you need not wait longer for the certainty of the news. The Great Cove is destroyed. James

Campbell left his company last night and went to the fort at Mr. Steel's meeting house, and there saw some of the inhabitants of the Great Cove, who gave this account : that, as they came over the hill, they saw their houses in flames. The messenger says that there are but one hundred, and that they are divided into two parts; the one part to go against the Cove, and the other against the Conolloways, and there are two French among them. They are Delawares and Shawneese. The part that came against the Cove are under the command of Shingos, the Delaware king. The people of the Cove that came off saw several men lying dead ; they heard the murder shout, and the firing of guns, and saw the Indians going into their houses before they left sight of the Cove. I have sent express to Marsh creek at the same time I send this; so I expect there will be a good company there this day; and as there are but one hundred of the enemy, I think it is in our power, if God permit, to put them to flight, if you turn out well from your parts. I understand that the West Settlement is designed to go, if they can get any assistance, to repel them. All in haste, from

Your humble servant,
BENJAMIN CHAMBERS.

These urgent appeals remained unanswered. The Provincial Government was too indifferent to heed these calls for help, and too weak to furnish arms and men for the protection of the frontiers. There was no alternative, but to abandon the settlement, or to remain, stand for its defence, and share its fate. To abandon it, was to insure its annihilation. To remain, and attempt to save it, was to imperil life. A stout heart and a cool head were needed, or all would be lost. But the path of duty is never long doubtful to the true man. The hour of trial is the crucible that refines human nature and lifts the soul above the dross of earth.

Mr. Chambers resolved to stand by his feeble settlement, to rescue it from the peril that threatened it, or to perish with it. He erected a fort at his own expense, and armed it with two cannon of four pound calibre and with such other offensive weapons as he could procure. He tempered his show of force, upon all proper occasions, with a friendly and conciliatory policy towards the Indians. It is true that his fort was not impregnable, and could not have withstood a fierce assault or held out against the rigours of a siege. But the unfaltering courage and iron will of its commandant made it strong enough to baffle savage vengeance, and to guard through long, weary years of desultory warfare the town which his energy and enterprise had founded.

About the year 1748, Mr. Chambers received the commission of colonel from the Provincial Government.

It would be most likely that he who had left his native land and established his home upon the frontiers of civilization; whose destiny it was to battle with the dangers of the wilderness; to toil, and struggle, and suffer; whose task it was to found and nurture into strength a prosperous town; whose clear head, wise counsels, and stern justice, managed and adjudged its affairs in peace, and whose unflinching bravery and unyielding fortitude defended it in war, would be a patriotic citizen, a good neighbour, a just man, a firm friend, a devoted father, and a devout Christian. Colonel Chambers possessed all these qualities in an eminent degree. In private life he was respected and esteemed for the purity of his character, the kindliness of his disposition, the soundness of his judgment, and for his austere love of justice. He was the recognized counsellor of the community in which he lived, and for many years a magistrate—the arbiter of all disputes, from whose judgment none cared to appeal.

The original settlers of Chambersburg and vicinity were almost exclusively Scotch-Irish Presbyterians, devout believers in the Westminster Confession, and imbued with the deepest reverence for the Sabbath and the sanctuary.

Mr. Chambers himself was a disciple of this creed, and built his settlement upon the solid rock of the Calvinistic doctrine and faith. Having a profound conviction that his settlement could only be stimulated into a sturdy and healthy growth by means of the ameliorating and enlightening influences of education and religion, he selected, at an early day, the most eligible and romantic site in the town, and by a deed dated in 1768 donated it to the religious society, " then and thereafter adhering to the Westminster Confession of Faith, and the mode of government therein contained, and for the purpose of a house of worship, session and school-houses, and cemetery."

At the commencement of the Revolutionary War in 1775, Col. Chambers was so infirm and advanced in years, being then about seventy years of age, as to be incapable of the fatigues and exposure of a campaign so distant as the heights of Boston. Patriotism shone forth in his family. His eldest son, James, raised a company of infantry from the neighbourhood, which he commanded as captain, and in 1775, marched, accompanied by his younger brothers, William and Benjamin, as cadets, to join the American Army, then encamped on the high ground of Boston, where the Royal Army was besieged. William was about twenty-two years old, and Benjamin twenty. His three sons remained in the army during the campaign; James having been advanced to the rank of colonel, and William and Benjamin to that of captain. They were also with the army during the arduous and trying campaigns of '76-'77 in the Jerseys, as well as at the battles of Brandywine and Germantown in 1778. On account of the infirmity of their father, and the embarrassed situation of his property and pecuniary affairs, which had been deprived of the necessary attentions of the young men, the younger brothers, William and Benjamin, returned home and attended to the farm and mills. They occasionally, however, assisted in the pursuits of Indians who had dared at times to make incursions upon the settlements about Bedford and Huntingdon.

James remained in the army until the close of the Revolutionary War, and afterwards was appointed a general of the militia, a brigade of whom, including a number of volunteers he commanded in the army to suppress the Western or Whiskey insurrection in Pennsylvania in 1794.

Col. Benjamin Chambers was married twice. His first wife, whom he married in 1741, and who was a daughter of Captain Robert Patterson, of Lancaster, was the mother of his eldest son, James. After her death, which occurred in a few years, he married Miss Jane Williams, the daughter of a Presbyterian clergyman, of the Virginia colony, from Wales. He died on the 17th of February, 1788, at the age of eighty years.

REV. THOMAS CRAIGHEAD.

ALTHOUGH this excellent minister spent only a small portion of his life in Cumberland valley, he properly deserves a place among its distinguished men. He was the pioneer of all its ministers, and was their general correspondent for bringing over and settling ministers from Ireland.

He was the son of Rev. Robert Craighead, a native of Scotland, who removed to Ireland, was a pastor in Derry and Donoughmore, was the author of several, even now, highly prized volumes in spiritual and controversial divinity, and twice a Commissioner of the Synod of Ulster at Loudon. Thomas was born and studied medicine in Scotland, but he soon became a preacher, and was settled for ten or twelve years in Ireland. Near this time a large emigration of Irish Presbyterians to America took place, in consequence of the oppression of the landlords, the sacramental test, and the marriage grievances, and Thomas Craighead was induced to unite with them.

His name occurs first, in 1715, among the ministers of New England. There were many immigrants from Ireland in that region, but Mather first notices him as a preacher at Freetown, about forty miles south of Boston. He was a relative of a Mr. Hathaway of that town, and had probably gone there at that gentleman's invitation. Some difficulties arose to prevent his final settlement, with reference to the payment of his salary, in respect to which they were quite delinquent and he was perhaps impatient. Mather writes, (5th month 22d, 1718, and 5th month 21st, 1719,) entreating the people, "to give a demonstration of the wisdom that is from above" by encouraging Mr. Craighead in his work, and says that they could not be insensible that he was "a man of an excellent spirit and a great blessing to their plantation," "a man of singular piety, meekness, humility and industry in the work of God. All that are acquainted with him have a precious esteem of him, and if he should be driven from among you, it would be such a damage, yea, such a ruin, as is not without horror to be thought of." These plans appear to have been unsuccessful, for, at least, in 1723 he is said by President Stiles, to have "gone to the Jerseys." In the year 1724, (January 28th,) he became a member of Newcastle Presbytery, which then included portions of Delaware, Pennsylvania and New Jersey. He was called both to Elk and to White Clay, but he accepted the invitation to the latter place, under the condition that he should give a portion of his time to Brandywine.

In 1733, Mr. Craighead removed to Lancaster county, Pennsylvania, and in September of that year he received and accepted a call to Pequea, where he was installed October 31. Donegal Presbytery, of which he now became a member, always speak of him as "Father Craighead," and appear to have had a peculiar veneration and love for him. He was very active in planting and building up churches in that region. His preaching was remarkably fervent and often attended with revivals. His theology was strictly conformed to the Westminster Confession, for which he displayed a special attachment, and which he subscribed first, both in Newcastle and Donegal Presbyteries.

Mr. Craighead's pastoral relation to the church of Pequea, was dissolved September 19th, 1735. On the 27th of the next month he was appointed by Presbytery to supply "the people of the Conodoguinit," by which was meant the congregation of Upper Pennsborough, whose place of meeting was a mile or two northwestward of Carlisle. After fulfilling this appointment, and a subsequent one at Hopewell, he received a call from the people of Hopewell, which he was prepared to accept, but as there were some difficulties respecting "the boundaries" between that congregation and that of Pennsborough, action in the case was delayed. He, however, supplied the people of Hopewell, whose place of meeting was at "the Big Spring," now Newville. Some difficulties followed him on account of his continuing to debar his wife from the communion. After quite a long consideration of the affair in Presbytery, Mr. C. declared his resolution to admit his wife to sealing ordinances for the future, and Mrs. C. expressed her aversion against overhauling former unhappy differences, declaring that "her husband lived in desirable peace and unity with her;" when Presbytery declared itself satisfied, and withdrew all action in the case. On the 17th of November, 1737, the call of the people of Hopewell was renewed and accepted, and his installation was ordered "at some convenient time before the next stated meeting." His pastorate there, however, was of only a short duration. He was now an aged man, though his earnestness and power remained unabated. A descendant of his, (Thomas Craighead, Jr., of Whitehill, Cumberland county,) declares that under his discourses not unfrequently so intense were the emotions of his hearers, that they were unwilling at the proper time to disperse. At such times he would continue his impassioned discourse while his audience were melted in tears. On one of these occasions, (near the close of April, 1739,) he became exhausted, and hastened to pronounce the benediction; waiving his hand he exclaimed, "Farewell! farewell!" and sank down and expired. His remains are reported to lie, without a monument, under the corner stone of the present house of worship at Newville.

Mr. Craighead had four sons: Thomas, whose daughter, Elizabeth, married Rev. Dr. Matthew Wilson, pastor of the First Presbyterian church of Philadelphia; Andrew, who died a bachelor, at White Clay creek; John, who was a large landholder near Carlisle, Pa., and whose descendants are numerous, two of them being eminent ministers in the Presbyterian Church. Jane, one of his three daughters, married Rev. Adam Boyd, whose descendants are well known in Baltimore and vicinity. Alexander, the third son, was early introduced into the ministry under his father, and was licensed to preach (October 8th, 1734,) and ordained and installed over the church at Middle Octorara, Presbytery of Donegal, November 18th, 1735. He was probably the first to whom the duty was assigned of supplying two Sabbaths, at three different times, (October 16th, 1734, April 4th, 1735, and September 3d, 1785,) for "the settlement over the river." He was, however, never an inhabitant of the Cumberland valley. He was an ardent supporter of Whitefield and the revivals. His zeal betrayed him into some irregularities which became the subject of much discussion before the Synod. Before any result was reached the Synod was divided, and he adhered to the New Brunswick party. On the refusal of that party to revive "The Solemn League and Covenant," he separated from them and attempted to establish churches in connection with the Reform Presbyteries. In 1749, he removed to Augusta county, Va., but his congregation being scattered on the news of Braddock's defeat, (1755,) he removed to Mecklenburgh county, N. C. In July, 1753, his name appears again on the roll of the New York Synod, and on that of New Castle Presbytery in 1754. In 1758, he became pastor of a congregation at Rocky River, N. C., in the vicinity of which he lived and died, (March, 1766,) much respected and beloved. He has numerous descendants in the South and West, and one of these, Thomas B. Craighead, was an eminent minister in Tennessee, though finally suspended for some errors in doctrine, (1824.)

REV. SAMUEL THOMPSON.

IN the minutes of the Presbytery of Donegal for Nov. 16, 1737, it is recorded that "Mr. Samuel Thompson, lately from Ireland, produced credentials and recommendatory letters," and on the next day, he was "received as a probationer and exhorted to diligence in his studies." He was at the same time appointed to "supply at Pennsborough, the first four Sabbaths to come." This is the first authentic notice we have found respecting the subject of this sketch.

He continued to supply the two churches of Upper and Lower Pennsborough, although application was made from the people at Falling Spring, (Chambersburg,) for his appointment there in 1738. It was during this period that some complaint was made of him before Synod, on account of a letter which he had written, in which were "some things very offensive to the honourable proprietor." On his being interrogated by his Presbytery, "he acknowledged his imprudence and inadvertency in writing said letter, which was designed to signify not his own but his people's thoughts, and which he never expected to go any farther than the one to whom it was directed." A number of the people of Pennsborough being present, "took the whole blame of the writing on themselves, and declared that they were provoked thereunto by their being credibly informed that some in authority had threatened to order a constable to pull Mr. T. out of the pulpit on the Sabbath, and drag him at an horse's tail to Newtown." This acknowledgment was, on the whole, accepted, but a member of Presbytery was sent "sharply to rebuke the people for constraining him to write the letter." The request of the two congregations of Pennsborough to have him ordained and installed over them was, for some time, declined on account of arrearages due to former supplies, but finally a satisfactory arrangement was made respecting them, and after "public advertisement at the meeting-house door, that if any would advance any lawful objection against his being set apart to the work of the holy ministry, it should then be given," he was publicly ordained and installed Nov. 14, 1739.

The pastorate of Mr. Thompson continued for nearly ten years, (1739–49.) In 1745, he was released from his charge of Lower Pennsborough, (Silvers' Spring,) "on account of bodily weakness," though he was still directed "to be generous and industrious in preaching there, according to his convenience and their necessity." Under his labours, the congregation of Upper Pennsborough became very numerous and influential. The building in which they worshiped was insufficient to accommodate the multitudes who assembled, especially on sacramental occasions, and not unfrequently, in fair weather, they collected in a grove on the high bank of the Conodoguinnett. He resided on the extensive glebe which the proprietors had given in fee simple to the congregation, and he is said to have cultivated it to a large extent with his own hands. He was, however, a good scholar, as was in fact indispensable to meet the high demands of his hearers and the ecclesiastical wants of that day. Cases of discipline were numerous in his church, which he appears to have managed with wisdom and fidelity. In two instances he was himself charged with immoralities, but after a careful investigation he was, in the one case, reproved for prevarication, but in the other was honourably cleared by his Presbytery and restored to his ministerial office, from which he had been suspended during the inquiry. So many "unhappy jealousies and disputes" had however arisen in the course of these judicial cases, that Mr. Thompson "doubted whether he could be further useful in this congregation," and at his own request and with his people's consent he was released from his pastoral connection with it, November 14, 1749.

It was during the pastorate of Mr. Thompson at Pennsborough that the first division of the Presbyterian church took place, (1743–58). He was made an object of special attack by those who charged ministers with unfaithfulness to their flocks, and a spirit of schism was strongly expressed among his people. He, himself, adhered to the Philadelphia Synod, or what was called the Old Side, but his congregation is said to have been among those which were "divided during the revival." There is no record of the organization of the church which was formed during these dissensions at Carlisle.

On his dismission from Upper Pennsborough, he went to reside at Great Conewago, in Adams county, near Gettysburg, where he was installed as pastor, and appears to have spent his time peacefully and usefully. On several occasions he was sent to supply destitute settlements in Virginia. He was dissatisfied with the arrangement of the Presbyteries on the re-union, (1758,) and for the remainder of his ministerial life attended but once on the meetings of the re-united Synod, and took no part in the meetings of his Presbytery. In the final adjustment of matters however, he appears to have acquiesced, and to have lived in harmony with his co-presbyters. In 1779, he requested leave to resign his charge "on account of his infirmities of old age," and the commissioner from his congregation reports that his people "have afforded a gratuity for his support, which is satisfactory to him, and acquiesce with him in his request." Although this request was complied with, he continued in this partial connection with that people until April 29th, 1787, when his death took place, after a ministry in this region of forty-six years.

He was probably married when he first settled at Pennsborough, as an inscription, accompanied by a coat of arms, on a tombstone in the old cemetery on the Conodoguinnett, reads: "Here lys ye body of Janet, wife of ye Rev. Samuel Thompson, who deceased September ye 29, 1744, aged 44 years." As the fruit of this marriage he had at least one son, William, who was sent to England for his education and there took orders as a minister in the Episcopal church. He was sent to this country under the support of the "Society for the Propagation of Religion in Foreign Parts," was the rector of St. John's church, in Carlisle, and was eminently useful in ministering to the distressed people of Cumberland and York counties, during the Indian wars. Among his descendants were James Hamilton, Esq., and Mrs. J. V. Thorn, lately of Carlisle.

ROBERT WHITEHILL.

JAMES WHITEHILL was born February 1st, 1700, and died at Pequea, Lancaster county, Pa., February 2d, 1766, and was the father of eleven sons and daughters.

Robert, his son, was born July 29th, 1738, in the Pequea settlement, before Lancaster county was organized. He enjoyed, when a lad, the advantages of a good elementary education, such as the common country schools afforded; but subsequently, by reading, enlarged his stock of useful information, which proved alike beneficial to himself and serviceable to his country.

In 1770, Mr. Whitehill purchased from the proprietaries of Pennsylvania, two tracts of land in Lauther Manor, which was not re-surveyed and divided into lots until 1766, though much of the land immediately west of the Manor had been taken up and settled thirty years before Mr. Whitehill moved to Cumberland county.

In the Spring of 1771, he left Lancaster county, and on the land thus purchased, erected the first stone house in the Manor, within two miles of the Susquehanna river; which he occupied till the time of his death, on the 8th day of April, 1813.

Mr. Whitehill long represented Cumberland county in various capacities. He was elected a member of the Convention held in Philadelphia, in July, 1776, in which the Declaration of Independence by Congress was approved, and other highly important measures were adopted, among which were the Constitution of Pennsylvania, the Bill of Rights, &c., &c. He was also a member of the Assembly held in Philadelphia, in November, 1776, which continued in session until the 18th of September, 1777, when it was removed to Lancaster, and assembled there the 29th of September, 1777, continuing in session until the 11th of September, 1778. Subsequently to this he was occasionally a member of both branches of the Legislature. He was a member of the Convention that adopted the Constitution of 1790, though in the printed Constitution his name does not appear, because he was so much opposed to some of its provisions that he refused to affix his name to it. He was also a member of the Convention that agreed on the part of Pennsylvania to the Constitution of the United States.

Mr. Whitehill was a member of the House of Representatives

during the stormy sessions of 1798, 1799 and 1800. In 1801, he was elected to the Senate, and was the Speaker during the trial on impeachment of the Judges of the Supreme Court. In 1805, he was elected to Congress, and was four times re-elected, and was a member at the time of his death. It is said he served longer, in a representative capacity, than any other man in Pennsylvania, and it was his proud boast that he never intrigued for a nomination, nor solicited a vote.

REV. JOHN CRAIGHEAD.

JOHN CRAIGHEAD was the second son of John and Rachel R. Craighead, who removed from Lancaster county, Pennsylvania, in the year 1742, and settled on a large tract of land four miles south of Carlisle. His great grandfather was Rev. Robert Craighead, a Scotchman, who went to Ireland as early as 1657 or 8, and was pastor first at Donoughmore and then at Londonderry. He subsequently resided in Dublin, and was the author of several volumes on Practical Religion, and on the Controversy with the Prelatists of Ireland. Rev. Thomas Craighead, son of Robert, was his grandfather, who came to New England in 1715, and after preaching eight years near Fall River, Mass., removed to Delaware and was installed pastor over the Presbyterian church at White Clay creek. In 1733 he accepted a call to Pequea, Lancaster county, Pa., and afterwards to Hopewell, (Newville, Cumberland county,) where he closed his ministry with his life.

The subject of this sketch was born in the year 1742, and passed his early youth on his father's farm. He pursued his classical studies at Princeton College, graduating in 1763. From Carlisle Presbytery, October 30th, 1765, he received a letter of recommendation to the Presbytery of Lancaster, within whose bounds he was prosecuting the the study of divinity. The latter Presbytery being in existence but a single year, he was transferred to Donegal Presbytery and appointed as a probationer, "to supply vacancies within its bounds." A call from Rocky Spring, near Chambersburg, Pa., was placed in his hands, April, 1767, as also an application for his services from Newcastle Presbytery. The latter invitation led to a correspondence between the two Presbyteries, the final result of which was an acceptance by Mr. Craighead, in October of the same year, of the call from Rocky Spring, at a salary of £100; when he presented a certificate of dismission and recommendation from Newcastle Presbytery (into which connection he had come by a new adjustment of the Presbyteries by Synod) to Donegal Presbytery, and "was cheerfully and heartily received." His sermon, exegesis, examinations in Greek and Latin, and the various parts of trial, are stated as having been "fully sustained;" and he was ordained and installed by Presbytery April 13th, 1768.

From the records of Presbytery it appears that Mr. Craighead continued without interruption and with great fidelity and usefulness in this pastoral relation until the year 1789, discharging not only his duties to his own congregation, but spending much of his time, as was the custom with these pioneer preachers, in organizing churches, and supplying settlements which had no regular means of grace. An interruption of his labours occurred for one year at this time, owing to ill health, which incapacitated him both *" in mind and body to attend to the duties of his office." But we find him again regularly in his place at the meeting of Carlisle Presbytery (which had been organized in 1786) in the Spring of 1791, when he was appointed its Commissioner to the General Assembly; and in the June meeting of 1792, supplies were provided for his pulpit in order that he might fulfil a *mission* on which he was sent by the Assembly. What this mission was, or the time occupied in its discharge, we are not informed. Most probably it was of a similar character to that which was frequently entrusted to the more prominent and experienced clergymen of this region—that of several months' missionary labours among the scattered members of Christ's flock who lived remote from organized churches, and were deprived of the sacraments. These missionary tours were made on horseback, over mountains and through forests, with nothing oftentimes to mark the road but blazed trees; and frequently they consumed months in their prosecution, and extended to a distance of several hundred miles.

The next mention made of Mr. Craighead is in 1793 when he was again chosen to represent his Presbytery in the Assembly; and it would appear he was in the performance of all his official duties as pastor until some time in 1795 or 6, when an application was made to the Presbytery for supplies on account of his inability " to discharge the ministerial functions." His ill health continuing, and the Presbytery believing " that there are not probable symptoms of his recovery, and that his temporal circumstances are comfortable," dissolved the pastoral relation on April 9th, 1799, " solely for inability." His death almost immediately followed, taking place April 20th, 1799. His body was laid to rest in the graveyard adjoining the church where he had so long and so ably preached the Gospel, and over it an affectionate people erected a suitable memorial, on which were inscribed his name, the dates of his installation and death, and that, " He was a faithful and zealous servant of Jesus Christ."

While on his way to join the American Army in New Jersey, and in passing through Lancaster county, he stopped with his company at

---

* He was subject to great depression of spirits at times, which unfitted him for preaching and pastoral duties.

the house of Rev. Adam Boyd, where he made the acquaintance of his daughter Jenny. After the close of the campaign they were married. His wife survived him, leaving no children.

Mr. Craighead, like nearly every other Presbyterian minister in the Cumberland valley, and indeed in this country, was an earnest patriot in the war for Independence. He could scarcely have been different, descended as he was from a Scotch-Irish ancestry, who in Scotland, Ireland, and in this country, were ever foremost in their resistance to all forms of oppression, and in their maintenance of civil and religious liberty. His uncle, Rev. Alexander Craighead, at as early a period as 1742, while residing in Lancaster county, published such advanced sentiments on the subject of political freedom that he incurred the displeasure of the Governor of the Province, and also of his fellow ministers; so that he finally removed to North Carolina, where his opinions and teaching were said to have been more influential than those of any other individual in the final production of the celebrated Mecklenberg Declaration of Independence.

The zeal and devotion of the subject of this sketch in his country's cause was similarly noteworthy. It is said of him that "he fought and preached alternately;" referring to his acting as captain of his company, when on the march and in the battle, and in camp, discharging the duties of chaplain to his soldiers.

Referring to a large oak tree which stood at the entrance to the mansion of one of his parishioners, Mr. Sharp, a writer* says: "Here also, in the early days of the Revolution, the brave and gifted Craighead gathered the men of this remote part of his congregation, and standing under its majestic branches, addressed them in favour of American Independence. In thrilling tones he exhorted his members to stand up boldly and let their slogan cry, "God and Liberty," forever ring from mountain to mountain. Roused by his fervid eloquence and patriotic example, they enlisted in defence of liberty, and their names may be found amongst those slaughtered at the "Paoli" and the "Billet;" who suffered at Valley Forge, and who fought at Brandywine, Monmouth, and other battles."

Still another writer states that he preached "in glowing terms, Jesus Christ, the only hope of salvation, and after the delivery of his sacred message, in eloquent and patriotic strains exhorted the youth of his congregation to rise up and join the noble band, then engaged under the immortal Washington, in struggling to free our beloved country from British oppression." On one of these occasions the patriot

---

*C. J. McClay, M. D.

preacher declaimed in such fervid and powerful terms respecting the evils his country was enduring, and presented such a description of each man's duty that "the whole congregation rose from their seats and declared their willingness to march to the conflict."

Besides inspiring others with courage and resolution, as is further evinced by a sermon still preserved in the Presbyterian Historical Society entitled, "Courage in a Good Cause," preached before Col. Montgomery's Battalion, August 31, 1775, Mr. Craighead, at the commencement of the war, "raised a company from the members of his own congregation, put himself at their head, and joined Washington's army in New Jersey." In many hard fought battles this clerical captain and his men "gave undoubted evidence that their courage was of no mean order."

The bold and faithful pastor subsequently returned to his congregation, and watched over it until increasing infirmities, and finally death severed the endearing relation.

REV. JOHN STEEL.

THE first notice we find respecting Mr. Steel is in the minutes of the Presbytery of Donegal for May 25th, 1736, when "the principal members" of the congregation of Nottingham "agree to carry into execution a method for supporting John Paton and John Steel." In 1742 he is called by the commission of the Synod of Philadelphia, "a probationer from Ireland, who offered himself to our care as a candidate for the sacred work of the ministry, but was under some difficulty with relation to a marriage promise claimed by a young woman in Ireland, as his testimonials set forth, and by reason of some steps taken by him in his marriage in this country. The commission finding in all things that his conduct at home and in this country has been fair and unblamable, those things excepted, do advise the Presbytery of New Castle to defer taking him on trials till December next, and in the meantime desire that both the young man and the Presbytery write to the Presbytery of Londonderry, in Ireland, to see if any further light may be obtained in said affair." In the year 1743, "the people of Great Conewago (Hunterstown, near Gettysburg,) supplicate for Mr. Steel, a probationer of New Castle," and the Presbytery of Donegal accordingly send to him their call, which after some months' consideration he declined. Next year (1744) the Presbytery of New Castle reported to the Synod that they had ordained him to the work of the ministry. He appears at once to have secured the confidence of his brethren in a high degree for his learning and practical judgment, for that same year he was selected by them as one of the trustees of the school under Alison and McDowall, for the education of young men for the ministry, and which afterwards was transferred to Newark, Del., where many able ministers received their education; and the next year (1745) he was appointed by Synod on an important committee to report a plan of union with the Synod of New York. While he was a licentiate (1743) he was sent to Virginia and to Conestoga, and after his ordination he was probably settled for about seven years at New London, Chester county, near the borders of Maryland and Delaware. In the year 1752, possibly earlier, he removed to West Conococheague, in what is now Franklin county, where he had charge of two congregations which, however, were yet in their infancy and differed from each other on the religious questions of the time. They were also in the midst of the perils of Indian depredations, which were then so terrible that not unfrequently the inhabitants of that part of Cumberland valley were obliged to quit their habitations and crowd into the more settled parts of the province. The people never ventured to assemble for worship without being fully equipped and watched by sentries against surprise. One of the meeting houses in which Mr. Steel preached was fortified as a fort, and after a while was burned to the ground. A number of whole families under his charge were barbarously murdered. Such was his coolness, courage and skill, that he was chosen to be the captain of the company formed among the settlers, and several expeditions are mentioned, under his command, into coves and over the mountains against the enemy. The government finally (1755) commissioned him as a captain of the provincial troops, and he was for many years active in the service. Under such circumstances it was impossible for him to to hold his congregations to regularity in worship, but ample opportunities were offered for his private ministrations among the afflicted. In the end his churches were broken up and he was obliged to seek a residence elsewhere.

In 1754, we find Mr. Steel preaching at Nottingham and then at York and Shrewsbury. As the congregations of Upper and Lower Pennsborough were then vacant he was sent to supply them, and in 1759 they united in calling him to become their pastor. In accepting this call he engaged to give a large portion of his time to Carlisle. This was resisted by Mr. Duffield, whose call was of an earlier date, and stipulated that two-thirds of his time should be given to that town, and by the terms of the recent reunion in the Presbyterian church, all care was to be taken to heal those divisions which had taken place in towns which were unable to sustain more than one minister. The efforts of Presbytery, however, were ineffectual and two houses of worship were erected in Carlisle, which had now become the centre of business for the region. It had become evident that the old meeting-house on the Conodoguinnett would soon be forsaken, and the congregation, which had for so many years assembled there, now gravitated toward the new town. From a letter of Colonel Armstrong, dated June 30, 1757, we learn that the people were to begin the next day to " haul stones for the building of a meeting-house on the north side of the square," and by a comparison of dates we must see that this was before either Mr. Steel or Mr. Duffield had begun to reside in Cumberland county, and was before the actual re-union of the general church. The New York Synod had, about that time, sent some ministers of their body to preach and to organize churches in this region, and it is very probable that a division had taken place in the church of Upper Pennsborough. On the organization of Donegal Presbytery, under the re-united church, Mr. Duffield was attached to it and soon afterwards a call was laid before it that Mr. Steel might become the pastor of the two churches of Pennsborough. This call was immediately accepted by him, and his installation took place early in April, 1759. It was a long time in the difficult circumstances of that period before the stone church on the square, in Carlisle, could have been tenantable, and we know that Mr. Steel's congregation must have had some other place of meeting in town. Tradition tells us of a "two-story dwelling," two doors north of the public square on Hanover street, in which Mr. S. resided, and some intimations are given that it was used also for public worship.

An unhappy state of feeling existed for a long time between these two ministers, and their congregations. Their complaints of each other were not unfrequently before Presbytery and Synod, generally referring, however, to matters of minor importance. And yet their congregations appear to have prospered and to have enjoyed evident tokens of Divine favour. There are no indications in the history of Mr. Steel's congregations that his ministry was attended with such powerful revivals as we read of in other churches, but his instructive style of preaching and his faithfulness in catechising and training the young were perhaps equally successful in keeping up the number of his communicants. Many of his sermons were in the possession of his great grandson, Robert Given, Esq., of Holly Springs, but were unfortunately consumed in a burning of the house which contained them. They were not only remarkable for a neat chirography and careful composition, but for calm earnestness, soundness in doctrine and a high tone of morality.

From an instrument, the original of which is in the possession of the Rev. Dr. Wing, it appears that the congregations of Upper and Lower Pennsborough, (Silvers' Spring,) agreed to pay him each seventy-five pounds on condition that each should receive an equal share of his labours. This was dated April, 1764, and we know that it continued at least three years and perhaps much longer. The disorders incident to the period of the Revolutionary War, broke up again his more peaceful occupations. His well known intrepidity and public spirit were more than once called into public service in repressing some popular commotions. In February, 1768, he was commissioned by Governor John Penn to visit with some others about 150 families who had settled, contrary to law, on the Redstone and the Youghiogeny rivers, and to induce them peaceably to remove. The mission was not altogether successful, but was performed on his part to the satisfaction of the civil authorities. The same year he co-operated with the justices of the county in endeavouring to restrain certain rioters from over the mountain who were rescuing two murderers of Indians from the jail in Carlisle. With a party of men he pursued after them, but was not strong enough to recover the prisoners.

During the pendency of measures for asserting the rights of the colonies against the mother country, he sympathized ardently with the patriots. A large meeting was held July 12, 1774, in his church, and was presided over by one of his elders, John Montgomery, in which the boldest sentiments were avowed, and active measures were taken to defend their rights. Three thousand men were organized, armed and furnished, and the Hon. George Chambers informs us that "the company which was in the lead was under the command of the Rev. Captain John Steel." He was however too far advanced in years for protracted service as a soldier, and we have no evidence that he was much in the field. His congregation, however, was almost completely disorganized in consequence of the number who went from it into the service. The common title of "Reverend Captain," which was given him by the popular voice, was never a reproach, for he was never known to act unworthily of either part of the designation.

Mr. Steel was never satisfied with the arrangement of ministers and churches in Donegal Presbytery after the re-union. He and others of what were called the Old Side, on finding themselves in a minority in that body, seceded, and when they found no relief in Synod, they continued for three years in a state of separation. Finally they were united with others of a similar affinity within the bounds of Synod, and formed into the Second Presbytery of Philadelphia. His punctuality in every duty would never allow him to be absent, and for twelve years, he was in the habit of journeying, in his own conveyance, at least annually, to the city of Philadelphia, to attend upon ecclesiastical meetings. He died in August, 1779, leaving a reputation for stern integrity, zeal for what he deemed truth and righteousness, and a high sense of honour. His remains lie interred in the Old Cemetery of Carlisle.

GENERAL JOHN ARMSTRONG.

PROBABLY no one among the early settlers of Cumberland county had more influence in directing its institutions and destinies than John Armstrong. He and a brother, William, (of whom we have no further information,) and a sister, Margaret, came from the north of Ireland some time before 1748, when a family record proves that he had become permanently settled in Carlisle. He first appears as a surveyor under the Proprietary Government, and we are informed that a large portion of the lands in middle Pennsylvania were first surveyed by him. The town of Carlisle which had been laid out at an earlier period, (1750,) was, with its adjacent lands, resurveyed and mapped out in its present form by him in 1762. In 1755, he was a Colonel, and had a controlling part in directing the defense of the settlers against the Indians. A commission now in the possession of his descendants, subscribed by Thomas Penn, and bearing the seal of the British Government in the reign of George the Third, gave him the powers of a Justice of the Peace. These powers were much more extensive then than those which belong to the office of that name now and for some time the county of Cumberland, over which his jurisdiction extended, included nearly all of Pennsylvania west of the Susquehanna. In the performance of these combined military and civil functions, when Indian ravages and border outrages were almost perpetual, he found sufficient occupation for most of his time, and for his utmost bodily and mental powers.

It soon became evident that a more aggressive policy was necessary in dealing with these Indians. In those merciless incursions in which the peaceable inhabitants were despoiled, captured and massacred, it was easy for their wily foe to elude opposition and punishment by retiring into the depths of the wilderness, there they had constructed a town called Kittanning, about twenty miles above Fort Duquesne, (Pittsburgh,) and about two hundred miles westward from Carlisle. This was known to be a rendezvous for their warriors, a depot for the stores with which the French liberally supplied them, and the fortress where their prisoners and plunder could be kept. It was there that Shingis and Captain Jacobs, two relentless and faithful leaders had their residences, from which they sallied forth at their will to desolate the frontier. About two hundred and eighty provincials were mustered under the command of Col. Armstrong, and sent (1755,) to surprise and destroy this stronghold. They succeeded in their scheme, for they came upon the Indians engaged in their revels at night, and in the early dawn set fire to their buildings and put to death the chiefs and most of the warriors. It was a terrible vengeance but indispensable even in the interest of humanity. This brilliant success gained for the commander distinguished honours, and the corporation of Philadelphia showed their appreciation of his skill and bravery by presenting him with a piece of plate and a silver medal, with a medal for each of the officers under him and a sum of money for the widows and children of such as had been killed. The Colonel had himself been severely wounded in the action by a musket ball, in consequence of which his shoulder was for a while disabled. Three years afterwards, however, (1758,) he marched with the advanced division of 3000 Pennsylvanians under Col. Bouquet, belonging to the expedition under Brig. General Forbes against Fort Duquesne. It was during this campaign that he formed that acquaintance with Col. Washington, which subsequently ripened into intimacy and warm personal friendship.

The previous year (June 30, 1757,) we find him engaged with his fellow-citizens in the erection of a "meeting house on the north side of the square," and the civil authorities are appealed to for help in this work on what he calls "political as well as religious grounds."

He had himself, perhaps, become a member of a congregation recently founded by what was called the New Side, in Carlisle, but he appears to have entered into the labour of "hauling stones" "out of Col. Stanwix's entrenchments," with the utmost public spirit, and we have reason to believe that his intelligence and wealth were freely contributed to give the structure its admirable strength and proportion. On the 12th day of July, 1774, he attended a meeting of citizens in that building to protest against the Act of Parliament "by which the port of Boston was shut up; to contribute for the relief of their brethren who were suffering from the oppressions of the mother country; to recommend the immediate assembling of a Congress of deputies from all the colonies; and to unite in abstaining from all trade or use of articles imported from Great Britain while these oppressions continued;" and he was appointed on the committee to correspond with similar committees from other provinces to co-operate in measures conducing to the general welfare. We have reason to believe that it was from a public meeting under his influence, that resolutions were sent up to the Provincial Assembly, calling upon that body to instruct those who represented the state in the General Congress to vote for an immediate declaration of independence of the mother country, and that here was the earliest voice raised in favour of such decisive action; and one which had no small influence in bringing about the final result. His commission as a Brigadier General in the Continental Army bears date March 1, 1776, and is signed by John Hancock. In 1777, he appears as a Major General in command of the Pennsylvania troops during the battle of Brandywine and in the military operations of that year in the eastern part of the State. In consequence, however, of some grievance which he believed himself to be under, he left (April 4, 1777,) the regular army, and at the battle of Germantown he commanded the Pennsylvania militia. He was a member of Congress in 1778–80, and also in 1787–88, having been recommended for that position without solicitation by General Washington.

From numerous letters of his which are published in the Colonial Records and Archives, it is evident that he was well educated, was endowed with much practical wisdom, and was much consulted and trusted by the Proprietary Government, and subsequently by the authorities of the state and nation. Among those which remain in manuscript in the possession of his descendants and others, are many from General Washington, not only upon official and public affairs, but upon subjects of private friendship. His own letters are all written in a beautiful hand, and indicate an accurate scholarship according to the literature of the time. The Hon. George Chambers, who was familiar with his general reputation, says of him; "He was a man of intelligence, of integrity, and of high religious and moral character. He was resolute and brave, and though living habitually in the fear of the Lord, he feared not the face of man." The style of his piety partook much of the peculiar characteristics of the people and period in which he lived, and hence might have seemed somewhat stern when judged by men of other associations, but we discover beneath this occasional indications of an admirably humane and tender sensibility. As a specimen of the religious opinions and spirit of the man and of the time, we may here give a letter which he wrote to his son James, on the occasion of the death of a favourite son of the latter:

"CARLISLE, *12th April, 1794.*

"DEAR JAMES:—I have seen your last to Polly, and see nothing wrong in it, only that it manifests an excess of grief, that for many important reasons ought to be moderated and suppressed; the various duties yet incumbent upon you and especially your own eternal concerns should take the place of that natural and paternal grief, which, in a certain degree, is rather laudable than sinful, but may readily become so by an undue indulgence and want of proper consideration; we must go to him (that is to the state of the dead,) but he will not return to us; therefore preparation for that solemn event is our principal business.

"From the nature and circumstances of this remarkable affliction, you may but too plainly and justly suspect, as I see you do, that God has a controversy with the parents of that child, and perhaps with his grandparents too, for so I desire to take it to myself. Now the immediate business which I most earnestly recommend to you is, with a faithful scrutiny, giving conscience its free course, that you may find out and be convinced of the grounds of this controversy, for examination and reflection (the divine word being still the standard,) are the first steps toward reformation in any man. And to assist you in this duty, take a retrospective view of your practical life from the first of your remembrance, more especially in the following particulars: In infancy you were presented to God in the ordinance of baptism—solemn engagements were therein entered into for your instruction, &c., in the faith and practice of Christianity; these vows and promises were to devolve on yourself at the years of discretion—ask yourself whether you have endeavoured to study the nature of that initiating ordinance, voluntarily taking these solemn obligations upon yourself and beseeching the free mercy of God through Christ, the Mediator, to enable you to perform these vows by giving you the spiritual blessing signified in and by that ordinance. Again, take a general survey of your life, how you have improven or misimproven your time and talents, together with the innumerable privileges, opportunities and admonitions received therein; but especially examine what has been the general and prevailing inclination or disposition of your *mind and will*, for this indeed is the touchstone of the state of the heart, either towards God or against him. And here, there is great reason to fear, you may find but too much cause for the controversy in question, for if a general shyness, a cold indifference or negligence toward God, the state of the soul, the Mediator, his ordinances and institutions, hath been prevalent and habitual, this fully marks an unrenewed state of the soul, involving in it infidelity, aversion and contempt of the gospel and the revealed will of God, (hence are men in a state of nature called haters of God.) Nor is this spiritual and moral disease to be healed by a better education, a few externals and transient thoughts. It requires the hand of the great Physician, the Lord Jesus by his Holy Spirit, and belief of the truth renewing the state of the mind and disposition of the heart as well, thereby leading the soul from a sense or fear of the wrath of God, the penalty of his broken law, and helpless in itself to flee to the merits of Jesus, that only refuge or foundation that God hath laid in his church, and who was made sin for us, (that is, a sin offering,) that all "believers might be made the righteousness of God by him." And this great salvation, though to be given freely, must be sought by adult persons, and earnestly too, only on the principles of pure mercy, because by nature we have neither title nor merit to procure it; at the pool of ordinances must we lie, if we expect to be saved, to which means, looking for a blessing upon them, I earnestly recommend your most serious attention. I conclude this letter by putting you in mind that although you have always had the call of God in his word, and perhaps often in his providence too, (though unobserved and therefore neglected,) God hath again condescended to add another providential call, much more sensible and alarming to us all, in removing a dear and promising child, but with double force to you, therefore, see that you endeavour to bear and improve it in the true sense in which it is designed, that is comparatively at least, that you weep not for him but for yourself and the rest of your family.

"I am your affectionate Father,

"JOHN ARMSTRONG."

He was not only a member but an elder in the first church which was organized in the town of Carlisle, and to which the Rev. George Duffield, D. D., who married his sister, was called to be the first pastor. His name appears as a representative of that church in the Presbytery of Donegal, for the first time near that period, and frequently afterwards until the date of his death. He was much interested in opposing the infidelity which became prevalent in this country soon after the American and the French Revolutions, and we find that he corresponded freely with Dr. Cooper, an eminent divine in this vicinity, to induce him to compose and publish a treatise which was directed against that tendency but still remains only in manuscript. Although the congregation with which he was connected here was not formed until after the great schism which ruptured the Presbyterian Church was consummated, and although he exhibited no evidences of a partisan spirit, he was thrown by circumstances and by what seemed a hearty preference among those who sympathized strongly with the New York Synod. He appears, however, to have taken a prominent part in the building of the house of worship on the public square, which, for some considerable time, belonged exclusively to the rival congregation. The epitaph on his tombstone in the Old Cemetery of Carlisle, which he himself originally surveyed and laid out, informs us that he was "eminently distinguished for patriotism, valour and piety, and departed this life March 9th, 1795, aged 75 years."

HUGH WILLIAMSON, M. D., F. R. S.

AMONG the early Scotch-Irish immigrants to the Province of Pennsylvania was John Williamson, from Dublin, who settled in Chester county about the year 1730. Soon after his arrival, he was united in marriage with Mary Davison, a native of Derry, who came to the same county with her father, George Davison, when a child of about three years of age. In 1752 he removed to Shippensburg, where he died a few years afterwards.

Of ten children—six sons and four daughters, who were the fruit of this marriage, and all of whom reached positions of respectability and usefulness,—one, at least, the eldest son, attained more than ordinary eminence, and from his residence with his mother for a considerable time in Shippensburg, after his father's decease, deserves a notice among the distinguished sons of Cumberland valley.

Hugh Williamson being slender and delicate his father resolved to give him a liberal education. After the common preparatory instruction, he was sent at an early age to learn the languages, at the academy at New London Crossroads, Chester county, under Rev. Francis Allison,—the Busby of the Western Hemisphere. Among the pupils of that seminary, may be mentioned Charles Thomson, Dr. John Ewing, Thomas McKean, and Benjamin Rush. After Dr. Allison's transfer to Philadelphia, Hugh Williamson went to the academy at Newark, Delaware, where he prepared for college. He entered the Philadelphia college in 1753, remained there for about four years, and graduated A. B. May 17, 1757. He was fond of mathematics, and became a proficient in Euclid. He became early impressed with a sense of religion, and while with his mother devoted much time to the study of divinity, under the auspices of Rev. Dr. Samuel Finley, with a view to the clerical profession. In 1759, he went to Connecticut, where he still pursued his theological studies, and was licensed to preach the gospel. He preached but a short time—not exceeding two years—when he found that his health and strength of lungs would not permit the duties of the office, and he was never ordained. Moreover, the memorable controversy in the Presbyterian church, between the adherents of Whitefield and the old orthodox party, proved a source of disgust to him, which induced him to withdraw from theological pursuits, to which he had been sincerely attached. He accordingly left the pulpit and entered upon the study of medicine.

In 1760, he received the degree of A. M. in Philadelphia college; and soon after, was appointed Professor of Mathematics in that institution; but continued his medical studies.

October 8, 1763, he gave notice of his intended resignation of the professorship; and in 1764, he went to prosecute his medical studies at the University of Edinburg. He afterward spent a year in London at his studies, and from thence crossed over to Holland, and completed his medical education at Utrecht. Having passed the usual examinations, and submitted a Latin thesis, he obtained the degree of Doctor of Medicine. Having spent some time in traveling on the continent of Europe, he bent his course toward his native country.

Upon his return, Dr. Williamson practiced medicine in Philadelphia for a few years. In 1768, he was chosen a member of the American Philosophical Society. His health failing, he resolved to try mercantile pursuits, but meanwhile, for a time, devoted himself to literary and philosophical investigations. In January, 1769, he was appointed by the Philosophical Society on a committee, with the Rev. Dr. Ewing, David Rittenhouse and Charles Thomson, to observe the *transit of Venus,* which occurred on the 3d of June in that year; and soon after to observe the *transit of Mercury,* which took place November 9, 1769. In that year, also, he philosophised on the comet. In 1770, he published observations on Climate, in the "American Philosophical Transactions." In 1772, he visited the West Indies, to collect contributions in aid of the Newark academy. In 1773, Governor John Penn certified to the "good credit and reputation" of Rev. John Ewing and Hugh Williamson, who were authorized to proceed to Europe to solicit further aid for said academy. They persevered under difficulties until the autumn of 1775, when hostilities with the colonies commenced. Dr. Ewing returned home; but Dr. Williamson resolved to remain, and make further efforts for the academy. Dr. Williamson was the first to report the destruction of tea, at Boston. On that occasion he ventured to declare his opinion, that coercive measures by parliament would result in civil war. Lord North himself declared that Dr. Williamson was the first person who, in his hearing, intimated the probability of such an event. Dr. Williamson, while in London, was the man, (probably with the aid, or at the suggestion of Sir John Temple,) who procured the letters of Hutchinson, Oliver and others, and caused them to be delivered to Dr. Franklin, who sent them to

Boston, for which Wedderburne, before the privy council, called Franklin a "thief."

After causing the Hutchinson correspondence to reach Dr. Franklin, it was deemed expedient by Dr. Williamson to take an early conveyance next day for Holland. It was supposed by John Adams, that Mr. David Hartly, a member of parliament, and a good friend of the Americans, was the person through whom the letters reached Dr. Franklin. On the Declaration of Independence, Dr. Williamson returned to the United States, and engaged for a time with a brother in trade with the West Indies. His residence then was at Edenton, North Carolina. In 1779-80, when the British took possession of Charleston, South Carolina, a large draft of military from North Carolina was ordered for the relief of South Carolina, on which occasion, the commander, Governor Caswell, placed Dr. Williamson at the head of the medical department. After the battle of Camden, August 18, 1780, which the doctor witnessed, he requested General Caswell to give him a flag, that he might go and attend to the wounded North Carolina prisoners. The General advised him to send some of the regimental surgeons, inasmuch as his duty did not require him to go. Dr. Williamson replied that such of the regimental surgeons as he had seen refused to go—afraid of the consequences. "But," said he, "if I have lived until a flag will not protect me, I have outlived my country; and, in that case, have lived a day too long." He went and remained two months in the enemy's camp, rendering good service to the sick of both armies, where his skill was highly esteemed. At the close of the war, Dr. Williamson served as a representative of Edenton, in the House of Commons of North Carolina.

He was next sent to Congress from "the old North State," where he continued for three years. Writing to President Dickinson, of Pennsylvania, from New York, while in Congress, January 14, 1785, about John Franklin and the other Connecticut intruders, at Wyoming, Dr. Williamson says in the conclusion of a letter:—"I have taken the liberty of giving you a full information, as I cannot cease to feel myself interested in the peace and reputation of a state which gave me birth." In the year 1786, he was one of the few delegates sent to Annapolis, to revise and amend the Articles of Confederation of the union; and in 1787, he was a delegate from North Carolina to the convention which framed the Constitution of the United States. Dr. Williamson was a zealous advocate of the new Constitution and was a member of the state convention which adopted it. He served in the first and second Congresses, and then declined a re-election. In January, 1789, he married Miss Maria Apthorpe, of New York, where he came to reside, and had two sons, who both died young. He continued industriously to write on various philosophical subjects; was an advocate of the great New York canal system; an active promoter of philanthropic, literary, and scientific institutions; and in 1812, gave to the world his History of North Carolina.

After a long life devoted to the best interests of humanity, Dr. Hugh Williamson died suddenly, at New York, on the 22d of May, 1819, in the 85th year of his age. Of him it may safely be predicated, that he was an ornament to his country, and one of the most eminent and useful men which it has yet produced. An interesting memoir of him was prepared and published by the distinguished Dr. Hosack, of New York, and has now a place in the transactions of the New York Historical Society.

GEN. JOHN ARMSTRONG, Jr.

GENERAL JOHN ARMSTRONG, Jr., deserves rank as one of Pennsylvania's distinguished sons of the earlier period, although he experienced severe criticism as well as a large amount of popularity at different periods of his career. He commenced his public activity at an age when his passions may have unduly influenced his judgment, and may possibly have given a hasty direction to his whole life. But no one can question the purity of his motives or the high order of talent which he give to his work.

He was several years younger than his brother James, having been born at Carlisle, November 25th, 1758. At an early age he was sent to Nassau Hall, and for a while enjoyed the instruction of Dr. Witherspoon, who entered upon the presidency of that institution during his course. Under such an influence the warm patriotism which belonged to his family was sure to be cherished, and we are not surprised to find that even while a student in college, at the early age of eighteen, he was enlisted as a member of a Pennsylvania regiment. Shortly afterwards he became an Aid-de-camp to the same Gen. Hugh Mercer who had served under his father in the expedition against the Indians at Kittanning. Associated with him, in the regiments under this gallant officer, were many youths belonging to the best families of Philadelphia and vicinity. It was at the disastrous battle near Stoney Brook, N. J., that the melancholy duty devolved upon Major Armstrong of bearing from the field and ministering to his dying commander during a week of suffering. Near the same time he became acquainted with Gen. Gates, who showed so much interest in him that he received an invitation to become a member of that General's staff. With the rank of Major he continued on that staff until the close of the war, a warm friend and admirer of his illustrious commander.

When the army was encamped at Newburgh, N. Y., in the winter of 1782-3, and while negotiations for peace were in progress, much solicitude was felt by the soldiers with respect to their arrearages of pay. Congress had passed resolutions not only for their payment, but for a half pay to officers who should serve to the conclusion of the war; but there were no funds for such a payment, and the needful ratification of nine states had not been obtained and now seemed improbable. Under these circumstances the officers and men became impatient of the long delay and the uncertainty of future payment, and an anonymous address was circulated through the camp calling a meeting to consider their grievances, which was followed on the next day by another, which set forth in forcible terms the complaints of the army. In this and in other papers the officers and soldiers were exhorted to decline the performance of any military duty during the remainder of the war, and to lay down their arms on the return of peace, unless Congress would satisfy their reasonable demands. It required all the wisdom of the Commander-in-Chief to restrain the impetuous spirit of the troops under these eloquent and apparently just appeals, and it was not until provision was made for the satisfaction of their claims that the danger passed away. These addresses were subsequently avowed by Armstrong to be his composition, at the request of many of his fellow officers, under the impression that the tardy movements of Congress needed some excitement. Washington at the time felt himself called upon to speak of these "Newburgh letters" in terms of great severity, but in after years he saw reason to change his opinion, and in a friendly letter to the writer's father he said, "I have since had sufficient reason for believing that the object of the author was just, honourable and friendly to the country, though the means suggested by him were certainly liable to much misconstruction and abuse."

On the return of peace he appears to have retired for a while to private life, though his brilliant qualities would not allow him to remain obscure. Unlike his older brother and his father, he became a warm partisan of the Democratic party, which subsequently supported Jefferson. For a time he held the office of Secretary of State in Pennsylvania under Gov. Franklin, and served at least one term as a member of the old Congress. In 1789 he married a sister of Chancellor Livingston, and took up his residence at Redhook on a beautiful bank of the North river, New York. This brought him into the most cultivated and refined circles of New York society, and he devoted his time ostensibly to agriculture, but more really to social and literary pursuits. By an almost unanimous vote of both houses of the New York Legislature he was elected in 1800 to represent that state in the U. S. Senate, but in 1804, before the expiration of his term, he was sent by President Jefferson as Minister to France. During the six years in which he retained that office he gained high honour from his government for not only his skill under difficult circumstances, but for many services for which he never received or sought compensation. For most of this time, as there was no Minister of the United States to Spain, he was called upon to act also in that capacity. His mission abroad closed at his own request in 1810. At the commencement of hostilities with Great Britain in 1812 he was commissioned a Brigadier General, and had command of the District of New York. In this position he came into conflict with many of his superiors, inasmuch as the whole policy pursued met with his decided disapproval. With great reluctance he consented in 1813 to assume the duties of Secretary of War, under President Madison, for he did not conceal his contempt of the qualifications of the Generals in command and of the principles of the campaign. He soon found himself in collision with those military officers on whom he was dependent for the execution of his orders, and not unfrequently with the President himself. The recollection of his "Newburgh letters" was revived against him, and the failure of a number of his schemes, unsupported as they were by his associates, completed his mortification. The ill success of the expeditions against Canada, and the capture of Washington, gave his enemies apparent reasons for demanding his retirement. In his subsequent defence he pointed out the reasons for his failure, and he bitterly complained of the President for allowing him to be misrepresented.

After his retirement from office he gave himself up to literary pursuits. He wrote and published two interesting treatises on farming and gardening, a severe review of General Wilkinson's memoirs, some biographical papers, and a History of the War with Great Britain. It is said also that he partially wrote a History of the American Revolutionary War, and we may well regret that a history, for the writing of which he was so well qualified, was not completed. With some obvious faults, for which allowance is easily made, it must be conceded that he was a genuine lover of his country, an incorruptible and able foreign Minister, a forcible and clear writer, and a virtuous and honourable citizen. He died April 1st, 1843, at his country seat at Red Bank, New Jersey, in his eighty-fifth year. A daughter still survives him, the estimable wife of William B. Astor, of New York city.

REV. GEORGE DUFFIELD, D. D.

THIS eminent patriot and divine was the third son of George Duffield who had left the north of Ireland and had settled first in Octorara township, Lancaster county, Pennsylvania, at some time between 1725 and 1730. He is supposed to have descended from a Huguenot family which had taken refuge under the British crown in consequence of the revocation of the edict of Nantz. At the time, however, in which the subject of this sketch was born, (October 7, 1732,) the family resided at Pequea, in the same county, on lands which still remain in possession of some descendants. The father died there at the advanced age of eighty-four years, having been "noted for his stern integrity and devoted piety."

The son, George, received his preparatory education at Newark, Delaware, and graduated at Nassau Hall in 1752. He then spent four years as a tutor in the academy and the college where he had been educated, but having become hopefully pious under the preaching of Dr. Robert Smith, of Pequea, he studied theology under the instruction of that divine, and was licensed to preach the gospel by the Presbytery of Newcastle, March 11, 1756. Three days before his licensure, he was married to Elizabeth, daughter of Samuel Blair, of Fogg's Manor, and in the autumn of that year, he was sent to supply some vacancies in the valley of the Shenandoah. During the next year he preached in some parts of New Jersey and Pennsylvania, and his labours were attended with revivals of religion, especially in the neighbourhood of Princeton and Fogg's Manor.

In consequence of those dissensions which had resulted in the great Presbyterian schism of 1741-58, a new congregation had been formed in Carlisle, but within the limits of the church of Upper Pennsborough. On the re-union, in 1759, Mr. Duffield had evidently been labouring for some time in this new congregation. When the call from Carlisle and Big Spring, (Newville,) was presented to him, early in 1759, he had become a resident of the former town, and had married for his second wife, Margaret, a sister (Webster says a daughter,) of John Armstrong, and an elder of the new church. A house of worship had been commenced, for we find that the Synod were grieved that year, at the divided state of the people in Carlisle and recommended that only one house of worship be erected in that town. He accepted of the call, engaging to give one-third of his time to the church of Big Spring, but he was not actually ordained and installed until the third Wednesday of September, 1759. He had entered warmly into the re-union and had himself chosen to be connected with the Presbytery of Donegal, though, as he declared at the time, "he hardly expected much comfort in it for awhile." Accordingly we find that for years an unhappy state of feeling existed between him and his neighbour, Rev. John Steel, and their respective congregations. More than once, causes of dispute were carried up to the higher judicatories of the church, who, "after mature and serious deliberations, unanimously agreed that the grounds on which these unhappy differences were built, were not sufficient to raise them to such a height as they have come to."

In April, 1760, two Presbyterian meeting-houses are mentioned as in existence in Carlisle. That in which Mr. Duffield preached was located on the east side of Hanover street, nearly opposite the present Second Presbyterian church. In spite of the contentions in which he and his people were involved, his preaching was attended with great success. He entered with all his heart into the revival spirit of that time, and was very popular as a preacher. His discourses were not generally written out in full, though from the specimens which remain, we should conclude that his manuscript was in the more difficult parts complete, while in others he trusted to the inspiration of the moment. They were highly evangelical in sentiment and urged upon impenitent men, especially, the claims of religion with unusual importunity and skill. Of a warm temperament and ardent in the assertion of his views, he often provoked controversy, but he was equally generous toward an opponent and ready to forgive. The whole population of the Cumberland valley was then exposed to the merciless ravages of the Indians, and not unfrequently, when preaching at some retired station, his congregation were obliged to assemble with arms in their hands. His sympathies with the suffering, and his courage in meeting danger made him a popular favourite. Dr. John McDowall, at one time Provost of the University of Pennsylvania, tells us that when he was but eight years of age he heard Mr. Duffield preach at Monaghan, (Dillsburgh,) from Zech. ix, 12, "Turn ye to the stronghold, ye prisoners of hope," when the preacher took occasion, from the entrenchments still remaining around the building, to illustrate the imagery of his text, and he ascribes his own conversion, under God, to impressions received under that discourse. The reputation he acquired brought him a number of calls to more important congregations. Twice he received invitations to the Second Presbyterian church, of Philadelphia, and commissioners were sent who urged the claim before Presbytery with much zeal. But his own judgment, as well as that of his Presbytery, appears to have been averse to his relinquishment of his charge at Carlisle. More than once he undertook long missionary tours into destitute regions, under the direction of his Synod, and in response to "the supplications" of the people. In 1765, he was sent to North Carolina, and directed to "tarry half a year in vacant congregations there, as prudence might direct," and the next year he was sent with his intimate friend, Rev. Charles Beatty, to preach for, at least, two months on the frontiers of Pennsylvania and Ohio. In 1769, he gave up his Big Spring congregation, and was installed for one-third of his time at Monaghan, (Dillsburgh.)

On May 21st, 1772, he received a call from the Third Presbyterian church, on Pine street, Philadelphia, which after five months' indecision and careful consideration, he deemed it his duty to accept. The Second Presbytery of Philadelphia, however, to which that church belonged, and which was composed of such as had sympathized with the Old Side during the schism, and having been unable to amalgamate with any of the Presbyteries and so had been joined together by themselves, were unwilling to receive him and refused to present the call to him. It was not until the Synod had reversed their action and had permitted the congregation to prosecute their call without the action of Presbytery, that it reached his hands and was at once accepted. For some time, nevertheless, his way was obstructed, until, by the action of Synod, both minister and congregation were transferred to the First Presbytery of Philadelphia, (May 26th, 1773.) An effort was made (November 11th, 1773,) by his former congregation of Carlisle to obtain his restoration to them, but without success.

During the political agitations which preceded the American Revolution, he took a prominent part on the popular side and became especially obnoxious to the official authorities. His large church edifice was on one occasion closed against him on the authority of the incorporated committee of the First church, who claimed a joint jurisdiction over it, but under the influence of a concealed political hostility. The house was opened by the officers of his congregation, and when his way was blocked up by the crowd which had assembled to hear him, he was introduced to his pulpit through a window. He had scarcely commenced the usual services, when a royal magistrate, (J. Bryant,) under the pretence of quelling a riot, commenced reading the Riot Act, and commanded the people to disperse. When other means of silencing this intruder had failed, one of the officers of the congregation seized him, bore him through the midst of the assembly out of the house, and ordered him to begone and to cease disturbing the worship of God; Mr. Duffield then went on with his preaching, but on the next day, he was required to give bail before the Mayor's Court for his appearance on the charge of aiding and abetting a riot. He refused not only to give such bail but to permit any one, even the Mayor himself, to give it in his behalf. He protested that he stood on the ground of principle, and that he was resolved to maintain the right of a minister of Christ and a worshiping assembly to be undisturbed while they were violating no law. He was allowed to withdraw and take the matter under consideration, but under the assurance that he would be soon called upon for his answer. The excitement of the people became intense as the news of this threat of imprisonment, spread, and the "Paxton Boys" who had formerly known him assembled and resolved to hold themselves in readiness to march a hundred miles for his rescue.

When the Colonial Congress held its sessions in Philadelphia, Dr. Duffield was for some time its chaplain, and when the British held possession of Philadelphia, and his church was occupied by them as a stable, he accompanied the American Army and shared in its distresses. He mingled with the soldiery, and by his ardent and patriotic addresses, did much to sustain their fainting spirits. During the dark period when Washington was in Pennsylvania, New Jersey, and on Long Island, he was with the troops, and more than once came nigh being captured. He had been honoured from the commencement of the war by having a price put upon his head, and by being numbered with some leaders who were excluded from the offer of amnesty. As soon as circumstances permitted he returned to his congregation and continued the pastor of the Third church until the day of his death. He returned more than once to his former home in Carlisle, for which he always retained the warmest affection, and his name is mentioned several times as a corresponding member at the meetings of the Presbytery of Carlisle. He took a prominent part in the new organization of the General Assembly, and in the formation of the new Constitution of the Presbyterian Church in the United States in 1788. He was the Stated Clerk of the Assembly from the time of its organization until his death, which took place February 2d, 1790, when he was in his fifty-eighth year. Although a man of slight frame and of small stature, he possessed a firm constitution and was capable of much endurance. He continued his ministrations until about a week before his death, when a severe pleurisy contracted at a funeral prostrated him. He was remarkable for the strictness and fervour of his devotional habits and for his valuation of the Sabbath. His confidence in the efficacy of prayer was such that he appeared to have no anxiety, though in the troubles of the time he more than once knew not where his day's bread was to come from. As he betook himself to prayer he would exclaim, "The Lord will provide," and his expectations were uniformly fulfilled. He was interred in the middle aisle of the church of which he was pastor, and his funeral sermon was preached by Rev. Dr. Ashbel Green, from Rev. xiv, 13.

Some manuscript sermons are to be found among his descendants and others, but we are not aware of anything published from his hand, except an "Account of his Western Tour," and a "Thanksgiving Sermon" on the restoration of peace. He received the honourary degree of a Doctor in Divinity from Yale college, in 1785. As the fruit of his second marriage, he left two sons, (two others having died in infancy,) the youngest of whom (George,) was Register and Comptroller General of the State of Pennsylvania under Governor Thomas McKean, and the father of Rev. George Duffield, D. D., for seventeen years the pastor of the First Presbyterian church of Carlisle.

MAJOR EBENEZER DENNY.

MAJOR EBENEZER DENNY, first Mayor of Pittsburgh, was born in Carlisle, Cumberland county, Pa., March 11th, 1761, and was the eldest child of William and Agnes (Parker) Denny.

His father and uncle, Walter Denny, removed from Chester county to Cumberland county in 1745, the latter settling near Carlisle, where he was the possessor of a large tract of land; subsequently he raised a company of volunteers for the Revolutionary conflict, and was killed at Crooked Billet. At this place also his son was taken prisoner. Another son, Rev. David Denny, was for many years pastor of the Presbyterian church at Chambersburg. William Denny resided in Carlisle, and was the first Coroner west of the Susquehanna, also a Commissary in the Revolutionary Army. His mother, a woman of unusual intelligence and energy, was the daughter of John Parker, and the grand-daughter of Richard Parker, who, as early as 1730, owned lands on the Conodoguinett, near Carlisle, which have remained in the possession of the family for three generations. Nearly all the male Parkers were participants in the struggle against the mother country, and throughout its progress were noted for their loyalty and heroism.

At the age of thirteen, Ebenezer was employed as a bearer of despatches to the commandant at Fort Pitt, and, though a mere lad, safely accomplished his journey over the Alleghenies, through a wilderness teeming with savage foes. He was afterwards employed in his father's store in Carlisle until he moved to Philadelphia, where he shipped as a volunteer in a vessel bearing a letter of marque and reprisal and bound for the West Indies. While acting in this capacity, for fidelity and valour, he was promoted to the command of the quarter-deck. Being tendered the position of supercargo for a second voyage, he decided to accept the offer, but, after crossing the Susquehanna en route to Philadelphia, received and accepted a commission of Ensign in the First Pennsylvania regiment. He participated in the action near Williamsburg, Virginia, where his captain and lieutenant having been disabled at the first fire, the command devolved upon him. On the night of October 14th, he was in the advance at the siege of York, and won such merited distinction that he was selected to plant the first American flag on the British parapet. He afterwards served in the Carolinas, under General St. Clair, and at Charleston during its investment, and also after its evacuation. Later he became Adjutant to Harmer, and Aide-de-Camp to St. Clair, and was repeatedly selected as the bearer of important despatches where courage, shrewdness and daring were required.

After his resignation, Major Denny resided in Bedford county, which he represented in the Convention of 1777, which formed the first Constitution of Pennsylvania. In 1794, he was commissioned Captain, and commanded the expedition to Le Bœuf. In 1795–96, he resided at his farm and mill near Pittsburgh, and was there nominated for the State Legislature and defeated, but in the following year, and by an almost unanimous vote, was elected Commissioner of the county. In 1803, he was Treasurer of Allegheny county, his name appearing first on the list of County Treasurers, and again in 1808 filled that position. In 1804, he was appointed a Director of the Branch of the Bank of Pennsylvania, established in that year at Pittsburgh, and which was the first institution of that nature west of the mountains. When this was merged into the office of the Bank of the United States he retained his Directorship, and was one of the few solvent men during the panic of 1819. For several successive years he obtained from the War Department the contract for the supply of rations for the troops at Fort Fayette and Presque Isle, and filled them satisfactorily while prosecuting also his mercantile and commission business in Philadelphia, on Market street. During the war of 1812, he successfully met the extraordinary demands upon him, and was appointed to furnish supplies to the North Western Army in addition to his own posts in Pennsylvania. At the close of the war he received a complimentary letter from General Harrison, in which he was cordially thanked for his valuable promptness, energy and ability.

When Pittsburgh was incorporated by act of Legislature, March 18th, 1816, Major Denny was elected the first Mayor, and, at the expiration of his first term, declined a re-election. He was Director in the Branch of the Bank of the United States, and afterwards of the Bank of Pittsburgh, in which he was a large stockholder. While visiting Niagara Falls in the summer of 1822, he was attacked by a sudden illness, and with difficulty reached his home, where he died July 21st, in the sixty-first year of his age. He was married July 1st, 1793, to Nancy Williams, daughter of John Williams, Sr., formerly of Carlisle, who participated as a Captain in the battle of the Brandywine, sister of Quartermaster-General John Williams, Jr., Charles Williams, of Lexington, Kentucky, and Hon. William Williams, late of Homewood; she died May 1st, 1806, leaving three sons, Harmer, William and St. Clair, and also two daughters.

DAVID WATTS.

DAVID WATTS, lawyer, was born in Cumberland county, Pennsylvania, October 29th, 1764.

His parents were Frederick Watts, a native of Wales, and Jane Murray, a niece of the celebrated David Murray, Marquis of Tullibardine, a partisan of the Pretender, Charles Edward, who, after the successful battle of Culloden, fled into France. About 1760, they emigrated to Pennsylvania, then a province of Great Britain. After a short residence in Chester county, they moved westward, and built a cabin on the western shore of the Juniata, near its confluence with the Susquehanna, a locality, in that day, on the extreme verge of civilization. It was about twenty miles from Carlisle, where Great Britain had, at that early period, erected a large brick barrack for the comfort of the soldiers employed in repelling the attacks of the aboriginal Indians.

Frederick Watts must have enjoyed the advantages of education in the mother country, for he soon became prominent among the disaffected of the colonists, and was an active partisan of the Revolution. He was appointed, and accepted the commission of General of a body of troops from Pennsylvania and Virginia, called "Minute Men," and served in that capacity during the war. When peace was declared, he became a member of the Executive Council of Pennsylvania—a provisional government formed prior to the adoption and establishment of the Constitution of the State. Under these unfavourable circumstances, the education of their only son, David, was a subject of much interest and difficulty. The duty chiefly devolved upon the mother, whose strong traits of Scotch character seemed to be deeply impressed upon the immature mind of her son, and showed their bearing upon his conduct in after life. Dickinson college, in Carlisle, was founded in 1783, and there he received as finished a classical and general education as the state could, at that time, furnish. He graduated in the first class which left its halls, and bore away with him a taste for, and appreciation of, the literature of Greece and Rome, that he retained throughout his subsequent life.

Attracted to the legal profession, Mr. Watts went to Philadelphia, where he entered as a student the office of that eminent jurist, William Lewis, and was admitted to the bar after the usual course of reading.

He then returned to his native county, and commenced the practice of his profession in Carlisle, where he soon obtained a large patronage, and took a prominent part in the political as well as in the legal questions which, at that period, occupied public attention. One of the most celebrated of these was what led to the so-called "Whiskey Insurrection," of 1794. That spirit was distilled in large quantities by the farmers of western Pennsylvania, and constituted their principal source of revenue. Therefore, when the United States passed acts levying an excise duty on the liquor, the measure was so distasteful to this generally peaceful class of the community, that they rose in open resistance to the law. So serious was the trouble that General Washington went to Carlisle, and reviewed there four thousand men under arms, preparatory to enforcing submission to the authority of the General Government. One of these was David Watts, who had joined a company of local infantry. He was fully alive to the threatened danger to the commonwealth, and so resolute in his opposition to the "Whiskey Boys," that when they had planted a "liberty pole" near Carlisle, and threatened to shoot any one who would disturb it, he shouldered the axe, and alone and unarmed rode to the spot where it stood, and felled it to the ground.

Mr. Watts was distinguished for courage and energy, and these characteristics, united to a thorough education, soon placed him at the head of the bar in Cumberland county, the acknowledged equal of Thomas Duncan, who had been for years the recognised leader on that circuit. They were both men of extensive and varied acquirements in professional and general literature, and both were distinguished for learning, polished manners and integrity. It is to be regretted that he should have passed away in the maturity of his intellectual powers, and left so few traces of his great ability beyond the printed volume of his arguments in the State Reports of Pennsylvania. In this early day, the lawyers were obliged to attend the circuit, extending over several counties, often exposed to inclement weather, traveling on horseback, and provided with poor accommodations. These exposures led to his early death, which occurred on September 25th, 1819.

He married, in September, 1796, Julia Anna Miller, daughter of General Henry Miller, an eminent soldier of the Revolution. They had twelve children, of whom the majority still survive. They were brought up in the doctrines of the Episcopal Church, of which their parents had been life long members.

COL. RICHARD M. CRAIN.

COL. RICHARD M. CRAIN, son of Joseph and Mary Crain, was born November, 1777, in West Hanover township, then Lancaster, now Dauphin county, and married Elizabeth, daughter of the Hon. Robert Whitehill, of East Pennsborough township, Cumberland county. His father, Joseph Crain, was a gentleman of high standing in the community, and an active and exemplary member of the Presbyterian church of Hanover.

Col. Crain, though more thoroughly acquainted with the business of the Land Office than any other man in Pennsylvania, consented to accept of, and served for the greater part of half a century in the subordinate position of Deputy Secretary, as it was considered good policy by the successive administrations during that time to confer the appointment of Secretary of the Land Office on a citizen of one of the western counties. He was also, during that period, elected by the Legislature Treasurer of Pennsylvania, and, as colleague of Major David Nevin, chosen to represent Cumberland county in the Convention which assembled May 2d, 1837, in the hall of the House of Representatives in Harrisburg, to propose amendments to the Constitution of the state, to be submitted to the people thereof for their ratification or rejection.

Of the esteem in which Col. Crain was held by his associates the following publication of their proceedings, on receiving information of his death, furnishes very gratifying evidence:

A meeting of the Governor, heads of departments and clerks, was held at the office of the Surveyor General of Pennsylvania at 5 o'clock on Friday, the 17th day of September, 1852, the object of which was stated by General J Porter Brawley, on whose motion Gov. Wm. Bigler was called to the chair, and, on motion of Major Thomas J. Rehrer, E. S. Goodrich was appointed secretary.

The following preamble and resolutions were then offered by L. G. Dimmock, Esq., which were read and, after a brief but eloquent address by Gen. E. Banks, were unanimously adopted :

WHEREAS, God, in his inscrutable wisdom, has removed from our midst Col. Richard M. Crain, late of the Surveyor General's office ; therefore be it

Resolved, That we deeply deplore the death of our esteemed associate and friend, Col. Richard M. Crain, who, during a long life of public service, sustained a character of unspotted integrity, and by his uprightness and affability, won the respect and confidence of all who knew him.

Resolved, That we tender the family of the deceased our sincere and heartfelt sympathy in their afflictive bereavement.

Resolved, That out of respect for the deceased the Land Department shall be closed on the day of the funeral.

Resolved, That as a mark of regard for our departed friend we will attend his funeral in a body.

Resolved, That the proceedings of this meeting be published in the papers of this borough, and the officers of this meeting and the Surveyor General be appointed a committee to present a copy thereof to the family of the deceased.

WILLIAM BIGLER,

E. S. GOODRICH, *Secretary*.

Chairman.

REV. ROBERT CATHCART, D. D.

THE REV. ROBERT CATHCART, D. D., was born in 1759, near Colerain, in Londonderry, Ireland. He studied at the University of Glasgow, and was licensed by the Presbytery of Ronte, in Ireland. He came to the United States in 1790, when he joined the Presbytery of Philadelphia, the year after the formation of the General Assembly. In October, 1793, he was installed pastor of the congregations of York and Hopewell by the Presbytery of Carlisle. Of the latter he was pastor forty-two, and of the former, forty-four years, these being his only pastoral charges. During these forty-two years, though Hopewell was fifteen miles from York, he never failed, when at home, to preach, but on one Sabbath. For forty years he never missed attending Synod but once, and then he was ill. For nearly thirty years he was elected a Commissioner to the General Assembly every year, and for nearly twenty years he was Clerk of the Assembly. The degree of Doctor of Divinity was conferred on him by Queen's (now Rutgers) college, New Brunswick, New Jersey.

For thirty years Dr. Cathcart was a Trustee of Dickinson college, and during all that time attended all their commencements. While a Trustee there, he obtained the degree of Doctor of Divinity for Dr. Scott, the commentator. The Rev. D. H. Emerson, D. D., one of Dr. Cathcart's successors at York, in a published letter says: "I knew Dr. Cathcart as intimately as any man can know a father. I visited him every week during nearly five years, unless prevented by sickness, and, with the best opportunities for becoming acquainted with his character, my deliberate judgment is, that he was among the finest and best of our American clergymen. * * * He was in the habit of reading, daily, at least two chapters in the Bible, in connection with Scott's Commentary. His reading, particularly for the last twelve years of his life, was immense. Having a strong constitution, unimpaired eye-sight, an insatiable thirst for knowledge, and a wonderfully retentive memory, he would read everything valuable within his reach, and would delight his friends with the stores of information which he would pour forth during a social interview. This habit of reading and of constantly exercising his mental powers, continued to the last moment of life."

All Dr. Cathcart's successors at York were greatly attached to him.

He was an *interesting* man. His manner, dry at first, opened more and more as one knew him better, and the attachment of his younger brethren gradually grew into respectful affection. One of his successors thus wrote of him, in a contemporary newspaper, at the time of his death:

"The most prominent trait of Dr. Cathcart's character, as impressed upon me, was his *gentlemanliness*. Perhaps it is because this high quality is less common now than it used to be. A more perfect gentleman at heart I never knew. His was not the polished exterior assumed for a purpose on an occasion, to veil selfishness, and then laid aside like a garment folded away to be used for a similar purpose. His character was genuine. Delicacy in regard to improper interference with the station or duties of another, was one of his most prominent features. His long connection (forty-four years,) with the York church, as their pastor, would have enabled him, as it has others similarly situated, to give his successor much trouble. If he ever had the slightest disposition to do so, he never manifested it, but gave the strength of his influence, in public and private, to sustaining him. The same trait was seen in all his intercourse. Where he had rights he maintained them; where he had not he was a law unto himself, in refraining from intermeddling. He was a 'gentleman of the old school,' nicely discriminating occasions, a principle of fine feeling running like a thread through his whole conduct.

"Dr. Cathcart was emphatically an *honest man*. His care and punctuality in pecuniary matters are well known. But this, which sometimes proceeds from mere regard to public opinion, was in him genuine honesty of heart. He was above suspicion. No man, even in his most secret thoughts, I suppose, ever took Dr. Cathcart for a disingenuous man. His sturdy and Puritan honesty made him almost uncharitable towards hypocrisy. He could not away with it. That a man should be genuine, that words and heart should agree, though he did not say as much about it as Carlyle, was to him the prime thing in a man. Indeed, it made him unsuspicious. Not feeling any movement of insincerity in himself, he was not apt to imagine it in others. And this was one of the sources of that tranquility of character for which he was remarkable. The 'mens conscia recti,' the straightforwardness of his temper, made him an excellent exemplification of that noble passage of Scripture: 'He that walketh uprightly, walketh surely.' If the bones of the prophet revived the dead by their touch, then could we wish the memory of the subject of this sketch to re-kindle in an age which mistakes hypocrisy for wisdom, and deceit for prudence, the pure, stern honesty which once characterized the Puritan of England and of Scotland. No one doubted the honesty of the Ironsides and the Covenanters. It will be a sad day for the Church if a Presbyterian's word ceases to be 'as good as his bond.'

"Dr. Cathcart's devotion to the best interests of the whole race of man, well entitles him to the name of philanthropist. No aspect of benevolent effort was uninteresting to him; no man knew so well what was passing throughout the world; no man's memory was so accurate a chronicle of the times. A thousand times has he sat down beside some friend, often some bright eyed youth or maiden—for he was one of those whose feelings never grew old—and given a complete review of everything contained in the newspapers of the week. But nothing interested him so much as the advance of religion in the world. He was devoted to the missionary cause, and contributed to the extent of, yea, and beyond his ability, as some thought, to the American Board. He watched its proceedings with intense interest, read every word of every Missionary Herald, and delighted to tell us how the missionary cause was progressing in every country where the messengers of the cross have gone. It is observable of some old men—and the same is true of ministers in more than one melancholy case—that they grow selfish as they grow old; animal appetites, as in original childhood, gain sensibly over intellectual and moral qualities, and they narrow down to a very minute sphere. Nothing of this kind was visible in Dr. Cathcart. Beautiful as is the York valley—a perfect gem of rich cultivated scenery—entirely as he felt at home there, long as he had resided by its clear river, its hills never bounded his sympathies. The feeling of Terence, expressing kindred with all mankind, or the still grander feeling, '*the field is the world*,' was the key-note to his constant habit of mind. He was devoted with singular attachment to the temperance cause, he watched with much anxiety the statistics of crime, he was deeply interested in all the aspects of politics, as connected, especially, with the onward progress of the human race, and while, to a considerable extent, a '*laudator temporis acti*,' he had yet ever a warm sympathizing feeling for anything that makes man wiser, better, holier, more active, industrious, or even comfortable.

"Dr. Cathcart was liberal, in the truest sense. Never was there a more thorough Presbyterian. Religion, in his mind, ever pursued its tranquil way along by Westmnister and Geneva, and he could hardly conceive of a connected or logical theology which was not Calvinistic. All other systems appeared to him defective, not indeed fundamentally erroneous, but defective in clearness, method and power. And as in doctrine, so in government, the republicanism of Presbyterianism struck him as beautiful and well ordered. Jerusalem to him, according to our forms, was builded as a city which is compact together. Our admirable Confession of Faith, our Catechisms, with their clear, racy and discriminating English of an age which had not yet felt foreign admixtures or domestic feebleness, was to him next to the Holy Word itself. But all this did not prevent a spirit of enlarged charity for others. Indeed, this liberality was a part of his Presbyterianism, as well as of his Christianity. He could not conceive of a religion without it. In the arms of charity, he embraced all who loved our Lord Jesus Christ in sincerity, and felt that under various forms and different rituals, and varying shades of doctrinal belief as to non-essentials, the same spirit of piety might and often did dwell.

"The character of Dr. Cathcart's piety was modified by the nature of the man. If his temperament were ever glowing, he restrained it. It appeared more in intellection and in action, than in feeling. It was observed, however, by those who knew him best and longest, that the further he went down into the vale of life, the clearer was his vision of celestial realities,—the nearer he drew to the gates of the city of God, the more he caught of the glories of the upper sanctuary upon his spirit. Does not this seem exceedingly beautiful, when every year mellows an old man's heart, and the softening radiance of God's angels is reflected upon his countenance, ere they bear him away forever? And true it is, that Dr. Cathcart's 'last days were his best days,' the whole Christianity of York being witness. And never was he so beloved, as just before 'he was not, for God took him.'

"We might dwell on other and more minute features of our departed friend, but it cannot be necessary. One was the conscience he made of punctuality, another was his untiring industry. He was fond of exertion, both physical and mental, and to this was, no doubt, owing— allowance being made for an uncommonly robust muscular frame—his long life, his long preserved vigour, and as an especial favour of Providence, the clearness of his eye-sight. He read constantly, literally from morning to night, and an uncommonly retentive memory enabled him to preserve almost anything that he read. But he was social also, retaining something European in his habits, in this respect. As long as he could walk, he would visit his old friends, and he loved to rekindle old recollections with them. Having known nearly all the celebrated men who were contemporary with him in America, he was very interesting in bringing out their characteristic traits, by anecdotes, told with marked vivacity, of circumstances occurring in his own intercourse with them. In short, he was a source of unfailing interest, and his withdrawal causes a vacancy which none but himself could fill as he did. He was original, every thing he did was his own, and no man who possesses this excellent trait can fail to be interesting.

Of the last moments of Dr. Cathcart it is not my privilege to speak, nor are they material. His life spoke for him. If to have every thought softened by a Christian atmosphere, to have every purpose connected with the advancement of Christianity and the best interests of men, to be much in prayer, and devoted to every gathering together of God's people,—if these be indications of a heart right with God, then our venerable father is walking in white above, with those who are worthy."

Dr. JAMES ARMSTRONG.

JAMES was the oldest of the two sons of Gen. John Armstrong, and according to a family record in the possession of his son, of Washington city, he was born in 1749. This must have been very soon after the emigration of the family from the north of Ireland. He was educated at Nassau Hall, afterwards Princeton College, where he graduated about four years before the Revolutionary War with honours as an accurate scholar. After leaving college he is said to have been *apprenticed*, according to the custom of the time, for five years, for the study of medicine with Dr. Morgan, at that time one of the most eminent physicians of Philadelphia. He commenced the practice of his profession with high testimonials of his ability and acquirements, from his late instructor, in the vicinity of Winchester, Va., but we infer from a correspondence between his father and Col. George Washington, in reference to a new location, that his prospects there were not encouraging. Being threatened with consumption, he made a voyage to London, where he became an admirer of the peculiar principles of Dr. Sydenham, which have since been so generally received, regarding the recuperative powers of nature. In his subsequent practice he favoured only such prescriptions as would assist the natural powers of the body in their own appropriate work. He, however, was induced from his admiration of Dr. Rush, with whom he afterwards became intimate, to make a free use of the lancet.

On his return, and when he was forty years of age, he married Mary Stevenson, a daughter of one of the oldest settlers in the valley, a man of wealth and eminent position in Carlisle. She was a woman of remarkable piety, could repeat both the Longer and Shorter Catechisms of her church, with their proofs, and insisted on her children being instructed in a similar manner. They had nine children, three of whom died in early life, and two still survive. Soon after their marriage they removed to the Kishacoquillas valley, then almost a wilderness, and there became possessors of a large tract of land on which they lived for nearly twelve years. In 1801 he sold his property there and purchased another called Richland Lawn, about six miles west of Carlisle. On this he resided for eight years, when (1809) he was induced by greater advantages for the education of his children, to return to Carlisle. There in the family mansion in which he had been born, and had spent his childhood, he lived in refinement, congenial society and the practice of his profession. He never sought political distinction, but while he resided in the Kishacoquillas valley he was requested by his fellow citizens to represent them in Congress. But as he was a Federalist of the Washington school in politics, as he disliked Jefferson, and was not in favour of the war with Great Britain in 1812, he had no great interest in promoting the public policy of the day, and after one term he retired again to private life.

Dr. Armstrong was well read in his profession, and familiar with general literature. A warm patron of education, he was, for thirty years, or thereabouts, the President of the Board of Trustees of Dickinson college, of which he had been one of the most active founders. He had no talent for the acquisition or the preservation of wealth. He had inherited from his own and from his wife's father a princely fortune, but he is said to have despised all ordinary methods of economy or of making money, and to have died insolvent. His home was a centre of lavish hospitality and of a generous patronage of all public enterprises. His talents and acquisitions might have secured him a high position in his profession, but a retirement from its active duties and a disinclination to those arts which are needful to popularity in it, prevented his attainment of a more than moderate success. His manner was studiously polite and dignified; his person tall and well proportioned; his dress was of the best materials, and fitted by the most artistic workmen; his wig with its somewhat antiquated queue was of the most scrupulous finish; and his conversation, though fluent, was carefully worded and high toned. To his friends and equals he was genial and agreeable, but common people could not approach him with familiarity. His keen gray eye, his large aquiline nose, his six feet stature, and a rather severe manner, made his presence uncongenial to such as were not of his own circle. And yet his strict integrity, his high sense of honour, his quick sympathy with the injured and distressed, his uniform interest in the public welfare, and his strict morality and religious principle made him valuable in every society.

Not a single vice has ever been attributed to Dr. Armstrong. The profaneness, and excess in drinking and in gambling, which were so common in his day, he detested and reproved with severity. He is said to have been passionately fond of horses and to have been himself an elegant horseman; "he always rode with whip and spur, and vaulted into his saddle with dignity and grace. He would as soon have thought of stumbling into a ball room as of mounting a horse awkwardly." He retained to the last most of his faculties of mind and body, free from infirmities usually incident to old age, his vision was distinct, his voice clear, his form unbent, his limbs were active, and only his hearing was impaired until his death. Until within a few years of his death he made an annual journey on horseback from Carlisle to Kittanning, a distance of two hundred miles. According to an inscription on his tombstone in the Old Cemetery of Carlisle, he "died in April, 1828, aged eighty-two." There is a slight discrepancy apparent between this inscription and the reported time of his birth in the family record. Having been brought up in the strictest principles and forms of the Presbyterian Church, he lived and died in its communion.

One who knew him well, both by personal acquaintance and reputation, writes of him: "A higher toned man than Dr. James Armstrong the state of Pennsylvania never produced. He was one who had an utter scorn for everything and everybody that was low or mean. He could not stoop to secure any favour. He would sacrifice everything to his self-respect. He would and did without a murmur dispense with not only the comforts but some of the very necessities of life rather than even appear to cringe. And yet he never boasted of his wealth, or family, or position in society. Wealth he held in light esteem, office had no allurements for him, and so reserved was he in speaking of his family that his surviving children were left in almost entire ignorance of its history."

HON. WILLIAM WILKINS.

THE HON. WILLIAM WILKINS, lawyer and judge, was born in Carlisle, Cumberland county, Pa., in 1779, his father, John Wilkins, having been a resident of that place. He was educated at Dickinson college, and studied law under the direction of Judge Watts, with whom he continued until his admission to the bar in Carlisle.

Settling in Pittsburgh in 1800-6, Mr. Wilkins practised successfully as an attorney, and was appointed judge by Governor Findlay. He was a General of the militia, also an influential member of the Legislature. He was elected to Congress upon two occasions, and for several years ably discharged the duties of United States Senator. During the administration of General Jackson, he was appointed by him Minister to Russia, and under the presidency of Tyler, became Secretary of War. Subsequently, although firmly attached to the Democratic party, he strenuously supported the Government during the war. While in his eightieth year, when the Home Guards were organized, he was mounted throughout the day, and took his position on parade.

During a period extending to more than sixty years, Judge Wilkins was the most prominent man in western Pennsylvania, was well known throughout the country, and was eminently influential as a popular chief and leader. As a lawyer he won high and widespread distinction, and participated importantly in public affairs, taking especial interest in the cause of education. He was twice married—to Catharine Holmes, of Baltimore, Md., and to Matilda Dallas, daughter of Alexander James Dallas, formerly Secretary of the Treasury. He died in June, 1865, in his eighty-sixth year, leaving as survivors four daughters.

WILLIAM CRAWFORD, M. D.

ONE of the most prominent citizens of Adams county, for the forty years between 1783 and 1823, was Dr. William Crawford. He was born in Paisley, Scotland, in 1760, and in 1781, on receiving his diploma from the University of Edinburgh, came to this country. He landed in Philadelphia, where he met acquaintances who induced him to settle near Gettysburg. For a time he lived in the town, which had not then become the county seat of Adams, but was one of the villages of York county. In 1794 he bought the farm on Marsh creek, on which he thereafter lived until death. In 1795 he returned to Scotland on a visit, and in 1796, on his return, was married to Miss Ann Dodd, who had come, with an uncle and other friends, from Scotland in the same vessel with him on his return voyage.

Dr. Crawford was an active practitioner for a long period, and his practice extended into the neighbouring counties of Cumberland and Franklin, and of Frederick and Washington, Maryland. His reputation was very high and especially in surgery. He became early interested in public affairs, was for several years one of the Associate Judges of the county, and was, for the eight years of Mr. Madison's presidential term, a Representative in Congress for the district of which Adams formed a part. On the expiration of his term of service he resumed the practice of his profession, in which he was actively engaged when overtaken by disease. His death occurred in 1823, in the sixty-fourth year of his age.

REV. CHARLES NISBET, D. D.

SOON after the close of the War for Independence the General Assembly of the Commonwealth of Pennsylvania chartered a college to be erected and established in the borough of Carlisle, to be forever called and known by the name of Dickinson college. The act recites that the honour of this name was conferred on Governor John Dickinson, in memory of his great and important services to his country, and in commemoration of his very liberal donation to the institution. In 1783 the country had been exhausted by a long and destructive war; there were few wealthy men, and the property of these few was small in comparison with that of the class called "rich men" in 1875. The donation of ten thousand dollars at that time was very liberal—as liberal, in public estimation, as the donation of ten times that sum in our day of large figures.

The original charter of the college contained some wise provisions, and a few otherwise. The Principal—as the President is called in the charter—was declared incapable of holding the office of trustee. This cut off from the Board the man who, of all others, best knew the interests and necessities of the college. Another clause was construed to give the students the right of appeal to the Board against the decisions of the Faculty in cases of discipline. This was the seed of bitter fruit, as the early history of the institution attests.

In 1784, Charles Nisbet, D. D., an eminent clergyman of the Presbyterian Church of Scotland, was elected President of the college. He was a man of vast and varied learning, tenacious memory, subtle and ready wit, remarkable conversational power and exemplary piety. He had been an outspoken friend of the American Colonies in their struggle for independence, and this fact, added to his great reputation as a scholar, made his appointment exceedingly popular in this country. The most flattering representations and promises were held out to him by leading members of the Board of Trustees to induce him to accept the presidency to which he had been unanimously elected. These were doubtless made in good faith, but without adequate knowledge of the endowment which was needed to support a first class institution of learning. Dr. Nisbet hesitated long to leave his native country, the cultivated society of which he was an ornament, the church and congregation of which he was the beloved pastor, and at the age of fifty years to engage in untried duties, on a new arena, among people whose habits and modes of thought were different from his own.

He finally yielded to the urgent solicitations of the trustees, and arrived in Philadelphia with his family in June, 1785. For three weeks he was the guest of Dr. Benjamin Rush, who entertained him with elegant hospitality, and introduced to his acquaintance the prominent citizens of Philadelphia. His first letter to his friends in Scotland proved that his impressions of America and Americans were very favourable; but subsequent letters indicate that the roseate hues of metropolitan society no longer gladdened his vision when he came to encounter the realities of his new office.

He arrived in Carlisle on the 4th of July, and was received with enthusiasm. He entered that ancient borough in charge of a committee of citizens, with an escort of cavalry, in time to observe the celebration of the anniversary of independence by noisy republicans.

He was installed in office the next day, and commenced the organization of an institution which he had been led to believe was to be the foremost college in America. During nineteen years he laboured as few men could have laboured, performing an amount of work that was truly prodigious, in the midst of discouragements under which most men would have succumbed. His efforts to obtain a high grade of scholarship were thwarted, his advice too frequently unheeded, and his recommendations unnoticed or rejected by the Board. His cherished hopes of success were not realized, and this profound scholar and Christian gentleman went down to his grave under a sense of disappointment, but with the serene consciousness that he had done his best for sound scholarship in Dickinson college, and in the firm belief that the seed which he had planted would spring up and bear fruit under more genial suns and skies.

During the whole time of his presidency Dr. Nisbet strove to elevate the grade of scholarship required for graduation, but a majority of the trustees dissented from his educational views, believing them impracticable in the existing condition of the country, and the minority acquiesced in the views of those who hoped to increase the revenue of the college by attracting that class of students who desire to obtain academic honours with the least possible outlay of time and labour.

Other causes, which it is not necessary here and now to enumerate, contributed to depress the college during the first two decades. "It had been," says Dr. W. H. Allen,* "organized before the country

---

*Historical Sketch of Dickinson college, read before the Philadelphia Conference of the M. E. Church.

needed it." The College of New Jersey at Princeton, and the University of Pennsylvania, were adequate to supply all the demand for collegiate education in this section of the country at that time.

But local interests or private jealousies prevailed then, as they have many times since, over the dictates of prudence and foresight. It is an American weakness to build half a dozen moribund colleges with no endowment but debt, with only the patronage necessary for one, and with half a dozen poorly paid Faculties to do the work of one, and to do it very imperfectly. It strongly resembles our sectarian weakness, which induces us to waste the Lord's money in building four or five churches in every little town which has no more population and wealth than are sufficient for the support of one, and placing in the pulpits as many starving preachers, who supply the half filled pews with spiritual food of about the same quality as the physical food which their sparse and sleepy congregations dole out to them.

Dickinson college was a premature birth, and with the most careful nurture its vital force in early life was necessarily feeble. The proverb says "money is the sinews of war," and it is equally true that money is the brains of a college, for without money brains will not come, or if they come, will not stay. Dickinson college had not a sufficient endowment to make it independent of tuition fees. This fact had then, as it always will have, a demoralizing effect on discipline. When students know that the Faculty depend on them for daily bread, and that their withdrawal or expulsion will close the doors of the institution, they have a firm conviction that they are masters of the situation. Dickinson College was in this precarious condition for nearly half a century. When it sought subscriptions from individuals, it was met with the charge of sectarianism; when it solicited donations from the state it was accused of political heresies and exposed to investigating committees; and when the number of students diminished and the Board could neither beg nor borrow, they reduced the salaries of the Faculty and lowered the requirements for graduation. This policy caused Dr. Nisbet to say that the people of this country seemed to know no difference between a college and a primary school for children.

In 1803 the college was consumed by fire, and a larger and more commodious edifice was erected in 1804, but Dr. Nisbet did not live to occupy it. This building is now called West College.

As already stated, Dr. Nisbet was a gentleman of vast and varied learning. Many of the most distinguished men of the country were trained under his careful and able supervision, and they always referred to him with profound respect for his character, and glowing admiration of his erudition and aptness to teach. Such a man could not die. His influence survives him in the vigorous impulse which he gave to education in its highest forms, and which has been, as it will be, transmitted from generation to generation.

Tradition still reports many striking and sparkling instances of the genuine wit which seems to have been a largely developed element of his constitution. This was a power which he could wield with tremendous effect, and which he did not hesitate often to bring into exercise. On one occasion whilst a member of the General Assembly, as he was replying to a speaker who had made an unfortunate address, he dealt out his caustic remarks with the introductory formula, oft repeated, "If I had said so and so, I should feel so and so." The Moderator was obliged to ask for an abatement of severity in the address. To his interposition the Doctor replied, with his peculiar tone and gesture: "And hasn't a man, Mr. Moderator, a right to say what he pleases about himself?" thus bringing down the house in irresistible laughter, and thus, perhaps, doing more to establish his cause than could have been done by an extended speech.

ROBERT DAVIDSON, D. D

ROBERT DAVIDSON, D. D., was the second President of Dickinson college. He was born at Elkton, Maryland, in 1750, and graduated at the University of Pennsylvania in 1771. When twenty-two years old he was *licensed* to preach by the Presbytery of Newcastle, and not long afterwards he was *ordained* by the Second Presbytery of Philadelphia. When twenty-three years old he was appointed an instructor in the University of Pennsylvania, and shortly afterwards chosen Professor of History, and assistant to Dr. Ewing, pastor of the First Presbyterian church of Philadelphia. In 1775 he composed a dialogue in verse, with two odes set to music, which were performed as an exercise at commencement, in the presence of the Continental Congress. In July of the same year he delivered a patriotic sermon on the war before the military in Philadelphia, and soon afterwards repeated it before the troops at Burlington. In 1784 he published an Epitome of Geography in verse, for the use of schools, which was highly valued at the time. When Dickinson college was founded he was invited to become one of the Professors. "His name will be of use to us," wrote Dr. Rush to Dr. Nisbet, "for he is a man of learning, and of an excellent private character." When leaving the University the Trustees of it testified their appreciation of his merits and services, by conferring on him the degree of Doctor of Divinity.

Dr. Davidson was thirty-four years old when, in the autumn of 1784, he became Vice-President of the college and Professor of History and Belles-Lettres, and also pastor of the Presbyterian church of Carlisle. This last relation he sustained with honour and success for twenty-eight years, greatly beloved by his flock. He was faithful and diligent in the discharge of his duties both as professor and pastor. In 1785 he composed a dialogue in blank verse, in honour of the patrons of the college, which was spoken in public and printed. He was noted for his systematic habits, and his achievements were correspondingly numerous and great. With eight languages he made himself acquainted; in theology he was well versed; and with the whole circle of science he was familiar, especially in astronomy, on which subject he published several papers, and invented an ingenious apparatus called a "*Cosmosphere.*" He was often called upon to deliver discourses on occasions of public interest, and always did it well. In September of '94 he preached a sermon on *"The Duties of Citizens,"* before the troops, on their way to suppress the Whiskey Insurrection, and soon afterwards delivered another on *"The Freedom and Happiness of the United States,"* before General Washington, Governor Mifflin, and the military bound on the same expedition. The authorities were so much gratified, that Governor Mifflin offered him an honourable position, which he respectfully declined.

In 1796, Dr. Davidson attained one of the highest honours of his church, in being elected Moderator of the General Assembly, the eighth in order, a position which he filled with his usual dignity and affability. When General Washington died, in 1799, Dr. Davidson delivered a eulogy on his life and services, which appears in a collection of discourses elicited by that event, and published in 1802, with the title *"Washingtoniana."* And upon the death of Dr. Nisbet, in 1804, he delivered a like tribute to his memory. During the five years succeeding the death of Dr. Nisbet, Dr. Davidson discharged the duties of the President of the college, and did so faithfully and acceptably. In 1809 he resigned, to give himself wholly to his pastoral charge, and received a vote of thanks from the Trustees for his long and faithful services. Dr. Davidson was a lover and composer of sacred music, and had a very decided taste and talent for drawing. In 1811 he published the 119th Psalm in metre, and the next year published a "New Metrical Version of the Psalms," with annotations—regarded as superior to Sternhold and Hopkins, improved by Rouse.

After a life of great activity and usefulness Dr. Davidson died in Carlisle, December 13, 1812, in the sixty-second year of his age. His funeral sermon, afterwards printed, was preached by his friend, Dr. Cathcart, of York. As a preacher, Dr. Davidson was eminently instructive, and, owing to extreme modesty, could command his pen much easier and better than his tongue. It has been well said of him, that, as a man of letters, his standing was high. His clear intellect and extensive acquirements made him a valuable instructor. As an evidence of his diligent and studious habits, he left twenty manuscript volumes of sermons and scientific lectures, in addition to all he had given to the public through the press. Dr. Davidson was married three times. By his second wife—daughter of the Hon. John Montgomery, of Carlisle—he had his only child, a son, the Rev. Robert Davidson, D. D., whose sketch will be found elsewhere in this volume.

REV. FRANCIS HERRON, D. D.

REV. FRANCIS HERRON was born near Shippensburg, Cumberland county, Pa., June 28th, 1774. He belonged to that honoured and honourable race, the Scotch-Irish, memorable in the history of the world, but especially in our country, for a thorough devotion to evangelical truth and constitutional liberty. The training of his early years bore rich fruit at a subsequent period of his life, making him so eminent among his brethren as an effective preacher and an orthodox divine.

Receiving the careful training indicative of his parents' high regard for knowledge, he entered Dickinson college, Carlisle, Pa., then under the care of that distinguished Presbyterian, Rev. Dr. Nisbet. Here he completed his classical course, and graduated May 5th, 1794. The prayers of his pious parents were answered by the influence of grace upon his heart, and he was led to study for the ministry of reconciliation. He studied theology under Robert Cooper, D. D., his pastor, and was licensed by Carlisle Presbytery, October 4th, 1797.

He entered upon the service of his Divine Master as a missionary, going out into the backwoods, as it was then called, passing through Pittsburgh, Pa., then a small village, and extending his tour as far west as Chillicothe, Ohio. Stopping for the night in a tavern at Six Mile Run, near Wilkinsburg, Pa., the people prevailed upon him to stay till the following Sabbath, which he did, and under the shade of an apple tree did this young disciple break the bread of life to the people.

His journey was resumed the next day, and with a frontier settler for his guide, he pushed on to his destination, through an almost unbroken wilderness, his course often guided by the "blazes" upon the trees. Two nights he encamped with the Indians, who were quite numerous near what is now the town of Marietta, Ohio.

On his return from Chillicothe, Ohio, he visited Pittsburgh. The keeper of the tavern where he lodged proved to be an old acquaintance, and, at his request, he consented to preach. Notice was sent, and in the evening a small congregation of about eighteen persons assembled. The house he preached in was a rude structure built of logs, occupying the site of the present First Presbyterian church. And such was the primitive style of that day, that, during the services, the swallows, who had their nests in the eaves, flew among the congregation.

At this time, the churches in that portion of our country were visited with a season of refreshing grace, and Mr. Herron entered into the revival with all the ardour of youth, filled with hopefulness and zeal. He preached for Rev. Dr. John McMillan, at the Chartiers church, during a revival season. He also preached at the Buffalo church, where his fervid eloquence made a deep impression, and the people presented him a call, and strongly urged it upon his attention He, however, concluded to return to the vicinity of his home, especially as a call from Rocky Spring church was awaiting him. This call he accepted, and he was ordained and installed as pastor of that church by Carlisle Presbytery, April 9th, 1800.

Here his life work commenced. The season of revival through which he had passed during his journey to and from the west, had given a spiritual unction to his preaching, which soon manifested itself among his people. His efforts in behalf of their true interests were systematized. Prayer meetings were inaugurated. He established the Bible Class, together with meetings for catechetical instruction. He devoted a large portion of his time to the "little ones of his flock." In scenes like these the first decade of his ministerial life passed away, the people grew in piety and spiritual strength, and the pastor in that power to influence the people, and to instruct and edify them.

During a visit to Pittsburgh, in 1810, he was invited to occupy the pulpit of the First church, then vacant by the recent death of Rev. Robert Steele. The people were charmed with his discourse; his ripening intellect, modified by that refined spirituality which was a prominent element in his ministration, had a powerful effect upon his audience. They urged him to preach for them a second time, which he did; the result was, a unanimous call was made out and presented to him in the usual manner.

The Presbytery of Carlisle dissolved the relation that existed between Rocky Spring church and Mr. Herron, and he was dismissed to Redstone Presbytery, April 3, 1811, and was installed pastor of the First Presbyterian church, Pittsburgh, Pa., the following June. In a few weeks he removed with his family to his new home, traveling in a large wagon with his wife, children, and all his household goods.

He joined Redstone Presbytery, June 18th, 1811. The importance of his new position was fully and truly felt. The commercial importance of Pittsburgh had given all kinds of business an impetus, and prosperity was advancing rapidly, but this outward show referred only to worldly affairs; the religious condition of the people was cold and almost lifeless. The church to which he was called was embarrassed with debt, and the piety of the people manifested a degree of conformity to the world which nearly appalled the preacher's heart. But the experience of his ten years' pastorate was to him invaluable, and girding himself, he entered upon his duties with a true heart and an earnest purpose. His preaching was the simple exposition of the truth as it is in Jesus—pointed, clear and unwavering—revealing the enormity of sin and pleading with the fidelity of one who loved their souls. This style of preaching was sustained by his efforts to establish the prayer meeting, which, strange as it now appears, met with much opposition, even among professors of religion; but this young pastor knew the holy influence of communion with God, and that God favoured a praying people; he therefore went forward, and, in connection with Rev. Thomas Hunt, who was pastor of the Second church, they persisted, though to avoid collision with the people the meetings were not held in the church, and a small room was used for that purpose in which Mr. Hunt taught a day school. The first meeting consisted of the two pastors, one man, and six women; and thus, for eighteen months, did these meetings continue without adding a single person to their number.

The chilling indifference of the people soon grew into a downright hostility, and husbands and fathers prohibited their wives and daughters from attending, and, finally, when the continued efforts of these pious people could be no longer borne, they waited upon Mr. Herron and told him that it must be stopped. His reply was the turning point in the spiritual condition of that people. He said, "Gentlemen, these meetings will not stop; you are at liberty to do as you please, but I also have the liberty to worship God according to the dictates of my conscience, none daring to molest or make me afraid." From that time a spirit of piety manifested itself among the members of the church, several gay and fashionable persons were hopefully converted, and an impression was made upon the whole community at once hopeful and healthful.

Besides his talents as a preacher, and his loveliness of character as a pastor, Dr. Herron was a practical man and a good manager. The debt which hung as an incubus upon the church increased the difficulties of his situation, and after various efforts to remove it or stave off the issue, the natural result arrived, and the church was sold by the sheriff in December, 1813. He attended the sale and bought the property in his own name for $2,819. In a short time he disposed of a corner lot to the Bank of Pittsburgh, whereon to erect a banking house, for $3,000. With this money he paid off the debt of the church, and placed the surplus, $180, in the treasury.

The church started on a new era of prosperity. Dr. Herron's intellect was in its full strength, and his influence was felt throughout the whole community, and his fame throughout the whole Church. The church became crowded with hearers, and the membership rapidly increased, so that an enlargement of the building was rendered necessary. This was done by removing the side walls and enlarging the width, so as to admit an aisle and an additional row of pews on each side. This alteration was completed in December, 1817, and on a resale of the pews, enough funds were realized not only to pay all the expenses of the alteration, but to alter the pulpit and erect a session-room in the rear of the church.

As a token of gratitude of the congregation to the pastor, and of the high estimate they put upon his practical efficiency and ministerial excellence, they raised his salary to fifteen hundred dollars—a large salary at that time.

Dr. Herron was a fine representative of a minister of the olden time. He was fond of the good old paths. He based his success, as a minister, upon catechetical instruction, Bible Classes and Sunday Schools. He believed, and acted out his belief, that the good old Presbyterian usage of drilling the children in the family and in the church, in the letter of the Shorter Catechism, is the best of all methods for impressing evangelical conviction, and for training a generation of sound, orthodox, intelligent Christians. This system, at first confined to the children, he extended, in 1823, to the adult members of his congregation. These meetings were conducted by the minister every Sabbath afternoon, and were, of course, highly blessed.

In 1825, the General Assembly resolved to establish a Theological Seminary in the west, and appointed a committee to select a place. Rev. Dr. Herron, with his naturally quick preception, in connection with the Rev. Dr. Swift, urged the claims of Allegheny city, Pa. He entered into the enterprise with his whole heart, and by much laborious and skilful effort, obtained a decision in favour of locating it there. Dr. Swift took charge of the instruction of the pupils, whilst Dr. Herron assumed the toils and anxieties of its sustenance. Though this involved a vast amount of time and labour, still Dr. Herron never for a moment withdrew from his post, but for every additional burden he seemed to be specially sustained by his Divine Master. Such a superabundance of toil suited the man, and with unwearied assiduity he laboured on for years, and to no one does the Western Theological Seminary of the Presbyterian Church, owe its influence, and success, too, in a greater degree, than to Dr. Herron.

In 1827 he was elected Moderator of the General Assembly of the Presbyterian Church, at its session in Philadelphia. During the autumn of that year a revival of religion manifested itself among his people, and eventually throughout the community. His ministrations were also blessed with outpourings of the Spirit in 1832 and 1835.

In 1850, Dr. Herron, having reached his seventy-sixth year, felt like the prophet Elijah, that he must soon depart. He therefore pressed his resignation upon his congregation, which they accepted with the understanding that he would accept a thousand dollars per year for life. He feel asleep in Jesus, and entered his rest on the 6th day of December, 1860. Though he had retired from active life for some years, his death was felt to be a public loss. A meeting was held of the ministers of the city of Pittsburgh, and the adjoining city of Allegheny, to give expression to their feelings. The Court of Common Pleas and the District Court adjourned, and the news spread as though a public calamity had befallen the city. The funeral was attended by all ranks in life.

The Rev. William M. Paxton, Dr. Herron's successor, delivered a memorial discourse in which he thus presented the aged patriarch as a man, a Christian, and a minister:

"As a man he was made for the times—a man of nerve, will, power, moulding rather than being moulded, breasting the current rather than floating upon its surface. Such men are generic forces, originating thoughts, creating circumstances, and propelling society in their own way and for their own purposes, stamping their impress upon the community in which they live, work reformation and originate eras of progress and improvement.

"As a Christian, he was distinguished by the vigourous growth and uniform development of the whole circle of Christian graces. His character was symmetrical, admirably adjusted, and equipoised in all its parts. His chief distinction as a Christian was his love for the person and his devotion to the glory of Jesus Christ. Secondly, his love for souls. Thirdly, he was eminently a man of faith. Fourthly, with a pure evangelical faith he combined a liberal catholic spirit, and fifthly, he was magnanimous in the highest and noblest sense the word can be used.

"As a minister, first, he was an experimental preacher; second, he was doctrinal; third, he was an awakening preacher; fourth, his preaching was tender and affectionate.

"As a presbyter, he was attentive, regular and prompt; thoroughly acquainted with rules of order, he very often presided over the Presbytery and Synod.

"As a public man, he was interested in every enterprise to promote the comfort of the people and the adornment of the city of Pittsburgh. He was one of the city's fathers, and no man loved it better or did more to advance its highest welfare. He not only loved his city, but also his state and nation. Patriotism was a part of his religion, and his heart was alike true to his country as to his God. He knew the worth of human liberty, and believed that these United States are a peculiar heritage of freedom."

Dr. Herron married in February, 1802, Miss Elizabeth Blain, daughter of Alexander Blain, Esq., of Carlisle, Pa. She died in 1855.

D. M'CONAUGHY, D. D. LL. D.

THE REV. DAVID M'CONAUGHY was born in Menallen township, York county, (now Adams,) about six miles from Gettysburg, on the 29th of September, 1775. His grandfather, David M'Conaughy, had settled in that region when Pennsylvania was a colony of Great Britain, and held the office of Sheriff of Lancaster county, under the royal government. In the revolutionary contest, however, he was on the side of the colonies, and proved himself a true patriot, although too far advanced in life to aid by his personal services. His son Robert, the father of the subject of this notice, partaking of his ancestral spirit, engaged actively in the service of his country; but how long, or in what capacity—whether as an officer or a private soldier—we are not informed. During his absence with the army, an incident is related of the remarkable preservation of his son David, then about two years of age, showing the special providence of God, in rescuing from death one who was destined afterwards to accomplish so much for Christ and his Church. His mother being temporarily absent, David, in company with the child of one of the labourers, wandered off to a mill-race in the vicinity, and falling into it, remained there for some time. When discovered and taken out, life appeared to be extinct. But after hours of unceasing efforts, suspended animation was restored, and he was given back, of God, to parental affection, to be reared for high and holy services in the kingdom of His Son.

In the vicinity of his parental home, under the tuition of a Mr. Monteith, he received the rudiments of his early education. When about ten years of age, he was sent to a grammar school in the neighbourhood, taught by a Mr. Boggs, which was one of the earliest classical schools established in the interior of the state. This school having continued but a short time, he was removed to a classical school in Gettysburg, taught by the Rev. Alexander Dobbin, a Scotch minister belonging to the Associate Reformed Church, and who is represented to have been a gentleman of extensive learning and devoted piety. In this school he continued in the diligent prosecution of his studies, until he was prepared to enter college. What degree of talent or aptness in the acquisition of knowledge he discovered, during this juvenile period of his life, we have no information. But his friends who knew him in his boyhood, represent him as possessing the same leading traits of character which he exhibited in after life. Quiet, patient and unobtrusive—though fond of the amusements usual with boys of his age—his conduct was ever marked by genuine politeness, and a regard for the feelings of others, which knew no distinction of rank or position.

His collegiate education he received at Dickinson College, Carlisle, where he was graduated on the 30th day of September, 1795, during the presidency of the Rev. Dr. Charles Nisbet, so celebrated for his various and extensive learning, and his salient and sparkling wit. He had the Latin Salutatory assigned him, which, according to the usage of the institution of that time, was considered the first honour. Among his class mates were Chief Justice Taney, of the Federal Court of the United States, and Justice Kennedy, of the Supreme Court of Pennsylvania, both distinguished as learned and able jurists, and the Rev. Joshua Williams, D. D., of Newville, equally distinguished as a profound and skilful theologian. To have been the successful competitor of such men, was no mean honour. But, even if we had not this testimonial of his scholarship, we might safely infer, from the accuracy and extent of his attainments in subsequent life, that he had laid a solid foundation, and industriously improved his advantages, during his preparatory and collegiate course.

Immediately after leaving college, he entered on his theological studies, under the direction of the Rev. Dr. Nathan Grier, of Brandywine, who had an extended reputation as an eloquent and popular preacher, and with whom many young men pursued their studies for the ministry. There he remained two years in the prosecution of his studies, when, on the 5th day of October, 1797, he was licensed by the Presbytery of New Castle to preach the gospel. The next spring he received permission from the Presbytery to itinerate six months without their bounds, and particularly within the limits of the Carlisle and Philadelphia Presbyteries. In accordance with this permission, he preached frequently in Philadelphia, and also in New York, whither he had gone, and where he was detained a considerable time by the prevalence of the yellow fever in Philadelphia, where it raged during the latter part of the summer, and the fall of that year. What proportion of time he spent in the Presbyteries of Carlisle and Philadelphia respectively, is not known, but the spring following, April 5th, 1799, he took his dismission from the Presbytery of New Castle, and on the 9th of the same month placed himself under the care of the Presbytery of Carlisle, his long residence within the bounds of which fully entitles him to a place in this volume.

Having received and accepted a call from the united churches of

Upper Marsh Creek and Great Conewago, within the bounds of that Presbytery, he was ordained and installed their pastor on the 8th day of October, 1800. In that same year the formation of Adams into a separate county took place, and Gettysburg became the county seat. This town was situated about three miles from the site of the Upper Marsh Creek church, and within the limits of that congregation. Increasing in wealth and population, and embracing within it a number of Presbyterian families, it was deemed too important a place to be left without the stated preaching of the gospel by Presbyterians. For a time it was supplied with occasional preaching by Dr. M'Conaughy himself, and also by Dr. Paxton, the talented and eloquent pastor of the adjacent church of Lower Marsh Creek, one or more of the families belonging to whose church resided in the town. After some years, however, the congregation of Upper Marsh Creek determined to remove their edifice to town, and in the year 1813, Dr. M'Conaughy preached his last sermon in the old church, previous to its demolition. From various causes, the new edifice was not ready for occupancy for several years. In the meantime, the congregation were kindly allowed the use of the Associate Reformed church, then vacant, until a pastor should be procured. Afterward, they worshiped in the Court House until the completion of their edifice. In the month of August, 1816, the house, having been completed, was solemnly dedicated to the worship of the Triune God. The congregation still retained its original chartered name of "Upper Marsh Creek," and still remained in union with Great Conewago, under the same pastoral care as before. In these united congregations, Dr. M'Conaughy continued, in the faithful and acceptable discharge of his ministerial duties, until the spring of 1832, when he was dismissed, at his own request, to connect himself with the Presbytery of Washington, and to enter on another, and in some respects, a more extended field of labour.

Dr. M'Conaughy watched over his flock with a shepherd's care, and was ever ready to bestow his labour and exert his influence for the advancement, not only of their spiritual, but also of their temporal interests. A few years before his removal from Gettysburg, the church in that place had suffered their debt to accumulate, until it had reached a larger sum than their real estate was worth. Under the pressure of such a debt, nothing but the most prompt and energetic efforts could save them from bankruptcy and ruin. At this crisis, Dr. M'Conaughy, with generous devotion to the interests of the church, undertook to relieve them; and by his untiring industry, great personal efforts, and the exercise of his large influence, succeeded in extinguishing the debt, with the exception of a very small and insignificant sum, which was paid after his removal from Gettysburg. In the accomplishment of this object he spared no labour. In addition to home exertions and influence, he visited the cities of Baltimore, Philadelphia, and New York, for the purpose of procuring funds. He also published a new edition of "Doddridge's Sermons," for which he procured a large subscription, from the avails of which he realized a considerable sum towards the liquidation of the debt. Providence smiled upon his efforts —the congregation were relieved, and before his death he had the satisfaction to see it, single handed and alone, able to support a pastor the whole of his time.

Of the spiritual results of his labours among the people of his pastoral charge, not having had time nor opportunity to procure the necessary information, we cannot speak with confidence. But if clear and able expositions of the gospel of the grace of God, if faithful pastoral instructions and prayers, and if the persuasive influence of a heavenly spirit and a holy life furnish any ground on which to erect a hope, we can hardly doubt but that many were brought to Christ through his instrumentality, and will appear as his "joy and crown of rejoicing, in the presence of our Lord Jesus Christ, at his coming."

Dr. M'Conaughy was the pioneer in the Temperance reform, in his native county. Preparatory to the formation of a society, and with a view of gaining access to all classes, he appointed meetings to be held at the Court House in the evenings, at which he read the Temperance essays of Drs. Rush, Beecher, and others. In this way he diffused information, and awakened attention in the community to the subject, and thus led to the formation of the first Temperance Society in Adams county, and of which he was elected the first president. In aid of the cause he preached a sermon from 1 Cor. vi, 10, "Drunkards shall not inherit the kingdom of God," which was published, and extensively circulated throughout that region. It contains an accurate description of the character of a drunkard, and a fearless and faithful exhibition of the certainty and justice of his exclusion from heaven. Its delineations are truthful and eloquent, eminently adapted to move and impress the heart.

In the year 1807, Dr. M'Conaughy commenced a grammar school in Gettysburg, for the purpose of thoroughly training young men to enter college. This school he continued until 1812, when he relinquished it in favour of a county organization. After the organization of the county institution, however, his services were occasionally solicited, and cheerfully rendered upon the failure of the board to secure other suitable teachers. In this respect he had nothing of the fastidiousness of some weak and vain men, who disdain to render aid to important institutions or enterprises, unless they are clothed with official rank, or their vanity flattered by some titular distinction. His heart and his hand were always open to the claims of learning and religion, and if, by any practicable service, he could give them increased force, he was ever ready to do it. As a teacher of youth, as well as a minister of the Gospel, he did much to elevate the character of his native county. His pupils were generally distinguished in the colleges to which they resorted for the accuracy and extent of their attainments. Many of them afterwards rose to stations of eminence and distinction in the different departments of society. Among these it will not be deemed invidious to mention the late Jeremiah Chamberlain, D. D., President of Oakland College, Miss.; the late Rev. John E. Annan, Professor of Mathematics in the Miami University, O.; and his brother, the Rev. Wm. Annan, the well known editor of the Presbyterian Advocate; the Rev. John Holmes Agnew, formerly Professor of Languages, in Washington College, and afterward Professor in the University of Michigan; the Rev. H. L. Baugher, D. D., President of Pennsylvania College, at Gettysburg; the Hon. Daniel M. Smyser, President Judge of the Bucks and Montgomery District; and the Hon. James H. Graham, President Judge of the Carlisle District, in this state. These, and others who might be named, laid the foundation of their eminence and fame under the tuition of this ripe scholar, and skilful teacher of youth. Indeed, as a thorough Latin and Greek scholar, Dr. M'Conaughy had few superiors; and as a teacher of the classics, the common verdict of those who knew him best, was, that he was eminently judicious and successful. It was the knowledge of this fact, and of his general scholarship, and high intellectual and moral endowments, that led to the suggestion of his name in connection with the Presidency of Washington College.

After the resignation of Dr. Wylie, and during the suspension of the operations of that institution, the Trustees were anxiously looking out for a suitable person to occupy that station. Having received the most favourable information respecting Dr. M'Conaughy, from one who had long been intimately acquainted with his character and qualifications, they unanimously elected him to the Presidency, on the 12th of March, 1830. This appointment, it was his inclination and purpose to accept, as he intimated in his communication to the board; but, shortly after his election, the unexpected death of a near relative produced such a condition of things in his family relations as to render it improper for him to remove. Of this he promptly and frankly informed the board, so that they might not be embarrassed, and their institution injured, by deferred expectations which might not be realized. Although the board deeply regretted the occurence which deprived them of his services, they admitted the validity of his reasons, and approved his course as ingenuous and honourable. The next fall the college was resuscitated, and its operations resumed under a temporary arrangement, which was to continue until a suitable principal could be procured. Failing in their efforts to secure such an one, the board again turned their eyes towards Dr. M'Conaughy. Having learned that the circumstances of his position were so changed as no longer to impose on him the necessity of remaining at Gettysburg, they again, on the 21st of December, 1831, unanimously invited him to occupy the post which he had before been obliged to decline. This invitation he accepted, and having removed to Washington, he was inaugurated as President of the college on the 9th of May, 1832. The number of students at the time of his accession was one hundred and nineteen. Under his mild and paternal administration the number continued to increase, and every year added to the strength and reputation of the institution in the minds of intelligent and well informed men. The whole period of his administration embraced seventeen years and six months, during which time eighteen classes were graduated; the first contained four, and the last thirty-six young gentlemen. And of the whole number who were graduated during his presidency—amounting in all to three hundred and eighty-eight—more than one-half belonged to the last six classes who received the honours of the institution, with his approving signature annexed to their diplomas. It is but justice to the memory of Dr. M'Conaughy that these facts be known. They tell their own story, and will enable those not otherwise familiar with the history of the college, to judge with what measure of ability and public approval its affairs were managed, under his superintendence.

The tender of Dr. M'Conaughy's resignation was made to the President of the board on the 1st of October, 1849, accompanied with a request that prompt action might be had upon it by the board, so that the way might be open for the choice of a successor, in time to meet the wants of the institution. Accordingly, at a special meeting of the board, on the 12th of October, his resignation was accepted, it having been ascertained that his purpose to retire was immovably fixed. At the special request of the board, however, and that the college might suffer no damage, he generously consented—in the event that a successor could not be immediately secured—to conduct the studies of the higher classes, as before, until other suitable arrangements should be made. This he did, unofficially, and as a matter of accommodation, during the greater part of the next two sessions—until the arrival of Dr. Clark, the President elect—much to the satisfaction of the board and the advantage of the institution.

The high respect and veneration entertained for Dr. M'Conaughy by the Board of Trustees, are indicated by the strongly expressive resolutions which were offered by the Hon. Th. M. T. M'Kennan, and passed immediately upon the acceptance of his resignation. In these resolutions it is declared, "that in accepting the resignation of Dr. M'Conaughy, the Trustees feel that it is alike due to him and to themselves to say that they part with him, as the presiding officer of the institution entrusted to their care, with undiminished confidence, and entertain for him feelings of the most profound respect and veneration, as a scholar, a gentlemen and a Christian minister;"—"that the fact of the graduating classes having increased from four—the number of the first class graduated after his accession to the Presidency—to thirty-six, the number of the last class previous to his resignation—furnishes the most honourable and gratifying proof of the ability and success of his administration, and of the high estimation in which the college and its learned Faculty are held by an intelligent public;"—"that, as a testimonial of their high appreciation of the intellectual ability, and ripe scholarship of Dr. M'Conaughy, the Board of Trustees do hereby confer upon him, the honourary degree of Doctor of Laws; and in closing their official relation with him, tender to him their best wishes for his future comfort, and their earnest prayers that the special blessing of Him, to whose glory his life and labours have been consecrated, may ever accompany and rest upon him."

These resolutions were not designed as an empty compliment, as is sometimes the case, but as the honest tribute of warm and generous hearts to genuine and unaffected worth. And they furnish a suitable close to an official connection, which had been distinguished by the most respectful and affectionate regard on both sides, and by important benefits to the institution which had been the object of their united prayers, labours and anxieties.

Dr. M'Conaughy's labours did not cease with the dissolution of his connection with the college. Although occasional attacks of disease and advancing years had impaired his bodily strength, his intellectual powers remained in all their original force. So far as the mind was concerned "his eye was not dim, nor his natural force abated." Hence, he pursued his mental labours with his accustomed activity. As evidence of this, during the next year after his resignation he prepared and published a volume of "Discourses, chiefly Biographical, of Persons Eminent in Sacred History." These are admirable discourses—"fine specimens of discriminating thought, lucid arrangement, vigorous style, and the skilful and profitable exhibition of sacred truth." Although, in his numerical divisions and some small matters of an artistical kind, the author may not have accommodated himself to the demands of modern taste, he has undoubtedly succeeded in the production of a work, which, in the estimation of competent judges, ranks with the very first of its kind.

In the year 1838, he published for the exclusive use of the senior class in Washington College, "A Brief Summary and Outline of the Principal Subjects Comprehended in Moral Science." This is a comprehensive and well digested outline, which, it is to be regretted he did not fill up, and thus have furnished our colleges with a convenient and reliable text-book on that subject. His other publications consist of some half dozen sermons, and a few of his Baccalaureate Addresses. These are all written with his accustomed ability, and were well adapted to the occasion and circumstances which severally called them forth. Since his decease, it has been announced that a couple of tracts from his pen have been issued from the press—one on the Doctrine of the Trinity, and the other on the Salvation of Infants. The subjects are important and their mode of treatment will, doubtless, sustain the well earned reputation of their author.

In his domestic relations, Dr. M'Conaughy was peculiarly blessed. In the spring of the year 1802, he was married to Miss Mary Mahon, daughter of David Mahon, Esq., of Shippensburg, Pa., a lady whose spirit was in harmony with his own, and with whom he lived most happily for fifty years. Her bereavement can only be mitigated by Divine Grace, and by the animating hope of, ere long, joining him again in their "Father's house," in heaven. Although without any children of his own, Dr. M'Conaughy's house was the constant home of some cherished young friend, towards whom he ever exercised a father's love and care, although without a father's name. Among his collateral descendants, and those of his wife, a number of names are registered as ministers of the Gospel, whose happiness it is to have the light of his bright example shining before them, to animate and cheer them in their work.

"If there was a man within the entire circle of our acquaintance who was entitled to the character of 'a good man,'" says the Rev. David

Elliott, D. D.,* "it was David M'Conaughy. Although from literary institutions of high reputation he had received the honourary distinction of 'Doctor of Divinity,' and 'Doctor of Laws,' the still higher and nobler title, that of 'a good man,' was conferred upon him by the united suffrage of the whole community. Nor was this title conferred upon him in the sense of disparagement, unless it may have been by some thoughtless charlatan, or by some transient observer, who knew but little of his character. But, Dr. M'Conaughy was reputed 'a good man,' in the most favourable sense of the phrase. The high qualities of his character, which lay transparent on the surface of his acts, commanded the respect, and won the admiration of all who had the capacity to discern, or disposition to appreciate, true moral excellence. His was no negative nor half-formed goodness, which, with doubtful features, glimmered out occasionally from the cloudy atmosphere with which sin envelops the soul; but it was goodness of a positive character, a living, active reality, looming out with a distinctness and maturity which vanquished doubt, and gave assurance of its divine, original and heavenly growth.

"There was, also, a sincerity and honesty in all his words and actions, which put to flight every shadow of suspicion that he was not what he appeared to be. Indeed, no man could be more free than he was from the deceptive practice of uttering words with a double sense, or concealing his real intentions by expressions of equivocal import or doubtful interpretation. What he said, he thought; his words being ever the faithful transcript of the thoughts and intents of his heart.

"There was, moreover, a completeness of character belonging to him, beyond that of most men. High qualities are often accompanied with great defects. That Dr. M'Conaughy was free from defects, we do not affirm; but, by the number and strength and vitality of his constitutional gifts and Christian graces, these defects were overshadowed and scarcely seen, or, if seen, but little regarded by those whose moral vision was not jaundiced by prejudice. And this living assemblage of excellent properties seemed all to be under the control of a gravitating power, giving regularity to their movements, and impelling them to a common centre, for the fuller and clearer manifestation of the whole. Hence, his character was one of great moral power, and his example was such as those within the sphere of its influence might safely and honourably imitate.

"The piety of Dr. M'Conaughy was eminently spiritual. It partook largely of the lineaments of its Divine Author. Formed by the Holy

---

* Commemorative Discourse, preached in Washington, Pennsylvania, March 21st, 1852.

Ghost, nurtured and strengthened by his abiding influence, it seemed to have largely outgrown and overshadowed the opposing principles of corruption in the soul, and to have brought him into a state of familiar fellowship with God, his Saviour. This spiritual feature of his piety, and its pervading and controlling influence over the mind, were often distinctly seen in his devotional exercises and acts. There were occasions on which, forgetting apparently the things of earth, he seemed to rise, in wrapt devotion, to the very throne of God.

"One of these occasions the speaker distinctly recollects, and will never forget. We had gone together, on a summer's Sabbath day, to preach and administer the Lord's Supper in the church of Mount Nebo, in the vicinity of your town. The morning service, including that of the communion, being over, Dr. M'Conaughy preached in the afternoon. By the time he closed his sermon the western sky was overcast with dark clouds, from the midst of which sheets of lightning burst upon the eye, the roar of distant thunder and the heavy sighing of the wind fell upon the ear, portending a fearful storm. The church (a building, as now recollected, of no great strength,) was in the woods, and the impulse, probably, of almost every mind in the house, was, that the service should close, to afford the people an opportunity to reach the neighbouring farm-houses, where they and their horses might find a shelter from the impending tempest. With Dr. M'Conaughy, however, all seemed to be clear sky. He raised his hands and his voice in prayer. He became deeply engaged. Pious thoughts seemed to crowd upon his mind; devout aspirations swelled his heart; time passed on, and still he prayed; while the indications of the approaching storm became more alarmingly distinct. And while others of weaker faith and less spiritual affections were anxiously observing the troubled atmosphere, our stronger and more devout brother had ascended from Nebo 'to the top of Pisgah,' and there, far above the reach of conflicting elements, and in view of the promised land, was holding sweet fellowship with his God. At length he ceased, and descending from the mount, closed the services with a hymn; we retired from the church, but, before we reached the nearest house, the storm was upon us."

On Sabbath, the 11th of January, Dr. M'Conaughy preached his last sermon, in the church of Washington, from Proverbs i, 22. He is reported to have been unusually animated and impressive, and all agreed in pronouncing the discourse one of the most solemn and powerful they had ever heard. On the next Sabbath he was confined to bed by a severe cold, but which, at first, created no alarm. After some days, however, his strength rapidly failed him, and he gradually sunk, until, at length, while his friends around his bedside were engaged in prayer that he might have a safe and easy departure, "the silver cord was loosed," and his ransomed spirit was "present with the Lord." His extreme weakness and difficulty of breathing, during his illness, prevented him from conversing much; but, in the language of one who was present, "the serenity of his countenance, and the few expressions which fell from his lips, betokened the heavenly sunshine of the soul within." His days were numbered, his work was done, and he has gone—as we confidently trust—to the enjoyment of that "rest which remaineth to the people of God."

He departed this life, at his late residence in Washington, on Thursday evening, the 29th of January, 1852, in the seventy-seventh year of his age, and the fifty-fifth of his ministry. He "died in a good old age, an old man, and full of years," having passed the ordinary period allotted to human life on earth.

JOHN MOODEY, D. D.

THE REV. JOHN MOODEY, was born in Dauphin county, Pa., July 4th, 1776. He graduated at Princeton College in 1796. His theological studies were pursued under the direction of the Rev. James Snodgrass. He was married to Miss Elizabeth Crawford. In 1803 he was installed as pastor of the Middle Spring Presbyterian church, about two miles north of Shippensburg. This was the only congregation of which he ever had charge. He served it for fifty years. During his protracted and faithful ministry, the degree of Doctor of Divinity was conferred on him by the Trustees of Washington College, Pa.

Dr. Moodey was a gentleman of stately personal appearance, and dignified bearing. He was eminently courteous in manner and sound in judgment. Apparently free from ambition, he was desirous only to be found faithful in the duties of the sphere to which Providence had called him.

His eldest son, Robert C. Moodey, was a physician, but died in middle life. His second son, John W. Moodey, also a physician, who long and successfully practiced his profession in Greensburg, Indiana, died there about five years ago. His third son, James C. Moodey, is a a lawyer of ability, and about ten years ago was a United States Judge for the district of Missouri. His fourth son, Joseph, departed this life in his youth.

Dr. Moodey, during his pastorate at Middle Spring, resided in Shippensburg, and much of the time in the building at the western end of the town, which is located within a few yards of the line dividing the counties of Cumberland and Franklin. Being the owner of some fields near to his dwelling, he carried on agricultural operations to some extent. His time, however, was mainly devoted to the spiritual interests of his congregation which was very large and scattered over a wide extent of territory.

As a preacher, Dr. Moodey had an excellent reputation. He was a logical, instructive, and able expounder of the gospel. He always read his sermons. With him there were none of the flourishes of oratory, or flashes of fancy, or efforts after novelty, which so often attract without any permanent interest or benefit, but his ministry was ever characterised by a plain, manly and edifying exhibition of the Word, and a bringing of things new and old out of his treasure, which saved his acceptableness in the pulpit from anything like abatement. A number of preachers of the Gospel were sent forth by his church. *One who grew up under his ministry, in a most admirable description of the old church, published in 1847, thus refers to its solid and solemn pastor:

> "Out from that pulpit's height, deep-browed and grave,
>   The man of God ensconced, half bust was shown.
> Weighty and wise, he did not thump nor rave,
>   Nor lead his folks upwrought, to smile nor moan.
> By him, slow cast, the seeds of truth were sown,
>   Which, lighting on good soil, took lasting hold.
> Not springing eftsoons, then to wilt ere grown,
>   But in long time their fruits increased were told;
> Some thirty, sixty some, and some an hundred fold."

Dr. Moodey died full of years. His remains now lie entombed in the same grave with those of the partner of his life, in the rear of the new church edifice which has taken the place of the old one in which his voice for half a century was heard proclaiming the way of salvation. Over the grave his congregation has erected a handsome monument, a fitting expression of their affectionate regard for one to whom their parents were so much attached, and whose memory is endeared to themselves by so many tender and touching associations.

---

*William M. Nevin, Esq., Professor of Belles Lettres, in Franklin and Marshall College.

REV. DAVID DENNY.

THE REV. DAVID DENNY was the third son of a Revolutionary soldier who fell in battle, when his eldest son, contending at his side, was captured by the enemy. He graduated at Dickinson College, while Dr. Charles Nisbit was Principal of that institution, and under that learned and classic divine began and completed his theological studies. He was a fond admirer of his distinguished preceptor, and often narrated anecdotes illustrative of his wit, learning and accomplishments. The sources of Philosophy and Divinity at that day were neither as copious nor accessible as at present, and the acquisitions of the students were consequently earned by severer toil and application than the facilities of learning now exact. The lectures of Dr. Nisbit were delivered at a modulated rate and tone, that the members of his class might be able to reduce them to writing as they fell from his lips. Mr. Denny, at his decease, left in his library seven quarto volumes of these discourses, in his own handsome and legible handwriting, which form together a respectable body of metaphysics and divinity. Whatever the present intrinsic value of these lectures may be, when the bounds of sacred and profane learning have been so much enlarged, the diligent reader will find in many pages of them strong marks of the erudition, original thought and classic taste of the author.

Mr. Denny was licensed to preach the Gospel about the year 1792, by the Presbytery of Carlisle, within whose bounds he remained until the close of his pastoral office. He was first installed over two congregations in Path Valley, that had lately become vacated by the death of the Rev. Mr. Dougal, where he continued until the year 1800, in the enjoyment of the esteem and affection of a much beloved people. In the year last mentioned, he was transferred to the pastoral charge of the Falling Spring Church, in Chambersburg, which he retained until the termination of his public ministrations—a period of thirty-eight years. His means derived from the ministry being inadequate to the demands of a large and growing family, he was obliged to combine with it, for a series of years, the labours of a teacher of the learned languages in an academy, and being master of economy he secured that enviable maintenance midway between poverty and wealth, so desirable to the good man, and that proves at once a defence against the inconveniences of penury, and the vices of profusion.

In the year of Mr. Denny's retirement from the active duties of the sanctuary, death snatched from his side the fond partner of his pilgrimage, a lady of exalted worth, and by the same stroke broke his cheerful spirit and firm constitution. Companions also who shared his better years and pastoral intimacy, had then dropped away one by one around him, until he was left almost alone, like the gray oak of the forest, surrounded by generations of a younger growth. He continued to languish under increasing infirmity, until repeated attacks of paralysis accelerated his decline and deprived him of the power of articulate speech. It was not until several months after this trying visitation, (December 16th, 1845,) that the mysterious hand which often chastens out of plenitude of love, called him, by a voice gentle and meek as the breathing of infant slumber, from the sorrow of his earthly state to the joyous assembly of the just. His person, cast in the finest mould for strength, activity and proportion, was well adapted to the air of dignity which nature herself had impressed upon it. His mind was of a strong and discerning order, always governed by candour and sincerity, and warmed by the love of truth. His views were expressed in the language of simplicity and earnestness, neither adorned nor obscured by the garnish of imagery or the flashes of rhetoric.

In doctrine Mr. Denny was a decided Calvinist, and conscientiously attached to the standards of the Presbyterian Church. Modesty and humility were interwoven with the very texture of his heart, and its liveliest sympathies were always in expansion for the sick, the suffering and the desolate. Neither inclemency of weather nor transient illness were suffered to detain him from the exercises of the pulpit, and he enjoyed, in no ordinary degree, the esteem and affection of the people among whom he laboured. He was actuated in social intercourse by a manly, tolerant and liberal spirit, and has left to all who stood in private or public relations to him, an example of many virtues with which humanity is not often adorned, which they may fail to imitate, but can never cease to admire and love.

JOHN BANNISTER GIBSON, LL. D.

JOHN BANNISTER GIBSON, late Chief-Justice of the Supreme Court of Pennsylvania, was born in Shearman Valley, Pennsylvania, November 8th, 1780. He was the son of Lieutenant-Colonel George Gibson, an officer of the Revolutionary Army, who fell in St. Clair's expedition against the Indians on the Miami, in 1791. He received his preparatory education in the grammar school attached to Dickinson College, and subsequently studied in the collegiate department, from which in due time he graduated. He entered the office of Thomas Duncan, who was afterward an Associate Judge of the Supreme Court of Pennsylvania, and passed through a severe course of reading for the legal profession, and was admitted as an attorney at law at the bar of Cumberland county, in 1803.

He first opened his office at Carlisle, Pennsylvania, and after a few years removed to the town of Beaver, in the same state. From this latter locality he changed to Hagerstown, Maryland, and shortly afterward returned to Carlisle. In 1810, he was elected by the (then) Republican party as a representative in the lower branch of the Legislature, and was re-elected the following year, during each session filling prominent stations on committees, etc. In July, 1813, he was appointed President Judge of the Eleventh Judicial District of Pennsylvania, and three years after was commissioned an Associate Judge of the Supreme Court, which, at that time, was considered equivalent to a life tenure, the appointment being "during good behaviour." At the death of Chief-Justice Tilghman, in 1827, he was appointed by the Governor to succeed him. In 1838, at the date of the adoption of the then New Constitution of the State, he resigned his office, but was immediately re-appointed by the Governor.

By a change in the Constitution making the Judiciary elective, his seat became vacant in 1851. During the same year he was elected an Associate Justice of the Supreme Court, being the only one of the former incumbents who was nominated by the Democratic party. He discharged the functions of his office until attacked by his last illness. He died in Philadelphia, May 3d, 1853. As a jurist he stood among the highest in the land. At home and abroad his transcendent legal ability was universally acknowledged. His judicial opinions are among the richest treasures of the country.

JOSHUA WILLIAMS, D. D.

DR. WILLIAMS had not the advantage of entering, at an early age, on a course of studies preparatory to the ministry. He was graduated at Dickinson College, in the year 1795, then under the presidency of Dr. Nisbit. His theological studies were pursued chiefly under the direction of Dr. Robert Cooper.

In the year 1798, in the thirtieth year of his age, he was licensed to preach the Gospel by the Presbytery of Carlisle. The year following, he received a call from the united congregations of Derry and Paxton, Dauphin county, which he accepted, and was ordained to the work of the ministry, and installed pastor of said charge, by the Presbytery of Carlisle, in the autumn of the same year. After having served the people of this, his first charge, for about four years, he received a call from the Presbyterian Church at Big Spring, left vacant by the death of the Rev. Samuel Wilson, which he judged it to be his duty to accept, and accordingly he gave up the charge of his former congregations, and was installed pastor of the latter in the year 1802. Under the labours of a prolonged pastorate, his general health declined, and a complication of infirmities reduced his physical strength. His nervous system, especially, became disordered, and, as a consequence, he often suffered great mental depression. A year or two previous to his release from his pastoral charge, under the impression that he was unable to perform, as they should be done, the duties of a pastor, he proposed resigning his charge. But the congregation earnestly remonstrated against his doing so, and assured him of their being well satisfied with such services as his feeble state of health permitted him to render. About the year 1829, at his earnest request, the pastoral relation between him and the congregation of Big Spring was dissolved. From the day of his installation till his resignation he lived and laboured among his people with uninterrupted harmony and growing interest.

After retiring from his pastoral charge, Dr. Williams did not at all abandon the duties of his office as a minister of the Gospel, but continued, as his health permitted and opportunity was afforded, serving vacant congregations in the bounds of the Presbytery, and frequently assisting his brethren on special occasions. In these labours of love he seemed to take great interest, often crossing mountains and riding a distance into neighbouring counties, to preach the Gospel to the destitute. Dr. Williams' last illness was only of about four days continuance. He had at various times expressed his fears of the dying struggle, but in his own case death seemed wholly disarmed of all his terrors. His end was peaceful, without a disturbed feature. On the morning of the 21st of August, 1838, he seemed literally to fall asleep in Jesus. The next day a very large concourse of persons (most of whom had been formerly the people of his charge,) together with eight or ten ministers, attended the funeral, and testified their very great regard for him, whom they had so much reason to love, and to venerate. His remains were deposited in the Big Spring churchyard, nearly in view from the sacred desk where he had so long preached to that people the Gospel of God, which brings life and immortality to light.

In the death of Dr. Williams the church lost an able and faithful advocate of the truth. His retired situation and unobtrusive disposition were, no doubt, the occasion of his being less publicly known than he justly merited. His talents and attainments as a minister of the Gospel were such as always to command the highest respect from all who knew him. He was naturally possessed of strong and vigourous intellectual powers. His judgment was sound and discriminating. He had a remarkable taste and aptitude for metaphysical discussions, which, however, never seem to have led him into erroneous speculations on the doctrines of religion.

As a steward of the mysteries of God, he was well instructed and furnished for every good work, above most others in the sacred office. His mind was richly stored with theological knowledge; with every part of Scripture he seemed familiar, and could quote any passage to which he wished to refer with great readiness and accuracy. He employed much of his time in reading instructive authors, and always with a view to the furnishing of his mind the more thoroughly for the duties of his office, and for his own personal edification.

As a preacher of the Gospel, Dr. Williams was grave and solemn in his manner, and highly instructive in his discourses. His usual method in his sermons was to explain his text, if it needed explanation, then state the subject or doctrine illustrated, and confirm this by Scripture and argument. And to make the truth bear upon the hearts of his audience, his first object was to instruct, then to persuade, believing that truth is in order to righteousness, and that there can be no correct practice till the mind be enlightened, and the heart sanctified through the truth of the Word of God.

In his manners and conversation, this excellent man was courteous and affable, yet always dignified. He was truly a lover of hospitality. It gave him great pleasure to have his brethren in the ministry visit him. Nor were such occasions suffered to pass without improvement. Very few men, we are assured, ever possessed in the same degree with Dr. Williams the happy faculty of communicating solid instruction in social conversation. Some useful subject was always introduced, and discussed in such a manner as to be at once interesting and instructive. The great doctrines of the Cross, which he professed to believe and which he preached, were not held by him as mere theoretical subjects, without a salutary and practical influence on his own heart. It was seldom, except to intimate friends, that he would freely unfold his imbued with the precious truths of the Gospel,—that he had felt intensely religious experience, but then it was manifest that his mind was deeply the power of that Word of God which he preached to others. Having fought a good fight, and kept the faith, he finished his course, leaving no room or reason to doubt that he passed to the possession of that crown of righteousness which the Lord, the righteous Judge, will give to all them that love His appearing.

GEORGE CHAMBERS, LL. D.

THE father of the subject of this sketch, Benjamin Chambers, was born in the year 1775, and was a son of Col. Benjamin Chambers, the founder of Chambersburg. When a youth of but twenty years, he enlisted in the company of his brother, Captain James Chambers, and marched with it to Boston. Soon after he joined the army he was commissioned a captain, and in that rank fought at the battles of Long Island, Brandywine, and Germantown, with credit and gallantry. During the retreat of the army from Long Island, the Pennsylvania troops were assigned to the distinguished but hazardous honour of covering the movement. While assisting in this delicate and perilous manœuvre, Captain Chambers had the great good fortune to arrest the attention of General Washington, win his commendation and receive from him, as a signal token of his approbation, a handsome pair of silver-mounted pistols, which have always been treasured as a precious heir-loom in the family, having recently been bequeathed to Benjamin Chambers Bryan, a great-grandson of the original donee.

But the diseases of camp and the rigours of military life compelled Captain Chambers to retire from the army; just at what period of the struggle is not definitely known. Although no longer engaged in regular military service, his skill and experience and great personal courage made him the captain and leader in many expeditions against the Indians, whose savage and bloody forays upon the settlements of Bedford and Huntingdon counties were constantly creating great consternation aud alarm.

At the conclusion of the treaty of peace with England he became extensively engaged in the manufacture of iron, and was the first to make iron castings in the country.

Influenced by the same enlightened liberality which characterized his father, he donated, in the year 1796, two lots of ground in Chambersburg as a site for an academy. A charter was procured in 1797, and shortly afterwards a suitable building was erected, and a select school organized and opened under the tuition of James Ross, whose Latin Grammar for many years maintained its distinguished position, without a rival, in the colleges and seminaries of our land.

Captain Chambers left upon record, among the last business acts of his life, his solemn testimony to the importance and value of education, by earnestly enjoining upon his executors, in his will, that they should have all his minor children liberally educated. This betokened a zeal for learning that was certainly very rare in that day. He died in 1813, crowned with the esteem, respect, and love of the community for whose welfare and prosperity he had taxed his best energies, and to whose development he had devoted the labour of a lifetime.

George Chambers, his oldest son, was born in Chambersburg, on the 24th day of February, A. D., 1786. It was not unlikely that such a father would put George to his books while very young. This seems to have been so. He must have been taught to read and write, and have acquired the other rudiments of a common English education, at a very early age; for when he was but ten he began the study of Latin and Greek in the classical school of James Ross. He subsequently entered the Chambersburg Academy and became the pupil of Rev. David Denny, an eloquent, learned, and much revered Presbyterian clergyman. He was ambitious and studious, and had made such progress in the ancient languages and mathematics that in October, 1802, he was able to pass from the academy into the Junior Class at Princeton College. He graduated from that institution in 1804, with high honour, in a class of forty-five, among whom were Thomas Hartley Crawford, Theodore Frelinghuysen, Joseph R. Ingersoll, Samuel L. Southard, and others who rose to distinguished eminence at the bar, in the pulpit, and in the councils of the nation.

He chose the law as his profession, and entered upon its study with William M. Brown, Esq., in Chambersburg. Having spent a year with him, he became a student in the office of Judge Duncan, in Carlisle, then in the zenith of his great fame. Having passed through the customary *curriculum*, he was admitted to the bar and sworn as a counsellor in the courts of Cumberland county, in the year 1807.

Shortly afterwards, he returned to Chambersburg and commenced the practice of his profession. When he entered the arena, he found the bar crowded with eminent and learned lawyers. Duncan, Tod, Riddle, and the elder Watts practiced there and monopolized the business. With such professional *athletes*, already crowned with the laurels of the profession, and clad in armor that had been tempered and polished by the lucubrations of more than twenty years, it seemed a hard, indeed an almost impossible, task for a young and inexperienced man to compete.

Mr. Chambers, however, courted notoriety by no adventitious aids. Indeed, he thought so little of all the usual methods of inviting public attention, that it is related of him that he dispensed with "*the shingle*," that ornament of the office-shutter which the newly-fledged lawyer is so apt to regard as an indispensable beacon to guide the footsteps of anxious clients. Nor did he advertise his professional pretensions in either card or newspaper. He was quite content to recognize in the law a jealous mistress, who would be satisfied with nothing less than the undivided homage of heart and mind.

His professional career was not distinguished by rapid success at first. Like almost all who have attained the highest honours at the bar, his *novitiate* was severe. He found the first steps of his journey toward eminence beset with difficulties and full of discouragements. After weary years of waiting, success came at last—as it must always come to true merit. When it did come—and, perhaps, it came as soon as it was deserved—he was prepared to meet its imperious demands.

Mr. Chambers had a mind most admirably adapted to the law. It was acute, logical and comprehensive, of quick perception, with strong powers of discrimination, and possessed of rare ability to grasp and hold the true points of a case.

Added to these natural abilities was the discipline of a thorough education, supplemented by a varied fund of knowledge acquired by extensive reading, which ranged far beyond the confines of the literature of his profession.

Besides all this, he possessed, in a most eminent degree, that crowning ornament of all mental stature, *good common sense*—without which the most shining talents avail but little.

It is not surprising, therefore, when the opportune time came that was to give him the ear of the court, that he should attract attention. From this time his success was assured, and his progress to the head of the bar steady and unvarying. This ascendancy he easily maintained during his entire subsequent professional life. Not only was he the acknowledged chief of his own bar, but also the recognized peer of the first lawyers of the state.

From 1816 to 1851, when he retired from active practice, his business was immense and very lucrative. He was retained in every case of importance in his own county, and tried many cases in adjoining counties.

He was well read in all the branches of the law, but he especially excelled in the land law of Pennsylvania. He had completely mastered it, and could walk with sure and unfaltering step through all its intricate paths. His preparation was laborious and thorough. He trusted nothing to chance, and had no faith in lucky accidents, which constitute the sheet-anchor of hope to the sluggard. He identified himself with his client, and made his cause his own, when it was just. He sought for truth by the application of the severest tests of logic, and spared no pains in the vindication of the rights of his clients. He was always listened to with attention and respect by the courts, and whenever he was overruled it was with a respectful dissent.

The writer of this tribute* came to the bar after Mr. Chambers had retired from it, and cannot, therefore, speak of him as an advocate, from personal knowledge. But tradition, to whose generous care the reputation of even the greatest lawyers has too uniformly been committed, has fixed his standard high. His diction was pure and elegant; his statement of facts lucid; his reasoning, stripped of all false and vulgar ornaments, was severe and logical; his manner earnest and impressive, and, when inspired by some great occasion, his speech could rise upon steady pinions into the higher realms of oratory.

His influence with juries is said to have been immense. This arose in part, doubtless, from their unbounded confidence in his sincerity and integrity; for he was one of those old-fashioned professional gentlemen who stubbornly refused to acknowledge the obligation of the professional ethics which teach that a lawyer must gain his client's cause at all hazards and by any means. While he was distinguished for unfaltering devotion to his client, and an ardent zeal in the protection of his interest, he was not less loyal to truth and justice. When he had given all his learning and his best efforts to the preparation and presentation of his client's case, he felt that he had done his whole duty. He would as soon have thought of violating the Decalogue as of achieving victory by artifice and sinister means. His professional word was as sacred as his oath, and he would have esteemed its intentional breach as a personal dishonour. He despised professional charlatanism in all its forms, and had he come in contact with its modern representative, he would have been his abhorrence.

Washington College, Pennsylvania, manifested its appreciation of his legal learning and personal worth by conferring upon him the degree of LL. D. in the year 1861. This honour, entirely unsolicited and unexpected by him, was a spontaneous mark of distinction, as creditable to the distinguished literary institution that bestowed it as it was well earned by him who received it.

Mr. Chambers having determined, in early manhood, to devote himself with an undivided fidelity to the study and practice of the law, and to rely upon that profession as the chief architect of his fortune

---

* J. McDowell Sharpe, Esq.

and his fame, very seldom could be enticed to embark upon the turbulent sea of politics. His tastes and habits of thought ran in a different channel. Office-seeking and office-holding were uncongenial pursuits. The coarse vulgarity and bitter wranglings of the *"hustings"* shocked his sensitive nature. Indeed, no one could be less of a politician, in the popular acceptation of that term. He was as much superior to the tricks of the political intriguer as truth is superior to falsehood. His native dignity of character, robust integrity, and self respect, united to an unbounded contempt for meanness, lifted him so high above the atmosphere of the demagogue, that he knew absolutely nothing of its undercurrents of knavery and corruption.

But in 1832, at the earnest solicitation of his party, he became a candidate for Congress in the district composed of the counties of Adams and Franklin, and was elected by a majority of about eight hundred. He served through the Twenty-third Congress, the first session of which, commonly called "the Panic Session," commenced on the 2d of December, 1833. The most conspicuous and distinguished men of the nation were members, and the Congress itself the most eventful and exciting that had convened since the adoption of the Constitution.

Mr. Chambers was again a candidate and elected to the Twenty-fourth Congress by a greatly increased majority, and at its termination peremptorily declined a re-election.

During his congressional career he maintained a high and respectable position among his compeers. He was not a frequent speaker, but his speeches, carefully prepared, closely confined to the question under discussion, and full of information, always commanded the attention of the House.

He served on the Comitee on the Expenditures in the Department of War, on the Committee on Naval Affairs, on the Committee on Private Land Claims, and on the Committee on Rules and Orders in the House. To the discharge of these public duties he gave the same industry, care and ability which always characterized the management of his affairs in private life. He was a conscientious public servant, zealous for the interests of his immediate constituents, and careful about the welfare and honour of the nation.

In 1836, Mr. Chambers was elected a delegate from Franklin county to the Convention to revise and amend the Constitution of Pennsylvania. This body convened in Harrisburg on the 2d day of May, 1837, and its membership was largely composed of the foremost lawyers and best intellects of the State.

Mr. Chambers was appointed a member of the committee to which was referred the Fifth Article of the Constitution, relative to the judiciary—by all odds the most important question before the Convention.

The controversy over this article was bitter and protracted, between the advocates of a tenure during good behaviour and the advocates of a short tenure for the judges. Mr. Chambers opposed any change in this respect of the old Constitution, and throughout the various phases of the angry discussion stood firmly by his convictions.

On the 12th of April, 1851, Governor Johnston commissioned Mr. Chambers as a Justice of the Supreme Court, to fill the vacancy caused by the death of Judge Burnside. He sat upon the Bench from this time until the first Monday of the following December, when under the amended Constitution, the new judges received their commissions. He was nominated by the Whig State Convention in 1851 for this office, but was defeated along with his colleagues on the same ticket, having received, however, from the voters of his native county, and of the adjoining counties, a very complimentary endorsement.

During the time Mr. Chambers was a member of the Supreme Court, he prepared and delivered quite a number of opinions, written in a perspicuous and agreeable style, and exhibiting his usual exhaustive research and extensive legal knowledge. Some of these opinions are interesting to the professional reader, and can be found in the fourth volume of Harris's State Reports. The most notable among them are the cases of Baxby *v.* Linah, in which the effect of a judgment of a sister State in the tribunals of this State is elaborately discussed; Louden *v.* Blythe, involving the question of the conclusiveness of a magistrate's certificate of the acknowledgment by *femes covert* of deeds and mortgages; and Wilt *against* Snyder, in which the doctrine of negotiable paper is learnedly examined.

Mr. Chambers never occupied any other public official stations; but in private life he held many places of trust and responsibility, giving to the faithful discharge of the duties they imposed upon him his best services, and to all enterprises for the advancement of the public good, and the promotion of education and morality, liberally of his substance.

In 1814 he was elected a Manager of the Chambersburg Turnpike Road Company, and afterwards its President, which positions he filled for half a century.

In the same year he was actively employed in organizing and establishing the Franklin County Bible Society, was elected one of its officers, and served as such for many years.

He was always a steadfast and consistent friend of the cause of temperance. By precept, by example, and by strong and eloquent advocacy of its principles, he strove to correct public sentiment on this subject, and to arouse it to a proper appreciation of the horrors of intemperance. He assisted in the organization of a number of societies throughout the country, to which he gave freely such pecuniary aid as they required, and before which he was a frequent speaker. The seed which he thus so diligently planted ripened into a rich harvest of blessed results, the influence of which remains until this day.

In 1815 Mr. Chambers was elected a Trustee of the Chambersburg Academy, and afterwards President of the Board, resigning the trust after a tenure of forty-five years, because of the increasing infirmities of age.

In the same year he was chosen one of the Trustees of the Presbyterian Church of Chambersburg, and in due time became President of the Board, from which he retired in July, 1864.

He was also for many years a Director of the Bank of Chambersburg, in 1836 was chosen its President, and annually re-elected until pressing business engagements compelled him to decline re-election.

The mention of these unostentatious but useful and responsible employments is not improper here, for it serves to illustrate how Mr. Chambers was esteemed in the community where he passed his entire life.

At the time of his death he was the largest land owner in Franklin county. He had a passion for agriculture, studied it as a science, and gave much of his leisure to the direction of its practical operations. His knowledge of soils, and of the fertilizers best adapted to them, was extensive and accurate. His familiarity with the boundaries of his farms, and the varieties of timber trees growing upon them, and exactly upon what part of the land they could be found, was so remarkable as to astonish his tenants frequently, and to put them at fault. He was not churlish in imparting all his knowledge about agricultural affairs to his neighbours, and he was ever ready at his own expense to lead the van in every experiment or enterprise which gave a reasonable promise of increasing the knowledge or lightening the labours of the farmer. For the purpose of exciting a generous emulation among the farmers, and facilitating their opportunity for gaining increased knowledge of their business, although at quite an advanced age, he expended much time and labour in organizing and putting into successful operation the first Agricultural Society of Franklin county, which he served as president for one year.

Mr. Chambers was proud of his native state, and a devout worshipper of the race whose blood flowed in his veins. These sentiments were deepened and strengthened by a diligent study of provincial history and an extensive personal acquaintance with the illustrious men whose lives adorned the first years of the Commonwealth. The knowledge which he thus acquired brought to him the sting of disappointment; for his sense of justice was wounded by the almost contemptuous historical treatment of the claims and deeds of that race which, more than all others, had helped to lay the broad foundation of state prosperity, to build churches and school houses, and to advance everywhere the sacred standard of religious liberty, which had loved freedom and hated the king, and had carried with it into every quarter the blessings of civilization, and the hallowed influences of the Gospel.

The spirit of his ancestry called him to the vindication of their race, and he determined—although the sand of his time-glass was running low—to round off, and crown the industry of a long life by a labour of love.

During the brief periods of leisure, which the almost constant demands of his business only occasionally afforded him, he prepared and had published, in 1856, a volume, which, with characteristic modesty, he entitled, "*A Tribute to the Principles, Virtues, Habits and Public Usefulness of the Irish and Scotch Early Settlers of Pennsylvania; by a Descendant.*"

This production discloses such a thorough knowledge of the subject, and withal breathes so great a filial reverence for those whose merits it commemorates, that it will doubtless long be read with increasing interest by their descendants.

Mr. Chambers was an ardent friend of the Historical Society of Pennsylvania, and impressed with the importance of the noble work, for the sake of truth, which it is now performing. The value of his efforts for the elucidation of the early history of the province and state, and his moral worth, were generously recognized by the Society in his selection to be one of its vice-presidents, which honourable office he held at the time of his decease.

By the request of the Society, Mr. Chambers undertook the preparation of an extended history of a considerable portion of the State of Pennsylvania, including the Cumberland Valley. It was also intended to embrace a compilation and analysis of the various laws and usages governing the acquisition of titles to land in the state, to be supplemented by an annotation of the changes caused therein by statutory law, and the decisions of the courts from time to time.

The manuscript of this work, which had cost much research and labour, was finished and ready for the press on the 30th of July, 1864, when the Rebels, under General McCausland, made their cruel foray into Chambersburg, to give the doomed town over to its baptism of fire.

It perished in the conflagation of that fearful day—which still haunts, and ever will, the memory of those who witnessed it, like the hideous spectre of a dream. Along with that manuscript perished also a biographical sketch, which was almost ready for publication, of Dr. John McDowell, a native of Franklin county, distinguished for his learning, usefulness, and devoted piety.

Mr. Chambers lost heavily in property by the burning of Chambersburg. The large stone dwelling-house built by his father in 1787, the house which he had himself erected in 1812, and in which he had lived with his family since 1813, together with four other houses, were totally destroyed.

But this pecuniary loss caused him, comparatively, but little regret. His private papers, an extensive correspondence, valuable manuscripts, hallowed relics of the loved and lost ones, many cherished mementoes of friendship, his books so familiar and so prized from constant study and use, the old-fashioned stately furniture, and the precious heirlooms that had come down to him from his ancestry, all shared the same common ruin. Such things are incapable of monetary valuation, and their loss was irreparable. In one half hour the red hand of fire had ruthlessly severed all the links that bound him to his former life, and thenceforth he walked to the verge of his time isolated and disassociated from the past. This calamity he keenly felt, although he nerved himself against its depressing influences with his characteristic cheerfulness and fortitude.

To this cause, also, must be atrributed the great lack of present materials for a proper biographical sketch of Mr. Chambers, and the difficulties and discouragements which the writer of this tribute has encountered in its preparation.

Mr. Chambers was deeply moved by the news of the bombardment of Fort Sumter. When he heard the startling intelligence, although in firm health, it seemed to stir a fever in his blood. He urged the calling of the citizens of Chambersburg together immediately, to take proper measures for assisting in the defence of the Government. He presided at the meeting, and made a touching and eloquent speech, which was responded to on the spot by the enlistment of a full company for the three months' service. A few years before he had presented a flag to a military company called in his honour *The Chambers Infantry*.

This organization formed the nucleus of the company now enlisted for the stern duties of war, and was among the first in the state to report for service at the headquarters at Harrisburg. From that hour, until the last Confederate soldier laid down his arms, Mr. Chambers stood steadfastly by the Union. The darkest hours of the war found him always the same unflinching supporter of the Government, the same staunch patriot, the same irreconcilable opponent of all compromise with treason, and the same defiant and implacable foe of traitors.

On the 6th day of March, 1810, Mr. Chambers married Alice A. Lyon, of Carlisle, daughter of William Lyon, Esq., Prothonotary and Clerk of the Courts of Cumberland county—a lady whose virtues and accomplishments cheered and solaced thirty-eight years of his life. Two sons and one danghter, the fruits of this marriage, still survive, and are residents of Chambersburg.

Mr. Chambers was of medium stature, of slender frame and delicate constitution. He was indebted for the physical strength which enabled him to sustain for so many years the burden of excessive professional labour, solely to his abstemious life, regular habits, and almost daily exercise upon horseback.

His classical training was excellent, and his knowledge of the Roman authors quite extensive. He was a well-read man, and familiar with the best literature of his own and past times—an acquaintance which he sedulously cultivated until a late period of his life. His library was large and well selected, and open at all times to the deserving, however humble might be their station.

Mr. Chambers cared for none of the arts of popularity. He was not one "to split the ears of the groundlings." He had no ambition at all for this. His bearing was dignified and his manners reserved. With the world he doubtless was accredited a cold and proud man; but to those who were admitted to the privileges of an intimate acquaintance, he was a sociable, kind, courteous and affable gentleman, and a genial and captivating companion. Having acquired a varied fund of knowledge from books, as well as from a close and intelligent observation of men, his conversation was exceedingly entertaining and instructive. His memory, going back into the last century, had garnered up many interesting reminiscences of the events of that age, and personal recollections of its illustrious men; and when in the unrestrained freedom of social intercourse he opened its treasures, they furnished, indeed, a rare intellectual entertainment to his charmed auditors. But so great was the elevation of his character and the purity of his nature, so intense his self respect, that I venture to assert that never at any time, under the temptations of the most unreserved conversation, did he utter a word or sentiment that might not with perfect propriety have been repeated in the most refined society.

He was a sincere and steadfast friend, a kind neighbour, and a good and useful citizen. His advice to all who sought it—and they were many, in every walk of life—proved him to be a willing, judicious and sympathizing counsellor.

In the management of his private affairs he was scrupulously honest and punctual. He required all that was his own, and paid to the uttermost farthing that which was another's. He scorned alike the pusillanimity which would defraud one's self, and the meanness which would rob another. But withal he was a generous man. His house was the abode of a most liberal hospitality. His benevolence was large and catholic, manifesting itself in frequent and liberal contributions for the advancement of education and religion. He was kind to the poor and deserving, and more than one child of poverty received a good education at his expense. But he did not publish his charities on the streets, nor give his alms before men. He reverently obeyed in this respect the scriptural injunction, "*Let not thy left hand know what thy right hand doeth.*"

It would be improper for us, by dwelling longer on his domestic virtues, to invade the sanctity of his home, where they grew into such eminent development. We know that he was a good husband, a devoted father, and an exemplar to his household worthy of the closest imitation.

Mr. Chambers was a devout man from his youth, and a sincere and unfaltering believer in the cardinal doctrines of the Christian religion. From childhood he was carefully trained in the tenets of the Westminster Confession and the Shorter Catechism. He drank in a reverence for the Sabbath day with his mother's milk, which so engrafted itself into his being that no earthly inducement could tempt him to profane it. In 1842, he made a public profession of his faith, and was received into the communion of the Presbyterian Church at Chambersburg. Thenceforth religion grew from a mere sentiment, or a cold intellectual belief, into the guiding principle of his life. It influenced his conduct towards others and governed his own heart. It kept him untainted from the world in prosperity, and solaced him in adversity. And when the twilight of his last days began to descend upon him, his pathway was illumined by the light of the Gospel, and he walked down to the dark river with a firm step, unclouded by doubts or fears, and with the eye of faith steadily fixed upon the Star of Bethlehem. He died on the 25th of March, 1866, in his eighty-first year, bequeathing to his children the heritage of an unspotted name, to posterity an enduring reputation, earned by a life full of good and virtuous deeds, and to the aspiring and ambitious youth an example worthy of the highest emulation.

HON. WILLIAM FINDLAY.

WILLIAM FINDLAY, the fourth Governor of Pennsylvania under the Constitution of 1790, from December 16, 1817, to December 19, 1820, was born at Mercersburg, Franklin county, on the 20th of June, 1768.

The progenitor beyond whom he never traced his lineage was Adjutant Brown, as he was called, who took part in the defence of Derry, Ireland, during its famous siege in 1566, and afterwards emigrated to this country with his daughter Elizabeth. The daughter married Samuel Findlay, of Philadelphia. A son by this marriage, Samuel, settled, some years before the opening of the Revolutionary War, at Mercersburg, a place which was then of more trade and importance relatively than now. It was an entrepot, where goods to be sent west of the mountains were brought in wagons and transferred to pack-horses. It is situated at the base of the Blue Ridge, in that great valley—the Shenandoah in Virginia and Cumberland in Pennsylvania—which stretches from the borders of Tennessee to the Hudson. In the year 1765, he was married to Jane Smith, a daughter of William Smith. She died in the thirty-fifth year of her age, the mother of eight boys, six of whom survived her. These lived to be men, and all of them attained respectable, and some of them distinguished positions in the communities where they lived. Had that young mother been spared to look on them in their manhood, she might have regarded them with the complacency of Cornelia herself. Her fine understanding, her piety, her maternal tenderness and affection, were themes on which those of her children who were old enough when she died to know and appreciate her virtues, fondly loved to dwell.

William, the subject of this sketch, was the second of this family of sons. The Scotch-Irish, the name by which emigrants from the north of Ireland were known, at an early day settled in great numbers in the Cumberland valley, and at Mercersburg they formed almost the exclusive population. Like the Scotch, from whom they were descended, they appreciated the importance of a good education. A knowledge of the common English branches they deemed indispensable for all their children, while one son in a family, at least, if it could be accomplished by any reasonable sacrifice, received a classical education. William, in his boyhood, displayed that activity of mind and thirst for knowledge which were the characteristics of his manhood. His leisure hours were devoted to reading such books as were accessible. They were few, but they contained solid and useful information, very different from many of those which a prolific and unscrupulous press supplies the youth of the present day. They were read with care, and their contents made the subject of reflection. It was the intention of his parents to have given him a collegiate education, in preparation for one of the learned professions, which, had he been allowed his choice, would have been that of the law. A fire, which consumed his father's store and dwelling, caused so severe a pecuniary loss that this cherished purpose had to be abandoned. His instruction was therefore only such as could be obtained in the schools of the neighbourhood. The meagre advantages afforded him were studiously improved, and the natural activity of his mind and his ambition to excel enabled him to make substantial aquirements. He wrote with correctness and perspicuity, had a general knowledge of American and English history and literature, and although not a technical lawyer, he acquired that "competent knowledge of the laws" of his country which Blackstone pronounces to be "the proper accomplishment of every gentleman."

On the 7th of December, 1791, he was married to Nancy Irwin, daughter of Archibald Irwin, of Franklin county, and commenced life as a farmer on a portion of his father's estate, which at the death of his father, in 1799, he inherited.

He was a political disciple and a great admirer of Mr. Jefferson, and at an early age took an active part in politics. The first office which he ever held was a military one, that of Brigade Inspector of Militia, requiring more of business capacity than knowledge of tactics. Military promotion led to political preferment. The election of a Colonel or Major was as fiercely contested as that of a Governor, and the candidates were often if not generally of opposite parties.

In the autumn of 1797, Mr. Findlay was elected a member of the House of Representatives of the State Legislature, which then sat in Philadelphia. He was then in the thirtieth year of his age, and found himself, if not the youngest, among the most youthful in a body where it was the custom to send men more advanced in years than at present. He was again elected to the House in 1803. He proved himself a leading member, and one of the most useful in the House, being placed in the most responsible positions.

On the 13th of January, 1807, Mr. Findlay was elected State

Treasurer, whereupon he resigned his seat in the House. From that date until the 2d of December, 1817, when he resigned to assume the duties of chief magistrate, a period of nearly eleven years, he was annually re-elected by the Legislature to that office, in several instances unanimously, and always by a strong majority, not uncommonly being supported by members politically opposed to him.

In 1817, Mr. Findlay was nominated by the Republicans as their candidate for Governor. General Joseph Hiester was selected by a dissaffected branch of the Republican party, styled Old School Men, to oppose him, who was supported also by the Federalists. The result was a triumph for Findlay, who was elected by a majority of over seven thousand votes.

In 1820, Governor Findlay again received the unanimous nomination of the Republicans for re-election, and Joseph Heister was nominated as before by the Republicans of the Old School, and was supported by the Federalists *en masse*. Under the Constitution of 1790, the patronage of the Executive was immense. To him was given the power of appointing, with few exceptions, every state and county officer. This power, considered so dangerous that, by the Constitution of 1838 and subsequent amendments, the Executive has been stripped of it almost entirely, was, in fact, dangerous only to the Governor himself. For while he might attach one person to him by making an appointment, the score or two who were disappointed became, if not active political opponents, at least lukewarm friends. Many trained and skilful politicians had been alienated from the support of Governor Findlay by their inability to share or control patronage. The result was the election of his opponent.

At the general elections of 1821, the Republicans regained ascendency in the Legislature. At the session of 1821–22, while Governor Findlay was quietly spending the winter with a friend and relative in Franklin county, he received notice that he had been elected to the Senate of the United States for the full term of six years from the preceding 4th of March. He immediately set out for the capital, where he took his seat and served the entire term with distinguished ability. While he was in the Senate, two of his brothers, Colonel John Findlay, of Chambersburg, and General James Findlay, of Cincinnati, Ohio, were members of the National House of Representatives. We are reminded by the following paragraph from the Harrisburg *Intelligencer*, of 1824, that travel to and from the capital then, even from contiguous states, was by no means so rapid and convenient as now:

"Mr. Findlay, of the United States Senate, also, left this place for Washington yesterday, by way of Baltimore, in a gig."

After the expiration of his senatorial term he was appointed by President Jackson Treasurer of the United States Mint at Philadelphia. This office he held until the accession of General Harrison to the Presidency, when, unwilling at his advanced age to be longer burdened with its cares and responsibilities, he resigned. The remainder of his life was spent in retirement with the family of his son-in-law, Governor Shunk, at whose residence, in Harrisburg, he died on the 12th of November, 1846, in the seventy-ninth year of his age.

In person, Governor Findlay was tall, with fair complexion and dark brown hair. He had a vigorous constitution and a cheerful disposition. He was affable and courteous in his address, fond of conversation, but did not monopolize it. He understood and practised the habits of a good listener. He exhibited great tact in drawing out the reserved and taciturn, and enabling them to figure well in conversation by giving rein to their hobbies. He possessed a remarkably tenacious memory of names and faces. After a long separation he could recognize and call by name a person with whom he had had but a short and casual interview. His acquaintance was probably more extensive, and his personal friends more numerous, than those of almost any other public man of his day.

In his domestic relations he was most exemplary, an affectionate husband and the best of fathers. He was pre-eminently an unselfish man. He was charitable in the largest sense. Thinking no evil himself, his unsuspecting benevolence was often imposed upon. He was a Christian in faith and practice. Baptised and brought up in the Presbyterian Church, he accepted its standards, and respected and hospitably entertained its ministers. In his inaugural address as Governor, in enumerating the duties which should be required of public servants, he included that of cherishing "by their example, the purity and beauty of the religion of the Redeemer."

HON. JOSEPH RITNER.

JOSEPH RITNER, the eighth and last Governor under the Constitution of 1790, from December 15th, 1835, to January 15th, 1839, was born in Berks county, Pennsylvania, on the 25th of March, 1780.

His father was John Ritner, who emigrated from Alsace, on the Rhine. During his early years Joseph was employed upon his father's farm. The only school advantage which he ever enjoyed was during a period of six months in a primary school at the early age of six years. At the age of sixteen he removed to Cumberland county, and was employed as a labourer upon the farm of Jacob Myers, near Newville. In the year 1800, he married Susan Alter, of Cumberland county. Their offspring were six sons and three daughters. Soon after their marriage they removed to Westmoreland county, and finally became settled upon a farm belonging to the wife's uncle, David Alter, in Washington county. What was unusual for farmers of that day, the uncle possessed a good library. The books were principally German works of a substantial character. Gifted with strong native sense, and a wonderfully retentive memory, this library proved to him a mine of wealth. Here, during his leisure hours, he delved, and what was wanting of privilege in school instruction, he, by diligence, himself supplied, affording a perpetual example to the young, of the fruits of industry and perseverance.

In 1820, Mr. Ritner was elected a member of the House of Representatives, from Washington county, and served in that capacity for a period of six years. In 1824, he was elected Speaker of that body, and was re-elected in the following year. In 1829, he received the nomination for Governor in opposition to George Wolf. It was a period of much excitement respecting secret societies, and great antipathy was exhibited towards them, especially the Masonic fraternity. So strong was this feeling that a political party was built upon it, known as the Anti-Masonic, and by this party Ritner was supported. He received a handsome vote, but was defeated. In 1832, he was again put in nomination, and though again defeated, made a great gain over his former vote. He was for a third time nominated in 1835, and was elected.

Ever the firm and devoted friend of the common-school system down to the close of his life he manifested a lively interest in this system, attending Teachers' Institutes in the county where he lived, and acting as presiding officer when upon the verge of eighty. In 1861, the Normal School at Edinboro', Erie county, was recognized and adopted by the State. Dr. Burrowes, who was then Superintendent, appointed his old friend and associate of a preceding generation, as one of the inspectors. Though then at the age of eighty-three he accepted the appointment, and made that long journey of more than five hundred miles by rail and stage, with the alacrity and pleasure of a boy of sixteen. And when he appeared upon the platform of the great hall of the Institute, in the presence of a concourse of upturned faces, it could but excite tears of gratitude, that his life had been almost miraculously lengthened out to see the day when a great institution devoted to the preparation of common-school teachers, a crowning feature of that system, should be inaugurated upon a spot which was an unbroken wilderness when the law was originally passed in his administration.

Governor Ritner always regarded his connection with the school system with singular satisfaction, and viewed the consummation of its adoption as the crowning glory of his administration. Even the progress which was made during the three years in which he occupied the chair of state was a subject of congratulation, which he thus presents in his last Annual Message to the Legislature: "The condition of the means provided by the State for general education is so flourishing, that little is required to be done by the present Legislature. Within three years the permanent State appropriation to this object has been increased from $75,000 annually to $400,000. Nor will this large outlay have been without its fruits. Instead of seven hundred and sixty-two common schools in operation at the end of the year 1835, and about seventeen academies, (the latter in a state of almost doubtful existence,) with no female seminaries fostered by the State, she has now five thousand common schools, thirty-eight academies, and seven female academies in active and permanent operation, disseminating the principles of literature, science, and virtue over the land. In addition to these, there are many schools, academies, and female seminaries of a private character, equally useful and deserving in their proper sphere."

Secretary Burrowes, *ex-officio* Superintendent of Common Schools, in his report to the Legislature at the same time that this message was delivered, pays the following just tributes: "The undersigned cannot close this report without bearing testimony to one fact alike honourable to the State and advantageous to the system. In his whole experience the blighting touch of party politics has never been detected upon it. All seem to forget their every-day differences, and to meet unitedly on this, as on a Sabbath ground of devotion to the public good. In no station of life has this right feeling been more obvious than among those in power. When the agitating divisions of the day shall have sunk into comparative insignificance, and names be only repeated in connection with some great act of public benefaction, those of GEORGE WOLF and JOSEPH RITNER will be classed by Pennsylvania among the noblest on her long list; the one for his early and manly advocacy, and the other for his well-timed and determined support of the FREE SCHOOL."

In the expression of his opinions in his messages upon national affairs, Governor Ritner was bold and outspoken, however unpalatable they might be to those whom he meant to reach. Upon the subject of slavery in any part of the national domain he uttered his condemnation in such clear and ringing tones that it arrested the attention of the philanthropist and the lover of freedom wherever it was read. His message of 1836 called forth from the Quaker poet, Whittier, the following spirit-stirring lyric:

> Thank God for the token!—one lip is still free—
> One spirit untrammeled—unbending one knee!
> Like the oak of the mountain, deep-rooted and firm,
> Erect, when the multitude bends to the storm;
> When traitors to Freedom, and Honour, and God,
> Are bowed at an Idol, polluted with blood;
> When the recreant North has forgotten her trust
> And the lip of her honour is low in the dust—
> Thank God, that one arm from the shackle has broken!
> Thank God, that one man as a *freeman* has spoken!
>
> O'er thy crags, Allegheny, a blast has been blown!
> Down thy tide, Susquehanna, the murmur has gone!
> To the land of the South—of the charter and chain—
> Of Liberty sweetened with slavery's pain;
> Where the cant of Democracy dwells on the lips
> Of the forgers of fetters, and wielders of whips!
> Where "chivalric" honour means really no more
> Than scourging of women and robbing the poor!
> Where the Moloch of Slavery sitteth on high,
> And the words which he utters, are—WORSHIP OR DIE!
>
> Right onward, oh, speed it! Wherever the blood
> Of the wronged and the guiltless is crying to God;
> Wherever a slave in his fetters is pining;
> Wherever the lash of the driver is twining;

Wherever from kindred, torn rudely apart,
Comes the sorrowful wail of the broken of heart;
Wherever the shackles of tyranny bind,
In silence and darkness the God-given mind;
There, God speed it onward!—its truth will be felt—
The bonds shall be loosened—the iron shall melt!

And oh, will the land where the free soul of PENN
Still lingers and breathes over mountain and glen—
Will the land where a BENEZET's spirit went forth
To the peeled, and the meted and outcast of Earth—
Where the words of the Charter of Liberty first
From the soul of the sage and the patriot burst—
Where first for the wronged and the weak of their kind
The Christian and statesman their efforts combined—
Will that land of the free and the good wear a chain?
Will the call to the rescue of Freedom be vain?

No, RITNER!—her "Friends" at thy warning shall stand
Erect for the truth, like their ancestral band;
Forgetting the feuds and the strife of past time,
Counting coldness injustice, and silence a crime;
Turning back from the cavils of creeds, to unite
Once again for the poor in defence of the right;
Breasting calmly, but firmly, the full tide of wrong,
Overwhelmed but not borne on its surges along;
Unappalled by the danger, the shame, and the pain,
And counting each trial for truth as their gain!

And that bold-hearted yeomanry, honest and true,
Who, haters of fraud, give to labour its due;
Whose fathers of old, sang in concert with thine,
On the banks of Swatara the songs of the Rhine—
The German-born pilgrims, who first dared to brave
The scorn of the proud in the cause of the slave:—
Will the sons of such men yield the lords of the South
One brow for the brand—for the padlock one mouth?
They cater to tyrants?—They rivet the chain,
Which their fathers smote off, on the negro again?

No, never!—one voice, like the sound in the cloud,
When the roar of the storm waxes loud and more loud,
Wherever the foot of the freeman hath pressed
From the Delaware's marge, to the Lake of the West,
On the south-going breezes shall deepen and grow,
Till the land it sweeps over shall tremble below!
The voice of a PEOPLE—uprisen—awake—
Pennsylvania's watchword, with Freedom at stake,
Thrilling up from each valley, flung down from each height,
"OUR COUNTRY AND LIBERTY!—GOD FOR THE RIGHT!"

At the expiration of his term of office Governor Ritner returned to private life, taking up his residence near Mount Rock, in the county of Cumberland. Possessed of a strong constitution and a powerful frame, he rarely complained of sickness, his system seeming to be proof against the ordinary inroads of disease. In 1840, however, he was attacked by cataract in both eyes, from the effect of which he was for some time entirely blind. By an operation performed upon the right eye, sight was completely restored so that he was able to read with ease the finest print. So painful was the operation that no consideration could induce him to submit to one upon the left, and that remained sightless to the day of his death.

He continued to take a lively interest in politics, and rarely failed to deposit his vote in the ballot-box in every important election. In 1848 he was nominated by President Taylor, Director of the Mint at Philadelphia, in which capacity he served for a short time; but before his nomination was acted on by the Senate, President Taylor died, and he retired, to make room for the favourite of President Fillmore. He was a delegate from Pennsylvania to the National Convention which nominated John C. Fremont for Pesident, and to the close of his life continued an active and ardent Republican.

Governor Ritner was endowed with a mind of great native strength. The faculty of memory was almost miraculous, for he seemed never to forget a name, an event, a date, or a fact. The impressions of his early and active life were retained with remarkable clearness, and he could recall occurrences in his official life, and repeat debates with surprising accuracy. He was remarkably temperate in all his habits, never using in any form tobacco or spirituous liquors. He was a man of strong convictions, and his opinions when once formed were rarely changed. His conscientiousness naturally inclined him to caution, and every subject requiring his decision received mature deliberation. He fortunately lived long enough to see many of the cardinal principles which he had advocated become the fundamental law of the land, and time, which "at last sets all things even," vindicated the soundness of his judgment. He died on the 16th day of October, 1869, in the ninetieth year of his age. His life was prolonged beyond that of any other Governor of Pennsylvania, though associated in this office with men wonderfully long-lived.

SAMUEL WYLIE CRAWFORD, D. D.

SAMUEL WYLIE CRAWFORD, D. D., was born in Charleston, South Carolina, January 7th, 1793. He was descended from Scotch ancestry, and from a family distinguished for their various services in the annals of Scotland.

He received his education in Philadelphia, and was graduated at the University of Pennsylvania in 1816. He commenced the study of medicine under the care of Dr. Samuel Smith, but soon relinquished it, and entered on the study of Theology under the Rev. Dr. Wylie, Professor of Divinity in the Reformed Presbyterian Church, and was licensed in 1818.

In connection with preaching, Mr. Crawford taught the English and Mathematical department of Grey and Wylie's Academy, until 1822, when he was sent by his Presbytery to Northern New York, and was ordained at Duanesburg, May 15th, 1823.

In June, 1824, he accepted an unanimous call from a congregation in Franklin county, Penn., and was installed their pastor in August of the same year.

This congregation was composed of members living in four localities, Fayetteville, Scotland, Waynesboro' and Greencastle.

At Greencastle and Waynesboro' the Presbyterian churches were used to hold the services in, and at Scotland and Fayetteville the school houses.

Mr. John Thompson, one of the elders of the congregation, living near Scotland, having offered to give the ground on which to build a church, Mr. Crawford's family connections in Philadelphia and New York, contributed the amount necessary, with the exception of some small subscriptions made by the Presbyterians in the neighbourhood of Scotland, and some work done by members. The present stone church was erected, and though belonging to the Reformed Presbyterian body, is, when not occupied by them, open to Presbyterian clergymen for the performance of religious services. The members were descendants of early settlers of Franklin county; the Thomsons, Renfrews, Burnses, Kennedys, &c., men of character and standing, some of whom served their country during the Revolutionary war, and some during the war of 1812.

The peculiar principles which the Reformed Presbyterians held (instilled into their minds by their Covenanter ancestors) on the subjects of Slavery, Psalmody, Covenanting, close communion, and civil government, prevented any intimate ecclesiastical relations with the Presbyterians, though as individuals there were among them many strong friendships.

Mr. Crawford resided for a time on Federal Hill, near Chambersburg, but the distance from the majority of his charge was too great, and he bought a farm four miles east of Chambersburg, near Fayetteville and removed to it in 1824.

Scarcely had he made the change when his house, which had been thoroughly refitted, was burned to the ground and most of its contents destroyed. This calamity rendered another change necessary, and his family went to New York while he remained to superintend the building of another home.

He consented at this time to take charge of the Chambersburg Academy, which he taught until the fall of 1830, when he resigned it, and demitted the charge of the Conococheague congregation to accept an offer from the Trustees of the University of Pennsylvania to become the Principal of the Academical Department of that institution, which had been founded by Franklin. In this position Mr. Crawford was eminently successful, and the Academy soon assumed the highest grade, hundreds of young men having been prepared for different colleges, and not one of his pupils offered for examination ever having been rejected. Many of them have risen to positions of honour and trust as statesmen, and as soldiers, and in the different professions, and have often traced their success in after years to the care and training they had received from their revered preceptor.

Mr. Crawford was the Moderator of the Synod of 1832, when the division took place (on the question of civil government) in the Reformed Presbyterian Church, and presided with dignity and judgment through very exciting scenes. He also installed the Rev. J. N. McLeod as successor to his father, Dr. Alexander McLeod, in New York city. This was soon after the division, and the question of church property not having been decided, there was an attempt made by the seceding party to hold the church, resulting in great excitement and almost uproar during which Mr. Crawford, though threatened with personal violence, proceeded with the installation service to its close, with determined courage.

In the beginning of his ministry Mr. C. was in the habit of preaching to the inmates of the Walnut street prison, Philadelphia, and became so interested in this work that on his return to the city, he, for several years, preached regularly in the Eastern Penitentiary and House of Refuge, visiting the cells and conversing with the prisoners. And very often through the week his afternoons were devoted to this good work, which he felt sure was blessed to the solitary inmates.

In July, 1835, a congregation composed of members from Dr. Wylie's congregation, and others, was organized at Fairmount, then a suburb of Philadelphia, and called Mr. C. to be their pastor. He accepted, and discharged the duties of this charge in connection with his Academical duties for eleven years, when, his health failing from over exertion, he was obliged to resign. This congregation built for him the church at the corner of Twenty-Third and Callowhill streets. From the small beginning of nineteen members it had increased to a membership of more than one hundred, and had a large and flourishing Sabbath school. Mr. C. had laboured among this people with his whole soul was deeply attached to them, and left them with great regret.

The degree of Doctor of Divinity was conferred on Mr. C. in 1844 by the Indiana University, at Bloomington. This University subsequently invited Dr. Crawford to be its President, which, though appreciating the honour, he was obliged to decline.

After an interval of more than a year, having regained his health, some of the members of Dr. Crawford's Fairmount church separated themselves from that connection, and with others were formed into a new organization over which Dr. C. was called to minister. This congregation erected a church edifice at the corner of Filbert and Seventeenth streets, Philadelphia. He remained with them until 1856, when his failing health made it imperative for him to leave the city. To both of these churches Dr. Crawford contributed largely of his means; and the attachment of the people to him was great, and fully reciprocated by him. In all his church relations he was earnestly seconded by his wife, whose sympathetic heart, active benevolence, and strong good sense made her well beloved and affectionately remembered by many.

Dr. Crawford for several years filled the chair of Church History and Pastoral Theology in the Theological Seminary, and, for two or three years after Dr. Wylie's death, the Professorship of Divinity; Dr. Wylie's son filling the chair of History.

In a list of facts one fails to convey to the reader the influence which such a man as Dr. Crawford exerts by his decision of character, scholarship, integrity, fine presence, warm sympathy, elegant culture, generosity and hospitality. During the greater part of his ministry he received his salary only to return it, or to use it for the various benevolent objects, brought so constantly to his notice. He was connected with the different benevolent societies now to be met with in all communities; organized a juvenile missionary society, which was the instrument of doing much good, and was honoured by God in being made the instrument of bringing many to a knowledge of the truth.

Upon the breaking out of the war Dr. Crawford was earnest in his patriotic support of the government. He saw that the issue forced by the South involved the very existence of the great principle for which he had contended through his whole life—the abolition of slavery—and he threw his whole soul into the struggle. Not content with seeing his three sons and son-in-law in the Union army, he sought and obtained a Chaplaincy for himself, and was only prevented from entering upon its duties by advancing age. Upon the passage of Lee's army through Chambersburg to Gettysburg, he remained at his home alone, and never shrank from asserting his principles and patriotism even when surrounded by the rebel host.

Dr. Crawford still lingers among us, though burdened with the increasing infirmities of advanced life. His former pupils entertain for him high veneration, and he enjoys the marked esteem of the entire church, of which he was the honoured, eloquent and influential minister, as well as the profound respect of the communities in which he has so long lived and laboured.

Dr. Crawford still lives at his retired and attractive home near to Fayetteville, retaining much cheerfulness even under the infirmities of four score years. Throughout his whole career he has been noted for his promptness and firmness in advocating the right and opposing what he considered wrong.

HENRY R. WILSON, D. D.

THE REV. HENRY R. WILSON, was born in the neighbourhood of Gettysburg, Adams county, Pa., on the 7th of August, 1780. He was graduated at Dickinson College, Carlisle, whilst the venerable Charles Nisbet, D. D., presided over that institution, in the days of its prosperity. He was licensed to preach by the Presbytery of Carlisle in 1801. After labouring for some months in Virginia, as a supply, he removed with his family to Bellefonte, Centre county, Pa., where Presbyterians had neither organized church nor house of worship. He commenced preaching in the Court House. His labours were greatly blessed in gathering here a church, as also another at Lick Run, twelve miles distant. Over these congregations he was installed pastor by the Presbytery of Huntingdon, in 1802.

In 1806, Mr. Wilson was chosen, at the early age of twenty-six, to fill the Professorship of Languages in Dickinson College. A part of the time, during his connection with the college, he preached to the Presbyterian Church of Carlisle, as colleague with President Davidson. In 1814, a call was presented to him by the congregation of Silvers' Spring, which he accepted.

In 1823, Dr. Wilson received a call from the church in Shippensburg. During his ministry there, the church enjoyed some precious seasons of refreshing, "and many were added unto the Lord." He was indefatigable and abundant in labours.

In 1838, Dr. Wilson was chosen the first General Agent of the Board of Publication, in which station he laboured arduously until 1842, when he resigned his office in that Board, and accepted a call from the church at Neshamony, at Hartsville, Bucks county, Pa. Here, with his accustomed fidelity, he continued to discharge the duties of pastor until the month of October, 1848, when, at his own request, the pastoral relation was dissolved.

For some months previous his health had become so infirm that he was seldom able to preach, except when carried from his bed to the church and placed in a chair, in which posture he delivered his message amidst much bodily weakness and suffering, but with his usual clearness of mind and earnestness of manner.

Dr. Wilson's health continued to decline, notwithstanding the cessation of his ministerial labours. After a sore conflict of forty-six hours, he died in Philadelphia on the morning of Thursday, the 22d of March, 1849, and was interred the day following, at Hartsville, the scene of his closing labours in the ministry. An appropriate discourse was delivered on the occasion by the Rev. Dr. Steel, of Abington, and the sympathies and affections of the people of his recent charge were abundantly shown toward one whom, though absent, they had not ceased to regard and love as their pastor.

The life of Dr. Wilson was an eventful one. More can be said of him than that he passed through scenes of some interest, grew old, and then died. From his earliest labours in the Gospel there was demand for a steadiness of purpose, and an energy of execution, that not every man is equal to.

The influence of such a man in the church we cannot duly estimate. He was a pioneer in the cause of the Gospel in central Pennsylvania, and his labours essentially contributed to lay firm and deep the foundations of those churches that adorn and bless the regions of his earliest toil. Ministers of Dr. Wilson's character stamp an impression upon the times in which they live. They give a fixedness to the order, the government, the instruction and standard of piety in the church, by which they, being dead, yet speak.

The ministerial labours of this venerable man were abundant. His preaching was in character with the man. It came down from a former generation, with all that seriousness of manner and weight of instruction that are the fairest ornaments of the Christian pulpit. His whole deportment and performance may truly be said to have been characterized by simplicity and godly sincerity. Eminently instructive, his preaching always made the impression, "these things are so, and religion is a serious and important matter."

Few men were less influenced in their ministerial work by changing circumstances, than Dr. Wilson. Whether the congregation was large or small, whether prosperity attended his steps, or disappointment was his portion, not in these was he to find the measure or the motive of his labours. He felt himself to be of that number to whom it has been commanded, "Go and preach," and whose the promise is, "Lo, I am with you alway." Not the increase, but the *work* was his. Not the measure of his success, but the command of Christ, and the assurance that God would bless and prosper his own truth—this was the rule and the measure of his toil.

Thus he *lived*, a laborious and eminently useful preacher of the

Gospel, the crown of his family, and an ornament to the ministry of reconciliation.

Thus he *died*, amidst great bodily suffering, with the language of praise upon his lips. Not weary with his ministerial labours, and his conflicts as a sinner saved, but in obedience to the Master's call, "It is enough, come up higher," he bade the world adieu, with a hope full of immortality, most beloved by those who knew him best, and lamented by all pious men of every name.

REV. ROBERT KENNEDY.

THE REV. ROBERT KENNEDY was born in Lancaster county, Pennsylvania, on the 4th of July, 1778. His grandfather, William Kennedy, with his brother Robert, emigrated from Ireland to this country in 1730, and settled in Bucks county, Pennsylvania. Robert had a son, William, who was a Major in the Revolutionary Army, and was killed by the tories near the commencement of the war. Some members of that branch of the family continued to reside in the Northern Liberties of Philadelphia up to 1836. William Kennedy, the brother of Robert, and grandfather of the subject of this memoir, had four sons—Thomas, James, Robert and John—and three daughters. James, the second son, was married in 1761 to Jane Maxwell, daughter of John Maxwell, and sister of General Maxwell of Revolutionary memory. They had twelve children, of whom Robert, afterwards the Rev. Robert Kennedy, was the ninth.

Of the early history of young Kennedy, the writer has no further information than that he received his elementary and classical education under the direction of a Mr. Grier, probably the Rev. Nathan Grier, pastor of the Presbyterian Church of Brandywine Manor, Chester county, Pa., and that tradition reports him to have been a youth of steady habits. He made a profession of religion in the church at Pequea, in his native county, but at what time is not known. His collegiate education was received at Dickinson College, Carlisle, where he graduated, September 20th, 1797, as the Rev. Dr. McGinley says; "the best scholar in his class." He studied theology with the Rev. Nathanael Sample, then pastor of the congregations of Lancaster and Middle Octorara. It was customary for young gentlemen looking to the ministry at that time, thus to prepare for their chosen work under private instruction, as Theological Seminaries had not then come into existence. And it may not be questioned that much as this method of preparation lacked the variety of modern facilities, it had some peculiar advantages. Being in due time introduced to the Presbytery of New Castle by Mr. Sample, Mr. Kennedy was taken under their care as a candidate for the Gospel ministry on the 12th of June, 1798, and on the 20th of August, 1799, he was licensed at Upper Octorara to preach the gospel. At the request of the church of that place, he was appointed by the Presbytery to supply them half of the time for six months. At the close of this time, by the leave of Presbytery, he traveled without their bounds, and spent the greater part of the time in supplying vacant churches in the Presbytery of Carlisle.

On the 30th of September, 1800, Mr. Kennedy was dismissed by the Presbytery of New Castle to put himself under the care of the Presbytery of Carlisle, and was received by this latter Presbytery on the 7th of October, 1800. On the 9th of September, 1802, a call was put into his hands from the united congregations of East and Lower West Conococheague, known as Green Castle and Welsh Run,* which call he accepted; and, on the 13th of August, 1803, the ecclesiastical banns having been published according to the custom of the time,† he was ordained to the office of the holy ministry, and installed the pastor of said churches. In these churches he continued to labour until the 9th of April, 1816, when, at his request, the pastoral relation between him and them was dissolved. His action in relation to this matter was believed by many to have been too hasty, as the circumstances were altogether insufficient to authorize so important a step. A very fulsome obituary notice of a young man of the congregation, who had been an officer in the army during the war which had just closed, had been published in some of the papers in that vicinity. Mr. Kennedy entertained a high regard for the character of the young man, but thought the production in very bad taste. Some one was so unfortunate as to misunderstand his views, and represented the matter to the family of the deceased in such a manner as to wound their feelings. Some remarks, also, which he made from the pulpit on a day of especial observance, were interpreted by prejudiced politicians as having a party aspect, and these things were caught up and repeated by the gossiping members of his church, in every circle in which they moved. Mr. Kennedy hearing them, and being of a sensitive nature, without con-

---

* See Historical Sketch.

† The call in which there is pledged " the sum of one hundred and thirty-three pounds, six shillings and eight pence yearly," is signed by James Mitchell, Alexander Gordon, Robert Marshall, Thomas Johnston, Thomas Mason, David Denwiddie, James Wilson, Joseph Davison, George Brown, Andrew Denison, James Downey, Sr., Nathaniel Martin, Thomas Waddell, Archibald Rankin, James Poe, William Bleakney, John Kennedy, William Scott, David Rankin, James Moore, John Lawrence, John Hargrave, Andrew Robinson, James Patton, John Edmiston, Isaac Far, Elias' Davison, James McCleno, James Watson, Edward Wishard, Thomas Wallace, Robert Robinson, John M. Davison, James Johnston, Abraham Smith, William Allison, James McLenahan, Jr., John Johnston, John John, Hugh McKee, James Downey, Jr., Robert Davison, John Watson, Thomas Brown, Robert Crunkilton, John McClary, Peter Shields, James McCrea, Alexander McCutchen, Samuel McCutchen, Samuel Crunkilton, Samuel McCutchen, Patrick Long, Nathan McDowall. The lineal descendants of the signers of this document may be found in nearly every state south and west of this point, many of them occupying positions of responsibility and honour.

sulting any of his friends, announced to his congregation, after preaching on the Sabbath, that he would apply to the Presbytery, at its next meeting, for a dissolution of his pastoral relation to his congregation. By the persuasion of his friends, however, when the matter became known, the application was either not made to the Presbytery, or, if made, was withdrawn. But he made an application to the Presbytery, at their meeting on the 9th of April, 1816, and his pastoral relation was dissolved.

"From the beginning of Mr. Kennedy's ministry," says the Rev. J. W. Wightman,* "the congregation seems to have been in a prosperous condition. The dangers of the frontier had been removed. The settlement was at rest and the population was increasing. And as a consequence, the congregation under the efficient ministry of Mr. Kennedy was speedily so strengthened in numbers, that to provide room for them, it became necessary to enlarge the church." Mr. Wightman also says, in referring to a classical school which, at that time, was conducted in the old "Study House" by a Mr. Boreland:—"This school was tenderly cared for by Mr. Kennedy, who was a man of sound and thorough scholarship, and who used his influence through his whole life to have young men equip themselves well for any good work."

During the month of May, 1816, Mr. Kennedy removed with his family to Cumberland, Maryland, where he had been invited to preach to a small church, and take the charge of the Academy. Upon his arrival there, he delivered an address before the Board of Trustees of the Academy, which was so favourably received that a copy of it was requested by them for publication. His geographical position, at the extreme western border of the Presbytery, cut off from intercourse with his ministerial brethren, left him to act alone, without the counsel or sympathy of those with whom he had been accustomed to consult and act. His situation was calculated to produce discouragement, and at one time induced him to project the organization of a new Presbytery.

In the midst of the loneliness of his position, however, he was not left without some token of the Divine favour. In 1820 his church and the town were visited with a precious revival of religion, during which a goodly number became subjects of Divine grace. But the next year, movements of a different character made their appearance. Theatrical exhibitions were introduced into the town by the young men of the place, to the great detriment of religion. Articles in their favour were written and published in the papers of the town. Mr. Kennedy fur-

---

* Historical Discourse delivered in Presbyterian Church of Green Castle, Pennsylvania, May 9th, 1869.

nished anonymous articles in reply, and so scorching was one of them, that the name of the author was demanded, with threats of punishment when he should be discovered. The name was given with his consent, but although it created great excitement they did not carry their threats into effect Mr. Kennedy firmly maintained his ground, in which, to their honour be it recorded, he was sustained by the pious Methodists and Lutherans of the town.

Finding that his salary from the church and the proceeds from the school were not enough to support his family and keep his son, John H., at the Theological Seminary at Princeton, he concluded to return to his former residence on a farm, within the bounds of the congregation of Welsh Run, which he did in the Spring of 1825. The church at Welsh Run being vacant—Green Castle having secured the whole of the labours of a pastor—Mr. Kennedy preached to them as a stated supply, giving part of his time to the congregation at McConnelstown. He continued in charge of these two churches until 1833, when his labours were divided between the Welsh Run church and some of the small towns in the neighbourhood. As none of these congregations could afford to give him much of a salary, he supported his family by his own exertions on a farm. He was one of the first advocates of temperance in Franklin county. He never would sell any of his grain to distillers. And in order to show that the farmers were in error, in supposing that they could dispose of their small grains profitably only by converting them into whiskey, he purchased cattle and hogs and fattened them with such grains and products of the farm as would not bear the expense of transportation to the distant railroad market. He also established the habit of cutting harvest without the use of liquor, against great opposition, both from the labourers and the farmers. At first it appeared as if he would lose his whole crop, on which his family depended, but he shouldered his cradle himself, assisted only by a hired lad of sixteen years, his little son of twelve, and a bound boy of eleven. After the first day, his daughter begged that she might be allowed to assist her father. This little party toiled on from day to day in the hot sun, without making much headway, until after the neighbours had cut their harvests, when they nobly came to his assistance, with their hands, and cut the whole of the remainder of his crop in one day. After the first year or two, he had no difficulty in getting as many hands as he required, and now no person in that neighbourhood thinks of taking liquor to the harvest-field.

Mr. Kennedy was twice married. His first wife, to whom he was united February 17th, 1801, was Jane Herron, sister of Rev. Dr.

Herron, formerly pastor of the First Presbyterian Church, Pittsburgh, Pa. She died May 31st, 1803. By her he had two sons, one of whom John H. Kennedy, became a minister in the Presbyterian Church.* He was married a second time, the 5th of June, 1806, to Mary Davidson, daughter of Elias Davidson, of Franklin county, Pa., by whom he had ten children, all of whom, but one son, are now dead. James Maxwell Kennedy, who married Sibilla S. Morris, daughter of Evan Morris, of Chester Co., Pa., and who was a gentleman of fine personal appearance, elegant and accomplished manners, and popular and distinguished as a dry goods merchant, died in Philadelphia, March 9th, 1848, leaving two children, Herbert Morris Kennedy and Amelia Theresa Kennedy. Elias Davidson Kennedy, the only survivor of the family, resides in the same city, and, as the reference made to him in the "Historical Sketch," in connection with the "Robert Kennedy Memorial Church," indicates, has shown a grateful appreciation of his deceased father's memory. His wife is a great grand-daughter of Matthew Shields, of St. Thomas, Franklin county, Pa., a gentleman belonging to a very respectable Presbyterian family, whose daughter Agnes, married William Clarke, of Cannonsburg, son of Thomas Clarke, of Chadsford, on the Brandywine creek, and whose oldest son, Thomas Shields Clarke, born at Cannonsburg, January 18th, 1801, after a very active and industrious life, particularly distinguishing himself in the transportation business, died at Pittsburgh, October 19th, 1867, leaving two children, Charles J. Clarke, and Mrs. Agnes Shields Kennedy, wife of Elias D. Kennedy.

In stature the Rev. Robert Kennedy was of medium size, slender, and of fair complexion, blue eyes, and very near-sighted. He was industrious, plain and unostentatious in all his habits. He was a man of vigorous intellect, and a fine scholar, especially in classical literature. He took a great interest in the success of Marshall College, which the following note will show was appreciated:

"GOETHEAN HALL, *May 9th*, 1836.
"REV. ROBERT KENNEDY.
"*Respected Sir :—*

"You are, without doubt, aware that a custom generally obtains amongst literary societies, of electing as honourary members, such persons as are distinguished for their literary taste and attainments. In accordance with this custom the 'Goethean Literary Society of Marshall College,' located at Mercersburg, Franklin county, Pa., entertaining a high opinion of your character as a gentleman, and duly appreciating your taste for literature and your devotedness to this cause, has taken the liberty to enrol your name

---

*See his sketch in another part of the volume.

on the list of her honourary members, and instructed the undersigned committee to communicate intelligence of this transaction. We are aware, that it is only by securing the influence and co-operation of such individuals as yourself, that we can give character and stability to our society, and whilst it affords us pleasure to be her organs on the present occasion, and whilst we are sensible the society has no other claims than such as are based upon your general devotion to the interests of literature, we trust that you will not only pardon the liberty she has taken, but willingly accept of her small token of respect.

"Wishing you health, prosperity and continued success in your literary pursuits, we have the honour to be, respected sir,

"Yours, respectfully,

"H. J. BROWN,
A. H. KREMER, } *Committee of the G. L. Society.*"
M. KIEFFER,

As a preacher Mr. Kennedy stood high in a Presbytery in which he had as compeers some of the ablest men in the Presbyterian Church. "His sermons," says Dr. Elliott, "were full of solid evangelical matter, well arranged, and forcibly expressed, were written in full, committed to memory, and delivered without notes. His style was earnest and persuasive, and he rarely failed to secure the fixed and sustained attention of his audience." The Rev. A. A. McGinley, D. D., another of Mr. Kennedy's co-presbyters for many years, says: "As a preacher he had few superiors. The plan of his discourses was as clear as the sun. He could pour a flood of light on almost every subject he discussed, and there was much pleasure and profit in attending to his sermons. They were always orthodox, always to the point, always instructive, and frequently very impressive." The following concluding sentences from a sermon on the Sacrament of the Lord's Supper, preached by Mr. Kennedy, at Welsh Run, and since published, will serve to show the fidelity and earnestness with which in the pulpit he urged men to the performance of their duty:

"I have now endeavoured to state the case in a plain and serious manner. What resolutions, my brethren, have you formed? Or what line of conduct do you intend to pursue? Are the arguments which have been mentioned, sufficient to convince you that you ought to do this in remembrance of Christ? And are you resolved by the grace of God, that you will not be disobedient to the heavenly command? Or are you determined to pay no attention to these things, and to treat them with contempt? You probably think that you are the sons of liberty and the lords of reason, and look down with scorn upon the bigotry and superstition of the religious part of mankind. But sober reason, in my opinion, blushes at your conduct, and clearly points to religion as its greatest perfection and brightest ornament. You may, indeed, live without religion, and perhaps even be happy, but if you should die without it, I shudder with horror to conceive the consequences. True religion is the friend of sober reason, and the man who chooses them as his guide and comforter, shall be happy in time and through eternity, but he that sinneth against Christ, who is the wisdom of God, wrongeth his own soul, and all that hate Him love damnation.

"Do any of you resolve, my brethren, that you will attend upon this ordinance, but decide to defer it to some future period? However foolish and unreasonable the excuse, it is so common and so often repeated, that I can scarcely think of any reply that will be likely to strike your attention. If the prison of hell were unveiled to your view, it would discover thousands who have made the same excuse, and who are now bound in everlasting chains of darkness and misery. If you are unfit for communion with God and his saints in this world, you must be unprepared to die, and unworthy of heaven. And surely, this is not a situation in which you may content yourselves, to live year after year. The table of the Lord we expect will shortly be spread in this house, and elsewhere for our brethren of different persuasions. We are sent to invite you to the Marriage Supper of the Lamb. Lay aside, we beseech you, your pitiful excuses. Make yourselves ready for the feast. And may the Spirit of the living God enable you to come to it in a worthy and reverential manner."

Not only was Mr. Kennedy, as already stated, a fine classic scholar, but, says the late Dr. Duffield, of Detroit, "he was also a man of real humour, keen wit, and not a little drollery. His sarcasm was delicate, pointed and always made a clear cut, like a sharp, smooth, highly sharpened razor." Living as he did during those times in which the whole Presbyterian Church was so deeply agitated with the schism which culminated in the unhappy division of 1837, he was, though quiet, modest and reserved, and generally disposed to eschew petty strifes ecclesiastical, brought into the discussions and agitations of that time. At the meeting of the Synod of Philadelphia, at Gettysburg, in 1834, the subject of the approval of the "Act and Testimony" coming under consideration, he delivered a speech which was so much admired, that he was urged to let it appear in the *Philadelphian*, then edited by Dr. Ely, and finally consented to its publication. The subjoined extract from the introductory portion of the speech, will show the peculiar character of his mind:

"With becoming deference to the General Assembly, let us examine whether the high charges contained in the Act and Testimony are just or not. It charges the Assembly with countenancing and sustaining *alarming errors*—yes, *alarming errors*. Now, sir, this Madam Alarm is as insidious an enemy as ever lived on the earth. You know how she deceived Demosthenes. At the battle of Cheronea, when Madam Alarm was driving him in full flight through the woods, his coat caught upon a thorn bush, and supposing it to be a Macedonian soldier he cried aloud to spare his life.

"From this it appears that the wisest and even the bravest of men are not entirely secure from the delusions of Madam Alarm. But some men are much more liable to her impositions than others, and these are sometimes men of a high degree of refinement and integrity. Some of our city clergy who have more study than exercise, have such a nervous sensitiveness, that the slightest touch seems to go to their hearts. Now, when the edge of controversy is brought to operate upon their nervous system in such a state of excitability, it immediately throws them into the *horrors*. While in this unhappy condition, mere straws become stumbling blocks, and a bramble bush or even a shadow, seen through the fog of their gloomy imaginations, appears like hydras, and gorgons, and chimeras dire. And when the pinions of these unfortunate brethren are once erected, it is impossible to smooth them down, either by the exercise of their own reason, or by the assurances of others. Every attempt to calm their troubled spirits only increases the fever of their alarm. It matters not how good, and wise, and judicious they may be on other occasions, their alarm now operates as an inverting lens, which turns every object upside down, and exhibits before them the most frightful monsters. A curious anecdote illustrative of this, is related in Cook's Voyages. When the crew put in at Tortoise Island to obtain a fresh supply of provisions, one of the sailors got lost, and was missing for several days. When ready to sail, they all set out in search of their lost companion. All day they searched in vain. In the evening they saw a large track in the sand, and being a good deal alarmed, they encamped for the night, kindled fires, and set out guards. About midnight one of the guards fired an alarm, and roused the whole crew, assuring them that he had seen something like a great bear creepiug towards the fire. The commander next espied the monster, and fancied it was as large as an elephant, and ordered out a sergeant with his picket to shoot it. But the sergeant was no alarmist. He wished to see what it was before he would shoot it, and he soon perceived that it was a man, and he joyfully recognized their lost companion, who was so famished that he could only crawl on his hands and knees. Had this sergeant been as much alarmed as his captain, he would have killed his companion; but he was a cold-blooded *fence-man*, and I, who am a fence-man too, beg leave to assure our alarmed brethren, that those whom they conceive to be heretics, are not monsters; they are really men like themselves, their companions in the Gospel ministry, and if they will fire on them and destroy them, they will do an injury to the cause of their Master and to their fellow-creatures which cannot be easily repaired."

"Mr. Kennedy's piety," says Dr. Elliott, "was intelligent and practical; the product of spiritual illumination and sanctifying grace, with great freedom from pretension on his part, It manifested itself in a clear comprehension of the system of Divine truth as revealed in the Word of God, and in a consistent and active obedience to the requirements of duty. Although we have no account of his conversion, or of the inward expression of his heart at this time, we have what is equivalent in a paper found among his manuscripts, bearing date December 8th, 1798, between eight and nine months previous to his licensure. This paper is denominated, 'A solemn dedication of all I have and am to the service of God.' In this solemn act of consecration, signed and sealed by his own hand, there is ample evidence of a deep and earnest exercise of soul, under the saving influences of the Spirit of God."

During Mr. Kennedy's extreme illness, the Rev. Mr. Davie said to him, "Father Kennedy, you have often administered the consolations of religion to others, will you leave to us, who are to stand in your stead, your feelings in dying?" He calmly replied, "I do not experience those rapturous feelings which some have spoken of in dying, but my faith in the efficacy of the blood and atonement of our Lord and Saviour Jesus Christ is as strong as ever."

Shortly before his death, and after his sight had fled, he requested his wife to call his children around his bedside, and when informed that they were there, he raised his head and said, "My dear children, I am about to leave you; may the blessing of God rest with you through time and eternity;" and in a few minutes thereafter he died.

His death was on October 31st, 1843, of a lingering disease of near a year's standing, caused by a fall, and from exposure to damp when his system was under the influence of medicine.

Thus passed from earth a faithful servant of the Lord, the light of whose example has not been extinguished by his descent to the tomb, but continues to shine with attractive lustre. How great the advantage of having godly parents! "I bless God," said Mr. Flavel, "for a religious, tender father, who often poured out his soul to God for me, and this stock of prayers I esteem above the fairest inheritance on earth." "A good man leaveth an inheritance to his children's children." "As for man, his days are as grass; as a flower of the field so he flourisheth. For the wind passeth over it, and it is gone; and the place thereof shall know it no more. But the mercy of the Lord is from everlasting to everlasting upon them that fear Him, and His righteousness unto children's children, to such as keep His covenant, and to those that remember His commandments to do them."

ROBERT JOHNSTON, M. D.

IN taking a retrospect of the families of Franklin county a hundred years ago, we find none more prominent for its patriotism and military ardor than that one to which Dr. Robert Johnston belonged.

He, and his three brothers, all held honourable positions in the Revolutionary Army. Colonel James Johnston commanded the regiment which marched from his section of the state into New Jersey, for the defence of that province.

Colonel Thomas Johnston was engaged in active service and was under General Wayne, when that General was surprised and defeated near Paoli by a superior force of the British, guided by American Tories. Major John Johnston, while a mere lad, raised a troop of horse, and offered it to the acting authorities. It was accepted, and ordered to report in Philadelphia, but when it reached Lancaster, on its way to that city, was met by a countermanding order, as the war was about to terminate.

Dr. Robert Johnston was a surgeon in the army from the beginning of the war until its close. He was with it at Yorktown, when Lord Cornwallis surrendered. He was one of the original members of the Society of the Cincinnati and greatly esteemed by his fellow officers.

At the close of the war, his migratory tastes continued and he went on a voyage to China, taking out with him a cargo of ginseng, at that time worth almost its weight in gold in the Chinese market. From this voyage he realized a large fortune and gained vast stores of general information. He brought home with him, what in that day was considered a great curiosity, a Chinese servant.

After his return, he married, and, purchasing a large estate in his native county, made there a home, which became the resort of many of the most distinguished men of the period, especially his former companions in arms. One of these, an old friend and fellow surgeon, the father of the present Mr. Horace Binney, died at Dr. Johnston's house. The doctor, probably using knowledge acquired in the East, embalmed the body of his friend and sent it home to his family.

Dr. Johnston, having no children of his own, adopted the youngest son of his only sister, Mrs. Elizabeth Boggs.

JOHN KING.

AMONG the records of the prominent citizens of Franklin county, a notice of the subject of this sketch is entitled to a conspicuous place.

By his industry and economy, first as an iron-master, and afterwards as a merchant, Mr. King acquired a large estate. Such was his fairness of dealing, and honesty of purpose, evinced through a life of multifarious business, that not the slightest imputation was ever made against his reputation, and all who knew him were ready to testify to his unbending integrity.

His time, services, and means were always ready to minister to the sick, comfort the afflicted, relieve the needy, advance the cause of religion and morals, and aid every work or enterprise that was esteemed of public usefulness. Connected with nearly all the religious, literary, charitable, and business institutions in Chambersburg, where much of his life was spent, he was always found to be a punctual, attentive, active and liberal member or officer, and many were the widows, orphans and others, who were witnesses of his kindness, friendship and assistance.

Mr. King, as a Christian, was meek and humble, and his firm and unassuming piety gained him the confidence and esteem of all. He was for many years a ruling elder in the Presbyterian Church of Chambersburg, and as a member of Session, his counsel and discretion indicated the soundness of his judgment. He was also a firm and uniform advocate and supporter of the order and principles of that church.

For many years he was President of the Chambersburg Bank, the affairs of which he administered with marked ability and success. He departed this life, July 8th, 1835. His estimable widow survived him a number of years. His eldest daughter, now deceased, was the wife of J. Ellis Bonham, Esq., a gifted member of the Carlisle bar, who was cut down in the midst of bright promise for the future. Another is the wife of J. McDowell Sharpe, Esq., a lawyer of foremost rank in Chambersburg. A third, who has remained unmarried, lives with the sister just named.

Mr. King's character and career present an useful example to others.

They serve to show, that good sense, sound discretion, diligence in duty, and unaffected piety, may accomplish more—unspeakably more—both for the good of mankind and the advantage of the possessor, than is ever achieved, in the absence of these qualities, by the most brilliant genius, the most vigorous intellect, or the profoundest erudition. Such men are an honour and a blessing to any community.

DAVID ELLIOTT, D. D., LL. D

DR. ELLIOTT spent his whole life in Pennsylvania. His grandfather, Robert Elliott, was a Scotch-Irishman, who came to this country in 1737, and settled on a farm about seven miles north of Carlisle. His father, Thomas Elliott, who was at that time about seven years old, afterwards, at the close of the Indian war, purchased a farm in Sherman's valley, now Perry county. He was first married to Catherine, daughter of William Thomas, of York county, and afterwards to Mrs. Jane Holliday, of the same race, who was born in 1745. David, one of the five children of this second marriage, and the subject of this sketch, was born at the Valley Home, February 6th, 1787.

He was not an exception to the providential law, by which a pious and faithful mother's character is reflected in the life of her son. Such a mother early taught him to repeat his prayers, as well as Catechetical and Scripture questions, and also gave him his first lessons in spelling and reading. From the age of six years onward he was sent to such schools as a rural neighbourhood, in those uncultured times, afforded. In all these schools Dillworth's Spelling Book, the Bible, and Gough's Arithmetic were the standard class books. Every morning the pupils were required to repeat one or more answers to the questions of the Westminster Shorter Catechism, and on each Saturday to recite the whole. It was partly due to this training at school, but still more to the maternal fidelity which set apart a portion of each Sabbath afternoon to religious training at home, that the future distinguished Professor of Theology, "at a very early period," could both "ask and answer the whole of the Shorter Catechism without the aid of the book."

Whilst he was attending one of the primary schools just referred to, at the age of seven or eight years, he experienced a remarkable providential deliverance from instant death, which not only made a powerful impression upon his youthful mind, of the sovereign goodness of God, but, through his whole life, was associated with his grateful memories of the unseen hand which, as he never doubted, both led and covered him. Passing through a grove of lofty oak timber, with his companions, on his way to school, a heavy storm of wind arose, which soon blew a perfect hurricane. During the sudden violence of one of the gales which swept through the woods they all stopped suddenly, as though apprehending danger. While thus stationary he heard a crash like the breaking of timber, but such was the noise produced by the tempestuous fury of the wind that he knew not whence it came, nor whether it was near or far off. At this moment, and without any assignable reason for doing so, he made a step forward, and as he moved, a large limb of a tree, six or eight inches in diameter, and of great weight, passed down behind him, brushing his shoulders and the skirts of his coat in its descent to the earth. Had he not moved when he did, at that very moment, it would have struck him directly on the head and killed him in an instant. Every thought of this providential escape, at the time, and long afterwards, brought him to tears, in remembrance of the mercy which snatched him from destruction.

In 1802, young Elliott entered a classical school in Tuscarora valley, Mifflin county, Pa., which was twelve miles distant from his home, and under the care of the Rev. John Coulter, pastor of the Presbyterian Church at that place. In 1804 he became connected with a school in Mifflin, which was in charge of Andrew K. Russell, afterwards a tutor in Washington College, and then a popular teacher and preacher in Newark, Delaware. The happiest of all the influences of the year spent at that place grew out of his residence in the family of the Rev. Matthew Brown, then pastor of the Presbyterian Church of Mifflin, and afterwards the distinguished President, first of Washington, and then of Jefferson College. In 1805, Mr. Brown having received an invitation to become at once the first pastor of the Presbyterian Church of Washington, Pa., and principal of the Academy at that place, secured his young friend as assistant instructor. This arrangement continued for one year, with great acceptance and benefit to the community and the pupils.

In April, 1806, Mr. Elliott left Washington for his home. His journey homeward, on horseback, owing to changes of weather for which he had not provided, brought on sickness and debility which hindered his entrance into college until January of the next year. But this was the most profitable interval of his life, as it was the crisis of his spiritual birth. At the end of his first session as a student in Dickinson College, the prostration following hard study induced him to pack his books, determined not to return. But the vacation inspired him with hope. Exercising great care, he was enabled to hold such a position in his class that on his graduation, September 28th, 1808, by the unanimous selection of his classmates, to whom the Faculty left the distribution of honours, he delivered the *valedictory*.

Dr. Elliott's first preceptor in theology was his pastor, the Rev. John

Linn, with whom he spent two years as a student. His last year was spent with the Rev. Joshua Williams, D. D., of Newville, Pa. He was licensed to preach as a probationer by the Presbytery of Carlisle, September 26th, 1811. Having preached several times to the congregation of Upper West Conococheague, at Mercersburg, Pa., he received a call, dated February 19th, 1812, to settle as pastor of this large, intelligent and influential church, which, a little while before, had been left vacant by the resignation of the Rev. John King, D. D. The call having been approved by the Presbytery, in April the young minister at once entered upon his labours, though he was not ordained until the next meeting in October, in his own church. In the meantime he was married, May 14th, 1812, to Ann, daughter of Edward West, Esq., of Landisburg, Pa. He laboured among the people of his charge with great energy, efficiency and success. As a specimen of many public movements in which the young pastor took an active interest, the Franklin County Bible Society may be cited, which, in 1815, originated in his appeal through the newspapers, was carried to great success largely through his exertions, and had the honour of representation in the Convention at New York, in 1816, which formed the American Bible Society.

In 1829, Dr. Elliott received an earnest call to the pastorate of the Presbyterian Church, Washington, Pa., where he laboured with great acceptableness and success. To him, during this period, more than to any other man, was due the resuscitation and prosperity of Washington College after its complete prostration. The trustees elected him president of the institution, in connection with his pastoral charge, less than four months after his arrival in Washington. This appointment he declined under the impression that the church demanded his whole time. He consented, however, to become "Acting President and Professor of Moral Philosophy," until a permanent president could be secured. The college was opened, accordingly, November 2d, 1830, with two additional professors, and some twenty boys of the vicinity exalted into students. And yet by means of extensive correspondence and other agencies abroad, and vigorous internal management, the third session under the administration of the temporary president ended with one hundred and nineteen young men enrolled, and the regular classes respectably filled. At that stage of progress he handed over the institution, in the spring of 1832, to Dr. McConaughy, by whom the presidency had been accepted.

In 1835, Dr. Elliott was called by the General Assembly of the Presbyterian Church, to take a professorship in the Western Theological Seminary, at Allegheny City, Pa. By an arrangement, this was the chair of Theology. In 1854, he was assigned by the Assembly, with his own cordial approbation, to the department of Polemic and Historical Theology. To this institution he devoted his best years and powers. To a Divine blessing upon his fidelity as much as to all other agencies, does the church owe the preservation of this school of the prophets, through a hard contest of fifteen years for its very life. "His great life work," said his colleague, Dr. Jacobus, in an address delivered at his funeral, "was his headship of this Theological Seminary during thirty-eight years. He came in his full prime—fifty years old—ripe in experience, and rich in solid resources for his generation. He found here only this venerable father who survives him, (Dr. Luther Halsey,) and who had taught the first regular class, and acted as the sole Faculty (a whole Faculty in himself) during seven years, and who, after a year of joint labours, gave up the charge to his hands. What labours! what struggles! what conflicts! what prayers and tears he gave early and late to this service! what a work to look back upon! Nearly a thousand men have gone forth from under his hand, a large majority of whom are to-day labouring as ministers of Christ throughout this land and in various foreign fields. Nearly a quarter of a century ago I came to his side, when his only associate Professor was commonly understood to be *in transitu*, and everything struggling up the hill. I have seen him in times of great darkness, but always his resource was in God. What dignity! what gravity! what simplicity! what suavity and urbanity! what fidelity in the most trying hours! As an instructor in Theology, in Church Polity, or in the Pastoral care, the church knew him to be wise and true, and all his pupils revered and loved him. As an ecclesiastic, he shone in the church courts, and lifted his voice most effectively in the administration and guidance of her affairs." Chief among his publications was a volume of "Letters on Church Government," which was well received at the time it appeared, and the work in which he rescued from oblivion in sweet biographical sketches the labours of Elisha McCurdy and the other noble pioneers of the Presbyterian Church in Western Pennsylvania, and which generations to come will read with interest and profit.

Dr. Elliott had many and marked evidences of the confidence and respect of his brethren in the ministry. He was frequently sent as a Commissioner to the General Assembly. He was Moderator of the Assembly of 1837, which held its sessions in Philadelphia. He was returned to the next Assembly, 1838, over which, after preaching an able opening sermon, he presided, under the rule, until its organization by the election of his successor. It was during this brief space that the rupture of the Presbyterian Church into the "Old School" and "New School" divisions was finally accomplished.

Dr. Elliott's private character was one of peculiar excellence. "This, after all," says Dr. Brownson,* "was the real stronghold of his influence. Vigorous and cultured intellect, superior wisdom, unfaltering energy, and a life-long service, all came to proportion and power in *the moral excellence of the man* to whom they belonged. In person he was above the medium size. He was genial and sympathetic in his feelings. His manners had the simplicity, candour, politeness and attractiveness of a true Christian gentleman. He was magnanimous and courteous, even in difference and contest. As he scorned unfair advantage in carrying his point, so he was ever able to detect and expose it in others. The law of uprightness ruled him both in public and private dealing with his fellow men. I have often heard from his lips the confidential story of his annoyances, and yet I never heard from him a purpose, or even suggestion, at war with the highest standard of truth and honour. He held the confidence of his brethren and the world, in full proportion to the intimacy which opened to their view the secret springs of his action. If even a foiled antagonist would attempt to cover his own confusion with the insinuation of artifice, where others saw only the sagacity of a man as truthful as he was wise, no words of defence were needed to beat back the base insinuation. His continued defence was in the estimation of good and discerning men. His friends were life-long in their trust and attachments. Both in secular and religious association, one principle animated him whose sure crown was the unqualified reliance of his fellow men upon his integrity. He did truth, and thereby ever came to the light.

"In *social sympathy*, Dr. Elliott's character deepened with advancing years. His home was always a centre of hospitality, even to serious encroachment upon his substance. So also poverty and sickness, trial and misery were sure of the offerings, at once, of his heart and hands. His thoughtful attentions to persons in humble life, his visits of tender affection to the abodes of distress, his letters of Christian comfort to the bereaved—enough to fill volumes if published—his constant fidelity in turning social opportunity to the end of the soul's salvation—all these habits of his active life grew upon him more and more as conscious infirmities foretokened 'the night, when no man can work.'

---

* An Address commemorative of the Life and Character of David Elliott, D. D., LL. D.

"On the eighteenth day of March, 1874, he gently fell asleep in Jesus—as gently as an infant upon its mother's breast. The sun of his life set in a cloudless sky, giving, in its lengthened rays, a sweet token to all who beheld him, of the glorious day without clouds or tears, upon which his immortal eyes were then opening. We could not weep, but only praise God, as we bore his precious body to the beautiful city of the dead, and reverently laid it down to rest by the side of his sainted wife, glad that even then their spirits were holy and happy together in the vision and fellowship of the glorious Redeemer.

> "'There no sigh of memory swelleth;
> There no tear of misery welleth;
> Hearts will bleed or break no more:
> Past is all the cold world's scorning,
> Gone the night and broke the morning
> Over all the golden shores.'"

JOSEPH JUNKIN.

WHEN the second George, of Hanover, was on the British throne; when the Susquehanna flowed from its sources to the Chesapeake, through an almost unbroken forest; and when Pennsylvania was a nascent province scarce sixty years old; there crossed that river at Harris' ferry, now Harrisburg, two young Scotch-Irish immigrants—Joseph and Elizabeth Junkin. They had come two years before, he from Monahan, in Ulster, and she from Tyrone, landing at New Castle, Delaware, and stopping for a time at the place where Oxford, Chester county, now stands. A previous immigration of Junkins had located at that place.

The name is probably of Danish origin, and it is likely that the family was descended from those adventurers from Denmark who centuries ago, took possession of parts of North Britain. The family had for many generations dwelt in and near Inverness. Most of them became Presbyterians and Covenanters, and during the persecutions under the House of Stuart, emigrated to the north of Ireland.

Elizabeth Wallace, wife of Joseph Junkin, was also of Scotch ancestry; her parents having come from Scotland to Ireland before the revolution of 1688. Her mother was left a widow, and was in Londonderry, and, with her family, endured the horrors of that siege, successful resistance to which gave William of Orange that vantage which established him upon the British throne, the champion of the Protestant religion and of regulated liberty. Said her great grandson: "She saw from the walls of glorious old Derry, the smoke of the most important gun ever fired—the lee-gun of the Mountjoy, which righted the ship, broke the boom, relieved the starving garrison and city, forced the allies to raise the siege and retreat upon the Boyne, where the arms of William and of liberty triumphed, and completed the blessed revolution of 1688."

Joseph Junkin and Elizabeth Wallace were married at Oxford, after their arrival in America; and not long after their marriage came to the Cumberland valley, then Lancaster county, and "took up" five hundred acres of land, including the site of the present town of New Kingston. He might have secured ten times that quantity of land, for more than that lay unoccupied around his claim, and the only cost of obtaining a title was that of surveying and the land office fees. But he invested his money in improvement, and in building a stone house, which is standing to this day.

In this house, Joseph Junkin was born, January 22d, 1750. He had two sisters older than himself, Mary, who became Mrs. John Culbertson, and Elizabeth, who died young; and one sister and two brothers younger than himself, John, who died without issue, and Benjamin, the grandfather of the Hon. Judge Benjamin Junkin, of Perry county.

During the childhood of the subject of this sketch, the valley was subject to stealthy incursions of the Indians, who were very bold and bloody, after the defeat of Braddock. Sometimes the family had to fly to Chester county in dread of Indian hostility; and often Joseph, when a child, and the other children were hidden in the flax patch or the corn field at night for concealment from the marauders.

The father of Joseph Junkin died during the war of the Revolution, in 1777; the mother survived till 1796. The first place of public (Presbyterian) worship in this part of the valley was upon her estate, just north by east of where New Kingston now stands, three hundred yards from the old stone house. It was known for many years as "The Widow Junkin's Tent," and consisted of rude seats beneath the forest shades, with a "tent" or shelter for the preacher, braced against the trunk of a huge black oak, furnished with a bench for a seat and a board for the Bible. There Black, and Cuthbertson, and Dobbin, and others, preached the precious Gospel.

The landed estate was divided between Joseph and Benjamin, the latter retaining the homestead and the eastern portion of the land. Joseph received the western portion of the estate, and built thereon, in 1775, a substantial stone house, which is still standing, and is the country seat of Mr. Kanaga, the proprietor of the Girard House, Philadelphia, whose father bought it from Mr. Junkin, in 1806.

When the war of Independence began, young Junkin, then in his twenty-fifth year, took a prompt and decisive stand in favour of the patriot cause, as did all the Scotch-Irish Presbyterians and their descendants. Many incidents in the history of the valley, connected with that struggle, might be related did space permit. The writer of this sketch has heard its subject detailing many, but one of which will we find space to record.

Just before he marched to New Jersey, viz: in June, 1776, a large assembly of the inhabitants of the valley met in the public square, in Carlisle, to confer about public affairs. The idea of independence had been broached in Congress a few weeks before, and it was proposed to discuss and decide this question in this meeting. An eminent lawyer of Carlisle, Mr. W., made an earnest address, setting forth the folly and madness of the attempt at independence. He portrayed the vast weath and military power of Great Britain, in contrast with the poverty, weakness, and want of military resources of the colonies. He urged that we should seek nothing beyond a reasonable redress of grievances, and assured his hearers that an attempt to gain independence would result only in disaster and ruin to the colonies. When he had closed, another lawyer, William Lyon, made a short address, controverting the views of his predecessor, and then proposed that all who favoured independence should move to the north side of the "diamond," and those opposed to it to the south side. The great mass of the people, young Junkin and his brothers John and Benjamin with them, moved to the north side, three or four remained in the centre, but *none went to the south side.*

A few days after this, there was a battalion drill near Silvers' Spring, at which nearly all the people of the lower end of the valley who were not already in the army, were present. Whilst the parade was in progress, (it was now the 7th of July,) and whilst the men were marching through the bushes, and many were putting green branches in their hats as a token that they were willing to volunteer, a horn was heard, and a courier dashed up the road at full speed, announcing that independence had been declared at Philadelphia, three days before. A hand-bill copy of the declaration was given by the courier and read to the men, who unanimously and by acclamation ratified it on the spot, and a large company was at once raised and marched to the front.

Of that company Joseph Junkin was an officer. They were ordered to Amboy, in New Jersey, where they were employed in guarding the coast against the enemy, then in possession of New York. Such was the spirit of old Cumberland in that trying time.

His military engagements interfered seriously with his farm improvements, and deferred his marriage till towards the close of the war. When the army went into winter quarters, in 1776-7, he returned home. Next year he again volunteered, and continued in active service till wounded and compelled to come home. His brother John marched to the front in the fall of 1777. In a letter to his son George, written in 1819, he says:

"The Battle of Brandywine was fought September 11th, 1777, in which I commanded a company. Our army was forced to retreat. Great confusion followed, both among the troops and in the surrounding country. The dead found an asylum, but there was none for the wounded. On the 16th, we had a sharp skirmish with the enemy near the White Horse tavern, in Chester county, in which I received a musket ball through my right arm, which shattered the bone. I could find no place to retire to for cure or subsistence. The army was in motion; I could not go with them. A horse was procured by Captain Fisher; a rope was my bridle; a knapsack stuffed with hay was my saddle; and thus equipped and wrapped in my bloody garments, I arrived at home—ninety miles—in three days. I then took boarding in Carlisle, put myself under the care of Dr. Samuel A. McCoskry,* and paid all expenses attendant upon my cure, besides losing a full year of the prime of my life. I was urged to place myself upon the pension list, under the law of 1787, but, being in good circumstances, declined it."

He does not mention in the foregoing letter, what he sometimes detailed to his children, the fact of his escape from the British lines after he was wounded. Having fainted from loss of blood, the enemy passed him by, taking him for dead. Night came on. A shower of rain revived him. He arose, and dreading to fall into the enemy's hands, made his way across woods and fields. At nightfall he approached a farm house faint and weary. As he opened the kitchen door, a stout Quaker, the owner of the house, promptly approached him and gently pushed him back out of the house. The Quaker had perceived at a glance that the new arrival was an American officer, and being a true patriot, desired to save him from capture and perhaps death. As he closed the door behind him, he whispered, "Friend, thee is in great danger; my house is full of British officers, and there, in my meadow, is encamped a squadron of British horse; but I will try to save thee." He took him first to his barn and made him a bed of hay. But in a few minutes after leaving him, he returned saying, "Friend, thee must out of this; the officers have demanded hay, and doubtless will take it in spite of my refusal: come!" He took the wounded man to a spring-house loft, unbound some bundles of flax and made him a bed. Shortly afterwards, the worthy Quakeress came to the wounded officer with some warm milk and bread and some linen cloths, with which last she dressed his wound.

Before daybreak the next morning, the patriotic Friend came to the wounded man, assisted him to disguise himself by putting his fatigue dress, (the hunting shirt,) over his other dress, and conducted him down the ravine formed by the spring run to the main road, and pointed him the direction in which Washington's army had retreated.

---

* Father of Bishop McCoskry, of Michigan.

The wounded soldier had made some progress by sunrise, and was full of hope of rejoining his regiment, when, as he was crossing a brook, two dragoons, dressed in British scarlet rode up, made him prisoner and ordered him to march between their horses' heads. They asked him if he belonged to the rebel army. A Covenanter could only tell the truth. They inquired what brigade and regiment he belonged to. He replied, " Gen. Jas. Potter's brigade, second regiment." They marched him about a mile, and he resolved not to endure the horrors of a British prison ship, but determined upon escape or death. He had fixed in his mind that, about the midst of a wood which they were approaching, he would make a spring into the forest, and hoped that he might escape the fire of his captors, and that they could not pursue him through the under brush. But just as his nerves were strung up to the effort, and within a few paces of the thicket into which he was resolved to plunge, his rude captors halted, pointed down a dim road through the forest, and said, "You will find your regiment encamped in a field just beyond this wood—we are Americans in disguise." The revulsion of feeling had well nigh proved too much for the enfeebled man; he sank to the ground, but was soon able, with the assistance of the perpetrators of the rough jest, to reach his company. The captors were scouts dressed in British uniform, and sent out for intelligence of the enemy's movements; and as young Junkin wore a hunting shirt over his uniform, they had mistaken him for a private. His descendants have never ceased to cherish gratefully the memory of the patriotic Quaker, GEORGE SMITH, and his gentle wife, who saved the life of the wounded soldier.

In 1778, the British Indians became troublesome on the head waters of the Juniata; and the subject of this sketch, although exempt from military duty, his wound not being fully healed, volunteered to repel them, and marched with the troops for that purpose. He assisted in building a fort near to where Hollidaysburg now stands.

In May, 1779, he was married to Eleanor Cochran, by the Rev. Alexander Dobbin, D. D., by whom he had fourteen children, ten sons and four daughters, all of whom, except the youngest, were born in the stone house built by him in 1775, and still standing. His youngest son was born in Mercer county, Pa. Eleven of his children reached adult life and married. Two of his sons, the fourth and the youngest, were ministers of the Gospel, two of his daughters were married to ministers, and, including these, with other sons and sons-in-law and grand-children, there have already been amongst his descendants fifteen ministers and sixteen ruling elders—in all thirty-one Presbyters, and he was himself a ruling elder in the Associate Reformed Church.

He continued to live at his home in the valley until the spring of 1806. He was a Justice of the Peace and a practical surveyor, and was a highly esteemed citizen. In 1806, he removed with his family to "Hope Mills," in Mercer county, where he continued to reside until February 21st, 1831, when he died, in the eighty-second year of his age. He was self taught, but a man of solid and accurate English education. He was remarkable as a clear, consecutive reasoner, and wrote with a vigorous style. He was a Calvinist in religion, a Democrat in politics, and was somewhat ready to defend, with voice and pen both classes of opinion.

CAPTAIN JOHN JUNKIN,

THE son of the foregoing, was born in East Pennsboro township, Cumberland county, on the 12th of September, 1786. He was the oldest of ten sons, and was of eminent promise from early boyhood. He and his brothers, Joseph, George and Benjamin, received their earlier education in a schoolhouse which long stood on the border of their father's estate. In 1805, the father having purchased extensive lands in Mercer county, including the future family seat, at Hope Mills, John and Joseph were sent out to commence the opening of a farm and the erection of mills at that place. They erected a cabin, and built a mill dam on the Neshannock creek, and returned to Cumberland, to accompany, the next spring, the entire family to the new home in the west. This migration was effected in the spring of 1806. In the entire enterprise the subject of this sketch was his father's most efficient and wise helper, and when the new home was in process of being established, the father and mother found, in their elder son, at once a safe counsellor and an energetic leader in the work.

From 1806 to 1811, John Junkin continued in his father's house, and in the energetic performance of the duties of an elder son; building the family mansion, which is still standing; building mills; opening out the farm, and the various employments incident to frontier life.

Meantime he was attracting notice in the new settlement as a young man of fine talents, great probity, industrious habits and public spirit. He possessed more of the elements of popularity than perhaps any member of the family. He was a universal favourite amongst the young men of the county, and had he lived and remained in civil life he would have risen to any position which he desired, and which was in the gift of the people.

But before the family had been six years in their new home the storm clouds of war began to darken the horizon of our country, and in 1812 the conflict with Great Britain began. At the time war was declared the subject of this sketch was First Lieutenant of the "Mercer Blues," a company which had been organized in the town of Mercer and vicinity. The company, to the number of some eighty-four men, volunteered to march to the defence of the northwestern frontier, left defenceless by the surrender of Fort Detroit by General Hull. The

Captain of the company resigned and sent a substitute, and Mr. Junkin was elected Captain and led the company, first to Pittsburgh, and thence, with Gen. Crook's brigade, to Fort Meigs, on the Maumee river, where they rendered effective assistance to General Harrison, in the defence of that fortress and frontier.

"The Mercer Blues" were a remarkable body of men—nearly all Presbyterians, and most of them professors of religion. They found their own uniform, rifles, bibles and psalm books; and morning and evening worship, unless interrupted by alarms or extra military duty, was kept up by the inmates in every tent with the exception of two, and in those two the Captain often officiated. But the company was remarkable as a model of *drill* and *military morale*. Gen. Harrison often commended them as models for imitation.

One of the most perilous expeditions of the campaign was as follows: Gen. Harrison had heard that the brig Queen Charlotte (the same that was afterwards captured in Perry's victory) was lying ice-bound in Lake Erie, off Malden, and as it was known that she was laden with valuable military stores, in addition to her own armament, the General laid a plan to capture her, possess himself of her stores, and burn the vessel. He sent for Captain Junkin, and asked him to lead the expedition, offering him the choice of the men to accompany him. Junkin accepted the offer, and picked his men chiefly from his own company and Captain Dawson's, from the same county. Provided with hand sleds to carry away the stores in case of success, and well armed and accoutred for the expedition, they set forth, reached the lake opposite Malden, traversed its frozen bosom until they came in sight of the brig, but, to their great disappointment, found a quarter of a mile or more of open lake between the *terminus* of their icy bridge and the object of their search. Having no boats they were constrained to return, but the same ground swell that had caused the opening of the ice on the Malden side had begun to crack it in their rear, so that it was with extreme difficulty and peril that they reached the American shore, having often to take the planks off their sleds to bridge the chasms in the ice field. By great presence of mind and skilful engineering the entire command got safely to shore.

Walter Oliver,[*] a brother-in-law of Captain Junkin, (having married his sister,) was First Lieutenant of the company. Mr. Oliver was also a native of Cumberland valley, having been born near Big Spring, (Newville,) about 1780. A millwright by occupation, he had come to Hope Mills in that capacity, and when the war broke out he left his

---

[*] Brother of Isabella Oliver, the Poetess, afterwards Mrs. Sharp, of Newville.

young wife and child and marched to the defence of his country. He was long a highly reputable citizen of Mercer county, represented her for many years in the Legislature of the Commonwealth, held other offices of trust, and was for several years the Captain of the "Blues," who kept up their organization for many years after the war was ended. Mr. Oliver died, as did also Eleanor, his wife, within a few days of each other, in 1836. Captain Junkin had married in 1800 his cousin Martha, the daughter of Hon. Wm. Findley, of Westmoreland county, and who represented that district in Congress for twenty-two consecutive years. Thus, also, Capt. Junkin left a wife and daughter behind him when he marched to Fort Meigs. It pleased Providence that he was never again, in this life, to see his young wife. She died during his absence. The daughter still survives, the wife of the Hon. Wm. M. Francis, of Lawrence county, and mother of the Rev. John Junkin Francis, of Freeport, Pa.

Joseph Junkin, brother of the Captain, was ensign of the company, and bore an active part in the campaign. He was born at the same place in Cumberland where all of the family save one were born, and his numerous descendants live some in Pennsylvania and some in Iowa.

The attention of General Harrison having been drawn to Captain Junkin, as a young man of marked military talent, he mentioned him favourably to the Secretary of War, and the result was that soon after returning from the northwestern campaign he received a Captain's commission in the regular army of the United States. Shortly after this commission issued, and whilst the Captain was away from home on business, east of the mountains, the people of Mercer county adhering to the Democratic party nominated him for a seat in the State Legislature. This nomination he declined, on account of his military engagements. He was ordered upon recruiting service in the town of Mercer, where his personal popularity soon drew into the service a large number of men; but before marching orders came a malignant fever broke out amongst the men in the barracks, and, in bestowing personal attentions upon the sick men, he contracted the disease, and died April 27th, 1814. The writer of this sketch has seen old men who had been under his command, shed tears to his memory long after his decease. One of these, nearly twenty years after the death of his beloved Captain, said, as he tearfully gazed upon his tombstone, "he was a father to his men."

GEORGE JUNKIN, D. D., LL. D.,

SON of Joseph, above named, was born at the family seat in Cumberland, November 1st, 1790. His godly mother had from his birth devoted him, in her thought and in her prayers, to the Gospel ministry. He received his primary education in the school-house mentioned in a former sketch; although the parents bestowed more than ordinary attention in assisting the education of their children. He removed, with the family, to Hope Mills, in 1806, and took an active and energetic share in the making of that new home. He entered Jefferson College, Pa., May, 1809; graduated in September, 1813; and shortly afterwards, viz: in the early part of October, set out from his home at Hope Mills, to repair to Dr. Mason's Theological Seminary in New York. He crossed the mountains on horse-back, the usual mode of traveling in that day. *En route* he visited his native place in Cumberland, and spent a short season there. He crossed the Susquehanna on a ferry flat at Harrisburg, and proceeded to Philadelphia. There he met his life-long friend, the late Rev. John Knox, D. D., who was also on his way to the Seminary, having already been there one session. Dr. Knox was from Marsh Creek, Adams county. The young students, after a few days' tarry in Philadelphia, proceeded to New York, by the "Swift-Sure" line of stage coaches, and reached Somerville, N. J., the first day, and New York by the evening of the second. Now we can pass from city to city in two hours.

In passing through Pittsburgh, the student met his soldier brother, and spent the night with him. It was their last earthly interview.

On account of the fact that a voluminous biography of the subject of this sketch has been written by his younger brother, and extensively circulated, it is not deemed necessary to enter minutely into the details of his laborious, eventful and useful life. The prominent points of his history is all we can find space for, and those in but meagre outline.

He continued at the seminary until September, 1816. During his sojourn in New York city, he assisted in the organization of the first Sabbath school. At the date just mentioned he and three other students, his life-friend, Joseph McElroy, and two others named Lee, set out for western Pennsylvania in a two-horse wagon, and by the 15th of that month arrived at Noblestown, in Allegheny county, where the

Presbytery of Monongahela (Associate Reformed) was met. He was examined, and presented all his trials, which all proved satisfactory, except his opinions upon Catholic communion. He did not hold to close communion. The Presbytery did, and refused to license him to preach on that account. He then asked a dismission to put himself under the care of the Big Spring Presbytery, in his native valley. Upon this the Presbytery reconsidered their decision and licensed him to preach the Gospel.

His first sermon was preached in Butler, Pa., on the 17th of September, 1816, and from that time till a few days before his death, he continued to preach, with scarce a Sabbath's intermission, and often during the week. His first ministerial settlement was as a missionary in the city of Philadelphia, where he began his labours in March, 1818. The centre of his operations was in Mrs. Duncan's church in Thirteenth street, an edifice erected in pursuance of the will of Mrs. Margaret Duncan, who had, during a storm at sea, vowed to build a house for God, if he would spare her life and the lives of her fellow voyagers. He was ordained as an Evangelist June 29th, 1818, by the Associate Reformed Presbytery of Philadelphia. The ordination took place in Gettysburg, in the very place where forty-five years afterwards he laboured amongst the wounded and the dying, the victims of the terrible battle fought at that place.

In October 1818, he visited Milton, Pa., and preached to a congregation of the Associate Reformed Church in that vicinity. His visit resulted in a call, and he became the pastor of that people the same year, and continued to serve them, and a congregation which he gathered in the borough of Milton, in connection with White Deer church, for eleven years.

On the 1st of June, 1819, he was married by Dr. Mason to Miss Julia Rush Miller, of Philadelphia, a most estimatable lady, who for thirty-three years proved to him, indeed, a help-meet. He was installed pastor at Milton in October, 1819. In 1822, steps were taken by the General Assembly and the Associated Reformed Synod for a union of the two bodies; and this was so far consummated by 1824 that Mr. Junkin united with the Presbytery of Northumberland. He was cordially received; for his power had been felt from the time of his advent to that region, in the co-operative work of the church. He was soon recognized as the leader in the Bible, Sabbath School, and Temperance causes, and was much beloved and well sustained in his efforts, by his brethren in the ministry, and by all good people in that part of the state. He spent eleven years in pastoral and other labour in that field, and was the instrument of many great reforms in the churches, and in the community. He was a chief instrument in founding the Milton Academy, which, under the Presidency of that celebrated teacher, Dr. Kirkpatrick, has given so many distinguished men both to church and state, at home and abroad. As auxiliary to the Missionary, Bible, Education and Temperance causes, he established a paper called the *Religious Farmer*, the editorial work of which he added to his other toils. Being a practical and scientific agriculturalist, he did much to improve the style and methods of husbandry in that part of the state. His pronounced advocacy of the right, and opposition to the wrong, of course, roused the resentment of the bad, and whilst the wicked respected him for his consistency, zeal and public spirit, they hated him as cordially as he was warmly beloved by the friends of good order.

Whilst at Milton he was pressed into a controversy upon the opinions of *Socinus*. A learned and accomplished Unitarian minister, an Englishman by birth, assailed the doctrine of our Lord's Divinity through the local press, and Mr. Junkin defended it with such ability and effect as to banish the errors and the errorist from that community.

In 1826, Mr. Junkin was seriously ill, and for a time his life was despaired of. Mrs. Junkin had asked a pious carpenter, who was building a barn for them, to conduct family worship in a room adjoining the one in which her sick husband lay, but in his hearing. On one occasion the carpenter, a Baptist, asked an apprentice of his to lead in prayer. The youth did it with so much unction and earnestness, as deeply to impress the mind of the sick pastor, and when the worship was over, and the men had gone to their work, Mr. Junkin said to his wife: "If God spares my life, that young man shall enter the ministry." He did recover speedily, and the pious Baptist generously released his apprentice from the remainder of his time, and Mr. Junkin assisted him to prosecute his studies. After attending the Milton Academy, the young carpenter graduated at Jefferson College and the Princeton Seminary, and was, together with the lovely John Cloud, the *first Missionary of the Church to Africa*, where they fell, early martyrs to the blessed cause. Previous to this Mr. Junkin had assisted the writer of these lines and others, in their preparatory studies; but it was MATTHEW LAIRD, whose case awakened fully in the pastor's mind that interest in the cause of ministerial training which led him to enter the field of education, in which he spent the greater portion of his life.

In the summer of 1830, Mr. Junkin had been elected President of the "Pennsylvania Manual Labour Academy," located at Germantown. He accepted the appointment, and bade a tearful adieu to the people of his pastoral charge, who fully reciprocated his affection, and early in August of that year repaired to Germantown and entered upon his public duties. There he laboured assiduously until the spring of 1832, when having been elected President of Lafayette College, an institution existing only on paper, he accepted, and removed to Easton and began the arduous work of founding a college. Most of the students of the Academy at Germantown accompanied him to Easton, and constituted the nucleus of the future college, an institution which under him and his successors, and especially under the present efficient President, Cattell, has risen to be one of the best colleges of the land.

The story of the founding of Lafayette College is a romance of real life, as thrilling in its details as the stories of fiction, but we have not space for it here. Let it suffice to say, that it is a story of toil, trial, heroic sacrifice, and of wondrous perseverance under discouragements that would have crushed any ordinary man. During his presidency at Easton, the great doctrinal and ecclesiastical difficulties, which resulted in the disruption of the Presbyterian Church, approached their acme. Every friend of Presbyterianism desired that, by some process, the strife should be ended and peace restored; but none seemed willing to assume the unpleasant responsibility of using the *regular discipline* of the church as an instrument of adjustment. At length, George Junkin, who had been doctorated by his *Alma Mater*, in 1833, felt it to be his duty to step forth and secure a decision of the church courts upon the question, "Is the New School Theology to be acknowledged as being consistent with the teaching of the Holy Scriptures and the Standards of the Presbyterian Church?" He, therefore, entered formal charges before the Second Presbytery of Philadelphia against the Rev. Albert Barnes, a member of the same, and pastor of the First Presbyterian Church of that city. We have not space to detail the particulars of this great and important trial in its various stages, in the Presbytery, the Synod, and the General Assembly. It is part of the ecclesiastical history of the times, and is fully recited in Dr. Junkin's biography. Suffice to say, the Presbytery, by a decided majority, acquitted Mr. Barnes; the Synod, by as decided a majority, found him guilty of the charges, and suspended him from the ministry; and the General Assembly, by a close vote, reversed the decision of the Synod, and restored Mr. Barnes to his clerical functions, but advised some modification of his terminology. This decision of the General Assembly convinced the Old School that they must either tolerate a Semi-Pelagian theology in the church, or take vigorous measures for eliminating it. The conflict went on and resulted in the excision of certain

Synods in 1837, and the secession of the New School party in 1838, when a clear majority appeared against them. It is due to Dr. Junkin to say, that even his opponents attested the *purity* of his *motives*, and the Christian spirit and temper exhibited by him. Mr. Barnes, himself, bore magnanimous testimony to the fairness and Christian spirit with which his prosecutor had conducted the trial. His biographer has shown that Dr. Junkin's motto, "Union in the truth," which he always avowed as the object of the prosecution, has been marvellously realized in the recent re-union of the two branches of the Presbyterian Church. Mr. Barnes and his prosecutor both lived to see a steadfast approximation to the simple and obvious interpretation of the standards. The former greatly modified the language of his books, and the latter rejoiced in the fact that, after the heat of the conflict was over, the great men of the New School, always sound themselves, were disposed to insist that the few erring brethren among them should pay greater regard to the nomenclature of the Standards.

In the spring of 1841, Dr. Junkin, upon unanimous election of its Board of Trustees, became President of Miami University, at Oxford, Ohio. The institution was a good deal demoralized in its discipline; and the Trustees requested him to restore discipline and elevate the standard of scholarship. This he did very effectively and accomplished a good work for education and religion during his sojourn in Ohio. Meanwhile there was growing up at Easton and in Lafayette College, a desire that the founder should be recalled to the head of that institution. In this the Trustees unanimously concurred—even those who had for a time assumed an unfriendly attitude. He was re-elected President in the fall of 1844, and such was his love for that favourite spot and enterprise, that he accepted and returned to Easton. Under his administration the College steadily grew in numbers and in influence, although still struggling with pecuniary difficulties.

Meanwhile his fame as an educator had spread over the nation, and his services were sought for elsewhere. In 1848, he was elected President of Washington College, Va., a well endowed institution, now Washington and Lee University. He felt it to be his duty to accept, and bidding another sad adieu to Lafayette and to Easton, he repaired with his family to Lexington, Va. There he spent perhaps the happiest period of his life. His toils were not arduous, at least in regard to the pecuniary interests of the College. He was surrounded by men of high culture, and his family had every social advantage. A volume, nevertheless, could be filled with interesting details of his labours in that field, for he was a man of work, wherever he was, and one whose public spirit led him to throw himself, heart and soul, into every scheme for doing good.

There he continued to labour until the deep mutterings of our terrible civil war broke upon his ear. He did all that man could to avert that calamity. He wrote, he spoke, he reasoned, he prayed against the madness of secession. His family had taken root in the South. Two of his daughters had married Virginians, the one Col. Preston, the other Major Jackson, both Professors in the Virginia Military Institute. Two of his sons were settled in pastoral charges in Virginia, and were married to Southern ladies. His property was there; there he had buried his beloved wife, a daughter, and other dear ones, and it was a sore trial to leave all. His daughter Eleanor had married the afterwards renowned Gen. (Stonewall) Jackson. Both his sons-in-law were with him in Union sentiment, up to the moment that an army was called out. Rockbridge county, the one of which they were citizens, voted more then ten to one against secession, and there was a large majority against it in the whole State. But the rabid politicians prevailed, Virginia seceded, the rebel flag was hoisted over his College, and George Junkin left her soil and came to the North.

His exodus from Virginia, with his widowed daughter and his niece, would constitute a touching episode in the history of the war. He was now nearly seventy-one years old. He drove his own span of horses in the family carriage from Lexington *via* Williamsport and Hagerstown, to Chambersburg. There he rested a little while with his friends, the Kennedys. He was now in his native valley of Cumberland, and terrible as the times were, he luxuriated in its beauties and its memories. He visited the birth place of his mother in Franklin county, he visited the room at New Kingston in which he had been born nearly seventy-one years before, and thence proceeded to Philadelphia, where, in the bosom of the lovely family of his third son and namesake, he found a pleasant home for the remainder of his days.

But George Junkin could not be idle, his heart was on fire with zeal for the Union and for that Government which his father had bled to establish, and he threw himself into the cause with all his eloquence and energies.

He wrote a book called, "Political Fallacies," in which he exposed the enormity of the doctrine of secession. He made addresses at public meetings, he wrote for the papers, and when blood began to flow he went to battle fields, and to forts and hospitals to minister to the bodily and spiritual wants of the wounded and the dying.

During the autumn and winter of 1862–3, and the summer of the latter year, he preached for the Canal street Presbyterian Church, New York, but did not abate his patriotic labours. The people were very fond of him and parted with him reluctantly, when an attack of illness compelled him to return to Philadelphia.

When the war was over, he threw himself into the cause of Temperance and the Sabbath, and performed Herculean work therein. Thus he laboured on until a few days before his death, preaching, writing, traveling and lobbying in the cause of God's day, and the Temperance cause. In these years he made many visits to different parts of the land, one especially, to his native place in the valley, spending part of his seventy-first birthday in the house in which he was born.

He was also busy with his pen, and published several valuable works of small size; such as his "Tabernacle," "Sabbatismos," "The Two Commissions," &c. But the chief labour of the last year was preparing for the press his Commentary on the Epistle to the Hebrews. This he completed three days before his death, and went to make arrangements for its publication, but these arrangements were not completed when he was suddenly called to a higher life. The work has since been published.

He died of *Angina Pectoris*, May 20th, 1868. His last recorded text was John XIV, 1. His last audible words were "Christ—the Church—Heaven!"

In 1856, Rutgers College conferred upon him the degree of Doctor of Laws, but he little prized earthly titles. He was a man of God, devout, humble, prayerful. A strong intellect, great powers of generalization and analysis, a keen and discriminating logic, a power of language always vigorous and clear, and often rising to the height of poetry, a glowing heart full of deep affection, a disposition firm as a rock when contending for the right, but gentle as a woman's in all social elements, made George Junkin the great and good man that he was, for all his powers were baptized with the Holy Ghost, and consecrated to Christ.

Amongst his published works are: A Treatise on Justification; A Treatise on Sanctification; Lectures on the Prophecies; Political Fallacies; Sabbatismos; The Gospel according to Moses; The Two Commissions; and his Commentary on the Hebrews. Many sermons and pamphlets might be added to this list; but it is deemed needless Cumberland valley need not be ashamed of him. He was a sojourner on earth; in Heaven he is at home.

REV. WILLIAM SPEER.

THE early life of Mr. Speer was spent in the neighbourhood where Gettysburg was afterwards built. He was born within the bounds of and connected himself with the Upper Marsh Creek Church, and pursued his Academical studies on ground which was since marched or fought over in the great battle.

He graduated at Carlisle, at the age of twenty-four, in 1788, and remained there until 1791, in the only Theological class taught by Dr. Nisbet, with whom he was a favourite student. He declined or prevented calls from several important points in the church, one of them to be a colleague of the venerable Rev. Dr. John Rogers, in the First Church, New York. His piety was of an ardent and self-denying type, and his style of preaching most searching and solemn. He accepted a call to the Falling Spring Church, Chambersburg, in 1794, but left it in 1797, on account of unwillingness of the people of that day to submit to evangelical discipline, and their persistence in customs as to the baptism of their children, and others of a kindred nature which he could not conscientiously uphold.

Being filled with a missionary spirit, he went with some excellent families to Chillicothe, the seat of the new government of the Northwest Territory, a vast and wild region in which his only predecessor was the Rev. James Kemper, at Cincinnati, and thus became the first chaplain of the infant state of Ohio. Domestic afflictions compelled him to return to Pennsylvania. From 1802 till his death in 1829, his life was spent in the united congregations of Greensburg and Unity. He was a friend of missions, and an earnest and effective advocate of sound and thorough education. For many years he was a Trustee of Washington College, and was the first Vice-President of the Board of Directors of the Theological Seminary at Allegheny. Mr. Speer was the first man to move in ecclesiastical opposition to the errors and moral evils of Free Masonry; and roused the Synod to adopt an able paper on the subject in 1820. On the committee to prepare it, of which he was chairman, were also the Rev. Dr. Matthew Brown, President of Jefferson College, Rev. Thomas E. Hughes, and Elders Thomas Hazleton and Thomas Davis. Mr. Speer was sent to the next General Assembly to advocate a memorial to it from the Synod upon the subject. There a debate of several days elicited strong pleas for and against the action of the Synod on the subject. It was decided against; but information was disseminated, and opposition aroused, which, within the next few years, arrayed in opposition to Free Masonry, as existing at that time, the emphatic religious sentiment of western and central Pennsylvania, then the conscience of many of the best people of western New York, Ohio, and other parts of the country, and in the end the political organization of a party which exerted much influence upon the history of the country.

Mr. Speer was the grandfather of the Rev. W. Speer, D. D., for many years a foreign missionary, but at present Secretary of the Board of Education of the Presbyterian Church, which position he has recently intimated his desire to resign with a view to continue labour among the Chinese.

HON. THOMAS DUNCAN.

THIS distinguished lawyer and eminent judge was a native of Carlisle. His father was an emigrant from Scotland, and one among the first settlers of Cumberland county. The subject of this brief notice was educated at Dickinson College. Adopting the law as his profession, he repaired to Lancaster and studied in the office and under the direction of Hon. Jasper Yeates, then one of the Judges of the Supreme Court of Pennsylvania. On his admission to the bar he returned to his native place and opened a law office. His rise in his profession was rapid. In a few years he was at the head of his profession in Cumberland and adjoining counties, which position he maintained until he was appointed a Judge of the Supreme Court of the State of Pennsylvania. This appointment was made by Governor Snyder, on the 14th of March, 1817, and was made in consequence of the vacancy on that bench created by the death of Judge Yeates, his preceptor.

After Judge Duncan's appointment to the Supreme Court he removed to Philadelphia, where he resided until his death, which occurred on the 16th of November, 1827.

At the bar Mr. Duncan was distinguished by quickness and acuteness of discernment, accurate knowledge of men and things, with a ready use of the legal knowledge he so largely possessed. He was also remarkably ready in repartee. An instance of this we will briefly state. Mr. Duncan's principal competitor at the bar was David Watts, Esq., a distinguished member of the Cumberland bar. Mr. Watts was a large and athletic gentleman, whilst Mr. Duncan was of small stature and light weight. On one occasion, during a discussion on a legal question in court, Mr. Watts, in the heat of his argument, made a personal allusion to Mr. Duncan's small stature, and said he "could put his opponent in his pocket." "Very well," replied Mr. Duncan, "if you do so, you will have more law in your pocket than you have in your head."

During the ten years that Judge Duncan sat upon the Bench he contributed largely to the admirable stock of judicial learning which the law reports of that period contain.

These opinions are contained in the Pennsylvania State Reports, commencing with the third volume of Sergeant and Rawle's Reports, and ending with the seventeenth volume of the same series, and they furnish an enduring monument to his great learning, industry and talents.

AMOS A. McGINLEY, D. D.

THE subject of this brief biographical sketch was born in the vicinity of Fairfield, Adams county, Pennsylvania, in the year 1778. He was the son of John McGinley and Jane McGinley, whose maiden name was Alexander. His grandfather, James McGinley, emigrated from Ireland at an early period in the settlement of what was then York county, and was one of the four persons who purchased from Carrol the tract of land known as "Carrol's Tract." His grandmother was a Hollander. Both his grandfather and grandmother, as well as his immediate parents, are represented as being intelligent, pious, and useful members of society and of the Presbyterian Church. Thus descended from pious parents, he was early dedicated to God in covenant. He was the subject of many prayers, and was trained up "in the nurture and admonition of the Lord." Nor did God fail in verifyiug to them his most precious promise:—"As for me, this is my covenant with them, saith the Lord; my Spirit that is upon thee, and my words which I have put in thy mouth, shall not depart out of thy mouth, nor out of the mouth of thy seed, nor out of the mouth of thy seed's seed, saith the Lord, from henceforth and for ever."

His conversion took place at an early period of life. We have no information in regard to the exercises of his mind when this great change occurred. But having experienced this change, it decided his future course. Having dedicated himself wholly to the Lord, and considering himself called upon to do all that in him lay for the salvation of sinners and the glory of God; and as no way suggested itself to him which was so full of promise and of hope as the work of the ministry, so did he feel himself called upon to prepare for this heaven-appointed office.

Having thus dedicated himself to the Lord Jesus for this service, he commenced his preparatory studies with this in view. His classical studies were pursued under the direction of the Rev. Mr. Dobbins, in Gettysburg, Pennsylvania. Having finished these, and occasionally teaching in order to meet the expenses incurred in receiving his education, he entered Dickinson College, then under the Presidency of Dr. Nisbet, where he was graduated in 1798. We have been told by an aged person who was present at the "Commencement" at which young McGinley was graduated, that his appearance was so extremely youthful, and he acquitted himself so handsomely on that occasion, in the speech which he delivered, that it was received with unbounded applause.

Completing his college course, he pursued his theological studies under the direction of his pastor, the Rev. William Paxton, D. D. He was licensed by the Presbytery of Carlisle, A. D., 1802, and having preached acceptably to the churches of Upper and Lower Path Valley, he was invited to become their pastor. He was ordained to the office of the ministry and installed pastor of these churches, A. D., 1803. These churches to which he was called, and in which he laboured the remainder of his days, are located in the northern part of Franklin county, Pennsylvania, in a beautiful, picturesque and fertile but secluded valley.

Dr. McGinley's preaching was entirely extemporaneous, or from brief skeletons which contained only the heads of the several divisions of his sermons, and they were not preserved after they had served their temporary purpose. They were very often elaborated on his way to church. His habit was to start early and ride slowly and alone, revolving in his mind the subject upon which he intended to preach. He always disliked the labour of composition, and during the latter part of his life, he ceased to write altogether. Once, on being asked by a young clergyman for a copy of one of his sermons, he told him he would have to take his head, for the sermon existed only in it.

His style was simple and unpretending, and conveyed his meaning clearly to the minds of his hearers. He studied brevity and possessed the power of seizing upon the salient points of a subject and expressing them in few well chosen words. This talent was sometimes turned to advantage in the deliberations of Presbytery and Synod. He would embody in short resolutions the main features or essential parts of matters under discussion, and they were not uncommonly adopted without change or amendment.

His colloquial talents were of a high order. He could talk to the young, and converse with those of maturer years, readily adapting his ideas and language to the capacities of each. He possessed also the faculty of making others talk, and could elicit sensible remarks from persons who were usually regarded as rather slow of understanding. He seldom appeared to so much advantage as when engaged in animated conversation. It had the effect of awakening the higher qualities of his intellect, and in the glow of excitement caused by the interchange of thoughts with another, he would give expression to grander sentiments and acuter observations than any that appeared in his more formal pulpit utterances. Not unfrequently his familiar discourses were enlivened by sallies of humour, but they did not verge unduly upon levity, and were never of a nature to wound the feelings of any one. Being free from egotism, he rarely made himself or his own affairs a topic of conversation—never offensively, and only when the circumstances or occasion rendered it necessary. It seemed to give him more pleasure to bring others forward than to appear personally prominent. He was not wont to monopolise in conversation, but was careful to observe the equities of it, and was as willing to listen as to talk. In his somewhat isolated situation, visits from his clerical brethren were a great source of enjoyment to him. They afforded opportunities for the discussion—always kindly—of theological and ecclesiastical questions, and the exhilaration of mind produced by these occasions, would sometimes continue very long after the visitors had departed.

Dr. McGinley's manner was uniformly polite and courteous, not artificial or studied—the offspring of a kind heart. Given to hospitality, his house was ever open to the visits of his people and their friends. Seldom did a week pass without bringing company, sometimes in considerable numbers, which always met a generous welcome. Young and old came and found entertainment suited to their respective ages. He sympathised with them in all their interests and affairs.

> "His ready smile, a pastor's love expressed;
> Their welfare pleased him, and their woes distressed."

He was a practical man, fertile in resources, skilful in adapting means to ends, and wise to compose difficulties. He was thus fitted to be the guide and counselor of his people, both in religious and secular matters, and was often called upon to exercise his talents in this way. They were wont to resort to him, whether it was a case of conscience to be resolved, some perplexity of business to be disentangled, or some difference between neighbours to be adjusted; and they seldom departed without being in some degree relieved of their troubles. In not a few instances, he wrote wills, and acted as administrator of estates and guardian of minor children, for which services he declined to receive compensation.

Dr. McGinley was a close observer of external nature, and quick to notice every change that occurred. His knowledge of meteorology, as it respected variations of weather, was somewhat astonishing, when it is considered that he acquired it by observation, unassisted by the instruments which are now used in noting changes of the atmosphere. He was the "Probabilities" of the neighbourhood, though his reports rarely circulated beyond his own family. He could, in any season of the year, prognosticate, with wonderful certainty, the kind of weather that would occur within any period of twenty-four hours. This knowledge he utilized in such a manner, that he was seldom interrupted by the state of the weather in his business or in the performance of his parochial duties, for he had usually anticipated and prepared for its probable condition.

Overtaken by old age and the infirmities of nature, and feeling himself unable to perform the duties of the pastoral office, Dr. McGinley resigned his charge, April, 1851, though he officiated as their stated supply until the ensuing October. For nearly fifty years he proclaimed the glorious Gospel of the blessed God to the same community, and then, sinking under the burden of years, he yielded his pulpit that others might occupy it, and hold up as he had done, Jesus crucified, as the hope of a guilty and perishing world. He died May 1st, 1856, aged seventy-eight years, leaving the wife of his youth and three children, one son and two daughters, to mourn his loss, but living in the expectation of a blessed re-union in heaven.

"The removal of Dr. McGinley from the church militant to the church triumphant," says one who recorded his demise, "is not only a loss to that portion of the church with which he was more immediately connected, but also to the church in general. In the Presbytery of Carlisle his loss is greatly felt. He was one of its most active and influential members, one of its wisest counsellors, and most judicious; a firm defender of the faith, and yet always kind and courteous, and conciliatory; one whom all who knew him loved and revered; one whose memory will be embalmed with filial affection in many a heart."

JOSEPH McELROY, D. D.,

AS another distinguished son of Cumberland valley. His parents were of the staunch and godly Scotch-Irish race. He was born near Newville, then called Big Spring, in 1791, or 1792. He obtained his primary education in the school of the vicinage ; but when quite a lad was deprived of his father by the hand of death. His mother, who was a woman of exemplary piety, and no little energy, removed her family to the county of Washington, near the borders of Allegheny. There he resumed his studies, and by great energy and industry, not only assisted his mother in the matter of livelihood, but at the same time was qualifying himself for entering college. At an early age he entered Jefferson College, Pa., and pursued his studies with that diligence which insures success. Soon after he graduated he proceeded to New York and entered the Seminary under that prince of theological teachers and preachers, Dr. John M. Mason. There he was the contemporary of such men as John Knox, W. W. Phillips, George Junkin, William R. Dewitt and others of like stamp, and he proved himself their peer in most of the elements of ministerial ability. Perhaps none of the students of Dr. Mason caught more of that great man's preaching power, than did young McElroy.

Having completed his theological studies, he returned to west Pennsylvania, and presented himself to the Associate Reformed Presbytery of Monongahela, as a candidate for licensure. His examinations and trial exercises were highly creditable, but, like George Junkin, he did not believe in *close communion*, and like that fellow student, he was on the point of being refused license for that heresy. But inasmuch as he had no disposition to propagate his opinions on that subject, and was willing, whilst a probationer, to abstain from preaching on a question so non-essential, they licensed him. This result was brought about by the intervention of the Rev. Dr. Riddle, undoubtedly the ablest man of the Presbytery and a man of the most Catholic spirit.

From the day of his licensure, Mr. McElroy became, as a preacher, a man of mark, not only in his denomination, but in the whole of western Pennsylvania. Possessing a tall and well proportioned form, a finely shaped head, long and gracefully moving arms and hands, a countenance expressive of benevolent earnestness, and a voice, firm, yet melodious and well modulated, he was from the first a very attractive and popular preacher. The writer of this sketch, then quite a small boy, has a distinct remembrance of the impression Mr. McElroy made upon an audience, when he first appeared as a probationer.

His services were, of course, eagerly sought by "the vacancies" in the Associate Reformed Church, but he declined all offers. Dr. Riddle, who served the largest congregation in the region of Pittsburgh, and who was beginning to feel the infirmities of years, desired him to become co-pastor with himself, but young McElroy preferred building on a foundation of his own laying, and he proposed to his venerable friend to commence a new enterprise in the city of Pittsburgh, then rapidly growing in manufacturing and commercial importance. Dr. Riddle approved of the undertaking. There was a small Associate Church, and a Covenanter, (Reformed Presbyterian,) in Pittsburgh, the former served by Dr. Bruce, the latter by Dr. Black; but no attempt had been made to establish an Associate Reformed congregation. Mr. McElroy undertook the enterprise single handed. He obtained from the County Commissioners leave to hold public service in the Court House, in Pittsburgh. It was customary, in all the western counties to use the Court House for such purposes; and all denominations shared in the privilege.

Mr. McElroy began his labours in 181–. His audiences were small at first, but did not long continue so. He was an eloquent preacher, a man of fine address and attractive manners; and his pulpit performances were a novelty in that Scotch-Irish city. With all the doctrinal exactness and logical arrangement of sermons demanded by the old fashioned Presbyterians, he added a freshness and energy of manner and an attractiveness of style, to which the people were unused. With all the disadvantage of Rouse's version of the Psalms, and the other peculiarities of his sect, the Court House became the point of attraction, not only for those who inclined to the Associate Reformed Church, but for the educated men and women of the city. Mr. McElroy was a *memoriter* preacher, yet never, or rarely wrote his sermons. He was a careful student, and never entered the pulpit without thorough preparation. Thus, independent of paper, and thoroughly master of his subject, he was free to add to the energy and graces of his style great force of delivery and action. Dr. Merron, the pastor of the First Presbyterian Church, the leading one of the city, was a good preacher, but was trammeled by manuscript. Mr. McElroy was free, graceful and energetic in delivery and action.

It was not to be wondered at, then, that he soon gathered round him a strong congregation, and that many men of high intelligence attended upon his ministrations. Such men as the late Judge Shaler, Judge Balwin, and others, became very much interested in his preaching. A commodious church was built, and thus was founded, by his labours, the First Associate Reformed Church of Pittsburgh. The great Mason, his theological preceptor, once rode on horseback from New York to Pittsburgh to assist his pupil at a communion season; which showed the appreciation of that gifted man of the subject of this sketch. When the Presbytery met for his ordination, objection was made on account of his opinions on Catholic communion; but a majority voted to ordain him; yet two ministers, who strenuously opposed the ordination, would not join in the laying on of hands, but remained during the solemnity in Bitler's tavern drinking gin.

Mr. McElroy was married to Miss Alison, of Canonsburg. George Junkin was his groomsman. The marriage was solemnized by the celebrated Dr. John McMillan, and when the groomsman tendered him the usual fee, he shook his head and declined taking the fee, quaintly saying, "No, no; dog won't eat dog." Dr. McElroy continued in a prosperous pastorate in Pittsburgh some years. Meanwhile his beloved wife died, leaving a daughter to his care. He subsequently married Mrs. Pointell, daughter of the late Judge Walker, and sister of the Hon. Robert J. Walker, late Secretary of the United States Treasury, and Senator of the United States. She was a woman of peculiar loveliness and talent.

Dr. McElroy was subsequently called to the church formerly served by Dr. Mason—the Scotch Church, New York—then located in Cedar street. The church had been weakened by various causes, one of which had been the organization of a new church in Murray street, for Dr. Mason; another was that the process of moving "up town" and leaving lower New York to trade, had already commenced. But under Dr. McElroy's eloquent and efficient ministry, and his great prudence and wisdom in counseling his people, the church rapidly grew in numbers and also in wealth, so that they soon contemplated a change of locality. As the result, the congregation purchased a site at corner of Grand and Crosby streets, and built a spacious and elegant church with marble front and pillars. There the Doctor's ministry was continued with eminent success, and the large edifice was filled with hearers, whilst the communion roll was vastly increased. Not many years had rolled around, when another migration of the congregation of the Scotch Church seemed necessary. Many of the people had gone far "up town" for their residences, and business was beginning to press around their place of worship. This change of locality was not so easily effected as the former. Many were slow to see the necessity of the change, but such was the influence and address of Dr. McElroy, and such the wisdom and skill of his management, that, with not many dissenting voices, the congregation agreed to the change. A site was procured upon that grand thoroughfare, Fourteenth street, near Sixth avenue, and the spacious and elegant brown stone structure was erected which is still occupied by the congregation. The church in Grand street was sold to another congregation of Presbyterians; and the Doctor's labours were transferred to the new locality.

There he continued to labour with great energy and success, until increasing years and failing health constrained him to seek assistance in the pastorate. He has had two co-pastors previous to the present one, Rev. Samuel M. Hamilton. Mr. McElroy still lives in a good old age. He has seen many afflictions, and has ripened under them for the better land. He has been four times married, and survives all his partners. They were all superior women; of eminent piety, prudence and social position. Miss McLanahan, a native of Cumberland valley, was his third, and Mrs. Jeffray, of New York, his fourth.

The subject of this sketch was a man of mark and of great influence, whilst strength remained. Not only was he a great preacher and attractive pastor, but he was a wise counsellor, and a man of great discernment, sound judgment and prudent discretion. He rarely spoke in the church courts, but when he did, it was with weight, such as usually secured the success of his recommendations. He was a man *for executive work*—knew men and how to measure them—knew things and how to manage them discreetly. He was, during his active life, a member of most of our Church Boards, and his counsels were always sought and heeded. His church was always amongst the most liberal in our body, and his business tact challenged respect in all affairs of public interest.

But he is passing away, and in a few weeks, or years at the farthest, he will be numbered with the distinguished sons of the valley who are no more on earth.

HON. JAMES HAMILTON.

JAMES HAMILTON was commissioned President Judge of the Ninth Judicial District by Governor McKean, on March 1st, 1806, and died at Gettysburg, the 13th of March, 1819, having gone there in the discharge of the duties of his judicial office. His age was sixty-seven years.

His wife was Sarah Thompson, a daughter of Gen. William Thompson, who was a man of distinction in his day, and an officer of our Revolutionary Army. Judge Hamilton had two children who survived him; a daughter, Susan H., who was married to the Rev. J. E. V. Thorn, of Carlisle, and died childless, on the 9th of November, 1867; and a son, James Hamilton, Esq., who died on the 23d of January, 1873; he never married, and the name and blood of Hamilton is now extinct in Carlisle. No one now at the bar of Cumberland county ever practised under Judge Hamilton. But few ever saw him. George Metzgar, Esq., now ninety-three years of age, but in the full possession of his mental faculties, is the only living member of the bar that practised when he presided.

Judge Hamilton was born and educated in Ireland, and was a lawyer when he came to Cumberland county. He held the office of Deputy Attorney-General or Prosecuting Attorney for several years before he was appointed Judge. In this office he gained the reputation of a most industrious officer. He prosecuted for conviction as unrelentingly as ever did a Crown officer in the land of his birth. So much was this the case, and so unpopular was the part he had taken, that when he took his seat on the bench he found inscribed on the walls of the old court house, in large letters, the words, "More Leniency."

It is likely that the education he received in Ireland had a part in forming his notions of duty, not only as a prosecuting officer but also as a presiding judge; for as soon as he assumed the judicial office, he required the sheriff and two tipstaves to escort him from his residence to the court house and thence back to his residence. This was a duty imposed on the sheriff which was not only new but irksome to him and the tipstaves, and one against which he rebelled, and, it is said, had himself relieved of by legislative interference. It was probably more waywardness of mind and the want of adaptation of manners to the disposition of the people, than lack of ability or confidence in his integrity, that led to his impeachment before the Senate. His trial took place and resulted in his acquittal, at Lancaster. His counsel was Wm. Hopkins, Esq., then an eminent member of that bar.

During his term the leading lawyers at the Carlisle bar were, David Watts, Esq., and Hon. Thomas Duncan, afterwards a Judge of the Supreme Court of the state. They were two of the most remarkable men then living in the state, of great fame and large practice. The characteristics of their minds were marked and widely different. Mr. Watts was a man of very positive character, of great grasp and vigour of mind, fonder of arguing his causes upon principle than hunting up cases with facts assimilated to the one at bar. Judge Duncan was a man of acute mind, of amazing industry, and was possessed of a retentive memory, and thus, when arguing a case in court, was ever ready with an authority at hand with which to persuade the court that the point was there ruled. Judge Hamilton also was a student, but lacked always self-confidence, and was more inclined to take what he was told ruled the case, than to trust to his own judgment or the reason of the law. This often led him, as it ever has done others, into error; and resulted in frequent reversals by the Supreme Court; and there is a legend here that the following strange Act of Assembly was passed at his instance, to get rid of the multitudinous authorities with which Judge Duncan was wont to confuse his judgment:

Be it enacted, etc., "That from and after the first day of May next, it shall not be lawful to read or quote in any court of this Commonwealth any British precedent or adjudication which may have been given or made subsequent to the fourth of July, in the year one thousand seven hundred and seventy-six. *Provided*, that nothing herein shall be construed to prohibit the reading of any precedent of maritime law, or of the law of nations." Approved the nineteenth day of March, one thousand eight hundred and ten. Pamphlet Laws, 1810, page 136.

Whether this was true or not, to any extent, it was no doubt certain that Judge Hamilton had a stormy time of it, holding the reins of justice with two such coursers as Watts and Duncan for leaders. As time advanced his career became more popular. It is likely that his manners changed, and the people began to recognize those excellent qualities which do not attract the casual observer; such as his industry, his prompt attention to the business of the court, and above all his unquestioned honesty. There has no blemish, not even the suspicion of a blemish, on his judicial integrity, come down to the present day. The universal judgment of men, from all that is known and all that is reported of him, is, that he was perfectly honest, impartial, just and upright.

JOHN BOGGS, M. D.

DR. JOHN BOGGS, born August 17th, 1787, was the youngest of six children.

Having lost his father at an early age, he was adopted by his uncle, Dr. Johnston, who was able to give him not only a classical education and the use of his extensive library, but the further advantage of association with his own cultivated mind. The boy thus adopted proved to be studious and reflective, and became a fine classical scholar. He was the college class-mate of Thomas McCulloh, Matthew St. Clair Clarke, John H. Clarke, and many others who were men of mark. After leaving college, Dr. Boggs studied medicine with Dr. McClellan, of Greencastle, and attended lectures at the University of Pennsylvania, in Philadelphia. Before he was through with his medical course, he was summoned home by the serious illness of his uncle, an illness which speedily terminated in his death. The will once made by this uncle, leaving John his heir, had been destroyed, and he found himself obliged at once to begin the practice of medicine. After trying Huntingdon county, Pa., and finding but a poor opening there for a physician, Dr. Boggs decided to try some other locality. He was offered great inducements in Cincinnati, but the declining health of his mother decided him to settle in Greencastle, and practice there as partner of his old preceptor, Dr. McClellan. He first went to Baltimore, passed an examination before the Medical Faculty of the University of Maryland, and received a diploma.

About this time, while the war of 1812 was in progress, a call came for recruits, and was promptly responded to by the young men of Franklin county. Dr. Boggs joined Company 3, Franklin county Volunteers, and went with it to Baltimore, September 8th, 1814. There his company, with several others, was formed into a regiment, of which Dr. McClellan was appointed surgeon, and Dr. Boggs assistant surgeon. They were emergency men, and their services were needed but a short time. After this Dr. Boggs returned to Greencastle, resumed the practice of medicine, and four years later married Isabella Craig, daughter of William Allison. His practice became very large and necessitated his traversing a wide circuit of country on horseback. He was singularly successful as a physician, and had a strong hold on the confidence and affection of the families under his medical care

Families, in times of sickness and affliction, looked as eagerly for the coming of Dr. Boggs, in his capacity of Christian friend and comforter, as in that of a healer of bodily illness.

In 1825, he was ordained an Elder in the Presbyterian Church of Greencastle, and in the discharge of the duties connected with this office was earnestly and actively engaged until his death.

A man of deep religious fervour and strong attachment to the church of his choice, he was yet wholly free from the narrowness of sectarian bigotry. Ministers of all denominations partook alike of the hospitality of his house—a house in which the "Prophet's Chamber" was rarely untenanted—and all were made equally welcome to his professional services. During his thirty years' residence in Franklin county Dr. Boggs received many proofs of the esteem and affection of the community, and now that more than a quarter of a century has passed since he joined the "great multitudes," his memory is still fondly cherished in many hearts.

On a monument in the burial ground of the "Old Red Church" there is an inscription, in few and simple words, that tells the sweet story of his life:

"John Boggs, M. D., born August 18th, 1787. Died July 12th, 1847.

"An eminent physician, a faithful elder, an affectionate husband, father and friend, a useful citizen, a humble Christian; his life was piety, his death was peace."

His wife died two years later, leaving five sons and three daughters.

HON. DAVID FULLERTON.

BORN in Cumberland valley, (1772,) and of the predominant stock, Mr. Fullerton was highly esteemed, and is, to this day, prominently remembered as one of the most honest, active and self-denying representatives who ever served the people.

He was for many years in the Senate of the state (in 1832) as representative from Franklin county, and also in the Congress of the United States, (in 1828.) While in the State Senate he gave much of his time and attention in opposition to the construction of the then projected railroad ("tape worm") from Gettysburg to Hagerstown, having as his most active opponent the late Hon. Thaddeus Stevens, of Lancaster. Mr. Fullerton, as he then stated in an address before the Senate, had "traveled over the mountains for upwards of fifty years, * * * and was confident the work was to cost double the amount of the estimate." He then produced and presented before that body careful estimates of the actual cost of the road, made after a personal survey of the whole route.

While in Congress Mr. Fullerton, in a matter of considerable agitation throughout the country, voted contrary to the views of some of his constituents, and for this act he was burnt in effigy in Carlisle. He was much incensed, and immediately resigned. He was urged to return, but declined. His whole career as a representative was marked by the highest integrity, combined with the most active measures for the good of the people.

Until near the close of his life Mr. Fullerton possessed considerable property in Greencastle and vicinity. He was also President of the bank at Greencastle, and conducted the leading mercantile business of the town. Certain irregularities of others in connection with the bank led him to make a total sacrifice of his very considerable wealth, soon after which he died, (February 1st, 1843.) The railroad and other improvements of Franklin county are in a great measure due to his disinterested energy in behalf of the public welfare.

In the support of the church he was always in the lead; an elder in the Presbyterian Church of Greencastle, a regular correspondent of Rev. Dr. Knox, of New York, and others prominent in the church, and the first superintendent of the earliest (1817,) Sabbath-school organization known of in the history of the place of his residence.

Mr. Fullerton was the father of the Rev. Matthew Fullerton, for a time the esteemed pastor of the Presbyterian Church in Hagerstown, but called from his earthly labours to his heavenly reward in his early ministry. He stood deservedly high in the community in which he so long lived. Many yet affectionately cherish his memory, as an intelligent, upright and useful citizen, keeping steadily in view life's great aim. Being dead, he yet speaketh.

COM. JESSE DUNCAN ELLIOTT, U. S. N.

JESSE DUNCAN ELLIOTT, was born at Hagerstown, Md., July 14th, 1782. His parents were Pennsylvanians by birth. Young Elliott lost his father when at a tender age. Colonel Robert Elliott, who was a contractor in the United States army, was killed in 1794 by the Indians, while traveling from Fort Washington to Fort Hamilton with his servant. The Colonel being somewhat advanced in life wore a wig. The savage who shot him, in haste to take his scalp, drew his knife, and seized him by the hair. To his astonishment the scalp came off at the first touch. The wretch exclaimed, in broken English; "damn lie." The body was recovered and was buried in the Presbyterian Cemetery, and was subsequently re-interred by his son, then Commodore Elliott, in the city of Cincinnati, and a suitable monument erected to his memory. The Colonel's pocket book, containing papers and a lock of hair, were purchased from the Indians by an American officer, at the Greenville Treaty, in 1795, who handed them over to the Colonel's son, since Commodore Elliott.*

Mrs. Elliott, by the death of her husband, was left in a destitute condition, and through the exertion of John Thompson Mason, a prominent citizen of that day, of Washington county, Md., Congress voted a small gratuity for the relief of the relict of a brave officer, and Thomas Jefferson, then President of the United States, deprecating the parsimony of the grant, forwarded warrants for midshipman in the Navy to young Elliott and his brother, St. Clair. The warrants were dated April 2d, 1804, and were accompanied by orders attaching the subject of our sketch to the Essex, Captain James Barron, while St. Clair was assigned to the President.

The Essex sailed for the Barbary States, on the Mediterranean, to humble them, negotiated a peace with Tripoli, and brought home the crew of the Philadelphia, who had been confined in the dungeons of that city. In 1807, Elliott was attached to the ill-fated Chesapeake, and again departed for the Mediterranean, which vessel while on her voyage, was attacked by the British ship Leopard, and as the attack

---

* In a letter received February 2d, 1875, from Mrs. Elliott, widow of Commodore Elliott, who is residing at York, Pa., at the advanced age of 83 years, she states that the scalp lock and pocket book spoken of are still in her possession, also the flag that was fought under, at Lake Erie.

was sudden, and from a vessel belonging to a nation with which our country was at peace, the Chesapeake was obliged to strike her flag.

Midshipman Elliott was promoted to a Lieutenancy on board the John Adams, April 23d, 1810, and was bearer of dispatches to our Minister, William Pinckney, at the Court of St. James. Lieutenant Elliott was a warm admirer of his country, and stood up for his flag in public and private. A little incident that occurred during his five months' stay in London, shows his spirit. After delivering some dispatches he was advised by Mr. Pinckney to take lodgings at Hatchell's Hotel, with a view of being near his residence. Whilst taking his tea, a stranger took a seat by his side, and noticing his uniform, which somewhat resembled the British, he observed, "I believe there is a Yankee frigate on the coast?" "Yes," was the Lieutenant's reply. "What's she after," he again observed, and added, "I reckon she's after the Chesapeake affair; they had better let that alone," &c. He then lavished all manner of abuse on the Yankees and their country. Lieutenant Elliott handed him his card, and said, "Sir, you are now addressing a Yankee, as you call us, and an officer of the frigate in the Downs. There's my card." The stranger not apologizing, Elliott stepped to the person in waiting, and said, "Sir, you put a scoundrel, instead of a gentleman in the box with me; he has grossly insulted me. There's my card; give it to him, and tell him I demand his." By this time the fellow had slipped out and was not heard of afterwards.

About this time, (1810–11,) Lieutenant Elliott conveyed an important message to Admiral Sir John Borles Warren, in the Patriot. This was the ill-fated schooner in which Colonel Burr's daughter was afterwards lost at sea. In 1812, he was attached to the command of Commodore Isaac Chauncey, at Sackett's Harbor, and on the declaration of war against Great Britain was sent by him to the upper lakes to purchase vessels, and make other preparations for the creation of a naval force in those waters. While he was at Black Rock engaged in the service, two armed British frigates, the Detroit and Caledonia, anchored, October 12th, 1812, near the opposite shore, under the guns of Fort Erie. A boat expedition was organized under Elliott's command, and the vessels were boarded and carried with but slight loss, a little after midnight, October 8th. The Caledonia was safely brought over to the American side, but the Detroit was compelled to drop down the river, passing the British batteries under a heavy fire, and afterward was burned by the Americans, most of her stores having first been removed.

He boarded, sword in hand, the two vessels of war, and carried them in ten minutes. He made one hundred and thi ty prisoners, with their officers, and released forty of his own countrymen from captivity. They belonged to the 4th United States regiment. Elliott entered, the first man on boarding, and opposed three of the enemy with no other weapon than a cutlass. The Hon. Henry Clay, when the new army bill was discussed in the House of Representatives, January, 1813, said: "The capture of the Detroit, and the destruction of the Caledonia, (whether placed to our marine or land account,) for judgment, skill, and courage on the part of Lieutenant Elliott, has never been surpassed."

For this gallant exploit Congress passed the following resolutions:

"That the President of the United States be and he is hereby authorized to have distributed, as prize money, to Lieutenant Elliott, his officers and companions, or to their widows and children, *twelve thousand dollars*, for the capture and destruction of the British brig Detroit; and also,

"*Resolved*, That the President of the United States be and he is hereby requested to present to Lieutenant Elliott, of the United States Navy, an elegant sword, with suitable emblems and devices, in testimony of the just sense entertained by Congress of his gallantry and good conduct in boarding and capturing the British brigs Detroit and Caledonia, while anchored under the protection of Fort Erie."

In July, 1813, he was promoted to the rank of Master Commandant, and appointed to the Niagara, a brig of about 20 guns, on Lake Erie. In Perry's engagement with the British squadron, September 10th, 1813, Elliott was second in command, and a gold medal was voted to him by Congress for his conduct on the occasion. This engagement has become such a matter of history, that we have been tempted to copy Commodore Elliott's own account of the part he took in the engagement, although it is of some length.

"On reaching the head of Lake Ontario I was shown a letter by Commodore Chauncey, received from Captain O. H. Perry, senior officer on Lake Erie, in which a call was made for one hundred seamen, and with me as their Commander, he was pleased to say, that he would insure victory on the waters of Lake Erie. The opportunity to me was too tempting to be permitted to pass away, and I consented, with the condition that, after the capture of the British fleet, I should be permitted to return and join him in the great action on Lake Ontario. Accordingly I departed for Lake Erie, taking with me more than one hundred efficient men. Meeting Captain Perry at Presque Isle, I at once took command of the Niagara, of twenty guns; directing all my efforts in the organization of a crew, and practising them constantly in the use of the battery, and I did not land at Erie until we had conquered the enemy. On the following day we proceeded to the head of the lake, off Sandusky, and received on board Gen. Harrison, the other general officers, Col. Gaines, the young and heroic Croghan, and the Indian chiefs who were with them. After their departure we proceeded to our new anchorage at Put-in-Bay, and there made our calculations for future operations. Our first move was to proceed with all our force in view to Malden, to challenge the enemy's fleet to combat, and to intimidate the Indians. But failing in our views, we returned to Put-in-Bay. Captain Perry then received a communication from General Harrison, stating that unless the difficulty of the British fleet on Lake Erie was removed, he might be compelled to go into winter quarters, and thus would reluctantly fail in his contemplated plans. This suggested the necessity of some desperate and effective act. Accordingly, Perry and myself agreed upon again going over and giving them a feeling shot, with the hope of thus drawing them out; and in the event of that failing, we were to procure boats and men from Gen. Harrison, proceed over in the night in two divisions, respectively led by each of us, and burn the British vessels under their own guns. However, after the second attempt to get them out, they appeared in the offing on the morning of the 10th of September, when we immediately got under weigh, and endeavoured to work out of port (having a head wind) for the combat. The wind soon favouring, we stretched out sufficiently clear, when signal was made to form the established order of battle; the Niagara in the van. Being to windward we had it in our power to fight them as we pleased, and with a kind of metal, if properly used, to make the action short. Believing from the frequent opportunities I had had of encountering the enemy, that I could successfully lead the van of our line, I previously solicited and obtained the position. But when approaching the enemy nearly within gunshot, Captain Perry made signal to come within hail. I backed my main-top-sails and edged off the line. Captain Perry then asked to converse with my marine officer, Captain Brevoort, of the army, whose family lived in Detroit, and he learned from him the name and force of each ship in the British line. The Detroit being in the van, Captain Perry remarked to me that as the enemy's senior officer was heading their line, he thought it his duty to lead ours, and ordered me to take his place, under the stern of the Caledonia. The change was accordingly made, and our line formed, as sworn to by all the witnesses examined on the point, before the Naval Court, at New York, in 1815. When within $1\frac{1}{4}$ miles of the enemy, their ship, the Detroit, with her long guns, commenced a fire upon the Lawrence, Captain

Perry, at the head of our line. A few minutes after, about 12 o'clock, M., (both lines on an angle of 150°)—the head of our line reaching only to the third vessel in theirs—the Lawrence rounded to and commenced firing, aided by the two gun boats on her weather bow.

"The British fleet was in the following order: Chippewa, Detroit, Hunter, Queen Charlotte, Lady Prevost, and Little Belt.

"The American, thus: Lawrence, with two schooners, Scorpion and Ariel, on her weather bow, distance from her two hundred yards; Caledonia and Niagara in close order with the Lawrence, perhaps half a cable's length apart, (about 120 yards,) and the four gun boats astern, distance three-fourths of a mile.

"Immediately after the Lawrence had opened her battery, the firing became general along our whole line. On perceiving the shot of all our carronades to fall short of the enemy, I ordered the long guns shifted over against them, knowing the distance to be too great, and observing the Queen Charlotte bear up from our fire, I determined to run through the line after her, and directed the weather braces to be manned for that purpose. But there stood by me as good a seaman perhaps as our Navy ever had in it; I allude to Humphrey McGrath, purser, and formerly a lieutenant in the service, who, observing my movements, asked me to pause a moment, and then directing my attention to the slackening fire of the Lawrence and her crippled condition, remarked that if the British effected the weather-gage we were gone. I at once saw the propriety of the observation, passed forward to the forecastle, (my flying jib boom over the stern of the Caledonia,) and ordered Lieutenant Turner to put his helm up sufficiently to allow me to pass. This he at first refused, stating that he was then in his station in the line. Afterwards, however, on a repetition of the order, he did so, changing his position perhaps fifteen yards, and letting me pass him, he again luffed up into his position. At this time the Lawrence ceased her fire entirely, and no signal being made, after the first, to form in the order of battle, I concluded that the senior officer was killed. The breeze now freshening, I observed that the whole British fleet drew ahead, cheering along their entire line. I then set topgallant sail, fore and aft mainsail and foresail, and passed within twenty yards of the Lawrence, still not seeing Captain Perry. Having now exhausted nearly all my twelve pound round shot, I ordered Mr. McGrath with a few brace men to proceed in my boat to the Lawrence and bring me all hers; and immediately steered directly for the head of the British line, firing continually my whole starboard battery on them as I passed. When I reached within two hundred and fifty yards of the beam of the

Detroit and ahead of the Queen Charlotte, I luffed on a wind, and commenced a most deadly fire, the Niagara then being the only vessel of our fleet in what I call close action. The British were just before cheering for victory, but their cheers were now turned into groans, and the blood ran from the scuppers of the Detroit and Queen Charlotte, like water from the spouts of your houses in a moderate rain. The Lady Prevost luffed from her station in the British line and attempted to cross our bow for the purpose, as I thought, of raking us. I immediately ordered the marines under Captain Brevoort to proceed to the bow of the ship and fire upon her, which had the effect to force her back into their line. While thus engaged, a boat was reported as coming from the St. Lawrence, and believing it to be my own boat with the shot, I directed Midshipman Smith to stand by and pass them out. He returned, however, with the report that it was not our boat, but one of the Lawrence's. I looked over the stern and saw Capt. Perry in it, whom I met as he came over the side, asking what was the result on board his brig. He answered, '*Cut all to pieces—the victory's lost, everything gone! I've been sacrificed by the gun boats.*' To which I replied, '*No, sir, victory is yet on our side. I have a most judicious position, and my shot are taking great effect. You tend my battery, and I will bring up the gun boats.*' 'Do so,' said he, 'for *Heaven's sake.*'

"I immediately passed over the side into his boat, and pulled by the Lawrence, passing between her and the enemy. I hailed each gun boat as I passed, ordering it to make sail, get out the sweeps and press up for the head of the line, and to cease firing at the small vessels of the enemy astern. I then returned to the headmost gun boat, the Somers. Capt. Perry now perceiving the two ships foul, (being rendered so by the attempt of the Detroit to wear round and bring her starboard battery into action, the larboard having been destroyed, in a great measure, by the imperfect construction of her gun carriages, and the Queen Charlotte running up under her lee, and thus becoming entangled,) and observing that the gun boats were rapidly coming up, made the signal for close action, and then bore up, passing between the Chippewa and the two ships, Detroit and Queen Charlotte, while I shortened sail, with the four stern-most gun boats in line abreast, under the sterns of the two latter; distance, perhaps, 150 or 200 yards. Soon after the British ensigns were hauled down. The flag of the enemy's commander being nailed to the mast it could not be hauled down, and consequently an officer came aft and waved a white handkerchief on a boarding pike as a signal of submission, when I ordered the gun boats to cease firing. After the enemy had struck, the headmost and sternmost vessels of their line, the Chippewa and Little Belt, put up their helms, made sail, and attempted to escape for Malden, but were pursued by the gun boats, captured and brought back.

"As soon as we had ceased firing I went on board the Detroit to take possession, and such was the quantity of blood on the deck that in crossing it my feet slipped from under me and I fell, my clothing becoming completely saturated and covered with gore. I went below to see Capt. Barclay, who tendered me his sword; but I refused it, and anticipated the wishes of Capt. Perry, by assuring him that every kindness would be shown himself and other prisoners. While on board the Detroit, I ordered my coxswain to go aloft and draw the nails which held the British flag to the mast. These nails I presented, through the hands of my old townsman, Dr. Richard Pindel, to the man who was so blessed as to gain the heart of one of Washington county's fairest daughters—the charming Lucretia Hart. It was to her illustrious husband, Henry Clay, of Kentucky, to whom I felt under obligations, for a high encomium pronounced the winter before, in Congress, upon the capture of the Detroit and Caledonia, that I presented the nails that were intended to hold the British flag aloft through victory.

"Returning on board the Niagara I was met at the gangway by Capt. Perry, who asked me if I was wounded; I answered him, 'No.' He then observed to me that 'he thought it was impossible I could have pulled down the line without being killed.' He further remarked, '*I owe this victory to your gallantry!*' I then asked him why he did not stand further on and let us get fairly into action. He said he found the enemy's shot taking effect on his crew, and therefore, to divert the attentions of his men from their fire, he rounded to sooner than he intended."

Capt. Elliott received the following complimentary letter from the officers of the Niagara:

U. S. Brig Niagara, Sept. 19th, 1813.

CAPT. ELLIOTT.

Sir:—We, the officers of the U. S. Brig Niagara, under your command, with the most profound respect, congratulate you on our late victory over the British squadron, well convinced that in you we were ably commanded, and that your valour, intrepidity and skill could not be surpassed. You have, sir, our most ardent wish for future prosperity and happiness, both in your official and private capacity, and may your future naval career ever be as brilliant as the present.

Receive, sir, the assurance of our greatest respect.

J. E. SMITH, *Lieut.*
H. McGRATH, *Purser.*
NELSON WEBSTER, *Lieut.*
J. J. EDWARDS, *Lieut.*
ROBERT B. BARTON, *Surgeon.*
H. B. BREVOORT, *2d U. S. Inf.*

All who are familiar with the history of our country, are aware that many persons thought, that to the decisive action and gallantry of Elliott and the crew of the Niagara the victory was due. Politicians of both parties fanned these embers of dissatisfaction into a flame, a fierce newspaper war raged, and some ill feeling was raised between Perry and Elliott.

Many years passed. The gallant Perry had made his last voyage. In the fall of 1843, Commodore Elliott visited his native place. His fellow-citizens invited him to a formal dinner, which invitation he saw fit to decline, but at their earnest solicitation delivered to them an address* and thus referred to his former comrade: "Permit me now, friends, to remark, in reference to Captain Perry, that up to the time I went on board my brig, the Niagara, after the battle had ceased, I found him to be noble, gallant, high minded and honourable; and no man in my presence shall say aught against him! Let history tell the balance! That history contains the registry of unceasing persecutions, dark and ingenious conspiracies, unmitigated and vindictive assaults upon me, by those who pretended to be his friends. But, so help me God, I do solemnly declare, that I believe him to have been the victim of their hollow hypocrisy, as I have been the object of their infamous and vile slanders! When the universal enemy had stricken him and laid him low, I taught my heart to cast away all unfriendliness towards his memory; and now that the grave holds him captive, there is a full, deep oblivion of all that has passed in my breast. In religious sincerity, I say, peace, eternal peace, to the brave and gallant Perry, and before my eternal Judge, I declare that there is no hand, instinct with life, that is more ready to deck his tomb with laurels, than this same one, which once grasped his when congratulating him upon our victory.

"There were many circumstances which impelled me to the movements I made in this battle. The recollection of a father, who had

---

* This address Commodore Elliott, after much solicitation, allowed to be published, as reported, and we here make a general acknowledgment to it.

fallen in defence of that frontier which was attempted to be wrested from us—its then exposed condition—the urgent necessity for decided demonstrations, the love of country, and my burning desire to emulate the gallantry of another Washington county boy, the brave Israel, who threw himself on board the Intrepid, at Tripoli, for the purpose of destroying the Tripolitan fleet, and who, when discovered, rather than yield himself a prisoner, with his brave companions, applied the torch to the magazine, and went in one common wreck to the other world."

These daring exploits form a brilliant page in our country's history, and they have been emblazoned in prose and song. In October, 1813, he succeeded Perry in command on Lake Erie, and in 1815, he commanded the Ontario sloop-of-war, one of the squadron of Commodore Decatur, employed against Algiers, and contributed to the capture of an Algerine frigate by a discharge of heavy fire into her. He was promoted to the rank of Captain, March 27th, 1818, and till 1824, was engaged in selecting sites for dockyards, light-houses, and fortifications, on the coast of North Carolina. Life at sea is fraught with many dangers. Captain Elliott had many narrow escapes from death. We have space for but one, which he thus relates:—

"When I left Norfolk to join General Bernard in the coast survey, I embarked in a small *pereauga*, or boom foresail schooner, heavily laden with cedar, wines, birds, &c., not having any other opportunity to suit my immediate wishes. During this voyage an accident occurred, which, had it not been for the efforts of a brave and affectionate tar, would have brought me to my last account. One morning, the sea being boisterous and running high, I took a seat on the davit projecting from the stern, and to which the stern boat is hoisted. In one of the schooner's heavy plunges this davit gave way, precipitating me overboard. I was soon carried out of the sight of all on board, and was given up as gone by all but the tar above alluded to, who determined to go where I was last seen at any rate. Accordingly he descended to the bow of the boat, she hanging by the tackle from the stern, and making a rope fast, came up on deck, hauled it taught, and cut the after tackle. When the boat lowered and swung by the bow, he descended into the boat, accompanied by another hand. The sea running high, the passengers (being nearly 30 on board,) endeavoured to dissuade him, and that it was useless to risk his life. The other man who was with him, being in the act of climbing up again, the noble tar reached up and cut the rope over his hands. The boat being full of water, with their hats they bailed it out.. Previously to this, one of the passengers had thrown a piece of white cedar to me, about 10 feet long and 12 inches through, of which I laid hold—commenced and pulled off all of my clothes except my shirt which I tied round my body with my handkerchief below; seized the timber, placed it under me and put before the wind, and went off at the rate of about two miles the hour, endeavouring to get to leeward of the vessel. My strength soon began to fail me, but yet the heart was strong. It seems in splitting this log, the axe had changed its direction, and enabled me to place my hand between the split and the log. Being at the season of the year when it is usual to transport mocking birds from the south, they were afloat, and the last recollection I have was brushing one off my head. This gallant tar came to me when life was about to be extinct, picked me up, and brought me back safely to the vessel. Such was my state, that for two hours I had not then, nor have I now, the most indistinct recollection of anything that passed. I have never placed my hands in a basin of water since without thinking of that scene."

The Commodore was in command of the West India Squadron from 1829 to 1833, and in the latter year, of the Charlestown Navy Yard.

Afterwards he commanded for several years the Mediterranean squadron, visiting the Holy Land and other places of interest, and bringing home with him many curiosities and live stock of different kinds. His conduct in this position, did not meet the approval of the executive, his actions being misrepresented by his political enemies, and he was tried by court martial in June, 1840, and suspended from duty for four years. In October, 1843, the period of his suspension which then remained was remitted by the President, and he was appointed to the command of the Philadelphia Navy Yard.

He died in Philadelphia December 18th, 1845, respected and admired even by those who in political life differed from him.

ALEXANDER SHARP, D. D.

REV. ALEXANDER SHARP, D. D., was born three miles west of Newville, Pa., June 12th, 1796, was graduated at Jefferson College in 1820; studied Theology one year under Dr. John M. Mason, in New York, and finished with Dr. Riddle, near Pittsburgh; was installed pastor of the Associate Reformed Church of Big Spring, at Newville, June 29th, 1824, and continued in charge of his congregation up to the time of his death, on the 28th of January, 1857.

His father, Alexander Sharp, of Green Spring, came to this country prior to the war of the Revolution, in which he served as a private soldier. He was a brother of General Andrew Sharp, who left Cumberland county at an early day and settled on the Muskingum river, where he was killed by the Indians while going down the river in a canoe with his wife and children. They, with two other brothers, James and Robert Sharp, were born in the county of Derry, in the north of Ireland, where their ancestors had gone from Scotland in the previous century. Dr. Sharp was, in 1830, elected Professor of Theology in the Associate Reformed Seminary at Pittsburgh, to succeed Dr. Joseph Kerr. He declined the offer, but it was no mean compliment to a young man but six years in the ministry, conferred by such men as Drs. McDill, Findley, Reed, Claybaugh and others like them. Dr. Pressly was then elected and continued many years in connection with the seminary.

The church at Big Spring, of which Dr. Sharp had charge so long, was organized as a Burger Associate Church as early as 1760, but had no settled pastor till after the formation of the Associate Reformed Church, in 1782. The first pastor was Rev. John Jameson, from the Burger Synod of Scotland, who was installed in 1784 or 1785, and remained about ten years, when he drifted west. The second pastor was the Rev. James McConnel, who was installed about 1796, and demitted in November, 1809, and preached long afterwards in Butler county, Pa. The third pastor was Dr. Sharp; the fourth, Rev. W. L. Wallace, the present pastor and beloved successor of Dr. Sharp. So well balanced was he in mind and character that it was hard to point out any prominent traits. The whole profile was so plump and round that there were no projecting points or sharp angles. In person large and commanding, of ready, fluent speech, but with a monotonous and unattractive tone. In manners and character, simple, kind, courteous, hospitable and a sure and reliable friend. His mind was clear, strong, comprehensive and grasping. As a preacher he was lucid, scriptural, exegetical and didactic. In his early ministry he formed the habit of collecting every passage in the Old and New Testaments confirmatory of his position, and committing them to memory, so that in a few years he had committed the greater part of the Bible, and become so saturated with the Scriptures that he could quote from memory readily and fully upon any point, and in preaching and praying used a great amount of Scripture language and imagery without directly quoting. He was modest, rather backward, and of humble, simple, unaffected and consistent piety; as a husband and father perhaps a little too indulgent.

Dr. Sharp left but little that has been published to the world, and as his manner, presence and oral discourses are not known to many persons of the present day, the inquiry is often made: What was it that gave him his commanding position? Perhaps a true answer would be: his pre-eminent amount of common sense and judgment in the management of men and business. He was very successful in the conduct of his own private affairs. He successfully and economically settled the estates of many of his friends and neighbours. He was frequently consulted by men who were likely to get into litigation, and managed to save them therefrom. He was applied to by men who had become infatuated with strange and unscriptural notions of religion, and dissipated their errors, relieved their doubts and placed their faith on a firm foundation. He was not afraid to labour with his hands and set an example of industry to the community and all that were about him; but whether at a public gathering, talking with his neighbours, or in the harvest field with the reapers, wherever situate or whatever doing, he was ever a marked man, one that the most ignorant would recognize as a Christian gentleman, and the most cultivated as his peer in every respect.

Dr. Sharp had a taste for classical literature, and for some years taught a number of young men in studies preparatory to entering college. Among these were Rev. Dr. Robt. Gracy, Rev. T. V. Moore, D. D., now both dead; the late Joseph Hannon, M. D., George Grove, M. D., and the Rev. James B. Scouller, to the last of whom we are indebted for the greater part of what is of much value in this article on Dr. Sharp.

HON. JAMES BUCHANAN.

JAMES BUCHANAN was born on the 23d day of April, 1791. His birth-place was a wild and romantic spot in a gorge of the Cove, or North Mountain, about four miles west of Mercersburg, and bearing the peculiar, but not inappropriate name of "Stony Batter." His father, James Buchanan, Senior, was a native of Ireland, and one of the most enterprising, intelligent and influential citizens of that part of the state. His mother, Elizabeth Speer, remarkable for her superior intellect and genuine piety, was born in the southern part of Lancaster county.

Five years after his birth his parents removed into the town of Mercersburg, then recently laid out, where he was brought up and fitted for college. He entered Dickinson College, Carlisle, then under the Presidency of the Rev. Dr. Davidson, in 1805, being at the time in his fifteenth year. In 1809, he graduated with distinction, and in the same year commenced the study of law in Lancaster, in the office of James Hopkins, Esq. Three years after, or in 1812, he was admitted to the bar. He at once opened an office in Lancaster, and was almost immediately successful in obtaining business; his studious habits, his fine abilities, his agreeable manners and correct deportment, all combining to attract clients to him. He in a very short time took his place among the foremost at the bar, and had the command of as much business as he could attend to. There were soon very few important cases, either in Lancaster, or the neighbouring counties, in which he was not employed, or at least, in which there was not an effort made to secure his services. In a very few years, besides deservedly acquiring the reputation of being one of the ablest and best lawyers in the state, or in the country, he had, from being the possessor of very little, amassed what he considered a competence, and withdrew almost entirely from practice.

His first public employment of any kind was that of Prosecutor for Lebanon county, a position to which he was appointed in 1813, by Jared Ingersoll, Esq., then Attorney-General of the state under Governor Snyder. This office he probably retained but a short time. In the next year, at the age of twenty-three, and only two years after admission to the bar, he was nominated by his friends for the State Legislature, and elected. In the following year, or 1815, he was again nominated and elected. In both the sessions of the Legislature in which he sat, he was one of the most prominent members; by the sensibleness and justness of his views, and the force of his high character and eminent abilities, exerting, though so young a man, not a little influence. He was always, as on a more extended area in after life, at his post, and took an interest in everything that was done. His mode of expressing his views was then, as afterwards, clear and convincing. In the same year in which he was first elected to the Legislature, he went as a private in a company of volunteers to Baltimore, to aid in defending it against an anticipated attack from the British; and thus he early, by a voluntary exposure of himself to danger, gave evidence of that fire of sincere and true patriotism, which, till the last day of his life, glowed fervidly in his bosom. In the year 1820, his fellow citizens of the Congressional district in which he lived, (composed of the counties of Lancaster, Chester and Delaware,) and without solicitation from him, conferred on him the further honour of electing him to the National House of Representatives. They elected him again in 1822, 1824, 1826 and 1828, when he declined further re-election. His term of service in the House expired on the 3d of March, 1831. He was from almost his first entrance into the House, one of its most prominent and leading members, taking rank with such men as Randolph, McDuffie, P. Barbour, and others, and expressing his views in a clear and forcible manner on all the important questions that came before it. His speeches then, as since, were models of lucidness, chasteness and force. One of the most remarkable of them was that delivered at the Bar of the Senate at the conclusion of the trial of Judge Peck, he being chairman of the able committee appointed to conduct the case before the Senate. This speech has rarely been excelled in ability and eloquence.

In the same year in which he ceased to be a member of the House, he was sent by President Jackson, as Minister Plenipotentiary to the Court of St. Petersburg, where he made a most favourable impression, both for himself and his country, and where he negotiated the first Commercial Treaty which this Government ever had with that of Russia. In 1833, he returned from Russia; and in the same year he was elected by the Legislature of Pennsylvania to fill a vacancy in the Senate of the United States, occasioned by the resignation of William Wilkins, who had been appointed to succeed him at the Court of the Czar. He was afterwards elected for the full term of six years; though soon after his second election, he resigned to take a place in the cabinet of President Polk. His whole term of service in the Senate was the same as it had been in the House; viz: ten years.

In the body of which he was now a member, he took a similarly high rank to that which he had occupied in the House. He frequently measured arms with Clay, Webster and others, and without discredit or disadvantage to himself. He was, during most of the time, the principal leader of the Administration party, and expressed himself at large, and very ably, on all the important questions under discussion. During most of the time, he was chairman of the important Committee on Foreign Relations.

In 1845, he was tendered by the then recently inaugurated President, James K. Polk, the position in his cabinet of Secretary of State. This position he occupied with great honour to himself and advantage to the country. While in the State Department, the Oregon boundary question was finally settled, the war with Mexico was carried on and successfully terminated, and California acquired.

In 1849, at the expiration of Mr. Polk's Presidential term, Mr. Buchanan retired to his country seat, near Lancaster, Pennsylvania, where he remained until 1853, when President Pierce tendered him, of his own accord, the mission to the Court of St. James. This mission he was averse to accepting, but, on its being pressed upon him, he at length accepted it. He remained in England till the spring of 1856. While there he was treated with marked respect by all classes, from the Queen down. Lord Clarendon had reason to respect his abilities; for he found him more than a match in his diplomatic correspondence with him. His dispatches, while Secretary of War and Minister to England, have not been excelled by those of any other Cabinet or other Minister.

In June of the year he returned from England, he was nominated, (again, without any effort on his part) by the Democratic National Convention, which met at Cincinnati, as their candidate for the Presidency, and in the following November he was elected. And thus, from an humble beginning, after having previously occupied an unusual number of distinguished and honourable positions connected with the Government, he found himself at the age of sixty-five exalted to what is perhaps really the highest political position on earth. The duties of this high office he discharged with ability, and though much blamed for his course during the last few months of his administration, (a period when the affairs of the country had come to the fearful crisis to which they had been long tending,) yet, in all he did, and in all he abstained from doing, he was actuated by the highest and purest motives of patriotism. He did that, and that only, which he believed he was authorized to do, and which he thought it best and his duty to do. He, himself, feared not the verdict of future times, as to his course and as to his policy, and on more than one occasion, within only a year or two of his death, he had been heard to say, that had he to pass through the same state of things again, he could not, before his God, say that he could act otherwise than as he did. In sincere and cordial love for the Union he was second to none. The principal respect in which he differed from many others was, as to what were the best and most legitimate means of preserving or restoring the Union.

At the expiration of his Presidential term, in March, 1861, he returned to his home at Wheatland, where he spent the remainder of his life, enjoying the society of his neighbours and friends, and employing himself with his books and pen. One of the books most frequently perused by him was the Bible; in the teachings of which he was a firm believer, and on the promises of which he cheerfully relied. He had always been a believer in the Holy Scriptures, and in the truth of the Christian religion, and besides being always strictly moral in his conduct, had been in many respects, a devout and religious, as well as a kind and charitable man. But he had never made an open profession of being a disciple of Christ until within the last few years of his life, when he became a communicant of the Presbyterian Church. He died calmly and peacefully on Monday, the first day of June, 1868. On the Thursday following, his remains were followed to the grave by such numbers of his fellow citizens, (including a large number of persons from abroad,) as indicated, that however he may have been censured by persons of opposite political opinions while living, he was yet one who, in public estimation, was both a *great* and a *good* man, one deserving for his acknowledged strict integrity and his well known benevolence, esteem and regard, as for his learning, statesmanship, eloquence and talents, he commanded deference and respect.

On opening his will, it was found that he had remembered the poor of Lancaster, as well as the church of which he was a member, and had arranged that a handsome addition should be made to the fund which he had appropriated for their benefit, years before. It may be added that in person he was large, in manners courteous and polished, and that his stores of knowledge and his powers of conversation were such that no one could be long in his company without being deeply interested, and without receiving valuable information.—*Rev. E. Y. Buchanan.*

JOSEPH McCARRELL, D.D.

THE following sketch of this eminent scholar and divine, is from the pen of the Rev. Dr. Forsyth, of Newburg, N. Y., (now Chaplain at West Point, N. Y.)

The Rev. Joseph McCarrell, D. D., son of John McCarrell and Mary McKnight, was a native of Shippensburg, Penn., and was born on the 9th of July, 1795.

His parents were warmly attached members of the Associate Reformed Church of that place, and the region was one whose history was connected with the earliest annals of the denomination, in the communion of which Dr. McCarrell lived and died, and for which he had an unchangeable affection. His mind was early turned towards the ministry of the Gospel; and he entered upon studies preparatory thereto, availing himself of such helps as were within his reach, though in the main he had to depend upon his own efforts, and was in fact, to a great extent, a self-made man.

While thus engaged, the war of 1812 came on. In the summer of 1814, Washington was burnt by the British, and Baltimore was threatened with the same fate at the hands of the barbarian, Admiral Cockburn, the wretch who promised his followers "the beauty and booty" of that city. The whole country was aroused; the adjacent counties of Pennsylvania sent as quickly as possible their militia to the point of danger; while from Shippensburg every person capable of bearing arms hurried to the defence of Baltimore. Joseph McCarrell was one of these volunteers. He thus not only had a taste of military life, but from the hill about two miles from the city, on which his regiment was placed, he witnessed the magnificent spectacle of the bombardment of Fort McHenry. And he was one of those who through the long night watched the garrison flag, and when the morning dawned, saw with inexpressible joy the glorious banner still waving defiance to the foe.

Soon after his return home, Mr. McCarrell entered Washington College, Washington, Pennsylvania, and graduated with high honours in the class of 1815. For several years after leaving college, he was engaged in teaching in Bellefonte, in Greensburg, and in Carlisle, while he was at the same time pursuing the studies that would fit him for the sacred profession to which he was looking forward. In 1818, he entered the Theological Seminary of the Associate Reformed

Church, then in New York, under the care of that distinguished man, Dr. John M. Mason. He brought to the Seminary an amount of attainment in certain branches of learning, which very few possess when leaving it, for he had made himself a thorough Hebrew scholar, and had read the whole of the Old Testament in that language. Having finished the prescribed course of study, he was licensed by the Presbytery of Big Spring, Pa., on the 21st of June, 1821. For several months he supplied the Associate Reformed Church in Murray street, New York, (vacant by the resignation of Dr. Mason,) with so much acceptance, that not a few of its members wished to call him as their pastor. But he was destined to spend his life in another sphere.

Dr. McCarrell came to Newburg in the autumn of 1822. He was soon after invited to assume the pastoral care of the Associate Reformed Church there, and on the 13th of March, 1823, he was ordained and installed. The old church erected in 1795, was in the extreme southern end of the village, on ground now owned by Capt. H. Robison. The present edifice was built in 1821, and had been dedicated a few months before Dr. McCarrell arrived in Newburg. He is, consequently, the only one who had served the congregation as a pastor since it began to worship in the church at the corner of First and Grand streets. His pastorate was nearly twice as long as the united pastorate of his four predecessors. The society, though one of the oldest in Newburg, was by no means large when he became its pastor, but from that time it steadily advanced in numbers, and has become the mother of two congregations. In 1829, the Seminary, which had been suspended for some years, was revived, established at Newburg, and Dr. McCarrell was chosen Professor of Theology. Towards the close of that year he entered upon his work of instruction, and from that period until near the end of life he continued to discharge his two-fold duties as Pastor and Professor. And all who saw him, as he went out and in among us for so many years, knew that they were looking upon a "living epistle of Christ."

From time to time he took part in the public questions of the day, discussing them in the pulpit and through the press, but only those in which he deemed that some great moral or religious principle was involved. His last years were made sad by various causes, which could not operate upon such a nature as his without reaching and affecting the fountain of physical life. The unfortunate separation from brethren with whom he had been so long and closely connected in ecclesiastical fellowship, the changes in the denomination to which he was so warmly attached, and lastly the loss of a beloved daughter, all helped to make a deep and visible impression upon him. During his last two years, it was obvious to all that his strength had been weakened in the way. Still he seemed to have derived so much benefit from a few months' rest, that about the beginning of his last year the hope was entertained that he might recover strength before he went hence. He did resume his labour and continued it for a month, but early in March he was obliged to give it up again. On two succeeding Sabbaths he was able to be in church, though declining to take part in the service. The last Sabbath of his life was the last day on which he conducted family worship, and it is worthy of note that the psalm then sung, in course, was the seventeenth, last four verses. He was mercifully spared all acute suffering and mental wandering during his illness. He was calm, serene, peaceful, and at last fell "on sleep," in Jesus, as quietly as an infant in its mother's arms. He died at an early hour on the morning of Tuesday, 29th of March, 1864, and was buried in Newburg, in the "Old Graveyard," in the centre of the city, where he is surrounded by his elders—who are also "waiting for the adoption."

Dr. McCarrell's private character I can hardly venture to portray. If I were to do so, I might be charged with presenting an ideal and not a real character. So, at any rate, I would have judged the Doctor's character, had I merely met with it in a description, and not enjoyed the felicity of knowing it. In all his familiar intercourses he was as simple as a child, and when engaged in conversation there was *naive* spontaneity and richness in his turns of thought that was exceedingly refreshing. In his speech there was no satire, just because in his nature there was no bitterness. Humour, quaint, fantastic, happy humour, like Paul Richter's—only more elegant—overflowed his table talk, imparted to it the richest flavour. Yet, over all his speech and manner, there breathed a sacred tenderness which flowed not from any earthly source, but was the fragrance of a heavenly spirit. His childlike faith imparted, at all times, a charm to his daily life. His nature so trustful, so affectionate and given to meditation, seemed to be ground well prepared for the seed of God, and surely in it that seed so grew and fructified as it is rarely seen on earth. He always appeared to me like the beloved apostle whose head lay confidingly on the breast of Jesus, and to whom were revealed the most glorious visions of the church's future. The spiritual insight, the purity of conscience, the ecstatic joy, the womanly gentleness of feeling which are especially attributed to that apostle, were all of them characteristic of this good old man.

No one could look upon Dr. McCarrell without receiving the impression that he was a man of power, though not of the sort which works with noise and observation. Such was the impression which he made upon the Professor of the Military Academy at West Point, many years, when the pulpit was supplied by the minister of the vicinity, during a vacancy in the chaplaincy. With his strong subjective tendency, his modesty and the comparatively sequestered sphere in which he moved, the occasions fitted to show the real grasp and vigour of his intellect were few and rare. But when one did arise, no one who heard him could doubt (though he might not agree with his reasonings,) he was a workman of a high order, and that there slumbered within him the fire of real eloquence. And so too no one could be brought into even casual contact with Dr. McCarrell without seeing that he was a good man. In all my intercourse with men never have I met with one in whom masculine vigour of intellect was combined with more of the gentler grace of the Gospel; nor one who surpassed him in childlike simplicity, unselfishness and profound reverence for all sacred things. He had his failings, no doubt, but even they leaned to virtue's side.

The ministers whom he helped to train are connected with various branches of the church, and occupy widely scattered fields of labour, but to all of them the tidings that their venerated professor was no more were sad indeed. The student who met him for the first time might get the idea that he was a man of dull and phlegmatic temperament, but he would soon discover that under that calm exterior there beat a large and very tender heart. He had the art of winning his pupil's love, without the least visible effort on his part to do so.

His method of instruction was modeled after that pursued by Dr. Mason, though with some modifications, which, perhaps, were not improvements. With both, the Bible in its original tongue was one great text book. Dr. McCarrell was very fond of treating subjects analytically, and he was a master of this mode of discussion; but it would have been of advantage to himself and his pupils, if he had combined it with the synthetic. Yet no student of right views and feelings, could pass through his hands without becoming a sound theologian, well instructed in the Scriptures.

As a preacher he was solemn, instructive, impressive. As a writer he was clear and forcible. Among his publications were "Sermons on Baptism," a sermon on "The Christian's Hope," and an "Answer to a Discourse preached by Dr. William E. Channing, at the Dedication of the Second Congregational Unitarian Church, New York, December 7th, 1826."

Dr. McCarrell was married to Jane B. Leiper, of Shippensburg, who still survives him. His family consisted of eight children, (four of them are still living,) and one grandson.

EDWARD CRAWFORD, ESQ.

EDWARD CRAWFORD, son of Edward Crawford and Elizabeth Sterritt, was born in 1758. In the year 1776, and at the early age of eighteen, he entered the military service of his country as an officer of the Revolutionary Army, in which he continued until the war terminated, and peace acknowledged us to be, what we had declared we were, an independent nation. Of his fatigues and exposure during this period nothing need be said; they were common to all who shared the honour and danger of the service, but the modesty and reserve of the deceased on this subject were so remarkable, that for many years it did not become known to his most intimate friends, (and it never was communicated to others,) that he received a severe wound during one of the battles in New Jersey, and came near to losing his life at the siege of Yorktown, in Virginia. Soon after the close of the war, and upon the erection of Franklin county, he was appointed to the several offices of Prothonotary, &c.; in one of which he was succeeded by Col. Findlay, of Mercersburg. To the capacity and fidelity with which the organization of these offices was made, the routine of business established, and the various duties discharged throughout the twenty-four years and upwards that he held them, the entire community could bear witness. In connection with Alexander Colhoun, he established the Chambersburg (now the First National) Bank, 1807. He was its first President, and was re-elected to this office for twenty-three years, until removed by death. In any project for the public good he was among the foremost, exerting his extensive influence, and devoting his personal services and pecuniary aid to promote the general interests, with a zeal and liberality not at all abated by advanced and advancing years, and the short hold he seemed to have upon the world.

In addition to the positions of honour, trust and usefulness, already referred to, Mr. Crawford occupied many others. He was a member of the Society of the Cincinnati; he was elected a manager of the Franklin County Bible Society, December 12th, 1814; he was appointed to meet the soldiers on their return from the defence of Baltimore, and addressed them; for some years he served as a Trustee of Falling Spring Presbyterian Church. As he was one of the oldest, so was he one of the most useful, and one of the most respected citizens of

Chambersburg. He died at the age of seventy-five years. So long a life necessarily carried with it more or less of the crosses and distresses of this world, from which he was not entirely exempt—but in his cup was mingled an unusual portion of all that makes life valuable—the respect of the whole community, the sincere esteem of his fellow-citizens to whom he was more intimately known, and the ardent and devoted affections of those intimately connected with him—these conspired in aid of a clear and excellent understanding, and a warm and generous heart, to encourage and invigorate the efforts of his life, and to give enjoyment and happiness to his declining years. He was a wealthy, hospitable, public-spirited, unselfish man, and when called to fall under the stroke that spares none, his loss was deeply and long deplored by the community with which he had so long been identified, and especially by those bound to him by closer ties.

Mr. Crawford was married twice. His first wife was Catharine Hostinger, of York, Pa. Thomas Hartley Crawford was a son by this marriage, who attained eminence as a lawyer, was elected to Congress from his district, became Secretary of Indian Affairs under President Jackson, and was afterwards Judge of the District Court, Washington, D. C. His second wife was Rebecca Colhoun. Their daughter, Elizabeth Sterritt, married Reade Washington, Esq., of Clark county, Va. His grandson, Edward Crawford Washington, was killed in the advance on Vicksburg, May, 1863.

COL. JAMES AGNEW.

DAVID ELLIOTT, D. D., LL. D., long an intimate acquaintance and friend of Col. James Agnew, amongst other words of commendation, uses this language of him in his obituary: "This venerable man was of a sound and vigorous mind, wise and sagacious in the management of business." An eminent and prominent citizen in his day, he is worthy of mention amongst the men whose history belongs in whole or in part to the Cumberland valley, and its borders.

He was of that brave, hardy, godly and persevering race, the Scotch-Irish. His parents came from the north of Ireland, and settled in Adams county previous to the War of Independence. In that struggle several of the members of his father's family bore an honourable and patriotic part, although a cousin of his father, Gen. James Agnew, was an officer in the British army, and fell at the battle of Germantown.

The subject of this sketch was born in Adams county, Pa., July 31st, 1769. His mother's name was Ramsey. An incident is related of her that illustrates the fact that Providential impulses for which we cannot account, are sometimes, for wise purposes, made upon the human mind. She was living, for the purpose of attending school, at the house of her brother, Col. Ramsey, in Franklin county. One day she felt a special aversion to going, and could give no reason for the feeling. It was, however, so strong and decided that she yielded to it, and remained at home. That day a band of hostile Indians came upon the school house, and murdered and scalped the teacher and all the small children, and carried the larger boys and girls into captivity. One boy, who had been wounded and scalped, had the self-control to lie still and pretend he was dead; the savages did not strike him with the tomahawk, and he lived to tell the tale. Had Miss Ramsey gone to school that day she would probably have been killed or taken captive. Eleanor Cochran, afterwards Mrs. Junkin, and mother of Drs. George and D. X. Junkin, was also detained at home and saved from the fate of the other scholars.

Col. Agnew's parents were of the Reformed Presbyterian (Covenanter) branch of the church, but at the time of the union of most of that body with the Associate Church, (Seceders,) forming the Associate Reformed Church of North America, they joined in the said Union.

Educated in the doctrines, and trained in the stalwart morality of that strictest sect of Presbyterians, Mr. Agnew, through a long life, was a man of unswerving integrity of devotion to the principles in which he had been brought up. He obtained under domestic instruction, and in the school of the vicinage, such elements of education as fitted him for business; and his remarkable self-control and perseverance enabled him to improve to the best advantage the limited opportunities he enjoyed.

An incident occurred in the beginning of his career that had an important influence on his own life and the lives of others. He and a young man of the name of George, had been companions from boyhood, and had grown up devoted friends. They were to leave home on the same morning for their respective points of destination. Agnew was disposed to go west, the other east and south. They were both greatly distressed at the prospect of separation. Having met, young George with strong persuasion, earnestly besought his early friend to turn aside from his purpose. At last "the lot," the whole disposing of which is of the Lord, was appealed to for decision. In a certain contingency, Agnew was to be the companion of his friend and go with him to Baltimore. In another contingency, he was to follow his first wishes. With beating heart young George cast the lot. With excited hopes and anxious looks, they sought the index of their destiny. It favoured the previous desires of Agnew. Long and sadly they talked with each other but at length parted and moved forward, each in the path predetermined. Mr. George closed, a few years back, a long and useful life in Baltimore, the city of his choice. His career as a merchant was successful, and he died a man of wealth and influence. But the friendship of the two, like that of Jonathan and David, never ceased nor grew cold in their hearts. The periodical visits of Colonel Agnew to Baltimore, cemented and strengthened the early ties of a friendship, strong and enduring as the hills.

His natural force of character, under agonizing pain, is well displayed in the following surgical operation:

Dr. John McClellan, of Greencastle, Pa., having been consulted about a small tumour that appeared on the Colonel's tongue, supposed to be cancerous, advised its excision. This was at once assented to, although informed that the operation would prove dangerous and painful. That it might be done most effectually and with least danger, he kneeled beside a table and protruded his tongue. It was then fastened thereto with an awl, the end opened and a portion cut off. The Doctor in old age pronounced his own act to have been rash, as an artery was severed and the profuse bleeding arrested with difficulty. It showed, however, the valuable traits that made him in his day one of the most eminent of physicians. After the Colonel's wound was partially healed he was out on his farm one day, when the artery burst and a spurt of blood gushed from it as when first cut. He was in much peril, but with great presence of mind, pressed the tongue firmly against the roof of his mouth, hastened home, seized a pen, requested a piece of sheet lead from the store, and with this compressed the artery and staunched the flow of blood. The Doctor, twenty miles away, could not have reached him to save his life, before this timely self applied remedy. The energy, unflinching nerve, power of will, and fortitude, displayed in the above operation, proved him to be a person that could be relied on as help in like emergencies. Dr. McClellan therefore, as also the physicians who subsequently settled in McConnelsburg, made him their companion in cases requiring these traits. To them he rendered valuable aid in the discharge of their painful duties, and was rewarded with their lasting friendship and regard.

His maternal uncle, Colonel Ramsey, owned an estate on West Conococheague, near Mercersburg, called Ramsey's, (now Heister's) Mills. At an early age young Agnew went to live with him, and assist in managing his affairs. Here he acquired, in part, those habits of business, energy, care and diligence, in the exercise of which, in after life, he constructed one of the largest fortunes in that part of the commonwealth. At the time of his advent to the vicinity of Mercersburg, emigration to western Pennsylvania had been inaugurated, and a considerable trade was carried on between the settlers west of the Alleghenies and the older settlements of the Cumberland valley. This trade was prosecuted by means of "pack horses," and the route corresponding pretty nearly with the present turnpike was called, "The Packer's Path." Passing through the Gap by Stony Batter to the Big Cove, it left the east side of the Cove Mountain and thence along Sideling, (or Side-long-hill,) to Pittsburgh. At "Stony Batter," an old Scotchman had a little store, in which he traded with the packers and others in salt, groceries, hardware, and dry goods. He subsequently moved into Mercersburg where he put his son James to school, and in time sent him to Dickinson College. That son, James Buchanan, afterwards became President of the United States. By the assistance of his uncle, Colonel Ramsey, young Agnew, about his twentieth year, established a trading post in the "Great Cove," seven miles west of Mr. Buchanan's store, on the "Packers' Path." At this station where McConnellsburg now stands, he built up a very prosperous business, and continued it the greater part of a long life. To the mercantile business which was his first and chief pursuit, he added a farm and tannery, the latter being at that early day, very necessary for the supply of settlers, and very profitable. His father had sunk a tannery on his farm in Adams county, and employed a man to work it for him. But when quite a lad James seeing something wrong in the management of the employee, of his own choice, and by his energy and attention, so thoroughly learned the details of the business, as to save his father from losses, and to make this knowledge afterwards a means of profit to himself.

By diligence, skill and energy in business, Col. Agnew prospered and became one of the wealthiest men in central Pennsylvania. At least twice in every year he repaired to the commercial cities, to make purchases. In these very early days this was done on horseback. Although he often carried large sums of money, and the mountains were infested with robbers such as Lewis and Connelly, and others, he was never molested by them. He put his trust in God, was a man of habitual prayer, and seemed never to fear, although other merchants and travelers were robbed along the same road.

When his first purchases were made, he was introduced by his relative, Col. Ramsey, to one or two merchants of Philadelphia, but had no character for business qualities established at this early period. One fact, however, in the very beginning operated in his favour—his caution. It at once secured the good will of the merchants. The goods selected made such large bills, that he feared to assume the responsibility of taking them. He directed the clerks to deduct certain portions. This was done until the amount was within a certainty of his ability to pay. When the heads of the firms learned these facts, they called on him, and on inquiry found out from himself the reasons of his procedure. They were confirmed in the opinion that he would be a safe and good customer, and insisted on his taking all the goods; assured him that he would not be harrassed about payment, and that if the time therefor was too limited, it should be extended to suit this exigency. The goods were bought; and now came a time of trial. Many were the obstacles in the way of meeting his engagements. The produce that availed in city payments was limited, banks were few in number, were widely separated, the circulation of their notes confined within narrow limits, and subject to heavy discount in the cities. Other hindrances pressed on him. Unwilling to fail in punctuality, he vigorously set to work; made sale of his goods, secured such collections as were possible, purchased horses, sold them in eastern markets, and made such energetic efforts in various ways, that success crowned his endeavours, and his contracts were fulfilled to the entire satisfaction of the men who had so generously trusted him. But the scarcity of money, together with the embarrassments arising in that early day from his isolated and mountainous position, was for years a source of anxiety and trouble in the fulfilment of his city purchases. Yet his ceaseless energy, fertile resources, capacity of business, rigid integrity and indomitable will, not only carried him safely through his difficulties, but secured him the increasing and life-long friendship of the men who first confided in him. These traits and these friendships, laid the foundation for such general esteem in the cities, that he could command almost unlimited credit. So wisely, so prudently, and so successfully did he manage his commercial transactions, that not many years elapsed before he was able to make all his purchases in cash. This policy he pursued until the close of his mercantile life.

In properly estimating his character, the early period at which his mercantile career commenced must always be kept in mind. The advantages were very few and limited, the difficulties great and many. Yet, by the force of his character, he made himself a popular and successful merchant. Seasons came when particular kinds of merchandise would become very dear and scarce for years together. They were articles that would be greatly needed, not only in the household but on the farm. The want of some would be sorely felt both by man and beast. Yet his foresight of these times was such that he met and successfully overcame obstacles that appeared insuperable. On one occasion the preparations made from garret to cellar of his house, and even in the erection of exterior buildings, were so extensive as to appear foolish and extravagant. The end foreseen, however, came, and proved the wisdom of his acts. He was able to sell his merchandise from twenty-five to two hundred per cent. cheaper than other stores for many miles around, and to keep up the supply until the exigency was past. Thus he not only made himself useful and popular but secured his own benefit without detriment to his fellow-men.

His fertility of resources was such that he created demands for large quantities of produce, greatly to the advantage of the farmers. Sometimes as many as one and two hundred sleds, in the town and vicinity, were coming and going and awaiting their turns for purchase and exchange. Not only was the whole day, but occasionally the entire night was consumed in the traffic thus created.

Col. Agnew became, at an early period of his life, a decided Christian, and was for many years a ruling elder of the church. He was remarkable for the soundness of his judgment, the punctuality of his attendance upon every duty appointed him, and for his direct, explicit and business-like manner of performing official duties. At the time of the troubles in the Presbyterian Church, which resulted in separation in 1838, he took decided ground with the Old School. He was a member of the Convention which adopted and signed "The Act and Testimony," and to his dying day was a firm and consistent believer of the sound doctrine, and the sedate and efficient order of the church of which he was a member and office bearer.

The congregation of McConnellsburg, of which he was in part the founder, was originally in connection with the Associate Reformed Church; but when that body united with the General Assembly, in 1825, it came cordially into the union. Dr. George Junkin, when a licentiate, several times supplied the pulpit of that church, and was once invited to its pastorate but did not accept. When at McConnellsburg he was the guest of Col. Agnew.

On one occasion an incident occurred which illustrates the character of both these men for brave and firm adherence to principle and law. It was before the days of canals and railways, and when the "Conestoga Wagons," with their stout draught teams, were the only mode of conveying freight from Philadelphia to Pittsburgh. These sometimes formed a long caravan on the road that passed through McConnellsburg. Very few gave to themselves and their horses the benefit of the Sabbath's rest; and what with the noise of the wagons and horses, and the boisterous voices and terrible oaths of the teamsters, became a serious nuisance to the Christian people along their route. The law of the State was against it; and many persons felt impelled by conscience to enforce the law. Colonel Agnew was one of these. This aroused opposition, and a portion of the community conspired to annoy him by nominating him for the office of constable. They supposed that, rather than accept it he would pay the usual fine. He was elected, and very soon they were disappointed and mortified with the results that followed. He accepted and took the oath of office. It *now* became his *sworn* and *official* duty to enforce the law; and he did it with firmness and zeal. One Monday morning, attempting to arrest a large and powerful teamster who had, the day before, violated both the law of God and the law of man, he was resisted. Colonel Agnew was a large, finely built man, over six feet, and very strong. The teamster was stalwart and violent, and withstood so fiercely that the Colonel was not equal to the task. Mr. Junkin was his guest at the time, and seeing the struggle could not resist the impulse of a generous nature to rush to the help of the officer. Though short of stature, young Junkin was a man of vast muscular strength and activity. With his help the giant wagoner was soon overpowered, and carried before the magistrate.

Colonel Agnew was an early and consistent friend of the temperance reformation. All the stores kept liquor, but he determined to banish it from his own. The person employed in the store to whom one-third of the profits was given, made objection, that it was a very profitable part of the business. He was directed however, to make a calculation of the usual amount of income from this source. This was done; the amount was added to his third, and the poison banished from the store. Through his example and influence the other stores, with one exception, discontinued the traffic.

In his prime he stood high in the confidence of his fellow-citizens, and was frequently called to execute important trusts, both civil and ecclesiastical; and he always, it is believed, did it to the full satisfaction of those who confided in him.

The subject of this sketch was one of the public spirited citizens of his region, who took a lively interest in improving the country. When he went to the Great Cove it was a wilderness, the settlers were few, the roads but paths, the wild animals numerous, and the houses cabins. But one or, at most, two log dwellings made the beginning of the village that was to be the theatre of his life. On the bank of a small stream was laid the foundation of his trading post and home. There, until a few years before his death, stood a tall elm under which the Indian had smoked his pipe, whilst he drew from the waters the fish that filled the streams in that early day. His latest dwelling of stone, was built as early as 1793. He lived to see great changes, and was active in promoting public improvements. "The Packers' Path" gave way first to the great State road, and that to the McAdamized turnpike, in the survey and location of which he had assisted; and before his decease, McConnellsburg had ceased to be on the great thoroughfare from city to city; the Canal and afterwards the Pennsylvania Central Railroad, having entirely superseded the Conestoga wagons in the great business of transportation. He lived many years after the great Cove was stricken from Bedford and included in the new county of Fulton, of which McConnellsburg became the seat of justice.

His home, though a private residence, was known as the "Minister's Hotel." This arose from the cordial hospitality with which clergymen of all denominations were received and entertained. This hospitality was practised for weeks and months at a time. Nor was it confined to persons only of the class named. They came from the cities and from all parts of the country north, south, east and west, and even from foreign lands. They were going to and from the Legislature, Congress, the "Springs," and various ecclesiastical bodies. A great amount of knowledge and of interesting incidents of men and things was thus obtained, that made his company instructive and entertaining. Had he done in this, as was done in another matter, a large amount of pleasant reading would have been left for his family and for others. He had kept, from an early period, a daily thermometrical and other records of the weather, and was so punctual in its performance, that even when from home it was not neglected. Carrying a pocket thermometer, he noted down in a small book the varying phases of the weather from day to day. A similar record of the above nature was once suggested to him by a person who had been greatly interested in his conversation, but he replied, that he was too old, and that his habits of writing unfitted him for the task.

Col. Agnew's systematic and strictly temperate habits assured a long life, and his death, the result of a fall down a flight of stairs, occurred on the ninth day of September, 1855, in the eighty-seventh year of his age.

As an appropriate conclusion of this biographical sketch we make the following extracts from the obituary notice written by the venerable Dr. Elliott, who knew him during a great part of their lives, including the period of their greatest vigour: "There was much in the character and conduct of Col. Agnew which furnished credible evidence of his being a child of God. In the discharge of religious duties, not only those of a public but those of a private nature, no one was ever more punctual. Family and secret worship were never omitted except on the ground of providential impediments. For both of these duties he had his fixed hours; and when these arrived neither company nor business were allowed to detain him from their performance, and when the place of his secret retirement was occupied, he has been noticed to retire to some spot out of the house where he supposed he was entirely secluded from observation, and there pour out his soul to God. The Sabbath he consecrated sacredly to religious duties. He was particularly attentive to the religious instruction of his children on that day, in hearing them recite portions of Scripture, and of the Shorter Catechism committed to memory. These exercises were followed by an earnest and solemn appeal to them on the subject of their personal salvation, which often affected them to tears. The writer has the declaration of one of his children, that if to any human instrumentality he was indebted as a means for his salvation, it was to the faithful instruction and appeals and prayers of his father. He also by his example gave constant sanction to the value of public ordinances and meetings for social prayer. His place in the church and the prayer meeting was never vacant until the illness which terminated his life. His last illness was protracted and severe. During its continuance he suffered intense pain, which he bore with remarkable fortitude and patience. By this protracted suffering God seems to have been detaching his affections from the world and raising them to higher and more enduring objects. His mind, as we are informed, was much exercised in reference to the state of his soul. With tears he lamented his shortcomings in duty, but while he had his doubts and fears, his eye was steadily fixed on the Saviour of sinners, and he expressed an humble hope of salvation through the merits of Jesus Christ. It was in Christ, and Christ alone, that he placed his reliance, and in him we trust he has found salvation. I only add that Col. Agnew long held the honourable office of ruling elder in the church, and was favourably known in the judicatories of the church, as a wise and judicious counselor.

He was married twice. His first wife was Mrs. Ochiltree, of Virginia. Her parents had emigrated there from Adams county, Pennsylvania. She became a widow about a year after marriage. Col. Agnew, who had too late addressed her when she was Miss Elizabeth Finley, a second time sought her hand, and became her husband. Of eight children left, the second son, John R. Agnew, is in the Christian ministry. After graduating at Dickinson College, he spent two years at Union Theological Seminary, Prince Edward, Va., and one year at Princeton, and was licensed to preach the Gospel by the Presbytery of East Hanover, in 1834.

His first public service was that of missionary to the Choctaw Indians, on the Red river, bordering on Texas, under no missionary organization and chiefly at his own expense, and at a time when it tried a man's soul to go out as a missionary.

His health having failed him there, he returned to the States, and was settled as pastor in Venango county, Pa., for nine years, when sore throat compelled him to seek a dissolution of the pastoral relation.

He then determined never again to accept a call to a church, and firmly adhered to this determination, though often urged to settle as pastor, preferring to preach to the masses as God might grant him opportunity.

Since 1846, he has served the church and his country in various capacities: as Agent for Lafayette College, Agent of the Board of Colportage at Pittsburgh, Agent of Lincoln University, Professor in Steubenville Female Seminary, and as Chaplain in the Penitentiary of Missouri.

While acting as Professor of Astronomy, at Steubenville, he invented an ingenious set of sectional globes, celestial and terrestrial, combined with an orrery in such a manner that all three in one more clearly and definitely convey to the mind of the student the movements of the heavenly bodies, than has been done by any other invention, and it will be a blessing to any school to be furnished with these appliances for illustrating geography and astronomy. While laid aside from preaching by physical infirmities, at Greencastle, Pa., he is completing these inventions.

In all the public positions he has occupied the Rev. John R. Agnew has proven himself to be a man of the very highest principles, faithful, earnest and conscientious in the discharge of his duties, and pre-eminently a man of faith and prayer, preferring the poverty and trials of the Gospel ministry to the many more lucrative positions which have offered themselves to him at various periods of his eventful life.

Col. Agnew's oldest son, James Finley, is an officer in the church, in western Pennsylvania. His youngest son, Samuel Agnew, Esq., of Philadelphia, was the real originator of the Presbyterian Historical Society, so far as the original suggestion is concerned. He urged upon the late lamented Dr. Van Rensselaer the importance of such an organization; and at his urgent request Dr. Van Rensselaer brought the subject before the General Assembly of 1852, and obtained a recommendation of it, and at every step of its progress he has been the devoted and indefatigable promoter of that society, and most of its success is attributable to his gifts, zeal and labours in its behalf. Mrs. Elizabeth Brown, and Mr. David Agnew, an elder with his father in the McConnellsburg church, are the other living children. William died early. Mrs. Sarah Patterson died a number of years ago, leaving a large family. His daughter Mary, a young lady of remarkable beauty and loveliness of character, died at an early age. His second wife was Mrs. R. Scott, of Gettysburg, Pa.,—Miss Patterson, of Lancaster county, Pa.

Dr. LEMUEL GUSTINE.

THIS distinguished physician's first residence in Pennsylvania was in the "Wyoming valley," in 1769. After the sad event which is known in history as the "Massacre of Wyoming," Dr. Gustine took up his residence in Carlisle. This was in July, 1778.

The circumstances of the invasion of the Wyoming settlement by the British and Indians; the battle and massacre; the conflagration of their dwellings, and the destruction of their property of all kinds, are well known to every reader of history, and need not be repeated here. But the personal action of individuals during such events is interesting, and may well be further noticed.

The British and their Indian allies had selected the time for the attack when the two Wyoming companies of Continental troops were absent from the valley, having been ordered to join the commander-in-chief "with all possible expedition." The number of men and boys able to bear arms to resist the enemy, was about four hundred, and these undisciplined troops marched forth to meet the British and Indians, the former consisting of British Provincials and Tories, were in number about four hundred men; and of Seneca and Mohawk Indians, about six hundred and fifty. The Wyoming men fought well, but were overpowered by the superior forces of the enemy. Dr. Gustine, the subject of this article, was an aid to Colonel Dennison, who, in conjunction with Colonel Zebulon Butler, commanded the Wyoming troops. Dr. Gustine and Colonel Dennison were the last to leave the field, and they were enabled with a few others to regain "Forty Fort," from whence they had marched to meet the enemy. When the fort was invested, Dr. Gustine accompanied Colonel Dennison to arrange the terms of the capitulation; and he is one of the signers of that document. Dr. Gustine was a man of great strength and activity, as well as of courage. When the British and Indians took possession of "Forty Fort," the latter commenced to plunder our people. An Indian attempted to take some property or apparel from the Doctor; he resisted, and giving the Indian a trip threw him to the ground. The other Indians were so much pleased at the Doctor's courage and activity that they handed him a rope, and said: "He is a drunken dog; tie him." Soon after the taking of possession by Major John Butler, who commanded the British and Indians, he said to Dr. Gustine, "I can protect you, and the others with you to-day, and for this night also, but I cannot promise you safety to-morrow." That night Dr. Gustine was enabled to procure a boat, and the next morning set off in it with his family and a few others down the Susquehanna. Landing for a short time at Fort Augusta, (now Sunbury, Northumberland county,) they pursued their journey down the river, and stopping for a few days at Fort Hunter, a few miles above John Harris' Ferry, (now Harrisburg,) they came to the Ferry; and from thence Dr. Gustine and his family proceeded to Carlisle, where he took up his residence, and remained until his death, which took place in 1807.

One of the terms of capitulation of the Fort at Wyoming, and signed by Dr. Gustine, contained the following: "that the inhabitants that Colonel Dennison now capitulates for, together with himself, do not take up arms during the present contest." Dr. Gustine did not return to the Wyoming valley, nor break his engagement by re-entering the military service. He pursued with great success the practice of his profession; his practice extending through a large extent of country in Cumberland valley.

Dr. Gustine was first married to a daughter of Dr. William Hooker Smith, a prominent citizen of Wyoming, who, among other official positions, was Surgeon in the Continental army. This lady died a few weeks before the "Massacre of Wyoming," and is buried at "Forty Fort." A daughter by this marriage, Sarah, was three years old at the time of the massacre, and was in the Fort when it was surrendered. This daughter accompanied her father, Dr. Gustine, to Carlisle. She subsequently, namely, in 1792, was married to the Rev. Nathaniel R. Snowden, then a licentiate of the Presbytery of Philadelphia, but who had for several years resided at Carlisle as a student of divinity under the eminent Dr. Charles Nesbit. Mr. Minor, in his History of Wyoming, (1845,) referring to the family of Dr. William Hooker Smith, says: "But there was another daughter, who was married to Dr. Gustine, whose name will be found to the capitulation of Forty Fort. Dr. Gustine removed to another part of the state, and an only daughter of theirs, who was in the fort at the time of its surrender, married the Rev. Mr. Snowden, father of James Ross Snowden. The heart leaps more quickly, and the life current flows more kindly at the mention of his name, when we recollect that the late honoured Speaker of the House of Representatives, and present Treasurer of the Commonwealth, is the descendant of one of the Wyoming sufferers."

Dr. Gustine, a few years after his removal to Carlisle, married Miss

Mary Parker, by whom he had several sons and daughters, most of whom removed to the state of Mississippi, where they became extensive and prosperous planters. And now there are none having the family name of Gustine residing in the Cumberland valley, albeit there are many in that region who are connected therewith by the ties of consanguinity and affinity, viz: the Hendersons, Loudons, Uries, Holcombs, Parkers, Snowdens, and others.

JOHN KNOX, D. D.

DR. KNOX was born June 17th, 1790, in Adams county, near Gettysburg. His father was Samuel Knox, M. D., a physician of high reputation. His mother was Rebecca Hodge. Dr. Knox received his preparatory instruction in preparation for college from his father and the Rev. Alexander Dobbin, pastor of "the Hill" Associate Reformed Church, of which, in early life, Dr. Knox was a member. In 1809, he entered the Junior Class of Dickinson College, and graduated in 1811.

Leaving college, he entered the Theological Seminary of the Associate Reformed Church in the city of New York, under the superintendence of the Rev. Dr. John M. Mason. He was licensed to preach the Gospel in 1815, and was ordained to the full work of the ministry, and installed collegiate pastor of the Reformed Dutch Church in the city of New York, on July 16th, 1816. In this charge he continued until his death on January 8th, 1858.

On May 11th, 1818, he was married to Euphemia Provost, elder daughter of the Rev. Dr. Mason. Mrs. Knox died July 6th, 1855.

In his private character Dr. Knox was the model of a Christian gentleman. Kind without an air of condescension, truthful without an ostentation of frankness, warm-hearted without credulity, scrupulously honourable, and punctiliously exact in the use of words, and in the performance of his promises, he won the friendship of those who knew him, and kept that friendship until the last.

As a preacher, Dr. Knox lacked what is commonly styled eloquence in delivery, but his manner had the best element of eloquence—which was persuasiveness. The matter of his sermons was always evangelical, and this was the chief secret of his long continuance in one charge, and of his undiminished influence throughout his pastorate.

As a philanthropist, he occupied a high position. He was a Trustee of Columbia College; of Rutgers College, New Jersey; of the Leake and Watt Orphan Asylum; Chairman of the Publishing Committee of the American Tract Society, and a member of several boards of his own church. In all these public relations, he evinced a steady diligence, and lent his influence and his wise counsels to the progress of their welfare.

"Dr. Knox was pre-eminently adapted to fill a large place in his day and generation. His noble, majestic form never disappointed the expectations which it could not fail to raise. The earthly house and the immortal tenant were well matched. He was *born* to exert a commanding influence. He was *consecrated* to exert a commanding influence for *good*. His comprehensive mind spurned all narrow, contracted, mean, petty and false views of any subject to which his attention was directed. He saw farther than most men; and as far as he saw, he saw clearly, and what he saw he spake, 'without partiality and without hypocrisy.' Then, too, his great heart was full of generous sympathies, which forbade him to yield his judgment to the special pleading of any *ex parte* advocate of selfishness and injustice. For these and similar reasons, his *wisdom* became the characteristic by which he was best known to the *world*—the secret of his power in the pulpit, and in pastoral visitation, over the understanding and hearts and consciences of his parishioners, a power which a long ministerial life but served to increase, and which will continue to be felt when all the popular eloquence of the times shall be forgotten; the secret, too of his election to so many important offices in the benevolent societies and philanthropic and educational institutions of his age, offices which, however arduous and thankless the labours devoted upon him in them, he could not be permitted, for any plea of increasing years, to resign; and the secret, moreover, of the innumerable applications to him, in person and by letter, for private advice, from kindred and connections near and remote; from members of his own congregation, and from his fellow-citizens generally; from his ministerial brethren; from strangers and foreigners; from high life, middle life, and low life, thronging his house, interrupting him at his meals, his devotions and his studies, and burdening him with cares enough to crush any ordinary man, though, truth to say, he seemed to thrive under them.

"For with all the public responsibilities which his sound judgment and discretion brought upon him, he found so much time for the enjoyment and duties of social life, that he was best known throughout the large circle of his *family* and *friends* for his *warm affection, constant and kindly solicitude*, and *bountiful hospitality*. Who that ever witnessed, can forget how his imposing presence was relieved by the beautiful combination in his manners of dignity, courtesy, affability and cordiality? His hearty welcome was sustained by his unwearied attentions to his guests, till his farewell left them more his admirers than ever. Among the multitudes entitled to his regards, or admitted to his confidence and favour, not one, in disappointment, perplexity or sorrow, ever applied to him for assistance, counsel or consolation in vain.

Many a time has he volunteered his thoughtfulness for them, and, when they least expected it, has soothed their griefs, guided them through their difficulties, and opened to them new avenues of usefulness and prosperity. And ever have they found him most deeply interested in, and most ready to promote, their spiritual and eternal welfare. He *watched* for their souls. If any man ever had a right to adopt the words of 'the greatest of all the men of the east,' it was Dr. Knox: 'When the ear heard me, then it blessed me; and when the eye saw me, it gave witness to me: because I delivered the poor that cried, and *the fatherless*, and him that had none to help him. The blessing of him that was ready to perish came upon me, and I caused *the widow's heart* to sing for joy. I was eyes to the blind, and feet was I to the lame. I was *a father* to the poor, and the cause which I knew not I searched out. Unto me *men gave ear, and waited, and kept silence at my counsel. I chose out their way, and sat chief,* and dwelt as a king in the army, *as one that comforteth the mourners.*'"

ALFRED FOSTER, M. D.

IN the old graveyard in the borough of Carlisle there is a monument with this inscription, "Alfred Foster, M. D.; born A. D., 1790; died A. D., 1847." On one side of it is written, "Purity of mind and integrity of purpose graced his great attainments in science and literature; and his character happily blended the guilelessness of childhood with the wisdom of mature years." On another, this: "His talents were various and brilliant; his learning extensive and accurate; but diffident of his own powers, he shunned that distinction which his abilities would have secured, had ambition prompted."

There is no place where the excellent qualities of men are more likely to be extravagantly portrayed than that which marks their last resting place. In this class would the above inscriptions be ranked by those who had no knowledge of the life and character of Dr. Foster, but to those acquainted with them, there is no word of extravagance in what is there written. He was a student from boyhood. He graduated at Dickinson College in 1809, was a classmate of Hon. James Buchanan and divided with him the first honours of the class. Here their lives separated. Mr. Buchanan soon became an eminent member of the bar and mingled politics with his profession; sought and obtained distinction in public life, and attained a name that will ever be remembered among men. Dr. Foster, with equal abilities and far greater acquirements, was never known beyond the limits of his own state; never known intimately but by people of his own town; and his memory now has faded from the recollection of many of the active portion of its population. But with those who had the good fortune to know him, there is an abiding love for his character, faith in his professional knowledge, and reverence for his intellectual attainments, that seldom cluster round the memory of the dead.

There is an atmosphere that always surrounds great minds, which is peculiar to them and noticeable by the observant. This pervaded the character of Dr. Foster more than that of any other citizen of Carlisle during his active career, although many men of distinction resided here at the same time, and they were generally his intimate friends. This exhibited itself in his case in many ways. Among others the following will serve as illustrations. With the members of his profession, when he was called into consultation, his judgment was considered unerring.

With the sick, and particularly with those whose ailments were as much mental as physical, when Dr. Foster said the danger was over or there was no real cause for alarm, the patient was instantly relieved; but more than all, in that circle composed of the leading men of his own profession, the leading men of the bar, the clergy and the professors of the college, he was ever regarded as the foremost.

There is a superiority which is seen and felt in the refined social circle that is not recognized by the multitude and not exhibited in a crowd or felt in a public assembly. It is the unerring deference which mind pays to mind, and that in the proportion each overshadows the other. Addison, in his Freeholder, tells us that his good genius once conducted him to the Temple of Fame and placed him where he could see all who were there and hear all that was said. He saw, seated at the table, the chief heroes and poets and philosophers of classic antiquity, heard their disputations, and noticed, when debate ran high, a nod from Homer settled the matter. In a large, refined and highly cultivated society existing in Carlisle, and embracing among others the members of the various professions, the Faculty of the college, distinguished officers of the Army and the Chief Justice of the state, the first place was unhesitatingly assigned to the Doctor. And the reason was obvious. There was no subject that engaged the minds of men in science, in philosophy, or in the line of the various professions, with which he was not familiar. Had a new planet been discovered? His mind glanced over the whole range of Astronomy from the Ptolemaic system to the last theory that had been advanced, and he illumined the subject with such stores of knowledge, that one who did not know him, would have felt satisfied he had spent his whole life in studying the courses of the heavenly bodies. Was the subject of pure mathematics introduced by some learned professor? He would begin with the history of that science and trace it through its three great periods, characterizing each by the introduction of its new methods, showing how geometry was almost exclusively cultivated during the era of Greek and Roman supremacy; how, after the decline of Rome, the sciences took refuge among the Arabs who translated and preserved the literary treasures of Greece, and introduced the second great period of mathematics by giving to Europe the decimal arithmetic and the algebraic calculus, both of Indian origin; and thence he would come down to what had in later years been done by Descartes, Newton, Leibnitz, and their successors, Euler, D'Alembert and Laplace.

Was some historic field of battle the subject of conversation? The men of military education were astounded at the accuracy of his knowledge of the details of that engagement and its influence on the war that was raging, and on the ultimate fate of the nations engaged; and so on through the whole round of human knowledge. There was no field with which he was not familiar, and no detail with which his mind was not accurately stored. And yet this great man was as modest as a child, as unobtrusive as it is possible to be, and so averse to adulation, that if any one offered to pay homage to his great attainments, he was apt to offend him, and if he dared to flatter him, was sure to make him angry. He never married, never strove for or attained wealth, was careless of money beyond his personal wants, and met promptly his pecuniary engagements. No man before him had ever in this place made such high attainments in learning and knowledge, and none since has ever aspired to them.

His family was, early in this century, prominent here, but he was the last of his name that resided in Carlisle.

JOHN CLARKE YOUNG, D. D.

JOHN C. YOUNG was born in Green Castle, Pa. His father was an excellent elder in the Presbyterian Church of that place. His mother was the sister of the Rev. John X. Clarke, and Hon. Matthew St. Clair Clarke.

His earliest training was received in his native place, from John Boreland, one of the finest scholars and most admirable teachers of the country. He was educated at Dickinson College, under the celebrated Dr. John Mason. His theological course was pursued at Princeton. In the third year he was chosen tutor in the college, along with the lamented A. B. Dod. After finishing his studies, and being licensed, he was first called to the church in Lexington, Kentucky. His preaching there made a profound impression, and his ministry was successful in a high degree.

After a few years, Dr. Young was called to the Presidency of Danville College, where his life-work was afterward spent. He was popular with the students, and greatly revered by the friends of the college. His ministry was greatly blessed to the awakening and conversion of the students. He organized a second church in Danville, to which he statedly ministered for many years, and where the students attended. He took an active and decided part in the discussions on slavery and emancipation in Kentucky, and was the author of a report on the subject in the Synod.

Dr. Young was Moderator of the Assembly which met in Philadelphia, in 1853, and presided over the deliberations of that body with great ability and universal acceptableness. The latter years of his life were marked by disease, which terminated his usefulness in 1857. He was twice married. His first wife was the daughter of Cabel Breckinridge, and sister of John C. Breckinridge. His second wife was the daughter of Hon. J. J. Crittenden, who still survives him. Two of his sons are, or were, in the ministry.

"Dr. Young," says his friend, Rev. D. H. Biddle, D. D., "was an able and sound divine, a faithful and successful teacher, of a logical mind and warm heart. His loss to the church and the cause of learning is deeply deplored, and his memory is fondly cherished by all who knew and loved him." Such men are ornaments to their age, and blessings to their country and the world.

JAMES S. WOODS, D. D.

THE REV. JAMES STERRETT WOODS, son of Samuel and Frances (Sterrett) Woods, was born in Cumberland county, Pa., April 18th, 1793. His parents were Scotch-Irish, and one of the best families in the Cumberland valley. They were remarkable for their intelligence, integrity and energy. Their piety was Scriptural and practical, resting on the sound basis of clear and thorough doctrinal knowledge. The greatest care was taken in the training of their children.

Samuel Woods, the father, was a man of the highest probity, courage and reliability. During the progress of the War of the Revolution he acted as Indian scout—a most perilous undertaking—in the service of the Government, or on behalf of the neighbourhood in which he lived, which was then the red man's undisputed home. The mother, whose maiden name was Sterrett, it is said, was a woman of devoted piety, and pre-eminent for her *faith*. The character of their children is their best eulogy. They worshiped in the Presbyterian Church, in Carlisle, Pa., under the care of Rev. Dr. Davidson, and subsequently Rev. Dr. H. R. Wilson. Here Mr. Woods first professed religion. James S. Woods received his classical education with Mr. John Cooper, Hopewell Academy, Pa.; graduated at Dickinson College, Carlisle, Pa., under the presidency of Rev. John McKnight, D. D. He obtained his theological education at Princeton, N. J., and was licensed by the Presbytery of New Brunswick, in 1817. His first settlement was in Mifflin county, Pa., whither he came in 1819. From this time until 1822 he laboured as an evangelist in the valley of the Juniata, from Lewistown to Shade Gap. Through this field, embracing McVeytown, Newton-Hamilton and Shirleysburg, he laid the foundations for the present churches. Here he is claimed as the father of Presbyterianism. Often he preached in private houses, school houses and barns. He mingled much with the people, catechising statedly and faithfully, and visiting the sick and dying wherever known. Many still live in the churches of McVeytown and Newton-Hamilton who count him their spiritual father, and hold him in the highest esteem. In the bounds of these places a work of grace was carried on for two years, which he considered one of the most powerful he had ever seen. He resided, at first, in the vicinity of McVeytown, and was called, in 1822, to take charge of the Lewistown and McVeytown churches. In the spring of 1823 he moved to Lewistown, and continued the pastor of the church there until the time of his death, a space of nearly *forty years.*

James S. Woods was married before he came to Mifflin county, to Marianne Witherspoon, a daughter of John Witherspoon, D. D., one of the presidents of Princeton College, and the only clergyman who signed the Declaration of Independence. He was a lineal descendant from the eminent Scottish Reformer, John Knox, and one of the most illustrious patrons of religion, liberty and learning in America. This lady, a native of Princeton, N. J., was possessed of fine mental powers, and great moral worth, and exercised, it is believed, an important influence in the formation of her husband's ministerial character. The fruit of this marriage was nine children, six sons and three daughters. In the religious training of these, Mrs. Woods was assiduous till the time of her death, which occurred in 1846, in the "sure and steadfast hope, which, as an anchor, entereth into that within the vail." Two of the sons have died: one, John W. Woods, while preparing for the profession of law; the other, Lieutenant James S. Woods, of the United States Army, while gallantly leading his company in the storming of Monterey, Mexico. The father of this family lived to see his children become, through the grace of God, his hope and his joy, and closed his life in the prospect of meeting his loved and loving ones in heaven.

"His household circle," says the Rev. David D. Clarke, D. D., in a sermon preached to Dr. Woods' bereaved church, by request of the elders and trustees; "his household circle was a rare example of unmarred communion. He was always its attractive centre. The appreciating visitor could not fail to see how each heart clung, as the tendril, to that true and trusted husband and parent, and fondly entwined each other. Even his grand-children were made merry and frisky as lambs under the charm of his smiles; and to take tea at grandpa's was counted a special honour.

"But it is not meet that I should enter further within the precincts of this stricken home! The bereavement by this death is first and greatly, but not solely yours. We tell it in two sweet words, 'Our father!' You knew him as none other did; you loved him as none other could. God gave him and took him. Bless his name that he was spared to you so long, to be the guide of your youth and the glory of your ripened years. His life, so consistent and beneficent, was a grand success. Much of its fruit has already been gathered and garnered in heaven, and more awaits the hand of the great husbandman. To sustain your relation to such a man and such a ministry is a heritage more precious than silver or gold. He did not live to become a burden to himself, or to you. God, whom he served, took him in his own time and way—always the best. He spoke not in death, but you know his life, and 'being dead he yet speaketh.' What more can you do—what more does God require than to bow down in trusting, hopeful submission, and say, ' Not my will, but thine, O Lord, be done !'

"We come now to survey a little further the public and professional life of our departed brother, as it was embraced in his pastorate here of *forty years*. Appearance, temper and manner, it is well known, are often elements of personal attraction and influence. Brother Woods possessed a commanding presence. His temper was warm, social and genial. There was a dignity, seriousness and kindness in his mien, which commanded attention and respect. His piety was stable and practical, his convictions earnest, and his purposes decided. For the authority of Scripture his regard was profound; to whatever he thought right his adherence was unwavering. Principle, duty, honour, he never sacrificed; yet he was not dogmatic or obstinate, but modest and humble. He did not seek his own praise in the disparagement of others. He was willing to be enlightened, and even led by others, in whose judgment and honesty he confided. He was punctual in all engagements—in pulpit and pastoral service, with his friends, and in his attendance on all the judicatories of the church. His desire was not fame, but to perform his duty and do good. Wherever you met him, his character was transparent, whether under his own roof, which was truly a minister's home, or that of others, in the sanctuary of God, or in the church courts, he was the same—the true friend, the agreeable companion, the Christian gentleman, and the conscientious servant of God. A conscience void of offence toward God and man made him fearless, and no one could despise him. He had a pleasant look and a kind word for all he met. It is easy to see that such a man would make friends, secure confidence, and have influence. No man in the county had a stronger hold on the veneration of the people. By his brethren of the Presbytery he was held in the highest esteem, and the Christian people of our churches were always glad to make him their guest. I deem it a great privilege to have enjoyed his acquaintance and regard.

"Dr. Woods was a patriot. While a student at college he joined a company, chiefly of students, to march to Baltimore when attacked by the British troops. He was not a perfect man ; we don't present him as such, for such he did not claim to be; but he was a rare man, a good man, a faithful man, a useful man, loved and honoured by God and man.

"If descent from an exalted ancestry, if a marriage alliance to one of the most renowned of American names, if personal worth and a long life of well-doing, entitle one to the grateful remembrance of posterity, Dr. Woods has a claim, and this record of his long, faithful and fruitful ministry fills one of the brightest pages of the church's history.

"Let us hear the testimony of those who knew him best: 'Dr. Woods,' says Rev. G. Elliott, 'was remarkable for his candor, his modesty and his magnanimity. His heart was the seat of kindness, and his home the scene of untiring hospitality. Those who had recently conversed with him familiarly could realize that he felt how precarious was his condition, and that he was growing in meetness for Heaven.'

"Dr. Engles, in *The Presbyterian*, says: 'An esteemed and venerable minister of our church, and a beloved member of the Synod of Philadelphia, has departed this life. After such a life, death is but a transition from labour to reward.'

"'We knew him well from early manhood,' Dr. McKinney, in *The Presbyterian Banner*, says. 'We were twenty-two years co-presbyters. Often did we labour together in religious services of great interest. He was a good man, a devoted minister, and an exalted though lowly Christian. He has turned many to righteousness, and will shine as the stars forever and ever.'

"But let us see how this high praise is supported by the long ministry which has just closed on earth. Much of the harmony of social life, and much of the success in every vocation, depend on the observance of the great law of *adaptation*, of properly fitting things. Ignoring this law commonly entails difficulty, disappointment and failure. He, whom we all mourn, was in the harmony of his relations, and in the success of his labours, a delightful example. Who was better suited to this field, in all its aspects, than he? Who could have endured so long and so well? Who could have so won the respect of all around, and the confidence and love of those especially committed to his spiritual oversight, binding them in the stability and repose of an intelligent and harmonious communion, and anchoring himself more deeply, with every revolving year, in the confidence and veneration of the community? In your just and appreciating tributes, brethren, in this appropriate and beautiful edifice, confessedly to a great extent the fruit of his judicious and patient efforts, in what he has done for the numerical and spiritual increase of this church, and through it for other churches, and for the general cause of God—in these is found the answer.

"To the work of preaching the Gospel he devoted his life. Whatever of talent or culture, whatever of gifts natural or gracious he possessed, were gratefully, and without reserve, laid at the feet of Christ. In the cross, as the symbol of the truth and power of God, he recognized the chief and sure agency for the reformation and redemption of our ruined humanity, the sovereign antidote to mortal woe. Baptized in the spirit of Him who triumphed as he expired on Calvary, at once the Saviour and Sovereign of the world, his was a faith that would give Christ the throne of the universe, his a charity that would make the world its beneficiary. Textual, evangelical, methodical and earnest, his preaching everywhere commanded attention and secured edification. In the early part of his ministry, he wrote out and committed to memory his sermons, dispensing with the manuscript in the delivery. His style was simple and unadorned, but clear and forcible. His good taste, his apprehension of spiritual and eternal things, and his desire to win souls, made him intensely anxious that all should understand what he spoke. But few men felt more fully than he did that the pulpit is the 'preacher's throne.' Out of it, he evinced the meekness of the lamb; in it, the boldness of the lion. He felt that he could teach his hearers. However striking their superiority over him in many things, he felt that in the most important of all things he had, as he ought to have, superiority over them. He could make the wisest of them more wise. He could reprove the most learned of them for their ignorance of 'the one thing needful.' 'Physicians, jurists, statesmen, must,' says an elegant writer, ' bow themselves before the pulpit, and must yield their dignified obeisance to him who is distinguished by the appellation, "*the mouth of God.*"'

"Dr. Woods loved his people, and while his strength supported him was much amongst them. His school house preaching, his regular catechetical instruction, his Bible-class exercises, and his wise, untiring and affectionate pastoral visitation constituted a most arduous and useful part of his long and fruitful labours. The Sabbath school, one of the best ordered and most efficient in the Presbytery, he considered a model Sabbath school. He loved the young. In the season of trial, in the chamber of the sick and the dying, his ready perception of propriety, his tenderness, his familiarity with the Bible, his rich fund of Christian experience, endeared him to all who, in those times, were privileged to enjoy the counsels and consolations of his benignant ministry. To exhibit Christ, to bring men to Christ, to confirm and comfort those who were in Christ, and to glorify Christ, was the Alpha and Omega of his labours.

"The cause of Temperance found in him an early and enduring friend. The evil of intemperance he regarded as one of the greatest which afflicts society. On this subject no one was better able than he to form a correct judgment. He lived before the commencement of the Temperance Reformation. He saw the evil in its fearful and unresisted progress. He carefully watched the working of the several plans of reformation. He considered the law defective, and as it is, badly enforced. His conviction was clear, that the true policy was *prevention*, starting with the *young*, and that but little dependence could be placed on any individual reformation, which was not supported by Christian principle. Views so sound will not be questioned, having the support of Scripture and facts.

"Two things are characteristic of this church under Dr. Woods, *order* and *growth*. It has enjoyed throughout his pastorate unwonted harmony. Its peace has been almost unbroken. But few cases for discipline have occurred, and rarely has it been found necessary to refer one for settlement to a higher court than the church Session. And while Dr. Woods had great confidence in a *true revival of religion*, refreshing Christians, and bringing many sinners to Christ, and while he never ceased to pray and wait for the special reviving grace of the Holy Spirit in his own congregation, and throughout the church, and was allowed of God to rejoice in many a special and glorious visitation of the Prince of Peace to this church, he relied mainly on the regular and usual increase, And seldom, in his long pastorate, was there a communion season without one or more additions to the membership.

"The honorary title of D. D. was conferred on him eight or ten years ago, by the Trustees of the College of New Jersey. Although he gave but little time to literary studies, after his entrance upon the work of the ministry, he was a good classical scholar. He taught a school while he resided above McVeytown; and for some time after his settlement here had charge of the Academy, a classical school he was instrumental in building. Among his pupils were Rev. M. B. Hope, D. D., Rev. Mr. Reed, Missionary to Siam, Rev. David McCay, Hon. R. C. Hale, Judge Benjamin Patton, and others of whom I have no record. Messrs. McCay, Milliken, and Woods entered the ministry from this church. One (McCay) has lately entered upon his reward; the others are still faithfully proclaiming that salvation which they were brought to know through the ministry of this sainted pastor. When Dr. Woods assumed the oversight of this church, William

McKay, Daniel Robb, Jacob Walters, and Anthony Young, were the Ruling Elders; these all are dead. Of the trustees not one lives. The members still living here are Mrs. Eleanor Doty, Mrs. Mary Jacob, Mrs. Waldron, and Ephraim Banks, Esq., venerable and beloved Christians! To you it has been given to receive your late pastor, and after waiting forty years upon his ministry, amid many changes and trials, to see him laid, full of years and of honours, in the grave! May the good Shepherd be near and keep you, 'make you to lie down in green pastures, and lead you beside the still waters; even in the paths of righteousness, for his name sake. And when you walk through the valley of the shadow of death, may you have no fear of evil, his rod and his staff comforting you, and your dwelling be in the house of the Lord for ever!'

"Here Dr. Woods began his pastorate; here it was closed. He found you weak; he left you strong. To your steadfast confidence, your cordial co-operation, and your generous forbearance, he felt his obligation. What a treasure is such a life to the world! How unvalued! What a glorious place will it fill in the grand reckoning of the judgment! The influence of every sermon and prayer, every exhortation and word of warning and comfort spoken in the closet, every visit to the bedside of the sick and the dying, or the silent and solemn utterance of a holy walk before the family, and in the circles of social life and of business, upon the young and the old, the educated and the influential, for individual and social good, for temporal and eternal happiness—the influence I say of all these, running through forty years' service, the full revelation of the last day will alone disclose! And in the impartial and final adjustment of all human character and deeds, the ministry of this dear pastor will receive the reward of grace, in the accordant salutation of those whom he brought to Christ, and in the transporting plaudit of the Master, 'Well done, good and faithful servant!'"

HON. JOHN REED, LL. D.

OVER a quarter of a century has passed since the death of Judge Reed, and yet the remembrance of him is distinct with the bar of Carlisle and the State, and with the people of this county; far more so than that of others, equally eminent in their day, who died years later.

He was born on Marsh creek, then York, now Adams county, in 1786. His father was General William Reed, who held a Major's commission in the later years of our Revolutionary war. Having a taste and genius for military life, he gradually rose to the rank of Major General of Militia. He was one of the representatives of the District of York and Adams in the convention which framed the Constitution of Pennsylvania, in 1790. He also represented the same district in the State Senate, from 1804 to 1808. Upon the declaration of war between the United States and Great Britain, in 1812, he was appointed by Governor Snyder, Adjutant General of the State. He immediately entered upon duty, and organized two divisions of the army; one at Meadville, Crawford county, which marched under General Tannahill for the Niagara frontier; the other, under General Crooks, was ordered to Fort Meigs. Owing to the exposure and fatigue incident to this arduous service, he sickened and died in Westmoreland county, 1813.

His son, John Reed, was prepared for college by the Rev. Mr. Dobbin, of Gettysburg. After completing his collegiate course at Dickinson College, he read law under the direction of William Maxwell, of Gettysburg. In 1809 he was admitted to the bar; and commenced the practice of the law in Westmoreland county. In a short time his practice extended through the counties of Somerset, Indiana, Armstrong and Westmoreland. During the last two years of his professional career in these counties, he performed the duties of Deputy Attorney General.

In 1815, Mr. Reed was elected to the State Senate, and at the expiration of his term declined re-election. In December, 1819, he was married to the daughter of Dr. John McDowell, a distinguished surgeon of the army of the Revolution; and on the 10th of July, 1820, was commissioned by Governor Findlay, President Judge of the Ninth Judicial District, then composed of the counties of Cumberland, Franklin, Adams and Perry. Judge Reed continued in that position until 1839, when, by change of the Constitution, his commission expired. He then resumed his position at the bar, and continued in active practice until the time of his death, which occurred in Carlisle, on the 19th day of January, 1850, when he was in the sixty-fourth year of his age.

In 1834, he was made Professor of Law in Dickinson College. The degree of LL. D. was conferred on him by the officers of Washington College, Pennsylvania, in the year 1839, and in 1849 or 1850, he was made an honorary member of the American Philosophical Society of Philadelphia.

It is a source of just pride to the friends of the dead to know that they are pleasurably remembered; and when this happens to be the case, the inquiry why it is so is most natural. In the case of Judge Reed there are a number of causes which unite in making his fame lasting. He was the President Judge of the Ninth Judicial District, and presided with dignity, ability and integrity, by virtue of a commission meant to be for life, conferred by a Governor able to discriminate as to character, and to know the importance of the grant he made. He presided for nineteen years, in a district where the bar was not inferior to any in the commonwealth or country; having among its number Thomas G. McCullough, George Chambers, James Dunlop, T. Hartley Crawford, John F. Denny, George Metzgar, Thaddeus Stevens, Andrew Carothers, John D. Mahon, Charles B. Penrose, Frederick Watts, W. M. Biddle, and others, all men of distinction, with whom he was not only officially connected, but with many of them intimately associated, and his fame and theirs will always commingle. He also, while on the bench, and afterwards, conducted a Law School, in Carlisle, with marked success. Among his students were such men as George P. Hamilton, Esq., H. N. McAllister, Esq., Hon. A. G. Curtin, Rev. Alfred Nevin, D. D., LL. D., who subsequently entered the ministry, Hon. F. W. Hughes, J. Ellis Bonham, Esq., Hon. Samuel Linn, Hon. James H. Campbell, Hon. John C. Kunkel and W. H. Miller, Esq., of Pennsylvania; J. L. Carey and Hon. Carroll Spence, of Maryland; Hon. W. N. Smithers, of Delaware; Hon. Alexander Ramsey, of Minnesota; and Hon. James Kelly, of Oregon; by all of whom his name has ever been held in reverence. His official position, and that of instructor of young men, gave him a marked position in society, and he filled it to the letter. His manners were refined and agreeable; his wit was quick and sparkling, and his home the abode of refinement; and there is no one that has ever come within the sphere of his influence that is not better for having done so.

SAMUEL AGNEW, M. D.

DOCTOR SAMUEL AGNEW was born at Millerstown, near Gettysburg, in Adams county, August 10th, in the year 1777, and was the son of James Agnew and Mary Ramsey.

He was of Scotch descent, or from that people who, encouraged by James I, migrated from Scotland and England to the confiscated estates in the province of Ulster. They were a rare people. Under their industry, intelligence and enterprise the desolated lands were reclaimed, towns grew up, and manufactures were extensively established. They were Presbyterians, and neither the tyranny of Charles II or James II, the dragoons of Claverhouse, nor the intimidations of the Papacy, could compel them to surrender their independence, or dishonour their manhood. These were the people who have made sacred the glens and moors of Scotland and Ireland, and who rather than yield their convictions of faith and duty, suffered the sharpest persecutions, and came to this side of the Atlantic to find a home more congenial to their tastes. Men of strong intellects, independent thinkers, intolerant of oppression, gentle in peace, terrible in war, they have left their impress upon all the institutions of the country of their adoption. The father of Dr. Samuel Agnew was quite as ready to resist oppression as his ancestors had been, and when hostilities commenced in the Colonies, he espoused their cause against the encroachments of Great Britain, took up arms as a soldier and was wounded in one of the battles of New Jersey.

The academical studies of Dr. Agnew were commenced under Rev. Matthew Dobbin, of Gettysburg; and after his graduation at Dickinson College, Carlisle, in 1798, he turned his attention to the study of medicine, under Dr. John McClellan, a prominent surgeon in Greencastle, Pennsylvania. In 1800, he took his degree of Doctor of Medicine in the medical department of the University of Pennsylvania. During the war of 1812 he served as a surgeon, and after its termination commenced the practice of medicine in Gettysburg, but afterwards, in 1807, located in Harrisburg, as in consequence of its selection as the seat of government the place promised to become one of importance. In this field he rapidly rose to deserved eminence, establishing a large and lucrative practice. His counsel and aid were sought after, not only by

his professional brethren in Harrisburg, but throughout the different counties of middle and western Pennsylvania.

In 1803, Dr. Agnew married Miss Jane Grier. Her mother was a Holmes—a prominent family of Carlisle. The issue of this marriage was six children, three sons and three daughters. Two of these children, a son and daughter, died in childhood. The oldest son, Rev. John Holmes Agnew, D. D., a sketch of whom will appear in this volume, became distinguished for his scholarly attainments and literary position. The next child, Mary Ann, died in early life, in Uniontown, Pa., where her brother was Pastor of the Presbyterian Church. She was regarded as a young lady of great loveliness of character, as well as devoted piety. A second son, the Hon. Judge James C. Agnew, died at Edina, Missouri, March 1st, 1870, greatly lamented by the citizens of Knox county, to whom he was well known, and among whom he had for many years occupied several responsible civil positions, and discharged the duties of Eldership in the Presbyterian Church. During the war of the Rebellion he entered the Union Army as Commissary of one of its regiments, his two sons entering with him, the one as Lieutenant, the other as a private.

His surviving daughter became the wife of Rev. John R. Agnew, at present of Greencastle, a man of fine culture as a scholar, and a noble Christian gentleman.

As a physician, Dr. Agnew possessed a rare combination of qualities. Thoroughly conversant in the literature, and familiar with the resources of his profession, his opinions were always received with respect by his medical friends. Though pressed with the arduous duties of an extensive and laborious practice, he occasionally contributed to the periodical medical literature of the day, and was often called upon to deliver literary, scientific, and religious addresses. His paper on the "Intermittents of the Susquehanna Region," is one of great merit, and attracted the notice of men eminent in the profession. The late Professor Samuel Jackson, of the University of Pennsylvania, spoke in the most complimentary terms of both his learning and skill, and on one occasion remarked to Rev. Dr. Dewitt, that "if he had an only son dangerously ill, there was no physician between Philadelphia and New Orleans whose services he would rather have, than those of Dr. Agnew."

The Rev. T. H. Robinson, in his "Historical Address on the Ruling Elders of the First Presbyterian Church of Harrisburg," says: " few men, have been better fitted in natural talents, in education, in personal character, and in public position, than Dr. Agnew, for a wide and permanent influence of the best and highest kind over their fellow-men. He was a man of notable qualities. In the eye of the world he was one of the marked men of society; and both in social and professional life, as well as in the church, he was promptly accorded a place as a leader.

"Though a charming social companion, and distinguished member of the medical profession, Dr. Agnew was not less prominent in the church. He led a consistent and godly life, and rarely allowed his duties as a physician to prevent his regular attendance on the public services of the sanctuary. He was a ruling Elder in the First Presbyterian Church of Harrisburg, for fifteen years."

As an evidence of the high estimation in which Dr. Agnew was held, at the special request and on motion of such a man as Jeremiah Evarts, he was, in 1826, elected a corporate member of the American Board of Commissioners for Foreign Missions. To any agency of the church, whether Sunday schools, Bible, Tract, or Temperance societies, he gave an active and hearty support. He was emphatically an active, earnest, public spirited Christian.

The Rev. W. M. Paxton, D. D., in a sermon delivered at Greencastle after the death of Dr. Agnew, from Psalm xxxvii, 37, "Mark the perfect man and behold the upright, for the end of that man is peace," took occasion to speak of him as one to whom this Scripture might apply with more than ordinary propriety. Quoting from that sermon, he says, "As a man Dr. Agnew exhibited an assemblage of interesting qualities. He had a mind sound, clear and discriminating, naturally vigorous but strengthened and polished by a regular course of collegiate discipline, expanded by extensive professional study and matured by the experience of a protracted life. His literary taste was cultivated and correct. To a vigorous and cultivated intellect he added all the finer qualities of heart. He was characterized by an expansive benevolence of feeling. To the old and the young of every class and condition he was uniformly tender and affectionate. His heart appeared to overflow with the milk of human kindness. In his domestic and social relations, he won for himself the most endeared affection; he was a devoted husband, a loving father, and an affectionate friend. The natural serenity and cheerfulness of his temper gave a charm to his old age, and the affability and dignified unobtrusiveness of his manners elicited the respect and esteem of all who knew him. He was esteemed as a public spirited citizen, was honoured as a generous, self-sacrificing philanthropist, and valued as a steadfast, sympathizing friend." Again, in speaking of the religious side of his character, he says: "It was as a *Christian* that Dr. Agnew shone preeminently. A warm hearted but rational piety was the great leading feature of his character; it was the pervading and controlling principle of his public and private life. He died on the 23d of November, 1849, in the seventy-third year of his life. His death was as gentle and as quiet as a summer evening; as calm as when an autumn sun sinks below the western horizon, and as its beams gild the bending sky, long after the great body of flame is out of sight, so do the delightful memories of his life linger in the thoughts and hearts of men.

JOHN McKNIGHT, D. D.

JOHN McKNIGHT was born near Carlisle, Pa., October 1st, 1754. He graduated at the College of New Jersey, under the Presidency of Dr. Witherspoon, in 1773. He studied Theology under the Rev. Dr. Robert Cooper, Pastor of the Middle Spring Church, was licensed to preach by the Presbytery of Donegal between the meetings of Synod in 1774 and 1775, and was ordained by the same Presbytery in the latter part of 1776, or early in 1777.

Mr. McKnight, soon after his licensure, organized a congregation in Virginia, on Elk Branch, embracing the country between Shepherdstown and Charlestown. In 1783, he accepted a call to the Lower Marsh Creek Presbyterian Church, in Adams county, Pa. In July, 1789, he was called to be a colleague Pastor with the Rev. Dr. Rodgers, of the United Presbyterian congregation of the city of New York. This call was accepted, and he was installed on the 2d of December of that year. In 1791, he was honoured with the degree of Doctor of Divinity from Yale College, and in 1795, was Moderator of the General Assembly of the Presbyterian Church.

Dr. McKnight remained in New York, in the earnest and faithful discharge of his pastoral duties twenty years, when he resigned his charge. On leaving New York, he removed to a small but beautiful farm in the neighbourhood of Chambersburg, Pa., which he had purchased for a residence. Though declining a regular call, yet he consented to be a Stated Supply to the church of Rocky Spring, which was about three miles from his dwelling.

In 1815, he was invited to the Presidency of Dickinson College, and accepted the invitation, but finding the fiscal concerns of the institution much embarrassed, resigned the office, and returned to his farm, preaching as opportunity offered, till his life terminated, October 21st, 1723.

Dr. McKnight published six Sermons on Faith, (recommended by Drs. Rodgers and Witherspoon,) 1790; a Thanksgiving Sermon, 1795; a Sermon before the New York Missionary Society, 1799; a Sermon on the Present State of the Political and Religious World, 1802; a Sermon on the Death of Rev. Dr. John King, 1811.

In the year 1776, he was married to Susan, daughter of George

Brown, of Franklin county, Pa., who survived her husband about nine years. They had ten children, two of whom entered the ministry.

In a letter dated Detroit, March 11th, 1853, the Rev. George Duffield, D. D., says :

"As a preacher Dr. McKnight was calm and dispassionate. Although there was very little variety in either his tone or gesture, yet his delivery was far from being dull or monotonous, it was well adapted to his matter, which was generally a lucid, logical exhibition of some important Scriptural truth.   *   *   *   *

"Dr. McKnight finished his earthly career surrounded by his family and friends, and among a people who still greatly reverence his memory. Having commenced his ministerial labours in the region where he died, at a very early period after its first settlement, his name was associated with the earliest and most important events connected with the church and cause of Christ within the bounds of the Presbytery of Carlisle. There are still living a considerable number who cherish a grateful appreciation of his services as an able and faithful minister of Christ."

REV. JOHN LINN.

JOHN LINN was born in Adams county, Pennsylvania, in the year 1749. His parents were Presbyterians, and were connected with the congregation of Lower Marsh Creek, in the Presbytery of Carlisle. He made a profession of religion while he was yet quite a youth. He was fitted for college by the Rev. Robert Smith, of Pequea, Lancaster county, Pennsylvania, and was graduated at Nassau Hall, during the Presidency of Dr. Witherspoon, in the year 1773.

After leaving college, Mr. Linn returned to Pennsylvania, and studied Theology under the direction of the Rev. Dr. Robert Cooper,* pastor of the congregation of Middle Spring, within the limits of what was then Donegal (now Carlisle) Presbytery. He was licensed to preach by the Presbytery of Donegal, in December, 1776. Not far from a year after his licensure, the congregations of Sherman's valley, in Cumberland (now Perry) county, invited him to become their pastor. He accepted the invitation, and was accordingly ordained and installed shortly after. Here he remained labouring faithfully and efficiently to the close of his ministry, and his life. He died in the year 1820, in the seventy-first year of his age.

Soon after his settlement in the ministry, he was married to Mary Gettys, a native of the neighbourhood in which he resided. She survived him a few years. They had seven children, five sons and two daughters. One of them, the Rev. James Linn, D. D., born in 1783, was the Pastor of the Presbyterian Church in Bellefonte, Pa.

"Mr. Linn," says Rev. Dr. Baird, "was about five feet and ten inches in height, portly and symmetrical in his form, and muscular and active in his bodily movements. He had great strength of constitution, and uncommon powers of endurance. His disposition was social and

---

* Dr. Cooper was born in the north of Ireland, in or about the year 1772, graduated at the College of New Jersey in 1763, was licensed by the Presbytery of Carlisle, February 22d, 1765, and was installed pastor of Middle Spring church, November 21st, of the same year, which church he served thirty-one years, resigning the charge on account of declining health. The degree of Doctor of Divinity was conferred upon him by Dickinson College, in the year 1792. He died April 5th, 1805, in the seventy-third year of his age. "As a preacher," says Dr. Moodey, "Dr. Cooper seems to have been distinguished rather for the solidity and excellence of his matter, than for elegant diction, or an attractive delivery. He was, however, in the earlier part of his ministry particularly, a more than ordinarily popular preacher, and, with the more intelligent and reflecting portion of the community, he retained his popularity to the last."

cheerful, he could easily accommodate himself to persons of different characters and conditions in life, and was cordially welcomed by every circle into which he was thrown. He was distinguished for sobriety of mind rather than versatility, was reflective rather than imaginative. He was accustomed to write his sermons out at full length, and deliver them from memory, except that in the summer, his morning discourse, which was a lecture on some portion of the New Testament, was usually delivered without preparation. He had a remarkably clear voice, and expressed himself with great solemnity and impressiveness. One of his manuscript sermons—a sermon occasioned by the death of the Rev. Samuel Waugh*—I have had the opportunity of perusing, and it shows that he was a correct writer, and an instructive, methodical and earnest preacher. He was uncommonly devoted to the interests of his flock, giving no inconsiderable portion of his time to pastoral visitation. In his family, and indeed in all his relations, he was a fine example of Christian dignity, tenderness and fidelity."

---

*Samuel Waugh was a native of Carroll's Tract, in Adams county, Pa., was graduated at the College of New Jersey, in 1773, was settled as pastor of the united congregations of East Pennsborough and Monaghan, in 1782, and continued in this relation until his death, which took place in January, 1807. One of his parishioners (Judge Clendenin) says of him:—"He was a sound divine, a very acceptable preacher, and highly esteemed by his people."

FREDERICK SMITH, ESQ.

ON the 3d of May, 1861, Frederick Smith closed a life of labour, honour and usefulness in Chambersburg. He was born in Friends' Cove, Bedford county, Pa., February 6th, 1796, and received his classical education at Washington College, After completing the study of the law, he removed to Chambersburg, and was admitted to the bar in 1818. Soon establishing a reputation, he was appointed District Attorney for Franklin county, and filled the office creditably for a number of years. A prominent member of the Democratic party, he served several terms in the Legislature, and was twice elevated to the Speakership. Although he abandoned active participation in politics, early in his career, he always occupied a high position in his party, and was frequently prominently brought forward as a candidate for gubernatorial nomination. During the greater part of his life, he enjoyed a lucrative practice at the bar, and won distinction in his profession. At the expiration of the term of Hon. Alexander Thomson's judgeship, he was unanimously recommended by his brethren at the bar for appointment to the vacancy.

An ardent friend of education, he took a lively interest in our schools and colleges, and was for many years Treasurer of Pennsylvania College, and one of its most energetic trustees. Although laboriously occupied in his profession, the concerns of his church, the Evangelical Lutheran, elicited his warmest interest, and he diligently attended upon its services and worked for its welfare. The Sabbath school engaged his best efforts, and for a long period he was its Superintendent—from July 13th, 1832, to February 3d, 1856.

No man of his day won more completely the confidence of the community, and none exerted a wider influence. A more stainless name was never borne in the society of his adopted home; his word was never weighed; his promises were accepted without questioning, and his endorsements passed without the discount of a doubt.

In manners he was remarkably plain, his demeanor was simple and unostentatious, his disposition exceedingly amiable and winning. With the agricultural community he was an especial favourite, and to him they flocked with their business, and came for advice in all the affairs of their lives, trusting him with implicit faith and veneration.

The beneficent influence which the lives of such men exert over their neighbours and acquaintances who come long under their operation, cannot be estimated; and it is not too much to say, that the good Frederick Smith did lives after him, and that his memory shall be loved and honoured when more brilliant citizens will be forgotten.

He brought up a large family, all but one of which survived him. The only exception was his eldest son, Alfred H. Smith, Esq., who graduated with high honour at Pennsylvania College, and was admitted to the bar of Franklin county. He died in his twenty-eighth year, after having acquired a billiant reputation as an editor, and as the most remarkable literary genius that his native place produced; having given abundant assurance of his becoming one of the most eminent men of letters of our day.

FRANCIS LAIRD, D. D.

THE REV. FRANCIS LAIRD, D. D., became the pastor of the churches of Plum Creek and Pike Run, in the Presbytery of Redstone, Pa., in 1800, where he continued till 1831, when he resigned this charge and accepted a call for the whole of his time to the church of Murrysville, Pa. Here he continued closely and lovingly devoted to the pastoral duties of his charge, till 1850, when he resigned on account of the infirmities of old age. He died April 6th, 1851, in the eighty-seventh year of his age—the fifty-fourth of his ministry.

He graduated at Dickinson College, during the presidency of the Rev. Dr. Charles Nisbet, and received the honorary title of D. D. from Jefferson College. He was a man of studious habits through life, well learned, especially inclined to biblical criticism, and well qualified for it. Many a young minister profited by his kind, clear and correct suggestions in this line. Even to the last days of his life, his supreme delight was the study of the sacred Scriptures in the original tongues. When his eyes had become dimmed, so that he could no longer read with the subdued light of his room, he would stand out of doors in the sun, its light blazing full on the page of the Hebrew Bible spread before him, while with quivering finger he essayed to follow the words of the Holy Book.

He strove to draw the truth from the very fountain head, and he was content with nothing less.

Equally well he loved to communicate it, when possible, in the very language in which God had given it to man. During the last moments of his life, this desire knew no abatement and was his ruling passion. Almost the very last words he uttered, faintly whispered into the ear of a sympathizing friend, were the Greek of St. Paul: *Ta panta kai en pasi Christos; Christ is all and in all.* Col. iii, 11.

THOMAS CREIGH, D. D.

THE HON. JOHN CREIGH, the grandfather of the Rev. Thomas Creigh, emigrated from Ireland to Carlisle, Cumberland county, Pa., in the year 1761, his paternal ancestors having left Germany about the year 1640, on account of the religious persecution then existing against Protestants. From a private letter from the minister of the Presbyterian Church at Carmony, Ireland, it appears that the great-grandfather of the Rev. Dr. Creigh was a ruling elder in that church in 1719, while his grandfather filled the same office in the Presbyterian Church in Carlisle. To this we may add that Judge Creigh was an ardent defender of the principles of the American Revolution, and his grandson, Dr. Alfred Creigh, of Washington, Pa., has his commission bearing date April 29th, 1776, "*in defence of American Liberty.*"

Such were the paternal ancestors of the Rev. Dr. Creigh, while his maternal ancestors—the Parkers and Dunbars—coming from Scotland, settled on the banks of the Conodoguinett creek, a few miles from Carlisle, near the old Presbyterian Meeting House, as early as 1730, some of whom filled the office of elder.

Dr. John Creigh, the father of the Rev. Dr. Thomas Creigh, was born in Carlisle, educated at Dickinson College, and received his degree of M. D., in Philadelphia, and after an eventful life, devoted exclusively to the arduous duties of his profession, died in Carlisle on November 7th, 1848. Dr. John Creigh and Ellen Dunbar Creigh, had six sons and four daughters, of whom Thomas was the *fourth* son, who was born in 1808; of these ten children, but three sons and one daughter survive.

Thomas Creigh received the best English education, which being completed, he entered the Latin Grammar school, and in due time became a student of Dickinson College. For four consecutive years he pursued his collegiate studies under Rev. Dr. Wm. Neill, (President,) Prof. Henry Vetake, Rev. Alexander McClelland, Rev. Joseph Spencer and Dr. John K. Findley, men who ranked high in their profession, and through whose instrumentality the graduates of that college were each prepared to act a distinguished part in the active duties of life. Among his twenty-one classmates who graduated with him in 1828, six became ministers, viz: Rev. Dr. Robert Davidson,

Rev. N. G. White, Rev. E. Y. Buchanan, Rev. Robert Bryson, Rev. J. G. Brackenridge, and himself.

Whilst attending college, Mr. Creigh attached himself to the Presbyterian Church of Carlisle, then under the care of Rev. Dr. George Duffield, and after he graduated, placed himself under the Carlisle Presbytery. He spent the usual time at the Theological Seminary at Princeton, and after being licensed to preach the Gospel by the Carlisle Presbytery, he received a call from the Presbyterian Church at Mercersburg, Franklin county, Pennsylvania, and was ordained and installed on November 17, 1831, in which church he has faithfully laboured for forty-four years. In this connection it may be added that this church has a peculiar history, worthy of being recorded. Although it had a nominal existence for many years, yet its first settled pastor was the Rev. John Steele, who served it about two years; the next was the Rev. John King, a licentiate of the Philadelphia Presbytery, who was installed pastor on the 30th day of August, 1769, and who resigned his charge in 1811, although his death from old age did not occur until July 15, 1813, then in his seventy-third year, having preached to that congregation forty-two years. His successor was the Rev. Dr. David Elliott, who was a licentiate of the Presbytery of Carlisle, and who was ordained and installed October 7, 1812; he resigned the pastoral charge of this church October 29, 1829, having filled the pulpit for seventeen years. Two years after the close of Dr. Elliott's ministry, or on the 17th day of November, 1831, the Rev. Thomas Creigh was installed its pastor; thus, for a space of *one hundred and six years*, this old Presbyterian church, baptized with the Spirit of God, and sanctified by His presence, has had but four regularly ordained ministers, and until the 18th day of March, 1874, when the death of the Rev. Dr. Elliott occurred, two of the three were alive to testify of God's goodness to the church of His own right hand's planting.

Mr. Creigh received the honorary degree of D. D. from Lafayette College, Easton, Pa., about 1853. It can be testified without flattery, that Dr. Creigh's high attainments in personal piety, his faithful exhibition of Divine truth, his sound judgment, his prudence, his constant study to promote the peace and purity of the church and neighbourhood by precept and example, his interest in behalf of education, and his constant desire to promote the extension of the church of his choice and of his fathers, handed down to him for so many generations, has enabled him, through the blessing of God, to strengthen the church entrusted to him by so many precious reminiscences, so many pious memorials, and to do a grand life-work.

In the town of his early years, of his middle age, and advanced life, Dr. Creigh's personal influence far exceeds that of any other person. His opinion on all subjects is considered sound and orthodox. As a member of Presbytery he occupies a high position. In subjects connected with the interests of the church his ministerial brethren almost invariably take his counsel and advice. And although age and honourable gray hairs have set their mark upon him, his health appears to be improving, and from present appearance he will, with the blessing of God, attain to his fiftieth year in the ministry.

MAJOR DAVID NEVIN.

TOWARDS the close of the last century, two brothers of the name of Nevin, came from England to this country, one of whom settled on the Hudson river, New York, in which region his descendants are still found, occupying high social positions, and the other of whom, Daniel Nevin, chose Cumberland valley for his home.

Mr. Nevin was united in marriage with Mrs. Margaret Reynolds, widowed sister of Dr. Hugh Williamson, elsewhere noticed in this volume, and lived at Herron's Branch, near Strasburg, Franklin county. The youngest child of this marriage was the subject of this sketch, who was born February 23d, 1782.

In his earlier years he received such education as the school in the neighbourhood could give, and assisted, as he was able, in conducting the operations of his father's farm, for which there was a greater necessity inasmuch, as his elder and only brother, John, was at the time a student in Dickinson College. It would seem that he had more than common desire for mental improvement, for often was he heard, in after life, by his familiar friends, to speak of books which he had read during the long winter evenings, and among which the Poems of Robert Burns held a conspicuous place.

After some training in mercantile pursuits in the neighbourhood of the place of his nativity, Mr. Nevin united with his young friend McCracken, afterwards General Samuel McCracken, of Lancaster, Ohio, in trading on the Ohio river, a business which, at that time, with its risks and toils, required an unusual degree of the spirit of enterprise. Returning, after some time, to Cumberland valley, to which he was strongly attached, he continued in mercantile life, in which his skill, industry, and perseverance were crowned with large success. On February 1st, 1810, Mr. Nevin married Mary Peirce, only daughter of Joseph Peirce, Esq., who resided on one of his farms above Carlisle, and who was an only son of one of the first and most enterprising settlers of Cumberland county. Mrs. Nevin survived her husband some fifteen years, after having reached the ordinary limit of human existence, three-score years and ten. After her decease, the following touching and truthful tribute to her memory was published by one occupying a distinguished position in the world, who knew how to appreciate her worth: "Few women have filled more honourably through life the proper sphere of woman's relations and duties. No one could well be more faithful as a wife, or more true and devoted as a mother. Her large family, mourning as they do her loss, may count themselves happy in her memory, as they all concur also in pronouncing it blessed. Nature and grace combined to make her more than usually loving and worthy of love. She seemed to live, move, and have her being, in the element of kindness. Her spirit was made up of gentleness and peace. The law of self-forgetting and self-sacrificing service entered largely into all her domestic and social relations; so that she appeared to be never so happy as in trying to make others happy. An atmosphere of trustful sincerity and hopeful benevolence always attending her, gave her presence for this purpose a special adaptation and force. She carried with her through life, one might say, the joyous simplicity of a child—a simplicity which was devoid of all affectation, and that knew no guile. What might have seemed to be thus in one view her weakness, became her great strength. Her passive nature clothed her with an uncommon amount of active resolution and power. Her work in life was great, and she did it well. Her praise is not with her own family simply, but with all who knew her as neighbours, acquaintances and friends. It may be doubted if she ever had an earnest enemy in the community to which she belonged; and it is certain that she has now gone down to the grave in the midst of universal esteem and regret. It is felt on all sides, that a "mother in Israel" has been taken away, and that a mournful void is created by her removal. There is something touching indeed in the spontaneous tribute that is everywhere paid to her acknowledged goodness. But her friends sorrow not for her as those who have no hope. She had consecrated herself in early life to the service of God; she showed herself an earnest Christian all her days; and she died at last in the full hope of a blessed immortality through Him who is the Resurrection and the Life. Retaining the full, unclouded use of her faculties to the end, and knowing well that the end was come, she rebuked the tears of those who stood sorrowing around her dying bed, professed her unwavering confidence in Christ—and in Him wholly and alone—and so, with peaceful serenity, surrendered her spirit into the hands of God. Death came upon her thus as the Christian's sleep. She died in the Lord."

In the war of 1812, Mr. Nevin, in the capacity of Major, with a large number of the citizens of Shippensburg, in which place he had then come to reside, marched to Baltimore for the defence of that city.

The scene at the separation on this occasion, as wives, mothers and sisters bade, though with sad hearts and tearful eyes, their loved ones go forth and battle for their country, is represented as peculiarly thrilling. All interests, however dear, seemed to be merged in that of patriotism. And hence, satisfied that duty called them to imperil their lives in the tent; on pestiferous plains, or amidst the death-missiles of the field of conflict, the brave men went forward with steady step and unyielding nerve to vindicate the right, and repel the invading foe. The principal elements of Major Nevin's character were courage, self-reliance, kindness, uprightness, enterprise, and decision. He was *felt*, in the entire section of the county in which his days were chiefly spent, to be a man of truth, wisdom, sincerity, justice and force. The Hon. George Sanderson, late Mayor of Lancaster, a life-long friend of Major Nevin, says of him: "He was one of the best known and most prominent men in the Cumberland valley. By his industry and energy he secured for himself the reputation—and deservedly so—of being one of the most successful merchants and business men of the community in which he resided. A man of the strictest integrity in all his dealings and intercourse with his fellow men, his word was at all times as good as his bond, and his character was beyond reproach. Kind and generous by nature, he was liberal to the poor, never turning a deaf ear to the appeals of the distressed, and his numerous charities were bestowed without ostentation or self-glorification. Take him all in all, he was a model man, and the place he occupied in Shippensburg and its vicinity it would be difficult to fill. In short, he was emphatically one of nature's noblemen.

"Major Nevin was a firm and consistent Democrat from principle, a sincere admirer of the doctrines promulgated and inculcated by Thomas Jefferson, and was withal a man of more than ordinary intelligence and of great influence in his party. He was a representative from Cumberland county in the Reform Convention, 1837–8, and assisted in remodeling the State Constitution. Although not a speaking member, owing to a diffidence in his own ability, his sound judgment and the liberal principles which he entertained gave his opinions, which were eagerly sought for by his colleagues, a weight in that assemblage of the talented men of the commonwealth, which few of his fellow members of greater pretentions possessed."

In person Major Nevin was tall, of robust frame, and commanding appearance. His countenance was indicative of benignity, quick perception, prompt action, and strong decision. His manner was dignified and somewhat reserved, ever exhibiting the culture which arose from frequent intercourse with the world, and much travel. His whole bearing, whilst utterly free from haughtiness, or any undue assumption of worth, was expressive of a consciousness of rectitude of intention, and a high degree of self-respect. He felt equally at home in associating with the great, and in mingling with the humble.

Major Nevin's health, during many of his last years, was feeble, by reason of a severe shock which his system had sustained from a protracted attack of malignant fever in 1823. But notwithstanding he was thus called to battle with physical prostration and suffering, few men were more active in attention to business. "*Perseverantia*," the motto on the family coat of arms, brought over by a kinsman from Scotland, seemed to be *his* actuating and ruling principle. With heroic spirit he bore up under a complication of maladies, thus, in all probability, as his physician told him, lengthening his earthly career, by not allowing himself to sink under the operation of causes which threatened, and, but for this reason, must have hastened its termination.

At length, after a long struggle with disease, he departed this life on May 27th, 1848, surrounded by most of his family, and in the full exercise of his mental powers. By special request of the military of the town, permission was granted them to march with his funeral, and after an admirable funeral discourse pronounced in his late dwelling in the centre of the town, by his nephew, John Williamson Nevin, D. D., LL. D., the very large concourse which followed his mortal remains to the grave showed that his hold upon the public regard was such as it is the privilege of but few to have, and that he was as extensively and deeply lamented by the community, when dead, as he was respected by them while living. His body is now entombed in the family lot in Spring Hill Cemetery, where also slumbers the dust of his wife, and eldest son, Joseph P., since deceased, and that of two young daughters, whom, in early life, he followed to the grave.

The surviving sons of Major Nevin, in the order of their age, are: Edwin H. Nevin, D. D., Philadelphia, Alfred Nevin, D. D., LL. D., of the same city, Samuel Williamson Nevin, Esq., and William Wallace Nevin, M. D., both of Shippensburg, and David Robert Bruce Nevin, Pension Agent, U. S. A., Philadelphia. The explanation of the giving of two such eminent Scottish names to two of his children, is to be found in the fact that the family, as reliable tradition affirms, are lineally descended from the Scottish heroes from whom these names are taken.

SAMUEL DUNCAN CULBERTSON, M. D.

AMONG the remarkable men of the Cumberland valley, no one is more entitled to distinction than Samuel Duncan Culbertson. Descending from the best blood of the best days of the Republic—the honest, steadfast, patriotic Scotch-Irish of the Revolutionary period—he lived to an old age, honoured for his great intellectual gifts, for his probity and his professional eminence; admired for his commanding personal appearance, his dignity of character, his energy and surprising business success; and beloved for his social attractions, benevolence and practical friendliness.

S. D. Culbertson's ancestors were fervent patriots, and were prominent actors in the War of Independence. His father, Robert Culbertson, was captain of a battalion of Col. Joseph Armstrong's command as early in the Revolution as August, 1776. Captain Culbertson was subsequently appointed Wagon Master for Cumberland county, (an office of much more dignity and importance than it appears in modern military grades,) on the 14th of August, 1780, previous to which he had been promoted to Lieutenant Colonel.

Col. Joseph Culbertson lived on an adjoining farm; of him we know nothing special. Col. Samuel Culbertson, a cousin of the foregoing brothers, and the most noted of the family, lived in the neighbourhood, raised a company of Provincial troops, and marched them to the spring running through Robert's farm, when he formed them in confronting lines on its opposite shores. Then clasping hands across the stream they swore fidelity to the cause of their country. This was a form of Scotch swearing which was deemed peculiarly solemn and irrevocable. After the vows were uttered, the oaths were confirmed by draughts from a tinful of whisky, which Robert supplied from his still house which stood at the head of his famous spring.

Colonel Samuel Culbertson was a prominent elder of the Rocky Spring Church, and was a member of the Assembly for a number of sessions. He died on his farm in the "Row," April 17th, 1817. A daughter married General John Rea, member of the Twelfth Congress. The Rev. James Culbertson, of Zanesville, Ohio, was his son.

Colonel Robert Culbertson was married to a daughter of William Duncan, who resided near Middle Spring, and whose family was among the earliest settlers of that neighbourhood. He was an active member of the Presbyterian congregation, then under the pastorate of Rev. Dr. Cooper, distinguished alike for his piety and patriotism. The Duncan name is found in the sessions of the Middle Spring Church, during the Rev. John Blair's ministry, in 1742. William Duncan paid an annual pew rent of £1 19s. 6d. in 1782.

The Culbertsons were connected with the Rocky Spring Church. Robert was an attendant of the Old Colonial Meeting House and paid to Rev. Craighead, £1 17s. 6d. as his annual pew rent, in 1776.

Samuel Duncan, son of Robert Culbertson, was born near Chambersburg, at "Culbertson's Row," on the 21st of February, 1786. His father dying when he was quite young, he was left to the care of his widowed mother, a woman of very superior character and culture. He received a classical education at Jefferson College, Cannonsburg, where, we believe, he was graduated. At that early day, means of conveyance to such a distant western point were limited and difficult, and our youthful student was accustomed to make his long way to and from the college on foot.

After quitting Cannonsburg, he began the study of medicine under Dr. Walmsley, a practitioner of reputation in Chambersburg, who removed to Hagerstown, whither his pupil followed him. Dr. Walmsley died soon after changing his location, when young Culbertson finished his course of study in the office of Dr. Young, of the latter place. During his pupilage, Mr. Culbertson spent one winter in attending medical instruction at the celebrated University of Pennsylvania, then, as now, the foremost medical school in America.

In 1836, the honourary degree of M. D. was conferred upon him in grateful recognition of his eminence and usefulness in the profession. Dr. Culbertson commenced the practice of medicine in Chambersburg, probably in 1808, and succeeded speedily to a large business and acquired great celebrity. His practice extended to a great distance from his home, as at that time the country was ill supplied with physicians, and diseases of a malarious origin were greatly more frequent than since the country has been opened up and settled. The luxurious vehicles, which carry the doctors so comfortably now, protecting them from the fierce beating of the sun and pitiless peltings of storms, were unknown to the rural physician, and he was compelled to make his laborious rounds on horseback. Wide spread epidemics of bilious fevers, dysenteries, and kindred diseases prevailed for a succession of years, making the work of the practitioner onerous and oppressive indeed. From a letter written in 1823, by a student of Dr. C., we learn that the Doctor had ridden from four o'clock in one morning until three of the next, three days in succession; and that his office was often so full that many patients had to wait for hours before they could get speaking to him. In connection with his profession, he opened, at an early part of his career, a small drug store, a custom which was quite common among doctors at that time. One sultry day, a worn and dusty footman walked into his shop, and begged a drink of water. The sympathetic proprietor stepped into his yard to get a cool draught from the well. While he was gone the ungrateful stranger robbed the till. A few years before the Doctor's death, he received from a Catholic priest a letter containing a sum of money, which the holy father said a rich penitent, in his extreme hour, had ordered to be sent to Dr. Culbertson as the principal and interest on the amount stolen more than fifty years before.

Growing weary, he sought to escape from his arduous duties, and went to Philadelphia in 1815, and engaged in merchandising, but being unsuccessful in his new pursuit, he returned to Chambersburg, and resumed his practice, in which he continued until 1831, when he finally relinquished it in favour of Drs. Lane and Bain. He then entered upon the manufacturing of straw boards, in conjunction with Mr. George A. Shryock (the great pioneer in that new branch of industry,) and others, in the first mill of the kind ever erected. Subsequently, he purchased the interest of his partners, and conducted the business alone, amassing a large fortune.

During the late war with England, Dr. Culbertson, true to his ancestry, was a fiery patriot, and shared in the struggle. With a little band of volunteers gathered from the neighbourhood, he left Chambersburg September 5th, 1812, and marched to Buffalo, where they lay until January, 1813, without any other winter quarters than their own rude huts. He held the position of First Lieutenant of his company until they reached Meadville. Then the First Pennsylvania Regiment was organized and he was appointed Surgeon, in which capacity he served until they were mustered out. On the return of the command, he resumed his practice. But his quiet life was soon again disturbed. In 1814, the country was alarmed by the intelligence that the British threatened Baltimore. The Doctor promptly called his neighbours to arms, raised a company rapidly, was chosen its captain, and marched hurriedly, with some eighteen hundred men of Franklin county, to the endangered city. Then he was once more elevated to the surgeoncy of the brigade. We have often listened with enthusiasm to the descriptions given of the tumultuous night in which the news was brought that the enemy were approaching Baltimore; when Dr. Culbertson turned out at midnight, and with drums beating, marched through the village streets, summoning his excited townsmen to the rescue; and have felt the glow of patriotic pride as we have heard how the dusky forms of responding citizens were seen falling with alacrity into the ranks of the swelling procession.

The love of country which warmed the bosoms of the Culbertsons in the days that tried men's souls, and which glowed in the ardent heart of their illustrious descendant in the vigour of his manhood, suffered no cooling amid the infirmities of his age. When the wicked rebellion massed its hosts for the overthrow of the Government and dismemberment of the Republic, he gave no equivocal support to the earnest, strenuous prosecution of the war for national existence, but uttered a full voiced advocacy of prompt, decided, unintermitting action.

As a business man, Dr. Culbertson is known to have been extraordinarily successful; but it was his professional career that made him eminent. In surgery he was very expert and daring; as an obstetrician he especially excelled. One who knew him well, says: " his medical qualification which most impressed me, was his wonderful readiness in discovering the seat of disease, its nature, and its probable issue. This rare faculty made his counsel extremely valuable. If a new disease appeared (or perhaps I had better say, an unusual disease, as a new disease is generally but the re-appearance of a disease itself not new,) no one was so apt to detect its character and tendencies, and hence none better able to suggest its treatment than Dr. Culbertson."

Dr. C. was not unknown as a medical writer. A lengthy report of a case treated by him, was deemed of sufficient value to be appended to a work upon kindred diseases by a writer of authority; and a communication of his on a vexed question in Physiology attracted, the hearty commendations of the celebrated Prof. Chapman. The style of his compositions was admirable, strong, chaste and easy. After he had retired from the practice, he was always willing to consult with his medical brethren, and, of course, his opinions and advice were frequently sought. In his intercourse with his medical brethren, he was ever respectful and courteous, observing its ethics with strict fidelity, and deporting himself with a delicacy that became proverbial. It was fitting then, from this view of his character, no less than out of regard to his acknowledged abilities, that the physicians of Franklin county, when they formed their first medical society, should have unanimously elected him their President.

Among the families he attended, he was looked up to as a general counsellor, and his advice has strengthened many a household struggling with affliction; and he was willing to give not advice only, but more substantial assistance.

The above sketch is written in no spirit of eulogy, but for the sole object of historical fidelity.

JOHN WILLIAMSON NEVIN, D.D., LL. D.,

WAS born near the village of Strasburg, Franklin county, Pa., February 20th, 1803. His parents were Christian people, members of the Presbyterian Church, and much esteemed for their uprightness and excellent character. His father, John Nevin, was a gentleman of more than ordinary intelligence, a graduate of Dickinson College under the Presidency of Dr. Nisbet, and fond of books, but in harmony with his tastes he spent his life in the noble occupation of a farmer, living for many years on his beautiful place near Shippensburg. For a time he served as a Trustee of the institution of which he was an Alumnus, and frequently he contributed articles to some of the public journals of his day. His mother was a sister of Dr. Hugh Williamson, a distinguished physician, patriot, and statesman during the Revolutionary war, who is noticed elsewhere in this volume.

Receiving his preparatory training from his father, John W. Nevin, when fourteen years old, entered the Freshman class at Union College, Schenectady, N. Y., of which the eminent Dr. Nott was President, and although the youngest member of his class, graduated with honour in 1821. His too much secluded life at college having told upon his health, study and books had to be in a great measure given up after his graduation, and the idea of pursuing a literary life seemed to be shut out forever. His health, however, gradually improved, and in the fall of 1823 he entered the Theological Seminary at Princeton.

Mr. Nevin remained at Princeton five years, three years as student of Theology, and two as teacher in the Seminary, Dr. Charles Hodge having asked him to take his place during his absence for this length of time at the Universities of Germany. Whilst occupying this position, at the earnest request of some friends of the Sabbath school cause, he wrote his work on *Biblical Antiquities*, which was afterwards adopted by the American Sunday School Union, and has ever since, by reason of its great merit, had a wide circulation.

Before leaving Princeton he was fixed upon as a proper person to fill the chair of Biblical Literature in the Western Theological Seminary, about to be established by the Presbyterian church at Allegheny City. In the fall of 1828 he was licensed to preach the Gospel by the Presbytery of Carlisle. Having accepted the invitation to the Seminary at Allegheny, he remained in connection with it ten years, during which, in connection with his colleagues, Dr. Halsey and Dr. Elliot, he performed a vast amount of work. In addition to his duties as Professor he also edited with ability a paper called *The Friend*, and frequently preached as opportunity offered. At the same time his attention was directed to the study of the German language, and it is but right to say, that no American scholar has done more in elevating the language and literature of the Fatherland to the high repute in which they now stand in this country.

On the 29th of January, 1840, the Synod of the German Reformed Church met in a special session at Chambersburg, and elected Dr. Nevin to the vacant chair of Theology in the Seminary at Mercersburg. This appointment he accepted, and entered upon his duties in the following May, with his characteristic energy. At the decease of Dr. Rauch, who was President of Marshall College, March 2d, 1841, both college and seminary were left solely in the hands of Dr. Nevin. He remained at the head of the college from the year 1841 to 1853, when it was removed to Lancaster. During this time, with the exception of the last two years, he discharged all his duties as a Professor of Theology, and until 1844, when the Rev. Dr. Philip Schaff was associated with him as Professor of Theology, he was the only Professor in the Seminary. Besides his official duties, he was a frequent contributor to the public press, preached often, and carried forward many important theological controversies.

When Marshall College was consolidated with Franklin College, at Lancaster, in 1853, Dr. Nevin was elected President of the new institution, but felt it to be his duty to decline the position. Removing to Lancaster, in 1855, he soon after built his beautiful home, Cærnarvon Place, in which he has ever since resided. During the period in which he had no official position in the church, he took an active part in bringing to completion the new liturgy or order of worship which had engaged the attention of the German Reformed Church, and had called out its best talent. His health being somewhat improved, he was induced, in 1861, to become Teacher of Æsthetics and the Philosophy of History in the college. Five years later, in 1866, he again became President of the college, by the general wish of the church as well as of its Trustees and Alumni.

Space will not permit us here to speak in detail of Dr. Nevin's numerous writings, consisting of books, addresses, sermons, and other articles prepared for the public press. In 1840, he prepared a series of articles for the German Reformed Messenger on the Heidelberg

Catechism, which excited general attention. They were published in book form in 1847, with the title: THE HISTORY AND GENIUS OF THE HEIDELBERG CATECHISM. This has become a standard work on that subject in the church. In 1845, he translated the Inaugural Address of Dr. Schaff, on *The True Principle of Protestantism as related to the Present State of the Church*, with an introduction of his own, commending the work, and a Sermon on *Catholic Unity*. In 1846, he published his *Mystical Presence; a Vindication of the Reformed or Calvinistic Doctrine of the Holy Eucharist*. This was by far one of his most important publications. It made him favourably known in England and Germany as a theologian of rare ability. His views of the evils and weaknesses of Protestantism are embodied in a tract entitled *Antichrist; or, the Spirit of Sect and Schism*, which was published in 1848.

We append here the titles of a few other productions of Dr. Nevin's pen, some of which have appeared in pamphlet form, others only in the Review: *Pa ty Spirit; Inaugural Address at Mercersburg; The German Language; Eulogy on Dr. Frederick Augustus Rauch; Baccalaureate Addresses; Early Christianity; Cyprian; Plea for Philosophy; Human Freedom; Address at the Formal Opening of Franklin and Marshall College, at Lancaster; Man's True Destiny; The Wonderful Nature of Man; Address at the Installation of Dr. B. C. Wolff; The Dutch Crusade; Some Notice of Dr. Berg's Last Words; The Lutheran Confession; Modern Civilization, by Balmes; The Anglican Crisis; Anticreed Heresy; The Moral Order of Sex; Wilberforce on the Incarnation; Review of Dr. Hodge's Commentary on the Ephesians; Christ and Him Crucified; The Liturgical Question; Vindication of the Revised Liturgy; Reply to Dr. Dorner, of Berlin, Germany; Revelation and Redemption; Revelation of God in Christ; Christ and his Spirit; Philosophy of History; The Old Catholic Movement; Review of Apollos by Bishop Cox; Reply to an Anglican Catholic; Christianity and Humanity*, read before the Evangelical Alliance; and other articles of a kindred nature. His lectures on *Æsthetics and Ethics*, and his *Notes on Theology* have not appeared in print.

Dr. Nevin still remains at the head of Franklin and Marshall College. He occasionally uses his pen and frequently preaches. He shows no abatement in his intellectual vigour. His discourses are full of unction and power, and exhibit a profound knowledge of the Scriptures, as well as great compass of thought. Most of the ministers of the

Reformed Church in this State, were at one time his students, and all regard him with much veneration and affection.

Since he left the Seminary at Princeton, his theology has undergone many and important changes. This could not well be otherwise. By some this has been regarded as an objection, or as a serious defection from the faith. He, however, does not think so, but maintains that all his changes have been simply parts of his progress in the true faith in Christ and Him crucified. This he has brought out in an interesting way, and with much seriousness and *naivete* in a series of articles in the Reformed Church Messenger, during the year 1871, under the title "My Own Life." Unfortunately they extend only up to the period when he was called to the Professorship in the Seminary at Mercersburg.

On the first of January, 1835, Dr. Nevin was united in matrimony to Martha, second daughter of the Hon. Robert Jenkins, a gentleman of excellence and influence, of Windsor Place, near Churchtown, Lancaster county, Pa. His eldest son, Captain W. W. Nevin, is now editor of "The Press," in Philadelphia, his second son, Robert J. Nevin, D. D., is the Rector of the Protestant Episcopal Church, in Rome, Italy, and his second daughter, Blanche, is an artist in the city first named. Two daughters remain at Cærnarvon Place. Three sons have died, one in childhood, the others in promising youth.

N. B. LANE, M. D.

NICHOLAS BITTINGER LANE was a native of Franklin county. He was born near Mont Alto Furnace, at the base of the South Mountain, in Quincy township, on the 15th day of August, 1802. His ancestors were emigrants from Holland, who came to this country at a very early period, and settled in Lancaster county, near Litiz. Samuel Lane, the father of the subject of this sketch, a wheelwright by trade, worked his way into Franklin county, and married the daughter of Nicholas Bittinger, a large land owner, who had signalized himself in the days of the Revolution as an ardent Whig, and who was captured by the British at Fort Washington. Inheriting a respectable property in Quincy township, from his father-in-law, he settled himself permanently near Funkstown. Daniel and Samuel Hughes, of Hagerstown, the latter a very distinguished lawyer, determining to erect a furnace on their mountain lands near that village, selected Mr. Lane as their superintendent, and under his directions were erected, and for a number of years operated, the " Mont Alto Iron Works," now so successfully conducted by Col. George B. Wiestling. Nicholas, the only son of Samuel Lane, was educated with as much care and instruction as could be provided him at home, and in the village of Waynesboro', where he was taught the mysteries of Surveying by John Flanegan, Esq., one of the most marked men of the county. In the spring of 1818, young Lane, then in his sixteenth year, commenced the study of medicine with Dr. S. D. Culbertson, of Chambersburg, an eminent practitioner of that day, with whom he remained until his medical course was completed in the spring of 1822, when he received the degree of Doctor of Medieine, not being twenty-one years of age, from the celebrated University of Pennsylvania, and winning the distinction of having his *thesis* published in a leading medical journal of that day, by request of the Faculty.

In 1824, Dr. Lane formed a partnership in the practice of medicine with Dr. Alexander T. Dean, then located in Chambersburg, who was one of the most accomplished physicians in the State, which association continued until Dr. Dean formed the design of removing to Harrisburg. The firm of Lane, Bain & Culbertson was then formed, but was of short duration; Dr. Culbertson relinquishing practice altogether, and Dr. Bain returning to Baltimore from whence he had moved to

Chambersburg. Dr. Lane, after the dissolution of the partnership, continued the practice of medicine for about twenty years, acquiring a large amount of business and gaining a reputation as a skilful physician excelled by none in the State, until he was disabled by the disease which closed his life on the 15th of April, 1853.

The life of a country physician is meagre of incidents of public interest, although so fraught with beneficence to individuals; his toils and anxieties, his days and nights of watching and care, his studies and habits of thought being devoted to the sole object of relieving sickness, healing wounds and averting the shafts of the last enemy. Great public affairs go on around him unparticipated and almost unobserved by him; other professions win applause and honours for their followers, large fortunes are made and high renown won by his fellows in other pursuits, but the worn and wearied country physician is almost submerged from public observation while he seeks to rescue the precious freight that this wrecked body yet bears. How many a splendid intellect, how much culture and sagacity in this grand class of workers have passed unnoticed, unsuspected! Among this class, Dr. Lane enjoyed an honourable position. He was a quiet, modest and courteous gentleman, fond of study, well posted in all the branches of his profession, wonderfully successful in the treatment of diseases, and as an operative surgeon cautious and skilful; besides, he had fine literary tastes, was a keen, forcible and ready writer, contributing frequently to the *medical journals* of his day, and in every scheme of reform and progress his pen could be relied upon as a powerful ally and advocate in his own community.

Dr. Lane took a deep interest in church affairs, although not a bigot in religion. While maintaining his own views firmly, he at all times yielded a respectful deference to the opinions of others; thus securing the good will and esteem of all denominations of Christians. He died in the faith of his fathers, a full believer in the doctrines of the Evangelical Lutheran Church.

Dr. Lane left a family of several sons and daughters. Two of his sons are engaged extensively in mercantile pursuits in the city of Pittsburgh. Two others have adopted the profession of their father and are pursuing the practice of medicine in their native county. Dr. William C. Lane, his eldest son, graduated in the University of Pennsylvania. As a physician he has received a thorough course of training—is devotedly attached to his profession and highly esteemed as an efficient practitioner in the community in which he is located. As a local historian he deserves more than a passing notice. No man in the State is better informed, or has written more, on the early settlement of this part of the Cumberland valley than Dr. Lane. Its first settlers, its Indian wars and depredations, its noted men and events, its early churches and forts, interesting facts and incidents, adventures, traditions, &c., &c.; in all this, he is a perfect storehouse of knowledge. He writes with great ease and elegance, and will dash off page upon page of local history, detailing events, giving dates, &c., with a rapidity and accuracy truly wonderful. His writings have appeared from time to time, for years past, in our local newspapers, and are of great value as contributions to our early history, and if compiled would fill volumes. During the war of the Rebellion he served as surgeon of the One Hundred and Twenty-second Pennsylvania Volunteers, and afterwards as surgeon of the Board of Enrolment of the Sixteenth District of Pennsylvania.

Dr. Samuel G. Lane, second son of Dr. N. B. Lane, received the degree of Doctor of Medicine in the University of Pennsylvania, graduating with the highest honours, and at once entered upon the practice of medicine. Young, talented and zealous, of undoubted integrity, fine social qualities, and a mind generously stored with varied learning, he soon took position in the very front rank of his profession, acquiring a respectable practice and the confidence and esteem of the entire community. At the breaking out of the Rebellion he received the appointment of Surgeon to the Fifth Pennsylvania Reserves, sharing in the full the active service and dangers of the campaign with that noted regiment. His energy and ability as a surgeon attracted the attention of Gov. Curtin, who called him from active service in the field and commissioned him Assistant Surgeon General of the State. In this responsible position, by his strict attenton to business, generous and impartial conduct, he was looked upon then, as now, with affection and gratitude by the entire medical corps of the state. As a writer Dr. Lane possesses remarkable ability, contributing much as correspondent and editor to the newspapers of his native town.

REV. JAMES BUCHANAN.

THE REV. JAMES BUCHANAN was a native of Chester county, Pennsylvania. He received his collegiate education in Dickinson College, Carlisle, where he was graduated September 28th, 1803. He studied theology with the Rev. Nathan Grier, D. D., of Brandywine, and was licensed by the Presbytery of Newcastle, when he was about twenty-three years of age.

Mr. Buchanan's first settlement was in the Presbyterian Church of Harrisburg, Pa., where he laboured some years with faithfulness and success. His health having become impaired, he resigned his pastoral charge, and spent several years in traveling, with a view to its restoration. At length, finding his health in some degree restored, and having received a call from the congregation of Greencastle, he accepted it, and became their pastor in the year 1816. In this pastoral charge he laboured with great fidelity and acceptance for about twenty years, when, on account of declining health, and his inability to discharge his pastoral duties to his own satisfaction, he resigned his charge, to the very great regret of his congregation, who were devotedly attached to him. In hope of retaining him with them, they generously offered to accept a diminished amount of labour, such as his weak health would allow, without any diminution of salary. But a sense of duty and a regard to their highest interests, induced him to withdraw, and open the way for the settlement of another pastor, who would be able to give them the full amount of labour. By changing his location, also, he hoped that something might be gained in point of health, and that his life might be rendered more useful in the service of his Divine Master. He accordingly removed with his family to Logansport, Indiana, where, in charge of the Presbyterian Church in that place, he laboured with encouraging success, until the Head of the church dismissed him to the possession of his reward. As pleasing evidence that he did not labour in vain, we have been informed that during the short period of his ministry there, the church increased from about twenty to an hundred members. His death took place at Logansport, on the 16th of September, 1843, at the age of sixty years. His disease, which was congestion of the brain, and which, at its first appearance on the Sabbath, obliged him to close abruptly the public services of the sanctuary in which he was engaged, terminated in death on the Saturday morning following, at five o'clock. The nature and violence of his disease incapacitated him for much satisfactory conversation. He gave ample evidence, however, of his resignation to the will of God, and that his hope of salvation was firmly fixed upon the atoning blood of Christ.

To strangers who did not know Mr. Buchanan, his appearance was rather harsh and repulsive. His delicate health and shattered nerves, often greatly affected his spirits, and gave to his countenance the appearance of severity and moroseness. But he was a man of a warm heart, and of a kind and generous disposition. In his friendship he was steadfast. Although he was generally grave, yet in the midst of his intimate friends he often relaxed, and was highly cheerful and sociable. His piety was of a retiring and unostentatious character. It was, however, eminently practical, prompting him to the diligent discharge of all incumbent duties. He placed a very low estimate on his own piety, and although no one else doubted its reality, he himself often did. His bodily complaints gave a melancholy complexion to his religious experience, and interfered largely with his Christian comfort; occasionally, however, he was favoured with seasons of comfort during which he greatly enjoyed the consolations of religion.

As a preacher he held a very respectable rank. His sermons, in their structure, were neat, systematic and short; in their matter, solid, evangelical and practical; and in their manner, grave, solemn and earnest. Although he could not be considered eloquent, he scarcely ever failed to interest and please those who were capable of judging correctly, and had a taste for good preaching. Indeed, very few men preached so uniformly well.

In the Judicatories of the church, Mr. Buchanan rarely spoke. This was not owing to any want of interest in the affairs of the church, or any want of readiness in communicating his thoughts, but to his nervous debility, which induced embarrassment, and rendered it exceedingly painful for him to make the effort. He was, however, a judicious counsellor, and did his part in this way, in the disposal of the business of the church.

In his doctrinal views, he adhered strictly to the standards of the church to which he belonged, which he believed to be in conformity with the Word of God. He eschewed all novelties in doctrines and forms of worship, being content to walk in "the old paths," and the "good way" in which his fathers had trod. He was a good man, and did a noble work for God.

HON. THADDEUS STEVENS.*

THADDEUS STEVENS was born at Danville, Caledonia county, Vermont, on the 4th day of April, 1792. His parents were poor, in a community where poverty was the rule and wealth the exception. Of his father, I know but little, save that he enlisted in the war of 1812, and died in the service. Upon his mother chiefly fell the burden of rearing their four sons. She was a woman of great energy, strong will, and deep piety. Early seeing the ambition and fully sympathizing with the aspiration of her crippled boy, she devotedly seconded his efforts for the acquisition of knowledge, and by her industry, energy and frugality largely aided him in procuring a collegiate education. He returned her affection with the full strength of his strong nature, and for many years after he had acquired fame and fortune in his adopted State, had the pleasure of making an annual pilgrimage to the home which he had provided for her comfort, and where she dispensed, with means he furnished, a liberal charity.

In the last year of his life, in writing his will with his own hand, while making no provision for the care of his own grave, he did not forget that of his mother, but set apart an ample sum for that purpose directing yearly payments upon the condition, "that the sexton keep the grave in good order, and plant roses and other cheerful flowers at each of the four corners of said grave each spring." In the same instrument, devising one thousand dollars in aid of the establishment at his home of a Baptist church, of which society his mother was an earnest member, he said, "I do this out of respect to the memory of my mother, to whom I owe whatever little of prosperity I have had on earth, which, small as it is, I desire emphatically to acknowledge."

After attending the common schools of the neighbourhood, he fitted for college at the Peacham Academy in his native county, entered the University of Vermont, and remained there about two years. The college suspending on account of the war, he proceeded to Dartmouth, and graduated at that institution in 1814. After reading law at Peacham, in the office of Judge Mattocks, for some months, he left his native State and settled in Pennsylvania, in 1815, first in the town

---

*From the Eulogy of Hon. O. J. Dickey, pronounced in the House of Representatives, Washington, D. C., December 17th, 1868.

of York, where he taught an academy and pursued his legal studies. The rules of court in that district having required students to read one year in the office of an attorney, he went to Bel Air, Harford county, Maryland, and was there examined and admitted to practice in August, 1816. He at once returned to Pennsylvania and opened a law office at Gettysburg, in the county of Adams, and entered upon the practice of his profession in that and adjoining counties. He was soon in the possession of an extensive and lucrative business, to which he gave his entire attention for some sixteen years.

Mr. Stevens first engaged actively in politics with the Anti-Masonic party of 1828-29, which he joined in their opposition to secret societies. He was elected to the popular branch of the Legislature of his State, in 1833, as a representative from the county of Adams, and continued to serve in that body almost without interruption until 1840, during which entire period he was the leader of the party in the Legislature, if not the State. During this service he championed many measures of improvement; among others the common school system of Pennsylvania, which, at a critical moment, he saved from overthrow by a speech which he always asserted to have been, in his opinion, the most effective he ever made.

By that single effort he established the principle, never since seriously questioned in Pennsylvania, that it is the duty of the State to provide the facilities of education to all the children of the Commonwealth. In behalf of this measure he joined hands with his bitterest personal enemies. He highly eulogized for his course upon this question, the chief of the opposing political party, Governor George Wolf, and denounced with all his power of invective the time-servers of his own party. Himself the child of poverty, he plead the cause of the poor, and by the force of his will, intellect, and eloquence, broke down the barriers erected by wealth, caste and ignorance, and earned a name that will endure as long as a child of Pennsylvania gratefully remembers the blessings conferred by light and knowledge.

In 1837-38, Mr. Stevens was a member of the Convention called to revise the Constitution of Pennsylvania, an assemblage which numbered as members many of the strongest men of the State, among whom Mr. Stevens stood in the front rank. This Convention, notwithstanding the able and strenuous opposition of a strong minority, led by Mr. Stevens, inserted the word "white" as a qualification of suffrage, thus disfranchising a race. On this account he refused to append his name to the completed instrument, and stood alone in such refusal. For the same cause he opposed, but unsuccessfully, the ratification by the people.

In 1842, Mr. Stevens, finding himself deeply in debt by reason of losses in the iron business, and liabilities incurred in numerous indorsements made for friends, removed to Lancaster county, one of the largest, richest and most populous counties in the State, and resumed the practice of his profession. His reputation as a lawyer had preceded him, and his income almost at once became the largest at the bar. In a few years he paid his debts and saved the bulk of his estate. In 1848 and 1850, he was elected to Congress from Lancaster county, when, declining to be a candidate, he returned to his profession until 1858, when he was again elected and continued to hold the seat without interruption until his death. His course upon this floor has passed into and forms no unimportant part in the history of a mighty people in a great crisis of their existence. But I have promised to leave to others to say what may be proper in illustration of his great achievements in his latter days.

To those here who judged of the personal appearance of the deceased only as they looked on him bearing the burden of years, and stricken with disease, though he still stood with eye undimmed and will undaunted, I may say that in his prime he was a man physically well proportioned, muscular and strong, of clear and ruddy complexion, with face and feature of great nobility and under perfect command and control. In his youth and early manhood, notwithstanding his lameness, he entered with zest into almost all of the athletic games and sports of the times. He was an expert swimmer and an excellent horseman.

When residing at Gettysburg, he followed the chase, and kept his hunters and hounds. On a recent visit to his iron works, I found the old mountain men garrulous with stories of the risks and dangers of the bold rider, as with horse and hound he followed the deer along the slopes and through the gaps of the South Mountain.

In private life among his friends, Mr. Stevens was ever genial, kind and considerate. To them he was linked with hooks of steel. For them he would labour and sacrifice without stint, complaint or regret. In his hours of relaxation there could be no more genial companion. His rare conversational powers, fund of anecdote, brilliant sallies of wit and wise sayings upon the topics of the hour, made his company much sought, and many of these are the current coin of the circles in which he moved.

Mr. Stevens was an honest and truthful man in public and private life. His word was sacred in letter and spirit, and was never paltered in a double sense. In money matters he was liberal to a fault, and out of his immense professional income he left but a meagre estate. In his private charity he was lavish. He was incapable of saying *no* in the presence of want and misery. His charity, like his political convictions, regarded neither creed nor colour. He was a good classical scholar, and was well read in ancient and modern literature, especially on subjects of philosophy and law. In his old age he read but few books. Shakspeare, Dante, Homer, Milton and the Bible, would, however, generally be found upon his table in his sleeping room, where he was accustomed to read in bed. He was simple and temperate in his habits. He disliked the use of tobacco, and for forty years never used or admitted in his house intoxicating drinks, and only then by direction of his physician.

Mr. Stevens was deeply loved and fully trusted by his constituents. He was often in advance of their views; sometimes he ran counter to their prejudices or passions, yet such was his popularity with them, so strong their faith in his wisdom, in the integrity of his actions and the purity of his purpose, that they never failed to support him.

Popular with men of all parties, with his own supporters his name was a household word. To them and among themselves, "Old Thad," was a name of endearment, while even his foes spoke of him with pride as the "Great Commoner." No man ever died more deeply mourned by a constituency than Thaddeus Stevens.

Having briefly selected some of the incidents that marked the history of my friend, I will, in conclusion, say a few words of him on the subject in connection with which he is probably more widely known than any other—slavery. Mr. Stevens was always an anti-slavery man. From the time he left his native mountains, to the moment of his death, he was always not only anti-slavery in the common acceptation of the term, but a bold, fearless, determined and uncompromising foe of oppression in any and every form. He was an abolitionist before there was such a party name. His opposition to American slavery never altered with his party connection, and was never based upon mere questions of expediency or political economy. He always viewed it as a great wrong, at war with the fundamental principles of this and all good governments, as a sin in the sight of God, and a crime against man. For many years, long before it became popular to do so, he denounced this institution as the great crime of the nation, on the stump, in the forum, in party conventions, in deliberative assemblies. On this question he was always in advance of his party, his State, and constituents.

Always resident in a border county, he defended the fugitive on all occasions, asserted the right of free speech, and stood between the abolitionist and the mob, often with peril to himself. This was one great cause of his having been so long in a minority, and of his entrance late in life into the councils of the nation, but for this, he was fully compensated by living to see the destruction of an institution which he loathed, and by receiving for his reward, and as the crowning glory of his life, the blessings of millions he had so largely aided to make free.

Mr. Stevens died on the 11th day of August, 1868, and his remains lie in Lancaster, Pa., in a private cemetery established by an old friend, in a lot selected by himself, for reasons as stated in the touching and beautiful epitaph prepared by himself for inscription on his tomb, "I repose in this quiet, secluded spot, not from any natural preference for solitude, but finding other cemeteries limited by charter rules as to race, I have chosen it that I might be enabled to illustrate in my death the principles which I advocated through a long life—equality of man before his Creator."

HON. FREDERICK WATTS.

N eminent minister of the Gospel once said, "the leading lawyer is always the most prominent member of the community in which he lives."

Whether this is always the case in large cities and commercial centres, it is no doubt generally so in agricultural communities; and it certainly is beyond dispute that Judge Watts was the most prominent member of the community in which he lived, for more than a quarter of a century. We find him in the Supreme Court of the State as early as October Term, 1827, arguing a case reported in 16 Sergeant and Rawle, page 416, and as late as May Term, 1869, as appears by the Cumberland Valley Railroad Company's appeal, reported in 12 Smith, 218, and all through that period of forty-two years (except the three he was on the bench) there is not a single volume of reports containing the cases from the Middle District, in which his name is not found, and few cases of importance from the counties in which he practised, in which he was not counsel for either plaintiff or defendant in error. Add to this the fact that, for fifteen years, he was reporter of the decisions of that court, and during that period, and before and after it, engaged in a large office business and in the trial of nearly all the important cases in the courts below, in his own county and Perry, and we have abundant evidence of a life of more than ordinary industry.

But this did not satisfy his love of labour. He was during this period President of the Cumberland Valley Railroad and continued in that office, discharging faithfully all its duties for twenty-six years. To his professional duties and those connected with the railroad, he added (what was always with him a labour of love) constant activity in agricultural pursuits, not only managing his farms, but as President of the Cumberland County Agricultural Society and an active projector of the Agricultural College of Pennsylvania, furthering the general agricultural interests of his county and State.

Judge Watts was born in Carlisle, May 9th, 1801, and is a son of David Watts, one of the most distinguished lawyers of his day, whose practice extended through all the middle counties of the State. His mother was a daughter of General Miller, of Revolutionary fame, who afterwards commanded the United States troops at Baltimore, during the War of 1812. His grandfather, Frederick Watts, was a member of the Executive Council of Pennsylvania, before the Revolution, and one of the prominent men of the province and subsequent State. Having been duly prepared, he entered Dickinson College, whence he graduated in 1819, and passed the two subsequent years with his uncle, William Miles, in Erie county, where he cultivated his taste for agricultural pursuits. In 1821, he returned to Carlisle and entered the office of Andrew Carothers, Esq., as a law student, was admitted to practice in August, 1824, became a partner of his preceptor and soon acquired a large and lucrative practice. In 1829, he and the Hon. C. B. Penrose, became reporters of the decisions of the Supreme Court, and they published three volumes, after which Judge Watts became sole reporter, and published ten volumes, and subsequent thereto, he and Henry J. Sergeant, Esq., published nine volumes. In 1845 he ceased reporting, and the same year became President of the Cumberland Valley Railroad. It is to his energy and able management that the people of the valley are indebted for a road which, when he took hold of it, was in debt, out of repair, unproductive, and in a dilapidated condition, but which, through his energetic and economical management, has been brought up to a high state of prosperity, having paid all its indebtedness and caused it to yield handsome returns to its stockholders.

On the 9th of March, 1849, he was commissioned by Governor Johnston, President Judge of the Ninth Judicial District, composed of the counties of Cumberland, Perry and Juniata. He retained the office until the Judiciary became elective, in 1852, when he resumed his practice. In 1854, he exerted all his influence and energy in favour of the Agricultural College of Pennsylvania, and upon its organization was elected President of the Board of Trustees, in which capacity he still acts. During the year 1854, he also projected the erection of gas and water works for Carlisle, and having formed a company, was elected its President, and remained such until its success was assured.

If asked for his most prominent characteristics, we would say, force of character and abiding self confidence. Whatever he undertook he did with all his might, and whatever he believed, he believed implicitly. He never sat down at the counsel table to try a case, that he did not impress the court and jury that he had perfect confidence that he would gain it; and if fortune did not seem to favour him, he never desisted until it was disposed of by the court of last resort. His temper was completely within his control. His equanimity was perfect, and he was ever ready to avail himself of any slip of his adversary. He had great powers of concentration, and always prepared his law points at the counsel table as soon as the evidence was closed. This he did with great facility, always directing them to the main points of the case. His power with the jury was very great. He knew and was known by every man in the counties where he practised, and was regarded as a man of large intellect, sterling integrity and unblemished honour. To these he added the impression of perfect belief in the justice of his cause; and this was effected by a manner which was always dignified, and in speech that was clear, strong, convincing and never tedious. He despised quirks and quibbles, was a model of fairness in the trial of a cause, and always encouraged and treated kindly younger members of the bar that he saw struggling honourably for prominence; and when he closed his professional career, he left the bar with the profound respect of all its members.

In 1860, Judge Watts removed to one of his farms, at some distance from town, and gradually withdrew from active practice, intending to devote his whole time to agricultural pursuits. In 1871, he was tendered the appointment of Commissioner of Agriculture, which he declined. The offer was renewed and he was finally induced to accept the appointment, and entered upon its duties, August 1st, 1871. He has ever since devoted himself assiduously to the practical development of the agricultural resources of the country. An admirable system pervades his department, and the three divisions are so arranged, that the most detailed and accurate information can be obtained with the greatest facility.

The country has not in its employ a more industrious, honest, faithful, and large hearted servant.

HON. THOMAS GRUBB McCULLOH.

NO name is remembered with warmer admiration by the people of Franklin county, than that of Thomas Grubb McCulloh, whose fame as the great lawyer was the pride of his community. He was born in Greencastle, on the 20th day of April, 1785. His grandfather, George McCulloh, born about 1710, at Killibegs, in the county of Donegal, Ireland, came to the American Colonies in 1728, settled in Lancaster county, and died in Little Britain, in that county, in 1806 or 1807. His father, Robert, was the eldest son of George, and was born in 1750. On the maternal side, he was a descendant of Thomas Grubb, whose father was one of the earliest emigrants from England to this country, coming over with William Penn. Thomas Grubb settled in Lancaster county, and his oldest daughter, Prudence, was united in marriage with Robert McCulloh, the father of the subject of this sketch, in 1778. About this time Robert McCulloh removed to Franklin county, where all his children were born.

Thomas G. McCulloh was educated in Greencastle, under the tuition of Mr. Borland, who afterwards became a very eminent Professor in a literary institution, in the state of New York. He studied law in Chambersburg, under Andrew Dunlop, one of the most distinguished lawyers of Pennsylvania, and was admitted to the bar in 1804 or 1805; and was married on the 1st of September, 1808, to Margaret Purviance. He practised law in Chambersburg about forty-three years, during part of which period he attended the courts of Bedford county, and was frequently called upon to try causes in other parts of the state, going as far as Pittsburgh even, being retained as counsel in important land suits, in which class of cases he had great celebrity. The reports of the Supreme Court of Pennsylvania furnish ample evidence of his immense practice, and bear convincing proof of his renown as a lawyer.

In 1821, he was elected to Congress, and during his service there his wife died suddenly, 26th February, 1821. For five or six terms, he represented his county in the House of Representatives of Pennsylvania, and was mainly instrumental with his colleague, James Dunlop, Esq., son of his preceptor, Andrew Dunlop, in having the Cumberland Valley Railroad extended to Chambersburg. He was the first President of this road, but resigned a few years before his death. At the time of his decease, he was President of the Bank of Chambersburg.

Thomas G. McCulloh was not only prominent as a lawyer, but he was a man of varied information, capable of discussing almost any subject brought before him. He was well versed in agricultural pursuits, and very attentive to the improvement of his farms, of which he had, at times, two or three. A man of public spirit and enterprise, he was always willing to lend a helping hand to all public improvements in his town or county.

To the day of his death he was a close student, reading works upon all subjects, particularly those of a legal character. He had a large, well selected library, miscellaneous and professional, and was constantly adding to its volumes.

When the first drum beat for volunteers to repel the British invasion of Baltimore, he stepped from his office into the ranks of the recruiting party, and marched with the company to the threatened city. When the regiment was formed he was appointed its Quartermaster. He took charge of the Franklin Repository, and edited it while its celebrated editor, Mr. Geo. K. Harper, was absent with the army, on the northern frontiers. He died at Chambersburg, September 10th, 1848.

Mr. McCulloh was always popular with the members of the bar, not only on account of his unusual legal attainments, but for his professional courtesy, which was especially extended to its junior members. As a public speaker he was not fluent, but was clear and logical, and his manner of speaking was of a conversational character, carrying great weight with juries. He wrote with skill and force. It is traditional that he was singularly independent of the stereotyped formulas of legal documents, and that his brief papers were remarkably pointed and unassailable. He has left behind him the reputation of being one of the ablest jurists of his day. His manners were exceedingly plain and popular, and he was always a favourite of his fellow citizens.

PATRICK ALLISON, D. D.

PATRICK ALLISON was born in Franklin (or what was then known as Lancaster) county, in the year 1740. His father, William Allison, immigrated to this part of Pennsylvania, early in the eighteenth century, from the north of Ireland. He was born in 1696, and died at his home in Franklin county, in the year 1778. His oldest son, John, inherited a large estate and on part of it laid out the town of Greencastle. William, the youngest son, lived and died on the paternal farm, and for many years exhibited the old house, so replete with ancient memories of border life.

Patrick Allison graduated at the University of Pennsylvania, in 1760. He commenced his theological studies shortly after he left the University, but in 1761 was appointed Professor in the Academy at Newark, Delaware, which office he accepted. He was licensed to preach by the Second Presbytery of Philadelphia, in March, 1763. In August of that year, he was invited to a church in Baltimore. He was ordained in Philadelphia, by the same Presbytery that licensed him, in 1765, but does not appear to have been ever installed in Baltimore, though he was always regarded as the pastor, during the long period (thirty-five years) that he continued to serve the congregation.

Mr. Allison received the degree of Doctor of Divinity from the University of Pennsylvania, in 1782.

Dr. Allison was married in March, 1787, to Wellary, daughter of William Buchanan, a gentleman who distinguished himself by his civil services during the War of the Revolution. She survived him about twenty years. He left an only child, a daughter, who intermarried with Mr. George L. Brown, and died in 1849, leaving six children.

"Dr. Allison's personal appearance," says Robert Purviance, Esq., of Baltimore; "was high, commanding and impressive. He was of about the medium height, and in every way well proportioned. His manners combined grace with dignity in an uncommon degree, so as to invite confidence on the one hand, and to repel all undue familiarity on the other. While there was nothing about him that savoured of ostentation, there was always that genuine self-respect, that considerate regard to circumstances, that cautious forbearance to give unnecessary pain, which never fail to secure to an individual a deferential respect from all with whom he associates. His moral character was entirely above reproach. Accustomed, of course, to move in the highest circles of society, he never forgot the sacredness of his calling, while yet he was a highly entertaining and agreeable companion. As he was himself remarkable for propriety of speech, he would never tolerate gross improprieties in others, no matter what might be their standing in society, and if an expression bordering on profaneness, or even indecent levity, were uttered in his hearing, it was very sure to meet with a deserved rebuke. His intellectual character was universally acknowledged to be of a very high order. His early opportunities for the culture of his mind were among the best which the country then afforded, and these diligently improved, in connection with his fine natural powers, rendered him decidedly eminent even among the greater minds of his profession. He was always a diligent student, and his studies, instead of being strictly professional, took a wide range. He was an elegant Belles Lettres scholar, and was very familiar with both ancient and modern history.

"The versification of Pope, and the chaste beauties of Addison, had great attractions for him, and I rather think that the style of Robertson, the historian, was the model on which he formed his own. His power of mental abstraction is said to have been so remarkable, that he experienced no interruption in the composition of a sermon by the presence and conversation of company. In the delivery of his sermons he always had his manuscript before him, and though his manner could not be said to be attractive to a stranger, yet to those who were accustomed to it, it was very agreeable. His discourses were generally didactic, often profoundly argumentative. I once heard an Episcopal clergyman of some note expressing rather a low estimate of some of the ministers of the day, but of Dr. Allison he remarked with emphasis, '*He* was a man of *matter*.' He was especially eminent in the judicatories of the church, and in all public bodies, being possessed of great penetration, the utmost self-control, and an admirable command of thought and language, the most appropriate and elegant. I remember to have heard that Dr. Samuel Stanhope Smith, then President of Princeton College, remarked to a gentleman of our city, ' Dr. Allison is decidedly the ablest *statesman* we have in the General Assembly of the Presbyterian Church.' And the late Dr. Miller, of Princeton, has left behind him a similar testimony."

Dr. Allison died August 21st, 1802, aged about sixty-two. His great aversion to appearing as an author induced him to leave, as one of his dying injunctions, that all his manuscript sermons should be committed to the flames; otherwise, doubtless, there might have been a selection made from them for the press, which would have done honour to our American pulpit.

JOSEPH POMEROY.

JOSEPH POMEROY, merchant, banker and politician, was born in Lurgan township, Franklin county, Pa., October 18th, 1804. Educationally his advantages were only such as the common schools of the district afforded. While a mere boy, he was placed in a store at Shippensburg, Pa., where he acquired a thorough knowledge of country business. Shortly after attaining his majority—that is, in 1826—he commenced business on his own account at Concord, Franklin county, Pa., continuing the same for twenty-five years, and becoming, in 1841, associated with William R. and John M. Pomeroy in a steam tannery at the same place. In April, 1851, he removed to Juniata county, where he had previously acquired considerable property, and where he resided until his death, conducting a very large business in merchandising, tanning, milling and farming.

In 1867, he was elected President of the Juniata Valley Bank, Mifflintown. He devoted considerable attention to politics, and was the recipient of several marked tokens of favour from his party—the Republican. In 1831, he was elected to the State Legislature as Representative from Franklin county; in 1861, Associate Judge of Juniata county, being the only successful nominee on the Republican ticket; and in 1872, the Representative of his Congressional District in the National Republican Convention, held in Philadelphia, in June of that year. Judge Pomeroy was a man of extraordinary enterprise and energy, of firm convictions and great tenacity of purpose, combined with strong common sense, good judgment and excellent address. To these qualities his success in life, which was without interruption, was wholly due, for he commenced with limited means and only such friends as his talents and character had won.

HON. HENRY M. WATTS.

HENRY MILLER WATTS, late Envoy Extraordinary and Minister Plenipotentiary to Austria, was born on the 10th day of October, A. D., 1805, in the borough of Carlisle, Pennsylvania. He cannot boast, as many justly do, of being a self-made man, having, under the Providence of God, derived his being from a most respectable and well-known parentage, able and ready to afford him all the advantages of education, wealth and position.

Frederick Watts, his grandfather, was an emigrant from Great Britain during our provincial days, and settled in Cumberland county, Pennsylvania, having previously married Jane Murray, of the lineage of David Murray, famous in the days of the Pretender. In the War of the Revolution he held the commission of a General, and was also a member of the Executive Council of Pennsylvania.

General Henry Miller was his maternal grandfather, and from him the subject of our sketch derived his name. When a Lieutenant, he organized a company in the borough of York, and marched it to Boston, where, as the only body of men from a section south of the Hudson, it participated in the skirmishes and battles with the British on Breed's and Bunker's Hills. His wife was Ursula Rose, one of the daughters of Joseph Rose, of Lancaster, Pennsylvania, who was called to the bar in Dublin, Ireland, as a barrister, and emigrated eventually to the United States.

General Miller was an active partisan officer during the Revolutionary War; was on intimate and confidential relations with General Washington and Colonel Hamilton; belonged to the Cincinnati Society, and during the course of his life held several civil offices under the Federal party. He died poor.

David Watts, the father, and only son of Frederick Watts, was a graduate of Dickinson College, during the presidency of the Rev. Charles Nisbet, D. D. He studied law in the office of William Lewis, and after his admission to the bar, began the practice of his profession in Carlisle, Pennsylvania. He was profound in classical lore, eminent as a lawyer, and distinguished in the wide circuit of his practice at the bar.

Henry Miller Watts, favoured with an ancestry so honourable, was carefully trained in the best schools; graduated at Dickinson College in 1824; studied law in Carlisle in the office of Andrew Carothers, who had been a pupil of his deceased father; was admitted to the bar as Attorney at Law, and removed to the city of Pittsburgh, and within a year thereafter, was commissioned as Deputy Attorney General of the State of Pennsylvania. This office he held under two successive Attorneys General, and then relinquished it for more general practice. His legal career, amidst many of the most eminent of the profession, was a rising one, and soon brought him distinction, and with it the confidence of the people.

In 1835, at the earnest solicitation of the electors of Allegheny county, he consented to represent that district in the popular branch of the State Legislature. He continued to serve for three successive terms, until in 1838, having married Anna Maria, second daughter of the late Dr. Peter Shoenberger, he determined to withdraw from the arena of politics and to remove with his family to Philadelphia, and there follow the more serene and congenial occupation of a lawyer. The period of three years, during which he represented his constituency, was distinguished by events of great public importance; the foundations of the system of canals and railways were laid; education by means of common schools was instituted; the Bank of the United States was re-chartered; there was made the first serious assault upon the existence of slavery in sister states by advocating the right of trial by jury of fugitive slaves; and the charitable institutions, which now redound so much to the credit of the great State of Pennsylvania, were enlarged and strengthened.

In 1841, induced by the position and reputation of Mr. Watts, President Harrison conferred upon him the office of Attorney of the United States for the Eastern District of the State of Pennsylvania, in which position he was duly confirmed by the Senate of the United States. He fulfilled the duties of this office to the entire satisfaction of the Government until the end of the term.

The incidents of a lawyer's life—devoted to his clients, wear and tear of mental and physical powers, an income too often inferior to his expenditures, and a disagreeable monotony—became in time irksome to Mr. Watts, until, weary of the practice of the law, in 1857 he crossed the Atlantic with his family for the purpose of educating his children, then eight in number, in the elementary schools of Paris.

Soon after the outbreak of the great American conflict, Mr. Watts became one of the founders of the Union Club of Philadelphia, an association of fifty patriotic gentlemen, who, in the darkest day of the war, about the close of the year 1862, determined to meet alternately at their respective homes in a social circle, in order to knit each other's hearts more closely in the holy cause of perpetuating the Union—the only condition of membership being *unqualified loyalty to the United States.* At a meeting of the Club in January, 1863, the articles of the association of the Union League of Philadelphia were submitted, duly considered, and subscribed by all present.

It was composed of nearly two thousand wealthy and influential citizens; was distinguished for its earnestness in the cause of the Union; for its liberality in the raising and equipping of several regiments for the war; and for the power it exercised in stimulating the whole country to active exertion. It still exists as a political and social organization, being incorporated by the laws of the Commonwealth.

In 1863, he took his eldest sons to Dresden, in Saxony, that they might enjoy the advantages of education to be derived in that metropolis of literature, and having acquired a knowledge of the German language, to become students in the School of Mines and Engineering located in that neighbourhood.

Mr. Watts devoted his time and talents, and made large contributions of money in behalf of the Union. Before the close of the war, he revisited Europe, and spent much of his time in the cities of Frankfort-on-the-Maine, Dresden, and Berlin.

After a sojourn of about eighteen months, Mr. Watts returned to Philadelphia, anticipating to quietly pass in that city the remainder of his life. Yielding, however, either to the promptings of a restless ambition, a taste for European habits, or to the wishes of his friends—perhaps to all combined—he accepted the honour of Envoy Extraordinary and Minister Plenipotentiary to the Empire of Austria. Accordingly, in August of 1868, President Johnson, with the unanimous consent of the Senate of the United States, forwarded to him his commission and letters of instruction.

Under the peculiar circumstances of this appointment, (with which the public mind is still familiar,) this testimonial of respect and confidence was very grateful to the recipient. His predecessor, the Honourable J. Lothrop Motley, had been recalled, much against the sense of propriety on the part of his numerous friends, upon some unfounded charges preferred against him by a certain McCracken, an epistolary myth.

The period at which Mr. Watts was accredited to Austria was unusually propitious. Our civil war was ended; the battle fields at home, and the signal naval victory in the British Channel, had falsified the confident predictions of European powers that our Union was a rope of sand, and incapable of the least strain. An American could now enter the courts of Emperors, Kings, and Potentates in simple costume, with the firm assurance of a man entitled to the highest respect.

Whilst Mr. Watts was engaged in faithfully discharging the duties to which he had been called, the unexpected announcement of the purpose of the President to send another Minister to Vienna, led to the following correspondence:

VIENNA, *May 12th, 1869.*

TO HIS EXCELLENCY HENRY M. WATTS:

SIR:—We, the undersigned, representing a number of American citizens, naturalized citizens, and others, who have served in the Army of the United States, now resident in Vienna, respectfully request the honour of your Excellency's company to dinner, upon such day as may suit your Excellency's convenience.

It would be presumptuous in us to make any comment upon the sudden and untimely removal, by the United States Government, of your Excellency from the high position you so worthily fill; but we may express our sincere regrets that, by your departure from Vienna, many of us lose a kind friend, and the Government a faithful public servant.

We have the honour to be your Excellency's obedient servants,

A. MEHAFFY,
EMILE SAMSON,
F. W. PAYNE, M. D.,
JOHN DE VELLO MOORE, M. D,
In the name of citizens.

LEGATION OF THE UNITED STATES OF AMERICA,
VIENNA, *May 13th, 1869.*

To Messrs. A. MEHAFFY, EMILE SAMSON, F. W. PAYNE, M. D, JOHN DE VELLO MOORE, M. D., Committee.

GENTLEMEN: I am honored by the receipt of your complimentary note of the 12th inst., inviting me on your own and on behalf of the citizens and soldiers of the United States, sojourning here, to a dinner prior to my departure from Vienna.

It is quite natural that I should agree with you that the recall of our Government was, under the circumstances, untimely, and that I should feel with you a little mortification at this sudden severance of our social and diplomatic relations.

No cause has been assigned for it, and all that take an interest in the event are left to conjecture.

There may, therefore, be no indelicacy on my part, or intention to disparage the motives of his Excellency the President of the United States, if I be allowed to say, that the removal was not occasioned by any differences between us in regard to public policy, the usual incident of a new administration.

It will be distinctly remembered that the vacation of this important mission, about two years ago, by my predecessor, Mr. Motley, left a disagreeable impression upon the minds of our people, and that President Johnson failed, in several successive efforts, to nominate one whose appointment would be acceptable to the Senate. At last he presented my name, and I was exceedingly gratified to know that it was promptly and unanimously approved.

Without yielding a blind acquiescence to every act of Congress, it was then well understood that my opinions in regard to the reconstruction of the late seceding States were decidedly in favour of the Congressional plan, and that it was this divergent policy that opened the wide breach that unhappily existed in the harmony of the Executive and Legislative Departments, whose administration commenced in peace.

I was not in Washington during the pending of my appointment, either before the President or the Senate; and when it was tendered to me, only nine months ago, I accepted it as a generous and honourable proof of the public esteem and confidence, and as firmly determined to avail myself of the high position to render some correspondent service to the great Western Republic, to which I was bound by every tie, and, if possible, to the great Eastern Empire, to which I was to be attached by an intelligent sympathy of a common brotherhood.

At this brilliant epoch of the world, when time and space are annihilated by the achievements of science and commerce, the arts and Christianity go hand in hand, spreading their softening influence over the asperities of man's rugged nature, there seemed no reason to me why the remote and young Republic I would have the honour to represent, should not be brought into closer affinity with the more ancient and venerable Empire to which I was to be accredited, and produce an amalgam of matter and spirit, which, in the Providence of God, might be congenial to both.

But my mission is at an end, and the shortness of it has not enabled me to finish the work I happily contemplated. I have, therefore, no claim to the distinction you so amiably intended for me, and I beg you will accept my declination of it, with the assurance of a perfect reciprocity of the deep interest you have so kindly evinced for me. I write this much—no more.

Truly yours, &c.,   H. M. WATTS.

On the first day of June, 1869, his Imperial and Royal Majesty accorded to Mr. Watts his last audience, during which the latter laid down all official authority, and took leave of his Majesty with mutual expressions of the unaffected sorrow, which the marked attention and courtesy that had been shown, both to himself and family by the Imperial Household, naturally occasioned.

After his departure from Vienna, Mr. Watts visited Poland, Russia, Sweden and Norway, Denmark, and other nations of Europe he had not previously seen, deriving much valuable information, and returned home greatly gratified with his experience, more convinced than ever that the Government of the United States is preferable to all.

Mr. Watts is at present largely engaged in the development of the iron and coal interests of the state of Pennsylvania; is distinguished for his charitable donations, and for the beneficial influence which he exerts on society. His intimate acquaintances recognize him as a truthful, honourable, and firm friend, of quick and comprehensive views, and decided courage in the performance of duty.

JOHN W. McCULLOUGH, D. D.

JOHN WILLIAMSON McCULLOUGH was born near Newville, Cumberland county, Pennsylvania, November 14th, 1801.

His grandfather, John McCullough, came to America from the north of Ireland, in 1770, and died in Cumberland county, in possession of about 1000 acres of its best land. His son, John McCullough, married Mary Williamson, daughter of David Williamson, of Cumberland county, formerly of Trenton, N. J. They named their son after his maternal uncle, Capt. John Williamson, of Charleston, S. C., and brought him up in the Presbyterian faith. Young McCullough received his early education in the country schools of the neighbourhood of his birth place. In 1819, he commenced the study of the Languages with Mr. John Cooper, of Hopewell Academy, and in September, 1822, entered Dickinson College, Carlisle, where he graduated in June, 1825. At a very early age he had decided to enter the ministry of his church, and after leaving college pursued his studies to that effect partly at Princeton and partly at Carlisle, under the Rev. George Duffield. He was first licensed to preach at Mercersburg, Pa., in April, 1828. In the same year he removed to Frederick, Md., as pastor of the church there.

On October 15th, 1829, he was ordained a minister of the Gospel in his church at Frederick. Upon this occasion, the sermon was preached by the Rev. Wm. Nevins, of Baltimore, presiding minister. The Rev. John Breckinridge, of Baltimore, gave the right hand of fellowship and made the opening prayer, and the Rev. Mr. Hubbard, of Taneytown, delivered the charge. During his residence at Frederick, he married Mary Louisa Duncan, daughter of Judge Duncan, of Carlisle. She died in 1839, leaving three children.

In 1830, he was elected pastor of the First Presbyterian Church, of Lansingburg, N. Y., where he remained until November, 1834, when he accepted the pastorship of the Presbyterian Church, at Ithica, N. Y. At this time he began to be assailed by grave doubts as to whether he had espoused the proper cause in religion, and having given the subject long, earnest and prayerful consideration, and being fully convinced that he was in error, in March, 1838, he resigned his charge at Ithica and withdrew from the ministry of the Presbyterian

Church. He at once applied for orders in the Protestant Episcopal Church and was ordained a Deacon in the same April, 27th, 1838, at Carlisle, by the Rt. Rev. Henry U. Onderdonk, D. D., Bishop of Pennsylvania. On the 3d of November of the same year, he was ordained Priest by the same Bishop, at Wilmington, Del., whither he had been called the September before as Rector of Trinity Parish. He found the parish in a languishing condition, but by his unwearied exertions he soon caused it to flourish as it had never done before since its foundation in 1698. In 1841, he married his second wife, Catharine Roberts Canby, daughter of James Canby, of Wilmington.

In 1845, he was was created a Doctor of Divinity by Columbia College, N. Y., having become conspicuous in the church for his talents and ability. In the spring of 1847, he resigned the rectorship of Trinity parish and accepted a call to St. John's Church, Lafayette, Indiana. Shortly after his arrival there it became necessary to elect a Bishop for that Diocese, and Dr. McCullough was persuaded by Bishop Kemper to become a candidate for the office. At the election he was defeated by one vote—his own.

During the winter of 1849 he received a most unexpected offer of the Professorship of Belles Lettres and Mental and Moral Philosophy in the University of Tennessee, at Jackson, together with the Rectorship of St. Luke's Church. After due deliberation he accepted the offer and continued in the discharge of his duties at Jackson five years. Meanwhile the University of East Tennessee was started and, unknown to himself, he was being strongly urged by his friends for the Presidency. The following letter picked at random from the papers of the Rev. Thos. W. Humes, of Knoxville, one of the Trustees, will show the estimation in which he was held by his fellows:

NEW YORK GENERAL THEOLOGICAL SEMINARY.
June 20th, 1853.

REV. AND DEAR SIR:—I understand that the Rev. J. W. McCullough, D. D., is spoken of for the Presidency of the East Tennessee University. May I venture to give my testimony in his behalf, as one who is well known to me and whose name is identified with personal worth, manly bearing, uncommon mental powers, and large attainments. As a writer he has few equals, as an executive officer none who knew him ever bring him before their thoughts except as presiding with dignity, with courtesy and efficiency. Had I time I could gather from this quarter, among the best and most honoured men, similar expressions of confidence and esteem. No university or college in our land but might be proud to secure his distinguished services.

I understand the election will take place very soon. I have just returned from a trip to the country and fearing even that this may be too late I send it at once. But be sure of this, had timely application been made, so high does the Rev. Dr. stand among scholars of my acquaintance, that any amount of most honourable testimonials could have been forwarded.

Most respectfully,
SAMUEL ROOSEVELT JOHNSON, D. D.,
Prof. Syst. Divinity in (Episcopal) General Theological Seminary.

At the proper time he was elected to the office; he at first declined it, but being persistently pressed finally accepted it. His reluctance, however, was well founded, for circumstances arose which rendered it impossible for him in justice to himself to retain the office more than one year. He resigned and removed to Baltimore, Md., where he remained till 1860. At that time his health being far from good he decided to try a change of climate, and accepted a call to the very pleasant though small parish at Waverly, N. Y. He resigned this in 1864, and accepted the Rectorship of St. Paul's Church, Alton, Ills., where he remained two years. At the end of that time his health having utterly failed, he resigned and removed to Detroit, Mich., where he remained about one year, during part of which he was in temporary charge of St. John's Church. In September, 1867, he started east, and on his way, while stopping at Waverly to visit his many warm friends, was taken ill and after a few days of acute suffering died October 14th, 1867. His remains rest in the Old Swede's Church-yard at Wilmington, Del.

Chs. B. Penrose

HON. CHARLES BINGHAM PENROSE,

SON of Clement Biddle Penrose and Anna Howard Bingham, was born on October 6th, 1798, at his father's country seat, near Frankford, Philadelphia.

In 1805, his father, being appointed Land Commissioner by President Jefferson, moved to St. Louis, Mo. In 1812, he enlisted as a private in one of the volunteer companies of that city; but the organization was not called into active service during the war.

In 1819, Mr. Penrose studied law in Philadelphia, with the late Samuel Ewing, Esq., and on being admitted to the bar, in 1821, settled in Carlisle. Here he at once took his place among the foremost in the number of eminent jurists of which that bar could then justly boast. Popular manners, legal erudition, close attention to business, and admirable oratorical powers, soon secured him a large practice.

In 1833, Mr. Penrose was elected to the State Senate, and on the expiration of his term was re-elected. In this capacity he achieved distinction, even among the men of ability who at that time were chosen to this office. In 1841, President Harrison appointed him Solicitor of the Treasury, which position he held until the close of President Tyler's Administration, discharging its duties with marked ability and fidelity.

When he resigned his office, returning to Pennsylvania, he resumed the practice of his profession in Lancaster, with success. In 1847, he settled in Philadelphia, his native city, and soon became largely engrossed in his professional pursuits. In 1856, he was elected as a Reform candidate to the State Senate, and against the earnest opposition of his family, consented to serve. He laboured most faithfully in aid of the good cause he had espoused, but the work and exposure were more than his constitution could bear, and after a short illness he died of pneumonia, at his post in Harrisburg, on April 6th, 1857.

The character of Mr. Penrose was distinguished by many strong and prominent points. He was emphatically self-reliant, depending on his own resources in the accomplishment of his plans and purposes. The earnestness of his temperament was indicated in everything he undertook. Whatever his hand found to do, he did with all his might. Such was the enthusiasm of his nature, that it kindled a warm sympathy on all sides in his favour, and greatly aided him in carrying forward his life work. To selfishness he was an entire stranger. " He looked not only upon his own things, but also on the things of others." Benevolence beamed in his countenance, and often found expression, not in good wishes merely, but also in acts of delicate and seasonable kindness. His mode of life was simple and frugal. Everything like ostentation was shunned by him, and he abhorred self indulgence of all sorts. His generosity was apparent to everybody, amounting almost to a fault. His manner, which was highly cultivated, was gentle, courteous, and genial, offensive to none, attractive to all. Especially was he gracious to his inferiors, careful of their rights, and considerate of their feelings. Best of all, he was a Christian. He was a consistent and exemplary member of the Presbyterian Church, recognizing it practically as "the whole duty of man to fear God, and keep His commandments."

Mr. Penrose was united in marriage with Valeria Fullerton Biddle, a lady of rare culture, attractive address, and lovely Christian character. Their home had every endearment which unity of counsel and plan, as well as tenderness and strength of affection could impart. It was pervaded by the very atmosphere of love. Their eldest son, William M. Penrose, now deceased, was an eminent member of the bar of Carlisle. Their second son, R. A. F. Penrose, as a sketch of him elsewhere in this volume shows, lives in Philadelphia, and has attained great distinction in the medical profession. Their third son, Clement Biddle Penrose, has a fine legal standing and practice in the same city. Their eldest daughter remains with the widowed mother, and the younger daughter is the wife of William Blight, Esq., all residents of Philadelphia.

ROBERT COOPER GRIER,

ASSOCIATE JUSTICE of the United States Supreme Court, was born in Cumberland county, Pa., March 5th, 1794.

He was the eldest son of Rev. Isaac Grier, and grandson of Rev. Robert Cooper, D. D., both of whom were Presbyterian ministers. In the autumn of 1794, his father took charge of the Academy at Northumberland, Pa., having a full complement of scholars. At the same time he taught a grammar school, preached to three congregations, and tilled his own farm for the support of his family. He was a superior Latin and Greek scholar, and, as may be imagined, a man of remarkable energy of character. He educated his son in the best manner, commencing with the Latin tongue at six years of age, and when he was but twelve years old he had mastered both it and the Greek language.

Young Grier continued his studies with his father until 1811, when he entered the Junior Class at Dickinson College, and graduated there in 1812. There he surpassed all his fellow-students in his profound knowledge of the Ancient Languages, besides excelling in Chemistry. He remained at the college, after he had taken his degree, for a year, and taught a grammar school therein. His father's health having failed about this time, he returned to Northumberland and assisted him in his educational establishment. After his father's death, in 1815, he succeeded him as Principal, lectured on Chemistry, Astronomy and Mathematics, besides teaching Greek and Latin. His leisure hours he devoted to the study of law. He was admitted to practice in 1817, and opened his office in Bloomsburg, Columbia county; in 1818, he removed to Danville, in the same county. His practice increased till 1833, when he was appointed by Governor Wolf, Judge of the District Court of Allegheny county.

Judge Grier now removed to Pittsburgh. On the 4th of August, 1846, he was nominated by President Polk, one of the Judges of the United States Supreme Court, and unanimously confirmed the next day. In 1848, he removed to Philadelphia, and continued to reside there until his death, which occurred September 25th, 1870.

Judge Grier was eminently distinguished for integrity of purpose, fidelity to his client, and benevolence to those of limited means, preferring justice to gain. He stood very high as a lawyer and as a judge.

The esteem of his legal brethren was exhibited in the great deference given to his decisions, and their warm personal friendship. At the death of his father, he took charge of his brothers and sisters, ten in number, cared for and educated all, as a faithful guardian, until they were settled in life.

In 1829, Judge Grier married Isabella, daughter of John Rose, a native of Scotland, who still survives him.

JAMES HUTCHISON GRAHAM.

JAMES HUTCHISON GRAHAM, Judge, was born September 10th, 1809, in West Pennsborough township, Cumberland county, Pa. At Dickinson College, in the same county, he received a careful classical education, graduating in the class of 1827. Upon leaving this institution, he commenced the study of law in the office of Andrew Carothers, a prominent member of the Carlisle bar, and was admitted to practice January, 1830. The skill he evinced in the management of his first cases, soon placed him among the most promising members of this very able bar, and in 1839, he was appointed by Governor Porter, Deputy Attorney-General of the State, a position he held for six years with signal credit, as was testified in 1850, by his election as President Judge of the Ninth Judicial District, composed of the counties of Cumberland, Perry and Juniata.

To this honourable part, Judge Graham was again elected in 1861, for another period of ten years, so that at his retirement from this office, in 1871, he had passed a score of years upon the bench. His decisions were characterized by marked ability and were rarely reversed by the Supreme Court upon review—probably as seldom as those of any District Judge in the State. After his retirement, he resumed practice at the bar in Carlisle, also actively interesting himself in giving instruction in the law department of Dickinson College. In 1862, his Alma Mater conferred upon him the degree of LL. D., an honour, in his instance, well merited by a profound acquaintance with forensic literature, and uncommon skill in bringing its principles to bear on the practical questions of life. He has been twice married, his second wife and a large family still surviving.

HON. R. M. McCLELLAND.

ROBERT M. McCLELLAND was born August 1st, 1807, at Green Castle, Franklin county, Pa.
Among his ancestors were several officers of rank in the War of the Revolution, and some of his family connections also distinguished themselves in the War of 1812, and in that with Mexico. His father was an eminent physician and surgeon, who studied his profession under Dr. Benjamin Rush, of Philadelphia, and practised it with great success until six months before his death, which occurred when he was eighty-four years of age.

Mr. McClelland graduated at Dickinson College, in 1829, among the first in his class. He was admitted to the bar, at Chambersburg, in 1831. He vigorously practised his profession in Pittsburgh for almost a year. In 1833, he removed to Monroe, in the territory of Michigan, where his legal practice was crowned with success. In 1835, was elected a member of the Convention called to frame a constitution for the proposed state of Michigan, and took a prominent and influential part in its deliberations. He was appointed the first Bank Commissioner in the state, by Governor Mason, and was offered the Attorney-Generalship, but declined both of these offices. In 1837, he was married to Miss Sarah E. Sabine, of Williamstown, Mass. He has had six children, three of whom now survive.

In 1838, Mr. McClelland was elected a member of the State Legislature, in which he soon became distinguished as the head of several important committees. He was elected Speaker of the House of Representatives in 1843. In the same year he was elected to Congress, where he soon took a respectable stand among the oldest veterans of that body. During his first term he was placed on the Committee on Commerce, and originated what was known as the Harbour bills, and carried them through. He was re-elected to the Twenty-ninth Congress by a strong majority. In this term he was placed at the head of the Committee on Commerce. The members of the committee, in appreciation of his services, and as an expression of personal regard, presented him with a beautiful cane. In 1847, he was elected for a third term to Congress, when he was placed on the Committee on Foreign Relations.

Mr. McClelland was in several National Conventions, and in the Baltimore Convention, which nominated Gen. Cass for the Presidency, in 1848. In 1850, he was chosen a member of the Convention called to revise the constitution of the state of Michigan, and took an active and controlling part in its deliberations. In the same year he was a member, and President of a Democratic State Convention. He was in the Democratic National Convention of 1852. He took an active part in the canvass which resulted in the election of General Pierce to the Presidency over General Scott.

In 1851, Mr. McClelland was elected Governor, and subsequently re-elected. His administration was regarded as wise, prudent and conciliatory. At the organization of the Cabinet by President Pierce, in 1853, he was invited to take the position of Secretary of the Interior, a place which he filled four years most creditably. He was again a member of a Convention to revise the constitution of Michigan, in 1867, in which his standing and experience made him conspicuous.

As a lawyer Mr. McClelland was terse and pointed in the argument of law questions, and clear, candid and forcible in his addresses to juries, with which he always carried great weight. In his political addresses before the people he was especially forcible and happy. In private life he is a genial companion, a good neighbour and earnest friend, and his great experience and extended knowledge of men and public officers enable him to observe with deep interest the great panorama of public events. His record is a good one, complimentary to himself, and creditable to his native valley.

DANIEL McKINLEY, D. D.

THE REV. DANIEL McKINLEY, D. D., was born in Carlisle, Pa., December 7th, 1800, in which place, and its immediate neighbourhood, he spent the period of his youth.

He was very early the subject of deep religious impressions, and so soon as his tenth year, thought he was the subject of special grace. He united with the Church of Carlisle, under the pastoral care of the Rev. George Duffield, D. D., who, perceiving his ardent piety and promising talents, encouraged him to pursue a course of liberal education with reference to the Gospel ministry, which he did at Dickinson College, being assisted therein pecuniarily by members of Dr. Duffield's congregation. During his course at college, a deep and powerful revival of religion occured in the church of which he was a member, and in it the college largely shared, and it is the testimony of those who were most deeply interested in these scenes, that young McKinley's efforts were untiring and invaluable.

Mr. McKinley graduated at college in the summer of 1824, and entered the Theological Seminary at Princeton the autumn of the same year. He was licensed by the Presbytery of Carlisle in the autumn of 1827, and was soon after installed as Pastor of the Presbyterian Church in Bedford, where he remained about four years, when he was compelled by bronchial affection to resign his charge, and desist from the labours of the ministry for about two years. The church in Bedford was gradually strengthened under his ministry, but there was no marked outpouring of God's spirit, such as attended his labours in subsequent years.

When the Second Presbyterian Church in Carlisle was organized, in 1833, Mr. McKinley was chosen as its pastor, and being encouraged by the improving state of his health, he accepted the call, and served the congregation for about five years. His labours in that field were eminently successful. He was zealous, earnest and untiring in his work. Considerable religious interest was manifested at several periods of his ministry; and during his pastorate there, seventy-six were added to the church on profession of faith. At the close of his labours there, the church was established and prosperous, and he greatly endeared himself to all classes of the congregation. About this time vigorous efforts were being made to arouse the church to the importance of the work of Foreign Missions, which was then comparatively in its infancy, and Mr. McKinley, on account of his well-known missionary zeal and fitness for the work, was urged to embark in it as an agent. This he consented to do, and for upwards of three years he served the board with a vigour, efficiency and success, which told powerfully upon the progress of the cause. He aimed especially to convince professing Christians of their duty to devote to the Lord a definite proportion of their stated income, and he may thus be regarded as one of the pioneers of systematic beneficence.

In the autumn of 1841, Mr. McKinley was chosen pastor of the Presbyterian Church, in Chambersburg, and he continued to sustain this relation for about nine years. About one year after his installation, a powerful revival of religion took place in that church, as the result of which thirty-two were added to the church at the succeeding communion on examination, and the effects of it were felt for years afterwards. Throughout all Mr. McKinley's pastorate at Chambersburg, he was eminently faithful, and during the years of his labours, one hundred and four were added to the church on profession of faith.

In the fall of 1850, he left Chambersburg to take charge of the Sixth Church, Pittsburgh, a new enterprise, and one which was supposed to afford a good field for the peculiar talents which he possessed. In this, however, he was partially disappointed, and after one year's labour, he asked to be released from his pastoral relation to the church and returned to the Presbytery of Carlisle.

This Presbytery had just then entered vigorously upon the work of church extension within its bounds, and in behalf of this enterprise enlisted the services of Dr. McKinley, which contributed greatly to its success.

After spending a year in this service, Dr. McKinley became Agent and Evangelist of the Board of Domestic Missions. For this he was well fitted, and in it he was eminently successful, until laid aside by the disease which proved fatal; a disease which was undoubtedly hastened in its development by his eagerness to labour, and his readiness to endure hardships and exposures. He knew not how to spare himself in his Master's cause, and especially when he saw tokens of the presence of God's spirit, he seemed to forget entirely the frailty of the earthly tabernacle.

Dr. McKinley was present in a number of extensive revivals of religion, in the interior of Pennsylvania. In these scenes he was in his element. His services were always eagerly sought by the brethren, and many interesting incidents in connection with his labours survive in the memories of those who were present at, or were subjects of these visitations of God's grace.

In the spring of 1855 he was obliged to desist from labour, by a return of his old tendency to bronchial affection, aggravated by other painful and threatening symptoms. Under the progress of a disease which baffled all skill, he departed this life in Chambersburg, December 7th, 1855, whither he had gone hoping to be able to attend the sessions of the Synod of Baltimore, but where, by reason of rapid decline, he remained to die.

There is no record of Dr. McKinley's death-bed experience and triumphs. The nature of his disease prevented any expression of what may have been his feelings. But his life was his witness, and his monument a life marked by eminent consecration, zeal, and success in his Master's work. He was, indeed, an exemplary Christian, and most devoted minister. His piety made a deep impression upon all with whom he had intercourse, and his efforts to save souls filled multitudes with thankfulness and praise. His mortal remains slumber in the grave yard at Carlisle, under a stone erected to his memory by members of the church in Chambersburg.

In 1831, he was married to Miss Mary Wyeth, of Harrisburg, and one daughter survives him, the wife of the Rev. James F. Kennedy, D. D., the gifted and popular Vice-President of Wilson Female College.

WILLIAM RANKIN, M. D.

WILLIAM RANKIN was born at Potter's Mills, Centre county, Pa., October 9th, 1795. His parents were of highly respectable social standing, and exemplary and useful members of the Presbyterian Church.

He graduated at Washington College, Pa., in 1814. For some time he thought of entering the Gospel ministry, but his native timidity as to his qualifications for this very responsible office, led him finally to relinquish the idea. One year after leaving college he commenced the study of medicine with Dr. Dean, an eminent physician of Chambersburg, and graduated at the Medical Department of the University of Pennsylvania in 1819. He practised his profession for two years in Campbellstown, Franklin county, Pa., after which he removed to Shippensburg, where, until within two years of the date of his death, he had an extensive, laborious and successful practice for more than half a century. March 3d, 1829, he was united in marriage with Caroline, eldest daughter of Major David Nevin, of the last mentioned place. Ten children, the fruit of this marriage survive him.

Dr. Rankin was endowed by nature with a singularly lovely temperament, which developed itself in a corresponding character. He was amiable and yet firm, dignified and yet familiar, peculiarly attentive to his own sphere of business and duty, and yet deeply interested in the welfare of his friends and neighbours, and in the prosperity of the community in which he lived. His spirit was generous and sympathizing. His manner was gentle and conciliatory. His bearing was respectful and attractive to persons of every rank and condition. Eminently pacific in his disposition, he "followed peace with all men," and often sought the blessing of the peacemaker in endeavouring to reconcile persons who were at variance. Prudence was one of his distinguished traits.

As a physician, Dr. Rankin occupied a high position. Well prepared for his profession by previous education, he never failed to keep abreast with its advances, through its current literature. To his large and ever-growing library, he added the various medical journals of the day, to some of which he made valuable contributions. In his judgment he was cautious but decided. His professional brethren, by many of whom he was often called into consultation, had the highest respect for his skill and attainments. The ethics of the profession were sacredly observed by him. His manner in the sick room was peculiarly gentle and sympathetic. His reputation reached far beyond the wide local range of his ordinary practice.

As a Christian, Dr. Rankin was consistent, useful and exemplary. He habitually "walked with God." Whilst making no affected pretence to religion, divine truth, as could easily be seen by all, was constantly moulding and fashioning his character. The "things which are lovely and of good report," adorned his walk and conversation. He occupied the position of ruling elder in the Presbyterian Church of Shippensburg for many years, and discharged its duties in a most faithful, conscientious, and acceptable manner. Often, in visiting his patients, when he found that earthly skill could not avail, he pointed them to the Great Physician, and sought his consoling and sustaining aid in their behalf.

Towards the close of his earthly career, Dr. Rankin was visited with a paralytic attack, which disqualified him for professional service. After two years' waiting his appointed time, his happy spirit, spared the agony of a painful conflict, was released July 15th, 1872, almost without a struggle, and passed to the reward of the just. By his death, there was removed from earth one, who, in the sweet and tender relations of husband and father, was excelled by none, and whose departure, even in advanced years, as a member of a community in which he had lived nearly fifty years, was universally deplored. It was a fitting and touching expression of this regard, by which all the places of business in the town were closed, whilst the mortal remains of the lamented dead were borne to their resting-place in Spring Hill Cemetery, where they shall repose till mortality is swallowed up of life.

RICHARD WOODS,

HE son of Samuel and Frances (Sterrett) Woods, was born in Dickinson township, Cumberland county, Pa., March 3d, 1804.

His parents were Scotch-Irish, and one of the oldest and best families in Cumberland valley. They were remarkable for energy, integrity and moral culture. Their children were trained with special care. The father was noted for reliability, courage, and probity. During the progress of the Revolution, he acted in the service of the government as Indian scout, an undertaking most dangerous. The mother was a woman of devoted piety. Their house, situated in the country, some miles from any place of worship, was often used for preaching and prayer-meetings.

Richard was always of a lively disposition. From his very childhood he was known as firmly adhering to the truth. This truthful character cleaved to him until death. He abhorred insincerity, equivocation, and deceit. His opinions were always uttered with such plainness as made them easily understood. His word was his bond. He was controlled by an habitual desire to *do right*. He strove to bring his entire life into subjection to this rule. It was evident to all who studied his character, that he was governed in all matters, even the most trivial, not by interest, caprice, or convenience—not by a thirst for popularity, but by elevated and unyielding Christian principle. Mr. Woods, being in stature about six feet, and of large frame, had an impressive appearance. His countenance, habitually thoughtful, was lighted with smiles during social and friendly intercourse. His manner was open, genial, courteous, and refined. He had an exuberant fund of information always at his command. Many a friend whilst visiting his hospitable home was instructed without the least tinge of pedantry, and made happy in the gushing flow of innocent mirth. Though never sent to college, yet by diligent study he had acquired a vast amount of theoretical and practical knowledge. He attached great importance to mental culture, and was guided by this conviction in the schooling of his children.

Mr. Woods, in his twenty-third year, on November 16th, 1826, married Mary Jane Sterrett, a native of Lancaster county, and a lady of great moral worth, whose Christian deportment told with moulding effect, not only upon her husband's character, but also upon that of her children. His happy conjugal relation threw an almost uninterrupted sunshine upon his domestic life, and surrounded him at its close with the consoling sympathies of a large and most affectionate family, whose love and reverence he had earned by a cordial participation in their feelings, and an ever active, yet well regulated interest in their welfare. His family numbered thirteen children, three of whom died in infancy, and another at the interesting age of nineteen, in the bright hope of a blessed immortality. Five sons and four daughters still survive, all of whom hold important positions in the several walks of life.

Mr. Woods always took an active interest in every good cause, contributing to their aid not only his energy but also his pecuniary means. He liberally assisted in the erection and support of Dickinson Presbyterian Church, in which, in 1836, he made a profession of faith living thereafter as a true and devoted Christian.

He inherited from his father the original homestead, which was among the oldest settlements of Cumberland Valley, and here, on an immense tract of land, he carried on his agricultural pursuits.

Mr. Woods had early and frequent evidence of public confidence. When but twenty-four years of age, and without his seeking, he was appointed Justice of the Peace for the district in which he lived, and was several times re-appointed, until he declined the position. In this office he was eminently useful, seeking always to be a peacemaker between the parties in litigation, and often succeeding, even against his own pecuniary interest. He was often called to serve as arbitrator. For many years he was called to be Treasurer of the Cumberland Valley Mutual Insurance Company, and by the force of his character much enhanced the credit of the Company. He was one of the original directors of the banking house of Ker, Brenneman & Co., afterwards changed to Ker, Dunlap & Co., and, finally, when the war came on between the North and the South, called "The First National Bank of Carlisle."

He was not only respected, but admired and esteemed by all his neighbours and friends. The regard and veneration he received was but a just return for the general benevolence by which he was actuated. He was a strenuous advocate on all occasions of the rights of his fellow-men, and as such, ever and earnestly opposed negro slavery. Firmness and courage were conspicuous traits in his character, yet with these was blended frankness, and a singleness of purpose which disarmed hostility, and disposed those most averse to his views to admire and love him as a man.

Mr. Woods was in feeble health for several years previous to his demise, which occurred February 29th, 1872, in the sixty-eighth year of his age. In his last illness, though afflicted with much bodily distress, he preserved unimpaired those amiable traits of character by which he was distinguished in health, frequently expressing a grateful sense of the kindness of those who ministered to his comfort and relief. In the full possession of his faculties, and aware of the fatal nature of his disease, he was perfectly calm and self-possessed; made arrangement of his affairs, spoke to his family as a tender husband and affectionate father solicitous for their eternal welfare, expressed his firm reliance on the mercy of God in Christ, and then departed in peace to his reward, leaving to his children an example worthy of imitation, and to the world an instance of useful living, and safe and happy dying.

FREDERICK AUGUSTUS RAUCH.

THE REV. DR. FREDERICK AUGUSTUS RAUCH, first President of Marshall College, was a native of Germany. He was born at Kirchbracht, Hesse-Darmstadt, on the 27th of July, 1806. His father was a clergyman of the Reformed Church, and continued in this relation, until Hesse, following the example set by Prussia, in 1817, resolved the two Confessions, Reformed and Lutheran, into one religious communion, known as the Evangelical Church.

Of the boyhood and youth of Frederick very few particulars can be given. Tradition says that he was bright and active, studious and apt to learn, and somewhat disposed to waywardness. He enjoyed all the advantages of education in his native country, applied himself diligently, and made rapid progress in his studies. At the age of eighteen he had graduated from the gymnasium, and was admitted to the University of Marburg, where he took his diploma in 1827. After this he prosecuted his studies for a year at Giessen. For a time, he was employed as an assistant in teaching, by an uncle who had charge of a literary institution at Frankford. Another year afterwards he spent as a student at the University of Heidelberg.

At Heidelberg, Rauch came under the special influence of the distinguished philosopher and theologian, Charles Daub. The two men were congenial spirits. Daub inspired Rauch with confidence, and Rauch at once awakened the liveliest interest of his great teacher. A friendship and intimacy, closer than is common between Professor and student, sprung up between them. The plastic influence of Daub on his life and habits of thought, philosophical but especially religious, was so powerful and permanent, that the association became an epoch in his spiritual life, to which Rauch was wont subsequently to refer with emphasis as a momentous one in his history.

On leaving Heidelberg, Dr. Rauch became Extraordinary Professor in the University of Giessen. At the end of a year, he was honoured with an invitation to accept a regular professorship in the University of Heidelberg. His prospects were bright, but in an unguarded moment they were dispelled suddenly. Dr. Rauch expressed himself too freely on a political question on some public occasion, at Giessen. He never liked to refer to the matter subsequently, and his most intimate friends in America remained ignorant of the precise character of the offence.

The result was that, instead of becoming ordinary Professor at Heidelberg, he drew upon himself the displeasure of the government, and regard for his personal safety imposed the necessity of fleeing from his fatherland. His departure was sudden. Time allowed him to make only a hurried visit to his father, between the hours of eleven and one at night.

Turning his face westward, he landed on our hospitable shores in the fall of 1831, being in the twenty-sixth year of his age. Dr. Rauch found his way to Easton, where he studied English assiduously, and for a livelihood, as he excelled in the science and act of music, gave lessons on the piano. Soon he was elected Professor of the German Language in Lafayette College. In the spring of 1832, he was appointed Principal of a classical school at York, which a few years before had been organized by the authorities of the Theological Seminary of the (German) Reformed Church, then located at that place. Several months later he was chosen Professor of Biblical Literature by the Synod of this Church, and ordained to the office of the ministry. For three years he laboured in this two-fold capacity at York. His chief attention was given to the classical school, which increased rapidly in numbers, and soon gained the position and character of a first class academy.

In the summer of 1833, Dr. Rauch was united in marriage with Miss Phœbe Moore, a daughter of Mr. Laomi Moore, of Morristown, New Jersey.

In the fall of 1835, the classical school which he presided over was removed to Mercersburg. Retaining his position, Dr. Rauch accompanied the institution. Measures were immediately taken to erect the school into a college. This was accomplished during the ensuing year, 1836, when Marshall College was organized. Dr. Rauch became the President, being continued at the same time as Professor.

Dr. Rauch was in all respects a remarkable man. "He was," says Dr. E. V. Gerhart, "a man of general intelligence and of general culture. A finished classical scholar, he was at home also in the science of the Fine Arts, in the department of History, in Bibical Literature and Theology. But his main strength lay in the department of Philosophy. For this abstruse sphere he was fitted by natural endowment. Upon it also he concentrated with affection his time and his studies, and here he attained to great eminence and great power. Acquainted with all the systems of Greek philosophy, and with the different phases of scholastic thinking developed during the medieval age, he was also thoroughly conversant with all the metaphysical systems of the modern world, of Germany, Scotland, and France, with Locke, Hume, Berkeley and Reid, with Condillac and Helvetius, no less than with Leibnitz, Kant, and Hegel. Yet whilst treading these labyrinthian mazes he never let go his firm hold on the verities of the Christian faith. He was not entrapped by the anti-Christian errors of philosophy.

He was not bewildered by the confusion of systems. He discriminated properly between man and psychology, nature and physics, the human reason and metaphysics, between a personal God and philosophical speculation concerning Him, between the truth revealed in Christ and theological science. Christ glorified was the anchor; the cable, faith, and the violence of no conflicts could break his moorings."

He published a work on *Psychology*, in March, 1840; and at the time of his death he had nearly completed his revision of it preliminary to a second edition. His *Psychology* was to have been followed by a work on *Christian Ethics*, and this by another work on *Æsthetics*.

We conclude this brief sketch of a noble man with a quotation from an eulogy on the life and character of Dr. Rauch, delivered by the Rev. J. Williamson Nevin, D. D., who was very intimately associated with him for a year at Mercersburg. He says, "I could not but look on it as a strange and interesting fact, that the infant college of the (German) Reformed Church should have placed at its head, there in Mercersburg, without care or calculation, or consciousness even on the part of its friends generally, one of the very first minds of Germany, which under other circumstances might well have been counted an ornament and honour to the oldest institution in the land."

The remains of Dr. Rauch were buried in a grove belonging to Marshall College. When Marshall College was consolidated with Franklin College, at Lancaster, 1853, measures were taken to remove the body. This was done in March, 1859. His ashes now repose in Lancaster Cemetery, and a few years ago a beautiful monument was erected to his memory by the Alumni, in the campus of Franklin and Marshall College.

ROBERT DAVIDSON, D. D.

DR. DAVIDSON, son of Dr. Robert Davidson, pastor of the Presbyterian Church in Carlisle, and President of Dickinson College, was born in Carlisle, Pa., February 23d, 1808. He graduated in Dickinson College in 1828, and in Princeton Theological Seminary in 1831. In 1832, he took charge of the McChord Church in Lexington, Kentucky. In 1840, he was made President of the Transylvania University, and the following year received the degree of Doctor of Divinity from Centre College, Kentucky. Resigning the Presidency in 1842, he was appointed by Governor Letcher, Superintendent of Public Instruction for the State of Kentucky. He was also offered a chair in Centre College; and was subsequently elected to the Presidency of Ohio University. All these offers were declined from preference for the pastoral office.

Dr. Davidson's pastoral charges have been, the McChord or Second Presbyterian Church in Lexington, Kentucky, 1832; the First Presbyterian Church in New Brunswick, New Jersey, 1843; Spring street Church in New York, 1860; the First Presbyterian Church in Huntingdon, Long Island, 1864. In 1868, impaired health required a temporary intermission of the active duties of the ministry, since which time he has made his abode in Philadelphia.

He served as Permanent Clerk of the General Assembly from 1845 till 1850. For a score of years he has been a member of the Board of Foreign Missions; and since 1867, a Director of Princeton Theological Seminary. In 1864, he was appointed one of the Committee on the Hymnal. In 1869, he was one of the delegation to the General Assembly of the Free Church of Scotland, in the city of Edinburgh, when they were complimented with a public breakfast.

His published works are the following: "Excursion to the Mammoth Cave, with Historical Notes," 1838; "History of the Presbyterian Church in Kentucky," 1847; "Leaves from the Book of Nature, Interpreted by Grace," 1850; "Letters to a Recent Convert," 1853; "Elijah, a Sacred Drama, and other Poems," 1860; "The Relation of Baptized Children to the Church," 1866; "The Christ of God; or, the Relation of Christ to Christianity," 1870.

Pamphlets—"The Bible, the Young Man's Guide;" "Reply to the (New School) Manifesto;" "A Vindication of Colleges," (Inaugural;)

"The Study of History;" "A Plea for Presbyterianism;" "Presbyterianism; Its Place in History;" "History of the First Presbyterian Church, New Brunswick, New Jersey;" "The Evils of Disunion;" "A Nation's Discipline; or, Trials not Judgments;" "On the Death of President Lincoln;" "History of the Presbyterian Church in Huntingdon, Long Island;" "Memoir of Governor Lewis Morris, of New Jersey;" "Piety not Incompatible with the Military Life." To this list might be added Funeral Discourses, Sermons in the *National Preacher*, and numerous contributions to *McClintock's Cyclopædia* and divers periodicals; besides his share in the preparation of the Hymnal.

Dr. Davidson's articles in the *Princeton Review* are the following:

1849. Review of Dr. Stone's Life of Dr. Milnor.

1850. Review of Seymour's Mornings with the Jesuits. Review of Layard's Nineveh, and Hawks' Egypt.

1851. Review of Trench on Miracles.

1853. Review of Arthur's Successful Merchant, and Van Doren's Mercantile Morals.

The Rev. J. A. Murray, D. D., author of the sketch of Dr. Davidson's father, published in another part of this book, fitly describes the son as "a distinguished educator and learned divine, who still lives, advanced in years, but physically and mentally in a wonderful state of preservation, and continues instructive and popular as a preacher, and no less brilliant in social life."

BENJAMIN SHRODER SCHNECK, D. D.

THE father of Dr. Schneck was a native of the Dukedom of Nassau, Germany. He was descended from a most excellent family, and emigrated to this country near the close of the last century. He first located in Reading, Pa., where he was married to Miss Elizabeth Shroder, a native of that place. They were both pious, God fearing parents, who brought up their children in the nurture and admonition of the Lord.

Their son, Benjamin, was born in Upper Bern Township, in the northern part of Berks county, Pa., March 14th, 1806. He received his early education from his father, and at the age of sixteen connected himself with the Reformed Church at Reading, then in charge of Rev. William Pauli. He pursued his studies in a private way, and having resolved to devote his life to the work of the ministry, he was placed under the tuition of the Rev. Dr. Frederick L. Herman, of Falconer Swamp, Montgomery county, Pa. His licensure to preach was received from the "Free Synod," in east Pennsylvania, on September 6th, 1825. His first pastoral charge in Centre county, consisted of seven congregations. In September, 1828, he transferred his ecclesiastical relations from the "Free" to the regular Synod of his Church. In 1833, his health becoming somewhat impaired, he resigned his charge in Centre county, but continued to labour for a season among destitute congregations in the same region. After having regained his health to some extent, in 1834, he accepted a call to the Gettysburg charge, which, however, declining vigour compelled him to relinquish at the close of the first year.

In September, 1835, Dr. Schneck took charge of the "Weekly Messenger," which had just been started in Chambersburg, and continued in this relation until 1844, when he resigned. In 1847, he resumed it, and continued in it until 1852. From the early part of 1840, the Rev. Dr. Samuel R. Fisher was associated with him in the editorship, who also became his successor. Dr. Schneck also edited at the same place until 1864, when it was removed to Philadelphia, the paper called *Reformirte Kirchenzeitung*, which grew out of the union of two papers, *Christliche Zeitschrift* and *Evangelische Kirchenzeitung;* the one previously published in Gettysburg, and the latter in east Pennsylvania.

Dr. Schneck, whilst editor in Chambersburg, took charge (in 1855,) of St. John's Reformed Church at that place. Sometime afterward he was Professor of German Language and Literature in "Wilson Female College." He was frequently honoured by his church. He was President of the General Synod in 1839. In 1843, he was appointed with the Rev. Dr. Theodore Hoffeditz, to visit Germany, to transfer, if possible, the Rev. Dr. Frederick W. Krummacher, of Elberfeld, to the Theological Seminary then located at Mercersburg, Pa. He was for many years an efficient member of the Board of Visitors of the Theological Seminary, and for a time also a member of the Board of Home Missions. A Professorship in the Theological Seminary at Tiffin, Ohio, was tendered him, which he was induced to decline. The honourary degree of D. D. was conferred on him by Marshall College, in 1845.

Dr. Schneck was married June 30th, 1836, to Rebecca Riddle, daughter of the Hon. James Riddle, of Chambersburg, a lady of fine culture and fervent piety, who proved to him a most worthy and excellent companion. He died, April 19th, 1874, in the sixty-ninth year of his age.

He was an earnest, instructive, practical preacher. As a pastor he never failed to attach his people to him. He was a genial writer, equally at home in the German and English languages. He published in 1844, *Die Deutsche Kanzel*, a selection of German sermons for each Sunday in the year; in 1846, he edited the *Forest Minstrel*, for Mrs. Lydia Jane Pierson; he also published *The Burning of Chambersburg*, and a volume on "Mercersburg Theology."

Dr. Schneck possessed attractive social qualities in an eminent degree. As a citizen, he was highly esteemed by the community in the midst of which he spent the greater part of his life. He was honoured by those who knew him best with various public positions of prominence. He identified himself with the general interests of the place of his residence. His strong hold on the affections of the people was indicated by the unusually large attendance at his funeral, and the general closing of business during the funeral procession. He was lamented by all, as a faithful man, who had done life's work well.

ALEXANDER TAGGART M'GILL, D. D., LL. D.

THE subject of this sketch was born at Cannonsburg, Pa., February 24th, 1807. He graduated at Jefferson College in 1826. After a short service in this college as tutor, he went to Georgia, studied law, and was admitted to the bar, receiving almost immediately afterward several important appointments from the Legislature of that state.

In 1831, Mr. McGill returned to Pennsylvania, relinquished the law for Theology, the study of which he pursued in the Theological Seminary of the Associate (now United Presbyterian) Church, then located at Cannonsburg. In 1834, he was licensed to preach, and in 1835, he was ordained and installed, at Carlisle, Pa., as pastor of three small churches, distributed through as many counties, Cumberland, Perry, and York. In 1837, he married Eleanor Acheson, daughter of Gen. George McCulloch, of Lewistown, Pa., Senator of Pennsylvania, and afterwards member of Congress.

In 1838, Mr. McGill became discontented with the peculiarities of the church in which he was born and reared, and connected himself with the Old School Presbyterian Church. Soon after this he became pastor of the Second Presbyterian Church in Carlisle, where he continued about three years, until his election as a Professor in the Western Theological Seminary, at Allegheny. On that work he entered with the greatest alacrity and pleasure, and very soon had ample evidence that it was the right vocation for him. But it was a situation of great labour and trial, in view of the struggling condition of the institution, and at length the toils and anxieties of the position told on his health. At the very time his thoughts were turning to the southern climate, which he had found so genial and sanative in the days of his youth, he received, without the slightest anticipation, a call to the Seminary at Columbia, S. C. After much hesitation he accepted this call. He spent the winter of 1852–3, at Columbia. In 1853, the General Assembly elected him again to Allegheny, where his family had remained, and he returned to that position. In 1854, he was transferred to the Seminary at Princeton, leaving Allegheny in a prosperous condition.

Dr. McGill's chair at Princeton, is that of "Ecclesiastical, Homiletic, and Pastoral Theology." He was Moderator of the General Assembly of the Presbyterian Church, (Old School) in 1848, Permanent Clerk, from 1850 to 1862, and Stated Clerk from 1862 to 1870. He received the title of Doctor of Divinity in 1842, from Marshall College, Mercersburg, Pa., and the title of Doctor of Laws from the College of New Jersey (Princeton,) in 1868. He has never had robust health, and the hard labours to which he has been called, and, still more, bereavements in his family, have stamped the appearance of old age upon him, without impairing at all his usefulness and the activity of his mind. His method of preaching always without a manuscript or brief before him, has been of great advantage to his popularity as a speaker, and still more to the vigour and freshness of his memory, especially in the use of Scripture. And owing to his zeal and efforts in training students to this method, it has gained largely of late years, both in metropolitan and country pulpits of the Presbyterian Church.

Dr. McGill is a finished scholar, and a superior preacher. With his pen, in the pulpit, and in the Professorships he has filled, he has rendered valuable service to the church of his adoption, and registered his name high on the record of her representative men, both for the present age and the generations to follow.

JAMES WALLACE WEIR,

WAS born at Harrisburg, Pa., August 9th, 1805. His great-grandfathers Weir and Wallace fought together in the siege of Derry; their grandchildren (Samuel Weir and Mary Wallace,) met on the bank of the Susquehanna a hundred years after, and were united in marriage.

The father of Mr. Weir was elected one of three elders of the Presbyterian Church, at Harrisburg, in 1794, at its organization. His death, in 1820, threw his son into the world to secure a living and an education as he best could. At the age of sixteen he had an offer of a clerkship, with some strong inducements to accept it, in the then great hotel of Matthew Wilson, but at that early age he was too much opposed to such a trade to embark in it even indirectly. The leisure hours of the business in which he engaged were devoted to mental improvement, so that when only sixteen and a half years old he found himself calculating the eclipse of February 21st, 1822.

In 1824, Mr. Weir undertook to edit a small religious paper, and with this view learned type-setting, proposing to make the editorial chair the ultimate point of his ambition. At this time he learned two or three modern languages, and read extensively in political economy, politics generally, and the various branches of literature. Whilst thus engaged, he received an appointment in a bank at Harrisburg, which he accepted. For five years he was clerk in the Branch Bank of Pennsylvania, located there; for eleven years he was teller in the Harrisburg bank, and now for thirty-one years he has been cashier of the same institution, known at this time as the Harrisburg National Bank. Under his cashiership, the value of the stock of this bank has been trebled, and the clear earnings have been on the average of the last ten years twenty per cent.; this, too, without ever shaving or buying a note, or paying interest on deposits. During all this time his name has never appeared on the books of the bank as a drawer or endorser.

Allibone's Dictionary of Authors refers to Mr. Weir as a writer of force and varied ability, and as the author of several poems of much merit. The principal productions of his pen, are "The Closet Companion," a "Treatise on Sabbath-school Instruction," "Duties of Laymen," and "Social Prayer," all of which were received with marked favour, and recommended by gentlemen of high literary standing. Of the many admirable hymns and poems which he has written, we take the liberty of introducing here his reflections on his seventieth birthday, written August 9th, 1875:

> "THREESCORE AND TEN"—the by-gone years,
>   How rise their memories to my thought:
> The joys and griefs, the hopes and fears,
>   That fill the measure of my lot.
>
> Yet these are but the wayside sheaves,
>   We glean upon the field of years:
> Oblivion, in its reaping, leaves
>   But here and there some scattered ears.
>
> Perhaps 'tis well we can but glean—
>   For could we harvest all the past,
> Joys too intense, and griefs too keen,
>   Were o'er our present being cast.
>
> Life's current duties must be met;
>   And 'tis but glances we can give
> The darkening past—the game is set,
>   And we must for the mastery strive.
>
> Gird up thyself, my spirit then,
>   In Him who gives all needful grace;
> Thou canst not now afford to spend
>   Thy closing years in idleness.
>
> The past thou canst not now regain—
>   The shortening future is thine own:
> To Faith and Hope and Love attain—
>   These spoils from Time may still be won.

The volumes just referred to were written by Mr. Weir in early life. As he became absorbed in the affairs of the institution over which he presided, he forsook the paths of literature into which his youthful aspirations and bent had led him, to devote himself entirely to the arduous duties of his high financial position. And yet he could not entirely relinquish his literary tastes, and was occasionally drawn from his business to preside at seminary commencements and other literary and educational occasions, on which the evidence of his genius and taste was among the most gratifying displays. Had his talent been permitted to follow its bent there is little doubt that he would have ranked with the poet banker Rogers, but he chose a more secluded life and contented himself with doing good in other directions.

Mr. Weir joined the Presbyterian Church at Harrisburg in 1830. In 1834, he was elected an elder, and has ever since filled this office.

He has been connected with the Sunday-school about fifty years, and has been Superintendent of the school of that church for over forty years. He was one of the first, firmest and most influential friends of the anti-slavery and temperance causes. In 1859, he was elected a corporate member of the American Board of Commissioners for Foreign Missions, and long continued to promote its interests in every way in his power.

During his long life Mr. Weir has always resided in the city of his birth, with the exception of but six months, and that was while moving among the printing offices of Philadelphia. His steadfast residence in his native place has only tended to increase his influence and to endear him more and more to his neighbours. On August 9th, of this year, (1875,) there was a celebration of his seventieth birthday. To this event a correspondent of a Philadelphia daily thus refers:

"Yesterday the personal friends of this distinguished financier united in an ovation of respect such as is not often paid to men who lead a purely private career. It was as genuine a surprise as a magnificent success. Before the bank opened the different employees of the institution waited on the cashier in a body and tendered him their congratulations in an address full of affection and respect, the address being accompanied by a photographic group of their portraits in a large frame. When the bank opened, at nine o'clock, a stream of visitors began to pour into the cashier's room, until it was found necessary to occupy other parts of the house, where the nieces of Mr. Weir had prepared a collation for the entertainment of his friends. The callers continued to appear until three o'clock in the afternoon, during which time over eight hundred people paid their respects. On behalf of the directors of the bank, Mr. Weir was presented with a solid silver tea set. Messrs. Dougherty, Brothers & Co., sent a swinging silver ice pitcher, and a large number of bouquets were received. One hundred and fifty congratulatory letters were laid on the cashier's table, and the day wound up with a dinner, at which nineteen of the old friends of the cashier were present, whose average age was seventy-five years."

Such a demonstration is in the highest degree complimentary to Mr. Weir, and is but the expression of a feeling of esteem which is universal. No man better deserves it than James Wallace Weir. No banker in the State has a more unsullied reputation, and no man in any community, reaching the age of seventy years, has a purer personal reputation. Uprightness, benevolence, energy, geniality, courage in duty, fidelity in earth's various relations, all sanctified and adorned by religion, eminently mark his symmetrical character.

SAMUEL R. FISHER, D. D.

THE REV. SAMUEL R. FISHER was born in Norristown, Montgomery county, Pa., June 2d, 1810, the sixth son of a family of seven boys, the three youngest and the eldest of whom are still living. His ancestors, both paternal and maternal, emigrated from the Palatinate in Germany, early in the eighteenth century. They fled from persecution and were among the first Germans from that section of Germany who settled in Pennsylvania, and aided in organizing the first Reformed Churches in this state. They settled on the wild lands, in what was then Philadelphia, but now Montgomery county, the former near Sumneytown, and the latter near Hatfield station, on the North Pennsylvania Railroad.

His paternal and maternal grandparents were all born in this country, his father being the youngest of a family of thirteen, and his mother, next to the youngest of a family of twelve children. His paternal grandfather, George Fisher, was a soldier in the Revolutionary army, and as such passed through many trying scenes. His maternal grandfather, Jacob Reed, was Lieutenant-Colonel of the Pennsylvania militia, and was in the battles of Trenton, Germantown, Brandywine, &c.

Young Fisher commenced going to school very early, his parents availing themselves of such facilities for educating their children, as were afforded by the schools then in existence. From his earliest years he was piously inclined, and had a desire to make the Christian ministry his vocation in life. His father's pecuniary circumstances, however, having become straitened, he had partially abandoned the idea, because of his supposed inability to acquire the necessary education. His aspirations were revived in this direction, by a proposition from his relative and god-father, the Rev. George Wack, to take him into his family, and give him such instruction as his leisure from other duties that were required of him, would enable him to receive. With this object in view, he entered his family in the spring of 1824, and continued there nearly five years.

In the spring of 1826, he attended a course of catechetical lectures with a view to confirmation. On the 27th of May of that year, he was confirmed in Boehm's Church, of which the Rev. George Wack was pastor, then lacking five days of being sixteen years of age, and admitted for the first time to the Holy Communion of the Lord's Supper, a privilege which he enjoyed with much deep, pious feeling. For his early religious impressions he is greatly indebted to the influence of his truly pious mother.

As he advanced in years, he became more deeply sensible of the responsible nature of the ministerial office, and of the great importance of a thorough Classical and Theological education to the successful discharge of its duties. Hence he contrived various methods to secure that which was so much the object of his heart's desire. He entered the Preparatory Department of Jefferson College, Cannonsburg, Pa., in the fall of 1829, in the twentieth year of his age.

After spending a year in the Preparatory Department, Mr. Fisher entered college, and graduated in September, 1834, in a class of thirty-four members, among whom were more than the usual number of excellent scholars. During his college vacations, he made frequent journeys on foot. The fall vacation of six weeks, in 1832, was in this way appropriated to a journey of eight hundred miles, in which was included the distance from Philadelphia and return. During the greater portion of his college course, he also traveled every Sunday sixteen miles on foot, superintending two Sunday Schools, and listening to two sermons in the summer, and one in the winter.

The fall after graduating, he entered the Theological Seminary at York, Pa., then presided over by the Rev. Dr. Lewis Mayer, with whom was associated the Rev. Dr. F. A. Rauch, and passed through the prescribed course in the institution, which, at that time, covered a period of two years.

In September, 1836, Mr. Fisher was licensed to preach the Gospel by the Synod of the Reformed Church in the United States, and having accepted a call to the Emmittsburg charge, Frederick county, Maryland, he was ordained to the work of the ministry and installed pastor of the charge, by a committee of Synod, on the 19th of October, 1836. In this charge he laboured with varied success until the close of the year 1839. During the first year he preached to six congregations. Subsequent to that time, the number was reduced to four. In performing his duties, he traveled over a large extent of country, and engaged in a great variety of active operations. The result of his labours was a large accession to the congregations under his care.

On the first of January, 1840, he became connected with the Publication Office of the Reformed Church, which had just been established in Chambersburg. On the first of April, he removed with his family to Chambersburg, and became associated with Rev. Dr. B. S. Schneck, in the editorship of the "Reformed Church Messenger." At about this point in his history, the degree of Doctor of Divinity was conferred upon him by Marshall College. From that time to the present day, Dr. Fisher has been connected with the publication interests of the church, having had the special management of them since 1845, and also editing the "Messenger," at intervals in connection with another, but during the greater portion of the time alone. In 1840, he became the Stated Clerk of the Reformed Church in the United States, and has continued in this relation until the present time.

Besides several sermons preached on special occasions, Dr. Fisher has prepared and published, the following works: "The Rum Plague," a temperance story, translated from the German of Zschokhe; "Heidelberg Catechism Simplified;" "Exercises on the Heidelberg Catechism;" and "The Family Assistant." The latter three of these works indicate marked ability in their authorship. They have had, and still have an extensive circulation.

Dr. Fisher has been twice married. His first wife was Miss Ellen C. May, eldest daughter of Daniel May, Esq., of York, Pa., to whom he was married on the fifth of April, 1837. The fruit of this marriage was one son and one daughter, the former of whom is engaged in the work of the ministry. The first Mrs. Fisher died in Chambersburg, on the 26th of January, 1842, in the twenty-sixth year of her age. On the 5th of December, 1843, he was married to his present wife, Mrs. Naomi Kerns, widow of Abraham Kerns, of Bedford, Pa. The second marriage has been without issue.

Dr. Fisher now resides in Philadelphia, the Publication Office with which he is connected having been removed to that city, after the burning of Chambersburg during the War of the Rebellion. Though his life has been one of earnest labour, he still retains remarkable vigour, and, in his diligence and persistence in the work to which he is called, is an example of fidelity and efficiency. He continues to wield great influence in the church which he loves, and by which he has ever been highly esteemed. His ripe scholarship, characteristic sincerity and honesty, long experience, genial spirit, and singleness of purpose, have won him a position of prominence and power, which, no one can doubt, he occupies with a solemn sense of his corresponding responsibility. Catholic in spirit, he is also popular with other denominations than his own, and leaves the impression wherever he is known, that all his varied talents are consecrated to the full and final triumph of Christianity.

JOHN HOLMES AGNEW, D. D.

THE REV. JOHN HOLMES AGNEW was born in Gettysburg, Pa., May 9th, 1804. Of his father, who subsequently removed to Harrisburg, and whose fame as a physician reached far beyond the range of his practice, a sketch is given elsewhere in this volume. Young Holmes's teacher at Harrisburg, writes, " He was a good boy, of good abilities, and learned well and rapidly." He graduated at Dickinson College, under the presidency of the distinguished Dr. John Mason, and taught the grammar school in Carlisle for some time after leaving the college.

Mr. Agnew pursued his theological studies in the seminary at Princeton, and was licensed to preach the Gospel by the Presbytery of Carlisle, April 11th, 1827. Having received and accepted a call to the pastorate of the Presbyterian Church in Uniontown, Pa, he was dismissed to the Presbytery of Redstone, October 29th, 1827. He was married to Miss Sarah Emeline Taylor, of Newark, N. J., April 18th, 1829. On account of a nervous affection which always seized him severely after preaching, and from which he never could get relief during his life, he had to abandon in a great measure the duties of the pulpit, and consequently resigned his pastoral relation to the church at Uniontown, after discharging its duties for a short time as efficiently and acceptably as his failing health would permit. A. W. Boyd, Esq., of that place, in a letter, says, "I find those who were members of the church during Mr. Agnew's pastorate, remember him with a great deal of pleasure. All say he was greatly beloved by the people, was an excellent pastor, and a very instructive and interesting preacher, a man of deep piety, and it was felt to be a great calamity to the church when he left."

After relinquishing pastoral work, Mr. Agnew was elected Professor of Languages in Washington College, Pa., January 12th, 1831. This position he resigned September 26th, 1832, on account of inadequacy of salary. The degree of Doctor of Divinity was conferred upon him by this institution in 1852. The Rev. George P. Hays, D. D., its present President, in writing to a friend, says: "He is spoken of here by those who knew him, as a gentleman of very high scholarship and excellent ability as a teacher. He probably made as much reputation in the short time he was here as any man who was ever connected with the college, in an equal length of time. His departure from the college was deeply regretted by both the Faculty and the Trustees."

After leaving Washington, which he did on account of inadequacy of salary, Prof. Agnew became connected with the German Reformed Institution in York, Pa. He was then elected a Professor in Marion College, Missouri, where he remained until the institution was dissolved, and subsequently he was chosen to a similar position in Newark College, Delaware, from which he withdrew, as did some other professors also, because the funds for the institution were raised by lottery. Next he became editor of the Eclectic Magazine, and the Biblical Repertory, a quarterly in the interest of the (then) New School Branch of the Presbyterian Church, with which he was connected.

After having had charge of a Female Seminary in Philadelphia for a few years, Dr. Agnew became Professor of the Ancient Languages, in the University of Michigan, in 1845, retiring from this position, in which he established his reputation as a thorough scholar, in 1852. He then selected as his field of labour and usefulness, Maplewood Female Seminary, Pittsfield, Mass. In reference to this portion of his history, the Rev. C. V. Spear, A. M., present Principal of that institution, thus writes:

"Professor Agnew became a partner and co-principal in the conduct of this Seminary some time during the Academic year of 1852-3. The school was enjoying a very good degree of success when he became connected with it, and remained one of the prominent institutions of the state while he was its sole Principal, as it has since. Its *name*, now and for all the years since he was here, was given by him. He was very highly esteemed by the pupils and patrons of the school, as a man of rare geniality and elegance of manners in social life, and thorough scholarship and cultivated taste—eminently fitted in many respects for his post here and its multiform duties, and lacking only in health, and a certain financial sharpness too often incompatible with the highest culture and intellectual ability. He possessed, in a rare degree, that high hopefulness which is o necessary to the commencement and the prosecution of any undertaking that is at all difficult and worthy of high ambition; and with adequate support would, but for failing health, have continued his work here much longer without doubt. His pupils, and the teachers and professors in the school, were very warmly attached to him, and among other reasons, for the unfailing kindness, forbearance and urbanity, that characterized all his intercourse with them. I need not say, what no doubt many voices will utter, that while many men in posts of honour are feared, and others respected, he was a man to be both honoured and loved. I recall, as I write, the presentation of a beautiful vase of silver—I think the gift of the teachers and professors—as a testimonial of their high esteem and affection for him, at the Summer Anniversary of 1856. The sincere warmth of the devotion then expressed was no transient feeling, and his retiring a year later was deeply regretted by many friends."

It may here be added that all Dr. Agnew's friends earnestly wished that he had retained his position at Pittsfield. After abandoning it, which he did, no doubt, from a desire to make himself more able to do good, and from other influences, he was induced, through his too great readiness to trust in his fellow-men, to engage in some speculations, from which, however, he would, in all probability, have come out safely but for disasters which overtook them by reason of the war, and made them issue in total loss.

In addition to the literary labours of Dr. Agnew, to which we have already referred, he was also editor of *The Knickerbocker;* the author of a small and valuable work on "The Sabbath," from the press of the Presbyterian Board of Publication; and assisted in the translation of Winer's Grammar of the New Testament. Whilst, too, occupying positions of mere literary responsibility, we find him using his graceful pen in efforts to do good in the religious sphere. During his Professorship at Newark, he contributed an excellent sermon to the *National Preacher*, on "Motives and Means of Peace to the Churches."

Dr. Agnew died of bilious fever, at Peeksville, N. Y., October 12th, 1865. His character is thus succinctly delineated by one who knew him thoroughly: "He was generous, benevolent, social, genial, gentlemanly, scholarly."

JAMES ROSS SNOWDEN, LL. D.

JAMES ROSS SNOWDEN, lawyer, statesman and author, comes from one of the oldest families in Pennsylvania. Although born in Chester, Delaware county, Pa., he was, as the sequel of this sketch shows, in early life identified with Cumberland valley, by descent, residence and education, and thus appropriately finds a place in this work.

His great grandfather, John Snowden, emigrated from Great Britain at some time previous to the year 1678, and first fixed his residence in Delaware county. In 1685, he removed to Philadelphia. Being a man of education he was employed in various public offices. In 1704, he was an elder of the ancient Presbyterian *First* Church, in Market street, and was the first Presbyterian elder ordained in Pennsylvania. His son, Isaac Snowden, born in Philadelphia, in 1732, was an active and useful citizen, a member of the City Councils before the Revolution, a County Commissioner during the Revolution, and a Commissary for supplying the army. After the close of the War of Independence, he was elected Treasurer of the city and county of Philadelphia, which office he retained for several years, and was subsequently a member of the Select Councils of Philadelphiaa, Trustee of the College of New Jersey, (Princeton,) an elder in the Second Presbyterian Church, and a member of the committee of which Dr. Witherspoon was chairman which formed the Constitution and Form of Government of the Presbyterian Church, in 1786. Four of his sons were graduates of Princeton College and entered the ministry; among these was Rev. Nathaniel Randolph Snowden, who was born in Philadelphia, in 1770, and graduated in 1787. He studied divinity under Rev. Charles Nisbet, D. D., at Carlisle, and there married a daughter of Dr. Lemuel Gustine, an eminent physician of that town. They had five sons and one daughter. Four of the sons became Doctors of Medicine, viz: Isaac W. Snowden, Charles G. Snowden, Lemuel G. Snowden, and Nathaniel D. Snowden. The daughter, Mary Parker, was married to James Thompson, the late Chief Justice of Pennsylvania. The youngest son, the subject of this notice, was educated chiefly under the tuition of his father, who, for some years had charge of Dickinson College before it passed into the hands of the Methodist Episcopal Church.

Choosing the bar for his profession, James Ross Snowden was admitted *ex gratia* at the early age of nineteen, and having taken up his residence at Franklin, Venango county, he was appointed Deputy Attorney General. Subsequently, and for several years, he was elected to the Legislature of the state; and was Speaker of the House of Representatives in 1842, and again in 1844. In 1845, he was elected State Treasurer, and re-elected in 1846. In 1847, he was appointed by President Polk Treasurer of the Mint, and Assistant Treasurer of the United States. In 1850, he returned to the bar, and fixing his residence at Pittsburgh, was appointed Solicitor of the Pennsylvania Railroad Company, which position he resigned to accept the office of Director of the Mint, in 1853, which office he held until 1861, when he was appointed Prothonotary of the Supreme Court of Pennsylvania. In 1873, he resumed the practice of his profession in Philadelphia. During these active duties Mr. Snowden has also been connected with many scientific, literary and historical societies; and being an elder in the Presbyterian Church, has taken an active part in the various courts of that denomination.

Among the many works of which Mr. Snowden is the author, are the following: Ancient and Modern Coins; Medals of Washington and National Medals. Both these works are illustrated with fac simile engravings; the latter also contains biographical notices of the Directors of the Mint from 1792 to 1861. The Coins and Money Terms of the Bible; the Corn-Planter Memorial, and Sketch of the Six Nations of Indians.

In 1868, he contributed to Bouvier's Law Dictionary the articles on the Coins of the United States and Foreign Nations. He has also at different times published addresses, pamphlets on currency, on international coinage, history, and other subjects. He early took an interest in military affairs and was elected colonel of a volunteer regiment in 1842. He presided at the State Military Convention of 1845, and wrote the memorial which produced a needed reform in that branch of the service. Although always a Democrat, he supported the War for the Union, and being in command at Philadelphia of a volunteer regiment he twice offered it for service in the field; but it was not accepted by the Government. In 1845, he received the degree of Master of Arts from Jefferson College. In 1872, Washington and Jefferson College conferred on him the honorary degree of Doctor of Laws.

During Colonel Snowden's administration of the Mint, many improvements were made, prominent among which was the re-construction of the Mint building, so as to render it fire-proof. A beautiful medal commemorates this event. On the *obverse* is the bust of the Director, with the inscription, "Presented to James Ross Snowden, Director of the Mint, by his personal friends, as a mark of their regard for him as an officer, and their esteem for him as a citizen." Beneath the bust is the date, 1859. On the *reverse*, there is a representation of the Mint edifice, with the legend, "The Mint of the United States of America, built 1832; rendered fire-proof, 1856." Colonel Snowden married, in 1848, Susan Engle, second daughter of General Patterson, of Philadelphia.

JOHN MICHAEL KREBS, D. D.,

THE son of William and Ann (Adamson) Krebs, was born in Hagerstown, Md., May 6th, 1804. He was religiously educated. His father was a member of the German Reformed Church, and his mother after her marriage became one, though she had previously been an Episcopalian. He received the best education the town afforded till he was between fourteen and fifteen. In this time he gave some little attention to the classics, though his attention was chiefly directed to English studies. His father, who was a man of great energy, integrity and respectability, was a merchant, and also held the office of postmaster, and at the age above mentioned this son became a clerk in the post office, at the same time rendering some service in his father's store, which had meanwhile been given up chiefly to his brother.

In 1821, the year before his father's death, his thoughts were intensely directed toward serious things, and after his father's death his impressions became deeper and stronger, and after many and severe struggles, of which those around him knew nothing, his mind gradually came to repose in the gracious provisions of the Gospel, and at the age of nearly nineteen, he joined the church under the pastoral care of the Rev. John Lind. He now formed a purpose to devote himself to the ministry. After studying under Mr. Lind's direction for some months, he entered an academy in his native town, and in February, 1825, entered Dickinson College, Carlisle, Pa. He graduated in September, 1827, under the Rev. Dr. William Neill, receiving one of the highest honours of his class.

He then began his theological studies under the Rev. George Duffield, D. D. Three or four months after this a vacancy having occurred in the grammar school attached to the college, he was appointed to fill it, and here he continued in the business of instruction for two years, at the same time improving his leisure in the prosecution of his theological studies.

At the end of two years from the time he was graduated (October, 1829,) he was licensed by Carlisle Presbytery. During the winter and spring after he was licensed, he preached by appointment of the Presbytery to various congregations in the neighbourhood. In May, 1830, he set his face toward Princeton, N. J., to pursue further theological studies in the Seminary. He received and accepted a call to Rutgers Street Church, New York, and was installed November 12th, 1830, having been ordained the week previous at Lancaster, Pa., by Carlisle Presbytery. This was his only charge.

Dr. Krebs was a man of rare gifts and of still more rare and varied acquirements, being learned not only in theology but in the whole range of sciences, and his learning was all made to bear upon the work to which he had devoted his life, that of the Gospel ministry. He was eminent as a preacher of the Gospel, and still more eminent in the councils of the church, being distinguished for his knowledge of ecclesiastical law, and his acquaintance with the ecclesiastical history of the denomination to which he belonged. He was regarded as one of the highest living authorities in regard to Presbyterian usages.

In 1837, he was appointed Permanent Clerk of the General Assembly, and retained the office till 1845. He had resigned it the year previous, but his resignation was not accepted. In 1845, he was Moderator of the General Assembly of the Presbyterian Church. He was elected Clerk of the Presbytery and Synod of New York, in 1841, and Director of the Theological Seminary at Princeton, N. J., in 1842, and was appointed President of the Board in 1866. He was a member of the Board of Foreign Missions from its organization till his death. His published works consist of about a dozen occasional sermons, which are marked by great energy, perspicuity and precision.

In 1866, Dr. Krebs was a member of the General Assembly at St. Louis, Mo., and was appointed Chairman of the Committee on the *Reunion* of the Presbyterian Church. Of this measure he was an earnest supporter, though his decline in health, which had previously commenced, prevented his active participation in the preparation of the plan of union in the successful consummation of which he was deeply interested.

He died at his residence in New York, September 30th, 1867. He was twice married; first, on October 7th, 1830, to Miss Sarah Harris Holmes, a daughter of Andrew Holmes, of Carlisle, Pa. They had two children. She died February 20th, 1837. His second wife was Miss Ellen Dewitt Chambers, daughter of John Chambers, of Newburg, N. Y. She died in 1863. Several children survive him.

REV. JOHN H. KENNEDY.

REV. JOHN H. KENNEDY was descended from a very respectable and pious ancestry. James Kennedy, his grandfather, emigrated from Ireland, and settled first in New Jersey, and afterwards in Pequea, Lancaster county, Pa., where some of the family still reside. Rev. Robert Kennedy, the father of the subject of this sketch, who is elsewhere noticed in this volume, was for many years in the ministry, and sustained a very high standing among his brethren for talents, learning and respectability.

John Herron, Esq., the maternal grandfather, who was the father of Francis Herron, D. D., lived and died on "Herron's Branch," Franklin county. At the house of this venerated grandfather, John H. Kennedy was born, November 11th, 1801. His mother (Jane Herron) was, in the mysterious providence of God, removed by death when John, her eldest son, was eighteen months old. After the death of his mother, he lived in his grandfather's family until his fifth year. During this period his health was very delicate, and little hope was entertained that he should attain to manhood. His recollections of his grandfather, and his residence in his family, were of the most pleasing kind. It was, he remarks, his "Vale of Tempe," and the time spent there, his "Saturnalia." About the close of his fifth year he was taken home by his father, who had married a second wife. He was early sent to school, but was not so fond of study as of play, and especially such sports as required vigorous exertion. These, though often exposing him to danger, and sometimes to injury, contributed to that remarkable health which he enjoyed until the last year of his life. In his ninth or tenth year, he commenced the Latin grammar with his father, under whose instruction he studied the Latin and Greek Languages. He was afterwards connected with the Academy in Cumberland, Maryland, of which his father, on his removal from Welsh Run, had taken charge, being at the same time pastor of a congregation in that place. In November, 1818, he became a student of Jefferson College, Cannonsburg, Pa. During his whole collegiate course he sustained a high standing as to talents and scholarship, and graduated with honour, May, 1820.

Mr. Kennedy spent the summer of 1820 at his father's, in general reading, and in efforts to do good, as he had opportunity. In October of that year he entered the Theological Seminary at Princeton, where he studied the regular term of three years. To this period he always reverted with endearing recollections. He commenced his theological studies with diligence and success, and was soon distinguished by his talents and acquirements. During the fall vacation of 1821, he was taken under the care of the Presbytery of Carlisle. During the winter or spring of this year, he visited Morristown, New Jersey, at the request of Mr. McDowell, pastor of the church there, a powerful revival of religion having commenced, which pervaded the whole country. In October, 1822, he was licensed to preach the Gospel—aged twenty years and ten months. Deeply impressed with the responsibilities of the work to which he was to be devoted, he set apart a day for fasting and prayer, a duty which he often practised in the succeeding years of his life. After his licensure to preach the Gospel, he continued his studies another year at Princeton. During this year, the doctrines denominated Hopkinsian were frequently the subject of warm discussions in the Seminary. In these discussions he took an active and decided part in opposition to what he believed erroneous in these doctrines. A debate prepared at that time on the subject of the atonement, was afterwards published in the first volume of the Christian Advocate. Its admission into that periodical by the venerable editor, Dr. Green, is no slight evidence of its intrinsic ability and excellence, though written by one who had just arrived at the years of manhood.

Leaving the Seminary in the fall of 1823, Mr. Kennedy itinerated in different directions about eighteen months. He preached for some time in Bedford and Uniontown, Pa., and traveled through some of the Western States. He traveled also to the South, and preached for some time at Wilmington and Fayetteville, North Carolina. In April, 1825, he again arrived at his father's, who had now returned to his former residence in Franklin county. In the summer he visited Philadelphia, preached in the Sixth Church as a supply for three months, received a call from that congregation, and was ordained and installed as their pastor, November, 1825, in the twenty-fourth year of his age.

Previously to his settlement in this church he had been appointed chaplain, to go out in the Brandywine, the Government vessel, appointed to carry Lafayette back to his native land. This appointment was by some means prevented from reaching him until after his installation. Had he received it sooner it might have given a new direction to the current of his life.

His settlement in Philadelphia was unsought, as it was unexpected, by himself. The station was one of great importance and responsibility, for so young a man. The Sixth Church grew out of a division of the Old Pine Street Church, of which Dr. Alexander had been pastor when called to Princeton. On the settlement of Dr. Ely this division took place, and the Sixth Church was formed. It contained a large portion of intelligence, piety and respectability, but its location in the vicinity of other churches, and certain pecuniary embarrassments, were unfavourable to its growth. It had become vacant by the resignation of Dr. Neill, who had accepted a call to the Presidency of Dickinson College. After labouring a year in this congregation, and discouraged at his prospect of usefulness, he determined to resign his charge. The Presbytery met, and with the concurrent desire of the congregation, persuaded him to remain. His intention was at this time to have gone to Liberia, and he often expressed his regret that he yielded to the advice to remain in Philadelphia, having then, as he remarked, "had a burning zeal in behalf of Africa, such as he never felt in behalf of any other object." In 1828, he was married to Miss Harriet McCalmont, of Philadelphia, whose intelligence, piety, and accomplished education, qualified her eminently for being to him a prudent counsellor and cheering companion. In December, 1829, at his own request, his connection with the Sixth Church, which had continued for four years, was dissolved. During this period he discharged the duties of his office with ability and faithfulness. The *visible* fruits of his ministry were not equal to his *desires*, and hence his frequent discouragements, which resulted in his resignation, yet his labours were blessed to the edification of Christians, and a *goodly* number added to the Church. The charge of a congregation in a city is one of great responsibility and hazard, especially to a young man, yet was Mr. Kennedy enabled to sustain a high and increasing reputation among his brethren, and the intelligent part of the religious community, as an able, lucid, and instructive preacher of the Gospel. It is known that he stood very high in the estimation of his venerable patron and friend, Dr. Green, who occupied a pew in his church, and sat with delight under the ministry of his young friend.

After Mr. Kennedy's connection with his congregation was dissolved he committed himself to the providence of God, without any definite object or plan as to future settlement. He was urged to make a tour to Missouri, with a view of settlement at St. Charles, and accordingly left Philadelphia with that intention. The severity of the season prevented him, and he was detained in Franklin county. A call was prepared for him from the congregation of Newville, one of the largest and wealthiest in Carlisle Presbytery. At this crisis, being uncertain and anxious as to the path of duty, he set apart, as was his frequent custom, a day of fasting and prayer, to seek Divine direction. It was the 11th of March, 1830. It is worthy of observation that on the evening of this same day, altogether unexpected to him, he received a letter from Cannonsburg, inquiring as to his views in relation to a Professorship in Jefferson College, in connection with the charge of a small congregation, about five miles distant from that town.

He was at first startled at the proposal of a Professorship of Mathematics, for which he considered himself less qualified than for any other department. On further consideration, with the hope that by diligent exertion he might be prepared for the service, he inclined to accept. He visited the place in May; received and accepted the appointment from the college, and the call from the congregation of Centre. He returned to Philadelphia, and arrived in Cannonsburg with his family, and entered on the duties of his profession, June, 1830.

Professor Miller, in view of whose resignation, on account of age, the appointment was made, still continued to officiate for some time. This afforded opportunity for Mr. Kennedy gradually to prepare himself for conducting the departments of Natural Philosophy and Mathematics, which he was enabled to do with great credit to himself, and to the entire satisfaction of all concerned. After the division of the departments of Natural Science and Mathematics, and the appointment of a distinct Professor for the latter, he devoted himself more exclusively to Natural Philosophy and Chemistry, in which he greatly excelled.

In a sermon on the death of Professor Kennedy, preached in the College Chapel, by the Rev. Matthew Brown, D. D., President of the institution, December 27th, 1840, he says:

"As an *instructor*, Mr. Kennedy was thorough, discriminating, accurate and lucid in his illustrations. As a member of the Faculty he was energetic, fearless, and always ready to share the responsibility of a disciplined government. As a *preacher*, he was *instructive*, solemn, searching and forcible. As a *pastor* he was laborious and faithful. As a *writer* he was characteristically lucid, simple and concise. "*Multum in parvo*," appeared to be his motto in all his productions. He wrote with great facility, and furnished for "the periodicals," a number of essays, which do him great credit. His *talents* were various, and in some respects of a high order. He had more of the *intellectual* than the æsthetic—more of argumentation than poetry in his composition—more of the instructive than the pathetic.

He was a man of great *benevolence* and *liberality*. This feature of his character was not generally understood. In his wordly transactions he was exact, but when proper objects of benevolence were presented, no man in the community in which he lived was more liberal, according to his means. Besides the public contributions, in which he was always among the first, he performed many acts of private liberality unknown to the world.

Considered as a *Christian*, "the highest style of man," his *soul-searching* experience, his conscientiousness and stern integrity, his self-denial, his steadfast faith on the righteousness of Christ, his abhorrence of sin, his desires and endeavours after holiness, and his habitual aim to glorify God, gave "lucid proof" of sincere piety while he lived, which was confirmed in his death.

His health began seriously to decline in the winter of 1839-40. A journey to the east during the summer proved unprofitable, and he returned home to die in the bosom of his family. He looked forward to the hour of his death without dread. Still he clung to life, and although with regard to himself he had no fears, and could say, "to be with Christ is better," yet when he looked around on his wife and little children, and the prospect of leaving them exposed and unprotected in such a world as this, he greatly desired to live. At length, however, he was enabled, with sweet acquiescence, to commit the precious charge to Him who said, "Leave thy fatherless children, I will preserve them, and let thy widows trust in me."

His old enemy did not fail to assail him in his weak state, and when near the close of life, with *doubts* as to the foundation of his hope. These, however, were soon dispelled, and he afterwards enjoyed uninterrupted calmness to the last. A few days before his release he spoke of his departure with great composure and confidence. When the weather permitted, he was usually taken out in a carriage. On returning, a day or two before his death, he said that *that* was his last ride; in his next remove he "would be carried by angels into Abraham's bosom." On the 15th of December, in the thirty-ninth year of his age, he died without a struggle, and "sweetly fell asleep in Jesus." His wife and two children yet survive. One of them, the Rev. Robert P. Kennedy, is Pastor of the Red Clay Presbyterian Church, near Brandywine Springs, Delaware. With him his mother and sister reside.

CONWAY PHELPS WING, D. D.,

BELONGS to a family which is traceable through five generations to the settlement of the first of the name, in 1632, at Lynn, but more permanently at Sandwich, Massachusetts.

His father was born in Conway, in that state, but after his marriage removed to a settlement on the Muskingum, twelve miles above Marietta, Ohio. There the subject of this sketch was born, February 12th, 1809, but when he was four years of age his father removed to Phelps, Ontario county, New York, and there remained until 1833, when he died, aged sixty-five, much respected; and for many years an elder in the Presbyterian Church.

After two years of preparatory instruction there, in an Academy at Geneva, N. Y., young Wing entered the Sophomore class in Hamilton College, where he graduated with a respectable standing in 1828. He then entered Auburn Theological Seminary, where he graduated in 1831. He was immediately called to settle at Lodus, Wayne county, where he laboured as a licentiate during the previous spring vacation. He was ordained and installed by the Presbytery of Seneca September 27th, 1832, and retained the pastoral relation four years with success.

In the early part of 1836, Mr. Wing received and accepted a call to a Congregational Church in Ogden, twelve miles west of Rochester, N. Y., which, however, immediately became and has ever since continued Presbyterian. He remained there four years, with but little diminution of his labours, and with large accessions to his church.

In the autumn of 1838, he removed to the city of Monroe, Michigan, where many of his relatives resided, and he was for more than three years pastor of the Presbyterian Church there. The long continuance of severe labour now began to tell upon his health, and he was obliged to seek its restoration by a voyage to the island of Santa Cruz, West Indies. After a few months' residence there, he removed with his family to Tennessee, (October, 1841.) Six months were spent at Pulaski, Giles county, and at Columbia, in Maury county, in that state, preaching however to Presbyterian churches in those places. In hope that his health was now sufficiently restored to endure at least the climate of the middle states, he ventured (May, 1843,) to return north.

At the urgent call of a church in Huntsville, Alabama, Mr. Wing was induced to forego his preference of a northern residence, and to return after six months to that beautiful town. Though informing that people that he was conscientiously opposed to slavery, should do all he wisely could to oppose it, and could never own or even hire a slave, they persevered in calling him and in sustaining him. His own people unanimously and heartily upheld him in his course to the very last, in opposition to perpetual threatenings and secret combinations on the part of men in the political world and in the other denominations. And when he expressed to them his conscientious conviction that he could no longer remain the pastor of a slave-holding church, every effort was made by his congregation to retain him. A call from the First Presbyterian Church, Carlisle, Pa., reached him just as he had made up his mind that he could no longer continue a pastorate where public sentiment would not permit Sessions to call to account those slaveholders who offended against the laws of humanity. He reached Carlisle, April 28th, 1848, and was installed in the fall of the same year.

Since his residence in Carlisle, Dr. Wing's congregation has enjoyed a high degree of prosperity, a number of interesting revivals have taken place in it, and he has deservedly had the reputation of great fidelity to his duties and marked earnestness and ability as a preacher. Besides performing the ordinary work of a large pastoral charge, he, for one year, (1849,) at the request of the Faculty and students of Dickinson College, supplied the place made vacant by the transfer of Professor Allen to the Presidency of Girard College, and has constantly been occupied with works in Theological literature. In 1856, in connection with Professor Blumenthal, he published a translation of "Hare's Manual of Ecclesiastical History," in the composition of which he bore a principal part. Among his other publications are articles in the Presbyterian Quarterly Review, the chief of which were two on Abelard, two on the "Historical Development of the Doctrine of the Atonement," one on "The Permanent in Christianity," one on "Miracles and the Order of Nature," in the Methodist Quarterly. He was also the writer of two elaborate articles on "Federal Theology," and "Gnostics and Gnosticism," in McClintock's and Strong's Cyclopædia, and in 1868, he translated with large additions Dr. C. F. Kling's Commentary on Second Corinthians, for Dr. Schaff's American edition of Lange's Commentary.

Dr. Wing was especially active in efforts for the Reunion of the Presbyterian Church, being a member of the National Convention in 1867, and of the Assemblies in New York and Pittsburgh when the churches united. He was also a member of the joint Committee of Reconstruction for the re-organization of the Synods and Presbyteries. He received the honorary degree of Doctor of Divinity from Dickinson College, in 1857. He continued in the midst of his usefulness, respected and beloved by those who knew him, as an earnest Christian, a cultivated and genial gentleman, an accomplished scholar, a graceful writer, and an able, instructive and impressive expounder of Divine truth, until October, 1875, when he resigned his charge.

COL. THOMAS A. SCOTT.

THIS gentleman was born at Loudon, Franklin county, Pennsylvania, December 28th, 1823, and received his education at the village school of that place. When ten years of age he went to work in a country store, near Waynesboro', and was afterward employed in Bridgeport and Mercersburg until about 1841. At this period he removed to Columbia, Pennsylvania, and entered the office of the Collector of Tolls of the State Roads and Canals. His connection with state improvements continued until 1851, in which year he was appointed to a position on the Pennsylvania Railroad. He was first stationed at the Junction, near Hollidaysburg, and was placed in charge of the business of the Company passing over the Portage road, and the Western Division of the State Canal. As the various portions of the Western Division were connected, their operation was assigned to him, and so satisfactory were his arrangements that on the completion of this Division he was made Superintendent, with an office at Pittsburgh. In 1858, further promotion was accorded him, and he was appointed General Superintendent of the road from Philadelphia to Pittsburgh, his headquarters being at Altoona.

In 1860, on the death of W. B. Foster, Vice-President of the Company, Colonel Scott was elected to succeed him. Subsequent elections raised him to the position of First Vice-President, his great ability, ceaseless activity, and rigid integrity having rendered incalculable service to the powerful corporation which he serves. Engrossed in his railway business, Colonel Scott has never allowed himself to be distracted from his legitimate pursuits by the allurements of political ambition, but when during the war the services of an experienced railroad man became an imperative need for the service of the country, he was too patriotic to shirk the responsibility, and therefore, with the weight of his other engagements upon his shoulders, he, in 1861, directed the construction of the road from Annapolis which did much to aid the troops and contributed largely to the protection of the Capital. In the fall of that year, the need of such services becoming more and more exigent, he was appointed Assistant Secretary of War, and continued so until 1862, when he returned to Philadelphia. He was again called on, however, after the battle of Chickamauga, and dispatched to Louisville to aid in the movement of the 11th and

and 12th corps, via Nashville, to the relief of Rosecranz at Chattanooga. This operation was so successfully performed that, in a few days, the army of the Tennessee was reinforced sufficiently to be able to compel the full retreat of the enemy.

Returning with undiminished vigour to his usual duties, Col. Scott at once resumed his active supervision of the Pennsylvania Railroad. In 1871, rival routes to St. Louis and Chicago having been brought under the same management, it was deemed expedient, for the simple and effective working of the lines west of Pittsburgh, that a separate company should be chartered, and this was accomplished by charter from the State Legislature of Pennsylvania on March 1st, 1871, Col. Scott becoming President of this company, viz: Pennsylvania Company. On the death of J. Edgar Thomson, Col. Scott was unanimously elected President of the Pennsylvania Railroad Company by its Board of Directors, and at the annual election by the stockholders held in March, 1875, he was again unanimously elected President and still holds that position. The prosperity of the great corporation with which Col. Scott is identified, has been shared with the state, the name of which it bears; local interests have advanced, and the general interests of the state and people have been largely benefited.

The giant labours of Col. Scott would be impossible to any one not possessing his peculiar temperament and sound physique. In manner he is genial, and possessing in a remarkable degree the art of refusing gracefully, both he and the numerous applicants for favours avoid the annoyances which are so worrying and wearing to many public men. By habit he is so peculiarly rapid in his disposition of business that "Col. Scott's style" has almost grown into a byword in certain quarters, and yet this rapidity is never allowed to degenerate into hastiness; it is the result of observation, memory, and an especial faculty for cutting mental Gordian knots without injuring the rope of which they are tied, a gift of great value and rarity. The result of such a temperament, and such habits, is, that extreme pressure of business does not weary excessively; on leaving his office, Col. Scott feels that his work is done *pro tem.*, and its cares are left in his portfolio. Another effect is that while he never regrets the unalterable, he is constantly devising new methods of conserving and advantaging the interests confided to him—a work which would be impossible to a man burthened by cares and regrets.

REV. MATTHEW SIMPSON CULBERTSON,

THE son of Joseph and Frances (Stuart) Culbertson, was born in Chambersburg, January 18th, 1819. He was a quick, intelligent boy; his mother had dedicated him to God, and she looked forward to his becoming not only a minister but a missionary. He was educated at the United States Military Academy at West Point, New York, after serving a full course of years, and whilst serving as a Lieutenant of Artillery, he made a profession of religion, and soon after laid down the sword and took up the cross.

He entered the Seminary at Princeton, N. J., where he graduated in 1844. He was licensed by the Presbytery of Carlisle, in 1844, and soon after ordained by the same Presbytery as a Foreign Missionary to China. Previous to his sailing he married Miss Mary Dunlap, of New York State. His career as a missionary was marked by extraordinary devotion and ability. In the midst of his labours he was taken with cholera, and after a short illness died in August, 1862. His widow and three children survive.

Among the fellow-students of Mr. Culbertson at the national military school, were Halleck and McDowell, Magruder and Beauregard, all of whom afterwards wore the insignia of Major-Generals, and bore a leading part in the most momentous war in the annals of modern history. In the progress of his course he was appointed drill officer, with the title of Captain, and also served for a time as Professor of Mathematics. When two cadets were chosen to be sent to France, at the Government's expense, to complete their education in the school which produced a Bonaparte, Culbertson was the first selected, and obtained the suffrages of all the electors. At the West Point Academy he earned for himself the beatitude of the peacemaker. Engaged to act as second for the afterwards famous Magruder, in an affair of honour, he adjusted the difficulty, and prevented a probably fatal encounter.

While at Princeton, according to the testimony of his venerable instructor, Dr. Hodge, he was regarded as among the foremost members of the institution, and when, at the close of his three years' curriculum, he, with three others of his class, embarked for a foreign mission, another of the Professors (Dr. J. W. Alexander,) singled him out, and wrote of him in these terms: "One of the four, Culbertson, was an army officer, and highly honoured at West Point—chosen to go on some military mission to France."

The Rev. W. A. P. Martin, D. D., of the same mission with Mr. Culbertson, in his funeral sermon, preached at Shanghai, China, August 31st, 1862, says:

"Of the excellencies of his character I need offer no delineation; they are attested, with one voice, by all the Protestant missionaries, of all ecclesiastical connections in the community. 'Our devoted brother,' they say, in a paper adopted a few days after his death, 'was a man of a meek and quiet spirit, and remarkable for his singleness of aim and straightforward energy and industry in his Master's service; he resigned a commission in the armies of his country, to become a missionary to the heathen. He set before himself the highest ends, and strove, both by preaching and example, to glorify God in the salvation of his fellow-men.

"'He laboured, in connection with the late Dr. Bridgeman, for several years, with assiduity and perseverance, in preparing a revised translation of the sacred Scriptures in the Chinese language, a labour of love which he regarded as the great work of his life, and it was a source of especial consolation to him, just before his departure, that God had enabled him to complete it. He also wrote a work, entitled, "Darkness in the Flowery Land." We recognize in these traits of character, and this Christian life, the devoted missionary, whose example is worthy of our imitation.'

"Happy the grave which is crowned with such a tribute! There is but one eulogium which a good man may covet more earnestly, and that is the 'Well done, good and faithful,' pronounced by his Lord and Saviour. This blissful welcome has no doubt greeted those ears, which are now deaf to the voice of human applause."

JAMES DUNLOP, ESQ.

THE name of James Dunlop has spread widely through the Commonwealth, as that of one of her most eminent legal sons. Like so many of the notable men of the valley, he boasted pure Scotch-Irish blood. He was born in Chambersburg, in 1795; his father was Andrew Dunlop, Esq., a very able attorney of that place, his mother was Sarah Bella Chambers, a highly accomplished and admirable woman, a daughter of General James Chambers, who figured in the Revolutionary army, and served as Colonel at the battle of Brandywine, and a granddaughter of Benjamin Chambers, the sturdy founder of Chambersburg. His paternal grandfather, Colonel Dunlop, also participated in that memorable engagement.

Mr. Dunlop received his classical education at Dickinson College, Carlisle, graduating in 1812. Judge Grier, of the United States Supreme Court, Rev. John Knox, of the Dutch Reformed Church, of New York, and Calvin Blythe were his class-mates at college; the first named his room-mate and special friend. His legal studies were pursued in the office of his father; and he was admitted to the bar in 1817, at the same time with the late lamented Paul I. Hetich, Esq. Although he soon acquired a large business and an extensive reputation as a lawyer, he was not content with the awards which his profession brought him, and he engaged also in the manufacturing of cutlery with his brother-in-law, George A. Madeira, establishing the celebrated Lemnos Edge Tool Factory, so long known under the firm name of Dunlop & Madeira.

But realizing that his special vocation was the law, he entered on a wider field of practice, and in the fall of 1838, moved to Pittsburgh, and speedily won a leading position at its bar. In 1855, he left Pittsburgh, and took up his residence in Philadelphia. When on a visit to his class-mate, Charles F. Mayer, Esq., at Baltimore, he was stricken with paralysis, and died in that city on the 9th of April, 1856. His remains were taken to Pittsburgh, and interred in the Allegheny Cemetery.

Mr. Dunlop was a member of the State Senate from Franklin county, about 1825, and was subsequently twice a member of the Lower House. In 1838, he was a member of the Convention which reformed the Constitution of the State, when, it is said, "he distinguished himself for the learning and ability displayed in debate." He was the compiler of Dunlop's Digest of the Laws of Pennsylvania, and of a Digest of the Laws of the United States, works which have given him a lasting fame. In 1825, he read at a meeting of the Council of the Historical Society of Pennsylvania an elaborate article on the controversy between William Penn and Lord Baltimore, respecting the boundaries of Pennsylvania and Maryland, which was of such merit as to be published in full in the "Memoirs of the Historical Society of Pennsylvania, Vol. I.," in which may be found a brief sketch of his life.

Before the removal, by President Jackson, of the deposits from the United States Bank, he was an active supporter of the Democratic party; but after that event, he shook off his partisan allegiance and became a formidable champion of the opposition, making a remarkable speech against General Jackson, which caused a great sensation at the time.

Mr. Dunlop was noted for his forensic power, great legal attainments, literary accomplishments, droll humour, and caustic, pungent wit. As a writer, he was exceptionally ready, and as an opponent exceedingly formidable. One who knew him intimately writes that he was a man of courteous manners, amiable and considerate, a tireless student, possessing unbounded knowledge, which he was always ready to impart; and unostentatiously benevolent.

He was violently opposed to slavery, both politically and for humanity's sake; often helping the trembling fugitive on his flight to Canada. He was known to purchase a slave to save him from a life of bondage.

Great as was his eminence as a lawyer, thorough and exhaustless his Classical and Belles Lettres accomplishments, fluent and graceful his pen, mirth-provoking his humor, and scathing his wit, the human love which made him the protector of the oppressed, gives him a dearer and more blessed fame than all the qualities of his genius.

THOMAS VERNER MOORE, D. D.

THOMAS VERNER MOORE was born in Newville, February 1st, 1818. Having received his academic education in his native village, he entered Hanover College in 1834, and afterwards became a student at Dickinson College, at which institution he graduated with honours in 1838.

For a short time after leaving college, he was in the service of the Pennsylvania Colonization Society as traveling agent. His theological studies were commenced at Princeton, New Jersey, in 1859.

Mr. Moore was licensed to preach the Gospel by the Presbytery of Carlisle. In June, 1842, he was married to Sarah, daughter of the Rev. Dr. Blythe, of Hanover, Indiana. In the spring of this year he was installed as pastor of the Second Presbyterian Church, Carlisle. In this charge he laboured with much acceptableness and success. In the autumn of 1845 he was chosen pastor of the church at Greencastle, where he was attractive as a preacher and useful as a pastor. During his residence at this place, he was called to mourn the death of his wife. His relation to this congregation was dissolved in 1847, with a view to his acceptance of a call to the First Presbyterian Church of Richmond, Virginia. His pastorate in that city was a great success.

' "There," says Dr. Rice, " he made full proof of his ministry; there he realized the idea of a Christian pastor; there he accomplished a great and blessed work worth living for.

"As a preacher he was uniformly elegant and attractive, persuasive and instructive, always earnest and solemn, often overwhelming in power. His discourses were perspicuous in thought and expression. His style was finished and elegant, bright with the flashes of a chastened imagination, and glowing with the fervour of a sincere piety. The hearer was ordinarily reminded of the beautiful, peaceful landscape, bathed in the pure white light of heaven, yet reflecting the fresh tints of the springtime, or the varied hues of autumn; but at times, when the occasion demanded, he seemed to hear the rush of mighty waters, as, with a resistless torrent of eloquence, sin, and especially all baseness, were swept away to merited shame and ruin. Yet he oftener loved to bear the soul away to the blissful scenes where

' Sweet fields beyond the swelling flood
Stand dressed in living green,'—

where the palace of our Father stands on high, with its many mansions; where the multitudes of the blessed sit down to the marriage supper of the Lamb."

Dr. Rice also says, in relation to Dr. Moore's authorship: "Here, in Richmond, amid the arduous labours of his pastorate, he redeemed the time to employ his elegant and vigorous pen for the instruction of the church at large, and future generations of Christians. Here he wrote and published his Commentary on the Prophecies of Haggai, Zechariah and Malachi—'The Prophets of the Restoration'—which has taken its assured place among the standard works of Biblical interpretation. For accuracy and extent of learning, and for clearness of insight into the meaning of the Prophets, it will compare favourably with the works of the ablest commentators. Before committing this work to the press, he had the pleasure of receiving the hearty commendation and highly prized counsel of his greatly admired preceptor, the late Rev. J. Addison Alexander. It was in connection with the publication of this work that the acquaintance and friendship of years deepened into the closest and tenderest intimacy, which was ended, only for a brief space, by the death of that wonderful man.

"Here, too, he published his popular exposition of 'The Last Words of Jesus,'—a work for which he possessed rare qualifications. Also, the little tract entitled 'The Culdee Church,' which has afforded so much delight and such confirmation of faith to so many readers.

"Also, his two lectures on the 'Evidences of Christianity,' before the University of Virginia, in addition to various excellent articles for several religious and theological Reviews and Magazines, with a number of occasional sermons. Here, too, in connection with his lifelong colleague, the Rev. Dr. Moses D. Hoge, he engaged in the difficult task of editing, for several years, the *Central Presbyterian*. Also, in association with Dr. Hoge, he bore his part in projecting and conducting the *Richmond Eclectic Magazine*, which promised excellent fruits for the literature of the South, and whose merging into another periodical was greatly regretted by the friends of elegant literature and graceful culture."

During his residence in Richmond, Dr. Moore married Matilda, daughter of Mr. Henry Gwathmey, an elder of his church. When he left that city, it was to become Pastor of the First Presbyterian Church, in Nashville, Tenn., where, a few years previously, he had presided over the General Assembly of the Presbyterian Church (South.) His term of service in this field of labour was short, being scarcely three years in duration, part of which he was absent, by the earnest and affectionate desire of his people, seeking the recovery of health and strength in more genial climes and under brighter winter skies. He died, August 5th, 1871, leaving six children. Yet, though his pastorate was brief, it was effective. "If disabled, in the providence of God, from working himself," says one of his co-Presbyters; "he did better, he succeeded in causing his congregation to work. He was enabled to infuse into the loved and loving people of his charge something of his own earnest spirit, and to impart something of the wisely regulated method with which he did his own work. If the impulse which he gave to the Christian activity of his people, and of his brethren of this Presbytery, can only be carried onward, no man can estimate the value of his short and painful sojourn among us."

DAVID N. RANKIN, M. D.

CUMBERLAND VALLEY is well represented in all the professions, and by no means least notably in the medical.

Dr. David Nevin Rankin, was born in Shippensburg, Pa., October 27th, 1834. He was the second son of William Rankin, M. D., and Caroline (Nevin) Rankin, eldest daughter of Major David Nevin, of that place.

His academical education was received at Newville. At the age of seventeen he commenced the study of medicine with his father, and graduated at Jefferson Medical College, Philadelphia, in 1854. After graduation, he practised his profession in partnership with his father in Shippensburg, until the breaking out of the Rebellion. Whilst engaged in a very extensive and laborious practice, he contracted a cold, which produced several attacks of hemorrhage of the lungs, and threatened serious results. This impaired physical condition prevented his entering the regular army, as Assistant Surgeon. He received, however, an appointment under Surgeon General Finley, United States Army, as acting Assistant Surgeon, United States Army. Whilst occupying this position, he aided in opening some of the largest United States Army hospitals during the war, among which were the "Mansion House Hospital," at Alexandria, Va., and "Douglass Hospital," Washington, D. C. He was afterwards placed in charge of Epiphany and Thirteenth Street Hospitals, in the same city, and later was stationed at Pittsburgh United States Army Hospital.

In 1863, during the height of the Rebellion, Dr. Rankin was selected by Surgeon General James King, of Pennsylvania, as one of thirty surgeons appointed from various parts of the State, to render aid to the wounded immediately after battle. This corps of surgeons was called the "Volunteer Aid Corps of Surgeons of Pennsylvania," and, as may be seen by reference to Surgeon General King's printed official reports to Governor Curtin, the members of this corps rendered very efficient and valuable services.

After the war Dr. Rankin located in Allegheny City, where a few years before, he had married Kate, daughter of Henry Irwin, Esq., and he has succeeded in building up a large and lucrative practice. During his residence there, he has filled some very prominent positions, such as Medical Examiner for United States Pensions, Physician to the

Western Penitentiary of Pennsylvania, Medical Referee for the Ætna Life Insurance Company, and Vice-President of the Society of Natural Sciences of Western Pennsylvania. He is also a permanent member of the Medical Society of Pennsylvania, and a member of the Allegheny County Medical Society, as well as the author of the reports of numerous interesting medical and surgical cases.

Dr. Rankin is yet in the prime of life. His standing as a physician is excellent. His career thus far has been successful in every respect, and his prosperous past betokens for him a promising and useful future.

HON. EDWARD McPHERSON.

EDWARD McPHERSON is a descendant, in the fourth generation, of Robert and Janet McPherson, who settled on Marsh creek, Adams county, (then York,) about the year 1735.

His great grandfather, Col. Robert McPherson, was an active and influential citizen, and filled many important positions, among which may be mentioned, Treasurer of York county, in 1755, and again in 1767; Commissioner, in 1756; Sheriff, in 1762; and Assemblyman, in 1765–67, and 1781–84. He was also a member, from York county, of the Provincial Conference of Committees, which met in Carpenters' Hall, Philadelphia, June 18th, 1776; and was also a member of the Constitutional Convention which met July 15th, 1776, and formed the first Constitution of the State of Pennsylvania. He was also a Captain in General Forbes' expedition to reduce Fort Du Quesne, in 1758. He died in 1789. His grandfather, Captain William McPherson, served honourably in the Revolutionary War, having been attached in 1776 to Miles' Rifle Regiment, and was captured by the enemy at the battle of Long Island. On his return, he discharged many public trusts. He died in 1832.

He is the youngest son of John B. and Catharine McPherson, the former of whom was, for forty-five years, Cashier of the Bank of Gettysburg, and who died in January, 1858. He was born in Gettysburg, July 31st, 1830, and was educated in the Public Schools of that town, and at Pennsylvania College, located in Gettysburg, graduating in 1848, at the youthful age of eighteen, with the Valedictory of his class. He early developed a taste for politics and journalism, but at the request of his father began the study of the law with Hon. Thaddeus Stevens, in Lancaster. But his health failing, he abandoned it; and for several winters was employed in Harrisburg as a reporter of Legislative proceedings, and a correspondent for the Philadelphia *North American*, and other newspapers. In the campaign of 1851, he edited, in the interest of the Whig party, the Harrisburg *Daily American*, and in the fall of that year he took charge of the Lancaster *Independent Whig*, which he edited till January, 1854. In the spring of 1853, he started the *Inland Daily*, the first daily paper published in Lancaster. His health proved unequal to these labours, and he relinquished them, as stated. Except for brief periods, he has not had since, active connection with the press.

His first important public service was the preparation of a series of letters, ten in number, which were printed in the Philadelphia *Bulletin*, in 1857, and afterwards in pamphlet form, to prove the soundness of the financial policy which demanded the sale, by the State, of its Main Line of Public Improvements. These letters analyzed the reports of the Canal Commissioners for a series of years, proved the falsity of the conclusions drawn from them, and demonstrated the folly of continued state ownership and management. These letters were never answered, and they formed the text from which were drawn the arguments in favour of the sale, which was accomplished in 1858. The next year he prepared a like series on the sale of the branches of the canals, which had a like reception. Both these were published anonymously, but were signed "Adams," after his native county. In 1856, he published an address on the "Growth of Individualism," delivered before the Alumni of his *Alma Mater*, in 1858, one on "The Christian Principle; Its Influence upon Government;" and in 1859, one on "The Family in its Relations to the State," both of which were delivered before the Young Men's Christian Association of Gettysburg. In 1863, he delivered an address before the Literary Societies of Dickinson College, on the subject, "Know Thyself; Personally and Nationally Considered."

In 1858, Mr. McPherson was elected to the Thirty-Sixth Congress from the Sixteenth District of Pennsylvania, embracing the counties of Adams, Franklin, Fulton, Bedford, and Juniata. In 1860, he was re-elected. In 1862, he was defeated, in the political re-action of that date, the district having been meanwhile changed by the substitution of Somerset county for Juniata.

Upon the completion of his Congressional term of service, President Lincoln, upon Secretary Chase's recommendation, appointed Mr. McPherson Deputy Commissioner of Internal Revenue, April, 1863, in which position he served till December, 1863, when he was chosen Clerk of the House of Representatives, Thirty-Eighth Congress, which office he has continued to hold, during the Thirty-Ninth, Fortieth, Forty-First, Forty-Second, and Forty-Third Congresses, being the longest continuous service in that post, from the beginning of the Government.

During his service in Congress, his principal speeches were as follows: "Disorganization and Disunion," February 24, 1860, in review of the two months' contest over the election of a Speaker in the Thirty-Sixth Congress; "The Disunion Conspiracy," January 23, 1861, in examination of the secession movement and the arguments made in justification of it; "The Rebellion; our Relations and Duties," February 14, 1862, in general discussion of the war; "The Administration of Abraham Lincoln, and its Assailants," June 5, 1862.

During his incumbency of the clerkship, he has published "A Political History of the United States during the Rebellion," extending from the Presidential election of 1860, to April 12, 1865, the date of Lincoln's death; "A Political History of the United States during the Period of Reconstruction," extending from 1865 to 1870; a "Hand Book of Politics for 1872;" and a "Hand Book of Politics for 1874." These volumes are a compilation of the political record of men and parties during this eventful period, and have received a high place in the confidence of all parties, for completeness, fairness, and accuracy.

During the summer and fall of 1861, he served as a volunteer aid on the staff of General McCall, commanding the Pennsylvania Reserves, with a view to study the organization and wants of the army, and to fit himself for intelligent legislative action on those subjects. In the Thirty-Seventh Congress, he was a member of the Military Committee of the House, and took an active part in legislation respecting the army. He also served as chairman of the Committee on the Library, and as a Regent of the Smithsonian Institute. In 1867, the degree of LL. D., was conferred upon him by Pennsylvania College.

Mr. McPherson was married November 12, 1862, to Miss Annie D. Crawford, daughter of John S. Crawford, Esq., of Gettysburg, and granddaughter, on her father's side, of Dr. William Crawford, a native of Scotland, who settled near Gettysburg about the year 1800, and who for eight years represented that district in Congress, and on her mother's side, of Rev. Dr. William Paxton, who for nearly fifty years served with distinguished ability the Marsh Creek Presbyterian Church. They have five children, four sons and one daughter.

ENGRAVED BY HALLPIN, FROM A DAGUERREOTYPE.

H Harbaugh

HENRY HARBAUGH, D. D.

NEAR the base of the South Mountain, which bounds Cumberland valley on the southeast, in the southern extremity of Franklin county, Pennsylvania, within a few hundred yards of "Mason and Dixon's line," and in sight of one of the crown capped milestones which mark that line, is located a large stone farm house, and in its immediate vicinity a large bank barn, such as are usually found on the farms of the thrifty Germans of Pennsylvania. In this farm house the subject of this brief sketch was born, on the 28th of October, A. D., 1817. His parents were George Harbaugh, and Anna, his wife.

His paternal and maternal ancestors were among the early German emigrants, who settled in eastern Pennsylvania. He accordingly was a direct descendant from original Pennsylvania Germans, of which fact he made great account, and which also did much to give cast to his character and habits of life, and mould his thoughts and predilections.

In his early infancy Henry was baptized by the Rev. Frederick A. Scholl, then pastor of the Reformed Church, at Waynesboro, Pa., at which place his father's family worshiped. He was trained up under religious influences, after the manner for which many of the Pennsylvania German forefathers were distinguished. His earliest years were spent with his father on the farm, amidst its beautiful surrounding scenery, which, as all scenery is educational, left its impress on his young mind, as was abundantly evinced in his subsequent life. He also worked some time at the carpenter and millwright trade. His early education was only such as could be acquired at the country schools, as they existed at that time.

When he reached the years of maturity, he felt it to be his duty to devote himself to the work of the Christian ministry. With this view he repaired to Mercersburg, in 1840, and entered Marshall College, and subsequently the Theological Seminary of the Reformed Church in the United States, which were then located at that place.

In the fall of 1843, he was licensed by the Synod of the Reformed Church in the United States, which convened in Winchester, Virginia, and was soon thereafter ordained to the work of the ministry, and installed as pastor of the Lewisburg charge, in Union county, Pennsylvania, by the Susquehanna Classis. In this field he laboured until

1850, when he accepted a call from the First Reformed Church, Lancaster, Pennsylvania. His pastorate in Lancaster continued during a period of ten years. In 1860, he was called to the pastorate of the St. John's Reformed Church, Lebanon, Pennsylvania, which had been recently organized in that place. In October, 1863, he was chosen Professor of Didactic and Practical Theology in the Theological Seminary, at Mercersburg, by the Synod which met in Carlisle, Pennsylvania, and soon thereafter entered upon the duties of the professorship, in which he continued until his death.

Dr. Harbaugh was no ordinary man, whether viewed socially or intellectually. He was a most genial companion. He enjoyed society and generally formed the centre of attraction in it. He possessed a rare fund of pleasing, original anecdotes, which he related with a peculiar zest, and infused life and cheer into all around him. He was ardent in his feelings and warm in his attachments. His friends also were bound to him by the strongest ties.

As a theologian, Dr. Harbaugh was strikingly prominent. He had made himself fully acquainted with the most difficult theological problems of the day. The person and work of Christ especially engaged his most earnest attention, and the results of his investigations are everywhere apparent in the more profound productions of his pen. His inaugural address on "Christological Theology" is a masterly production of its kind. It evinces how deeply and earnestly his heart was enlisted in the vital points of the Christian system. As a teacher of theology, he always maintained a living sympathy with his students. His peculiar talent for popularizing even the most abstruse subjects made his lectures specially acceptable to them. They seemed eagerly to imbibe the very feelings, as well as thoughts of their professor.

Among other productions of his pen were, "The Sainted Dead," "Heavenly Recognition," "Heavenly Home," "The Life of Michael Schladter," "The Lives of the Fathers of the Reformed Church in America," "The Lord's Portion," "The Harbaugh Annals," "The Birds of the Bible," "Union with the Church," "Harbaugh's Poems," &c. He edited for many years the *Guardian*, and the *Child's Treasury*.

Dr. Harbaugh was twice married. His first wife was Miss Louisa Goodrich, of the vicinity of New Hagerstown, Ohio, and a sister of the Rev. William Goodrich, of Clearspring, Md. His second wife was Miss Mary Louisa Linn, daughter of James F. Linn, Esq., of Lewisburg, Pa., who survives him. He had two children by his first marriage, one of whom, a daughter, survives him, and ten by his last marriage, six of whom, four sons and two daughters, also survive him.

His constitution was vigorous and his general health good, until near the close of his life. The illness which ended in his death, was protracted and severe. He died in Mercersburg, Pa., on the 28th of December, 1867, at the age of fifty years and two months. His death was deeply lamented by thousands, and especially by the church, in whose Seminary he was Professor. His remains were interred, attended with appropriate solemnities, in the yard in front of the Reformed Church, in Mercersburg, on the last day of December. A fitting monument, erected to his memory a few years afterwards, by the Synod of the Reformed Church of the United States, marks their resting place.

HON. JAMES X. McLANAHAN.

THE HON. JAMES XAVIER McLANAHAN was a descendant of the Scotch-Irish stock which figured so prominently in the early history of the Cumberland valley, and contributed so many strong men to the Commonwealth.

The McLanahans of Franklin county, for several generations, have been a large, wealthy and influential connection.

James McLanahan, grandfather of James X., settled when young in the country near Green Castle, at a section called "the Marsh," from its topographical peculiarities. His son William inherited the "paternal acres," and lived and died there respected by his neighbours. William married a daughter of Andrew Gregg, a statesman of distinction in the annals of Pennsylvania, who represented the state in the United States Senate, 1807–1813, and was the Federal candidate for Governor in 1823. Andrew Gregg was the grandfather of ex-Governor Andrew Gregg Curtin.

James X. McLanahan was a son of William, and was born on the ancestral estate in the year 1809.

At a proper age, young McLanahan entered the Hagerstown school, and afterwards Dickinson College, where he graduated with honor in 1826. Resolving from his early youth to make the law his profession, immediately after graduating he commenced his legal education in the office of Andrew Carothers, an eminent member of the Pennsylvania bar, residing at Carlisle. Removing shortly afterwards to Chambersburg, Mr. McLanahan completed his studies in the office of the Hon. George Chambers, afterwards Judge of the Supreme Court of Pennsylvania.

Mr. McLanahan's well known intellectual powers, and his warm and generous nature, at once drew around him troops of friends, and he was soon offered a position in the political party to which he avowed his attachment. This, however, he declined, determining to devote his exclusive attention to the practice of his profession. It may be well to pause here in our brief narrative, to admire the wise and prudent course pursued by the young lawyer in this particular. Too many of our young professional men have ruined their prospects in life by entering too early into the battle and the strife of politics. Flattered by the attentions of men of high position, their company courted by the throng, the duties of their profession become irksome to them. They rebel against its stern demands. Mistaking the deceit of the politician for the truth of friendship, they offer themselves perhaps as candidates for the legislature, and are elected. Their minds not yet matured, lacking discretion, they serve their term with no credit to themselves nor benefit to their constituents, and are trampled upon by the next new comer. Then awakening from their stupor, they behold others, their inferiors in intellect, far on the road to wealth and distinction; and thus drooping with disappointment, they die in dissipation, or live pensioners on their respective parties.

Mr. McLanahan, by strict attention to his business, was soon in the enjoyment of a lucrative practice. Scarcely a case of any importance occurred in his county, after he came to the bar, in which he was not engaged.

In 1841, in Pennsylvania, the waves of political excitement ran mountain high. Both parties strained every nerve to secure the State.

At the preceding session of the Legislature, the Senatorial District in which McLanahan lived, had been formed with the avowed intention of preventing the election of any one of the political party to which he was attached. In opposition to his personal feelings, he was nominated for the State Senate, and in despite of every effort to the contrary, was elected by a large majority, running far ahead of his ticket. From the time he entered the Senate he became a prominent member and the leader of his party in that body. His profound research, depth of thought, and elegance of diction, soon placed him amid the foremost men of Pennsylvania. He served his Senatorial term of three years, and declined a re-election. In 1843, Mr. McLanahan was married to an accomplished daughter of Mr. James McBride, a wealthy merchant and estimable gentleman, of New York city.

He continued at the bar until 1848, when he was elected to Congress. Shortly after taking his seat as a Representative, he was unexpectedly and involuntarily drawn into a discussion, and delivered himself of a speech that riveted the attention of the House, and won the applause of the country. His closing appeal in behalf of the Union was most eloquent, and deservedly found a place in several of our American class-books.

Mr. McLanahan was re-elected to Congress in the fall of 1850, notwithstanding a most bitter opposition. At the commencement of the session his name was favourably mentioned as a candidate for the Speakership. This he very becomingly declined. He was, however, placed at the head of the Judiciary Committee. The duties of this responsible position he filled with marked ability. He projected several important reforms in that department of the Government, which met with the concurrence of the House and the nation.

Mr. McLanahan's fine personal figure, joined to a voice of great compass and power, and a countenance strongly marked with feeling as well as thought, gave him advantages as an orator which not many public men in this country possess. To say that he cultivated the rare intellectual gifts which nature endowed him with up to the fullest extent of their capacity, would be to make an assertion which nothing but the blindest friendship could excuse. A scholar he was, and a ripe one, too, but he was not a learned man in the common acceptation of the phrase. He early dropped the speculative sciences, and gave his mind only to those practical pursuits which in a country like ours are so much more useful. His quick perceptions made him a man of true sagacity; his ardent temperament, (we might say his strong passions,) gave uncommon energy to his character, and his clear reason purified his tastes, and made his judgment, though certainly not infallible, yet in the main altogether reliable.

But the strong hold he had on the affections of his constituents and his friends, is better accounted for by his attractive, social and moral qualities. The unselfish and generous impulses of his nature did not permit him to serve any one by halves, and yet his opponents never had cause to complain that his demeanor towards them was wanting either in justice or in courtesy. Sincerity, that first of virtues, was the characteristic trait of his mind. His whole conduct was full of transparent truthfulness. His speeches were marked with a sort of daring plainness. Concealment of his opinions, whatever might be the effect of their utterances upon himself or others, seemed with him to be out of the question. It could be said of him:

<blockquote>
His heart's his mouth.
What his breast forges, that his tongue must vent.
He would not flatter Neptune for his trident,
Or Jove for his power to thunder.
</blockquote>

Mr. McLanahan retired into private life, residing in New York city, where he had many warm personal friends. He resisted there all inducements to enter political office, preferring the quiet enjoyment of the family circle to the excitement of the arena of politics. He died December 16th, 1861, sustained by Christian hope. His wife, and only son, reside in the city just named. Though dying in the prime of his life, he had already earned the title of an able lawyer, an incorruptible public servant, and an honest man. Of such a character it is fit that the dignity should be vindicated and the value made known.

HON. GEORGE SANDERSON,

IS a native of Cumberland county, and was born in Dickinson township, about seven miles southwest of Carlisle. His parents were in humble circumstances, and he lost his father when only twelve years of age. His widowed mother, who was a woman of remarkable energy, managed to give him a common English education, which he afterwards improved by his own exertions and application to study.

In his seventeenth year young Sanderson was apprenticed to the coopering business, but, on becoming free, the business being very dull, he was induced to commence teaching school, in which honorable employment he was remarkably successful, and continued to follow it in Shippensburg and vicinity until 1836, at which time he became editor and proprietor of the Carlisle Volunteer, the recognized organ of the Democracy of Cumberland county, and continued to publish it for a period of nine years.

From 1839 to 1842, Mr. Sanderson was Prothonotary of Cumberland county, having been first appointed by Governor Porter, and afterwards elected by the people. From 1845 to 1849, he held the office of Postmaster at Carlisle, having been appointed by President Polk. In 1849, at the earnest solicitation of James Buchanan, whose name was then beginning to loom up prominently for the Presidency, he removed to Lancaster and took charge of the Intelligencer, the long established and influential organ of the Democracy of that county, and continued to conduct the paper until 1864, a period of fifteen years.

In February, 1859, he was elected Mayor of the city of Lancaster, and so satisfactorily did he discharge the responsible duties of the position, that he was re-elected for nine consecutive terms, and retired from the office in October, 1869, having been at the head of the municipal government for nearly eleven years, a much longer period than any of his predecessors who were elected by the people. Since he retired from the Mayoralty he has been engaged in the book and stationary business, and still continues to reside in Lancaster. In addition to the offices above mentioned, Mr. Sanderson held several minor positions of trust and responsibility in Cumberland and Lancaster counties, such as School Director, Assessor, Notary Public, &c., and was twice nominated as a candidate for the Legislature, but, owing to his party being in a minority, he failed of an election. In all the offices he held, he conducted himself to the entire satisfaction of the public, and with a degree of popularity in each which few persons can command.

In politics, Mr. Sanderson has always been a firm and unwavering Democrat of the real Jackson stamp, neither turning to the right hand nor to the left, and has a record politically as well as morally above reproach. He has now nearly completed his three-score years and ten, but still retains, in a great degree, his vigour of mind and body, and, as a political writer or speaker, would not be unwilling to break a lance with any of his opponents. In person, he is somewhat above the middle height, erect and well proportioned, and bids fair to live for several years to come.

JAMES I. BROWNSON, D. D.,

THE subject of this sketch, was born at Mercersburg, Pa., March 14th, 1817. His honoured and pious parents jointly represented an ancestry which had shared in the settlement of the beautiful and historic Cumberland valley. To their son and themselves, the Rev. David Elliott, D. D., LL. D., who was for a number of years Pastor of the Presbyterian Church at Mercersburg, thus refers in a letter written to the First Presbyterian Church, Washington, Pa., on the occasion of their Quarter Century Celebration, December, 1873: "With your present Pastor I have been acquainted from his earliest childhood, for I baptised him, when he was an infant. His excellent parents, Major John Brownson and his wife, were amongst my most intimate friends. The Major was a ruling elder in my first pastoral charge. He was a man of more than ordinary intelligence; and from his having been in the army, and mingled largely with the world, he had acquired an experience of human nature in its various forms of practical development, which qualified him to be a valuable assistant in the administration of the government of the church."

In his childhood, young Brownson was reduced by sickness to the borders of the grave, and for three months the question of his life was daily in doubt. At that time his father dedicated him upon his knees to God for the ministry, binding himself in a covenant which he ever afterwards held sacred. Its only two conditions were, the son's preservation and the Master's call. The parental heart which made that vow ceased to beat whilst the son was in the Senior class of college, but was unspeakably gladdened in death with the promise and process of its fulfilment. Mr. Brownson's union with the church by a profession of faith had preceded this bereavement by a few years, during a powerful work of grace which had sealed the early ministry of his Pastor, the Rev. Dr. Thomas Creigh.

Having completed his academical preparation at home, chiefly under the instruction of the Rev. Robert Kennedy, he was sent to the care of the friend of his parents already named, (Dr. Elliott,) then pastor of the Church at Washington, and in his sixteenth year entered the Freshman class of the college in that place, from which, in 1836, he was regularly graduated. After a year spent in the Bucks county Academy, at Newtown, Pa., as a teacher of the Ancient Languages and Mathematics, he entered the Western Theological Seminary, in which Dr. Elliott had now become a Professor, as a student for the ministry. His licensure to preach, in 1840, by the Presbytery of Carlisle, was followed the next year by his installation as the Pastor of the United Congregations of Greensburg and Mount Pleasant, Pa., in the Presbytery of Redstone. In this charge he laboured with great acceptableness and success for eight years.

A call was made out on the first Monday of December, 1848, by the Presbyterian Church of Washington, Pennsylvania, for Dr. Brownson's services as its pastor. This very important position was accepted by him with great diffidence of his ability to meet its demands. With a college on the one hand, and a female seminary on the other, the field was justly felt to be one involving a large responsibility, requiring special fitness for its cultivation. But the pastorate thus assumed, at once, as it has ever since, proved itself to be one of Divine constitution.

One of the best evidences of Dr. Brownson's marked success in the charge which he has occupied for more than twenty-five years, was furnished at the celebration just mentioned. On that occasion, Thomas McKennan, M. D., in an address in behalf of the elders and deacons, said:—

"Many whom I see around me, and many who have gone before, could bear testimony to the deep solicitude of our pastor in our behalf, and to the earnestness of his public and private appeals that we would come to Christ. In this, indeed, he has been a true and faithful pastor. Need we speak of his clear and cogent arguments *to convince our judgments* in behalf of religion and a religious life; of his gentle and tender ministrations at the bedside of sickness, and his still more tender ministrations in the houses of mourning and death; of his labours in behalf of every good enterprise; of his deep concern in all proper and important projects (educational and otherwise) connected with the welfare of this community; of his true, yet judicious, patriotism? All these are known and acknowledged by every one."

Such testimony, in such circumstances, speaks for itself. And whilst it is eminently complimentary to Dr. Brownson, an important lesson which it teaches should not be overlooked, viz: *That the pastors who make for themselves a large, and warm, and firm place in the hearts of their people, are those who preach simply and plainly the pure Gospel.*

Dr. Brownson is above medium size, and of commanding personal appearance. He is of a genial disposition, and in his deportment happily unites suavity and dignity of manner. By constitutional temperament he is conservative in spirit, and cautious in movement. His scholarly attainments are highly creditable. For a season, while the Presidency of Washington College was vacant, he very satisfactorily discharged the duties of the position. As a writer he is clear, logical and cogent. As a preacher he is instructive, forcible and impressive, always preparing his discourses with great care, and delivering them with pathos and power. By his brethren of the ministry, to whom he is known, he is justly held in high esteem for his uprightness, ability and usefulness.

WILLIAM HENRY ALLEN, M. D., LL. D.

WILLIAM HENRY ALLEN, M. D., LL. D., President of Girard College, was born near the city of Augusta, Maine, March 27th, 1808.

He is the son of Jotham and Thankful Allen, and his paternal grandfather was a descendant of the Braintree branch of the Allens of Massachusetts. His early life was spent at home on a farm until he entered the Wesleyan Seminary, (Maine,) where he received his education preparatory to entering Bowdoin College, which he did at the age of twenty-one, graduating therefrom after a four year course. Immediately after leaving college, he was called to take charge of the Greek and Latin classes at the Oneida Conference Seminary at Cazenovia, New York, where he remained for two and a half years; when his worth and ability being appreciated by his own townspeople, he was invited to return to Augusta, and preside over the High School in that city.

He remained in this latter locality, however, but six months, as he had been tendered the Professorship of Chemistry and Natural Philosophy at Dickinson College, Carlisle, Pennsylvania, which he accepted. This chair he occupied for ten years, and was then transferred to that of English Literature in the same institution, which he filled for three years. During much of the time he resided in Carlisle, he was a regular contributor to the Methodist Quarterly Review. He also wrote and delivered numerous addresses and lectures on educational and general subjects. He has delivered lectures in several cities of the Union, among them Philadelphia, Boston, Baltimore and Indianapolis. In January, 1853, at the request of the municipal authorities of Philadelphia, he pronounced a Eulogy on America's greatest statesman, Daniel Webster. This eloquent and able discourse was highly esteemed by the public. It was published, and took rank with others delivered by prominent men throughout the country.

In January, 1850, he was appointed President of Girard College, succeeding Judge Jones, who had held the position from the opening of the institution two years previously. The Board of Directors found in him a gentleman whose education and superior administrative abilities admirably fitted him to become the executive of an institution of this peculiar character. His duties there were entirely different

from those required in the same positions in other colleges. Here he was called on not only to organize and harmonize a staff of professors for the educational department of the college, but there devolved on him also the organization of what may be termed a "household staff" of officers—ladies and gentlemen—whose duties were the care of pupils when not engaged in school. It was also his duty to officiate in all the religious and devotional exercises of the institution, as the will of Stephen Girard, the founder of the college, prohibited the admission of clergymen within its pale. No sectarian teachings were to be introduced, and the minds of the pupils were to be kept free from denominational bias, so that when they should leave the institution by reason of their advanced age and education, they could better choose the creed which they would adopt for the future. Thus it will be seen, that there devolved on him the supervision of the school, the home, and the moral training of about five hundred boys. It was a great task, when it is considered that they embraced those ranging from the tender age of eight years to the active and impulsive youth of seventeen. How well and admirably he performed his manifold duties, how complete the satisfaction of the Directors, his long continuance in office testifies, and how well he has succeeded in gaining and keeping the respect and esteem of the numerous professors and officers of the institution is also proved by their many years of service under his administration. Last, but not least, the love and regard in which he is held by hundreds of the graduates of the institution, adds another link to the testimony, all going to show that in him the college has found a man equaled by very few and surpassed by none in his peculiar fitness for the position.

In December, 1862, he resigned the position which he had filled so acceptably for thirteen years, and retired to the walks of private life, taking up his abode on a farm on the banks of the Delaware, not far from the city. Here he remained for two years, when he received a call from the Pennsylvania Agricultural College to become its President; he accepted it, and continued in the position two years. In 1867, he was recalled to Girard College, thus receiving the most emphatic endorsement of the efficiency of his former administration. In religious belief he is a Methodist, and has been for many years a member of that church. He was honoured, in March, 1872, by being elected President of the American Bible Society, which position he continues to hold. In 1850, the year he was first inaugurated as President of Girard College, the degree of Doctor of Laws was conferred upon him by Union College, Schenectady, New York, and also by Emory and Henry College of Virginia. He has been married four times. First, in 1836, to Martha, daughter of Bishop Richardson, of Toronto, Canada; his second wife was Ellen Honora Curtin, of Bellefonte, a sister of Governor Curtin; his third, Mary Quincy, of Boston; and his fourth and present wife was, at the time of her marriage, Mrs. Anna Maria Gemmill, the widow of one of Philadelphia's most successful and highly esteemed merchants.

JOSEPH CRAIN AUDENRIED,

SON of the Hon. William Audenried, and his wife, Jane M. Wills, was born at Pottsville, Penn., November 6th, 1839. His father was a member of the State Legislature from 1822 to 1824, and of the Senate of Pennsylvania from 1824 to 1828, during which period he originated the idea of a specific fund for the support of the common schools of the state, which only failed in being brought to a successful issue, from the fact that, to quote from the press of that day, "those associated with him had not the moral courage to adopt his suggestions or carry out his proposed reforms."

His grandfather, Lewis Audenried, came to America from the Republic of Switzerland, in 1789. On his maternal side he is descended from Robert Wallace, who came to America from the county of Londonderry, Ireland, before 1738, and settled on Swatara creek, then Lancaster, now Dauphin county, in 1738. This Robert Wallace, together with the Rev. William Bertram, Hugh Wilson, and others, received from the proprietors, Thomas and John Penn, a patent for one hundred acres of land, upon which they erected the church of Derry, the first Presbyterian Church in that part of the country. This patent is recorded at Harrisburg, and is dated July 18th, 1741.

At the death of Robert Wallace, in 1783, his plantation, as it was called, passed to his son James, who had married Sarah, a daughter of the Rev. John Elder, of Paxton and Derry Church. This James Wallace served in the Revolutionary army, was appointed, in 1807, one of the first Brigadier Generals under the new Militia law; was a member of the Legislature of Pennsylvania, from 1806 to 1810, and of the Congress of the United States from 1815 to 1821.

When the Manor of Lowther, now in Cumberland county, was surveyed and divided into lots, in 1767, lot No. 4 was taken up by Moses Wallace, the eldest son of Robert Wallace, for which he paid to the proprietors, Thomas and John Penn, three hundred and eighty-one pounds, ten shillings. The warrant for this was granted in 1771, and the patent in 1774.

Moses Wallace married Jean Fulton, daughter of Richard Fulton, of the township of Paxton, in the county of Lancaster. Moses Wallace was born in 1741, and died in 1803. Jean Fulton was born in 1748, and died in 1786. They are both buried in the Paxton graveyard. Robert Wallace, born 1712, died 1783; and Mary, his wife, born 1721, died 1784, being buried in Derry Church graveyard. Out of several children born to Moses and Jean Wallace only one survived them, and this was Isabel, born 1776, who married Alexander Wills, the son of James and Mary Wills. In 1809, Alexander Wills was commissioned by Governor Snyder, as Justice of the Peace for Allen township, Cumberland county, and this office he held for nearly forty years.

They had three daughters, the eldest, Jane M., born June 8th, 1808, married the Hon. William Audenried, of Schuylkill county, Pa., the second, Rebecca Y., born January 23d, 1811, married Dr. Joseph Crain, son of Richard M. Crain, Esq., (a Captain in the War of 1812,) and grandson of Captain Ambrose Crain of the Revolutionary army. The third daughter, Caroline, born April 12th, 1817, married Dr. Matthew Semple, afterwards Professor of Chemistry in the Homœopathic College of Philadelphia.

From the marriage between Jane M. Wills and the Hon. William Audenried comes the subject of this sketch, who, in 1857, was appointed to the United States Military School at West Point, from the Congressional District of Pennsylvania embracing the counties of Cumberland, Perry and York. After a course of study of four years, he graduated at that institution June 24th, 1861, and was commissioned a Second Lieutenant in the then Fourth, now First Cavalry, but afterwards he was commissioned as First Lieutenant and Adjutant of the Sixth Cavalry, the commission dating from June 24th, 1861. The following, taken from General Cullom's biographical history of the officers and graduates of West Point, Vol. II, will give his military record: " Served in the rebellion of the seceding States, 1861–1866; in drilling volunteers at Washington, D. C., June and July, 1861; in the Manasses campaign, of July, 1861; as Aide-de-Camp to Brig. Genl. Daniel Tyler (second in command); being engaged in the action at Blackburn's Ford, July 18th, 1861; and battle of Bull Run, July 21st, 1861; in the defences of Washington, D. C., July, 1861, to March, 1862, being attached to the Second Artillery until December, 1861; as Adjutant of the Sixth United States Cavalry, December 1st, 1861, to July 21st, 1862, during which time he was detached in the Virginia Peninsular campaign (Army of the Potomac), as acting Assistant Adjutant General of the First Cavalry Brigade, from March, 1862, to July, 1862, being engaged in the siege of Yorktown, April 5th to May 4th, 1862; battle of Williamsburg, May 5th, 1862;

action of Hanover Court House, May 27th, 1862. On July 10th, 1862, he was appointed Aide-de-Camp to Major General E. V. Sumner, and promoted to the rank of Captain and additional Aide-de-Camp, August 20th, 1862. Served with General Sumner in the Maryland campaign (Army of the Potomac), September, 1862, being engaged in the battle of Antietam, September 17th, 1862, (when he was wounded, being shot through the left leg, and brevetted Captain in the regular army for gallant and meritorious services;) in the Rappahanock campaign (Army of the Potomac), December, 1862, to April, 1863; being engaged as Aide-de-Camp to General Sumner in the battle of Fredericksburg, December 13th, 1862. Major General Sumner dying in March, 1863, he was ordered to Major General John E. Wool, commanding Department of the East, New York city, and remained on his staff during the month of April, 1863, when he was ordered to report to Major General Ulysses S. Grant, then at Vicksburg, Mississippi, as Aide-de-Camp. Served with Major General Grant from June 20th, 1863, to October 1st, 1863, being engaged in the siege of Vicksburg, June 20th, 1863, to July 4th, 1863, and present at the surrender of the Confederate General Pemberton's army, at Vicksburg, July 4th, 1863.

Major General William T. Sherman being ordered from Vicksburg to the relief of the army under Major General Rosecranz, at Chattanooga, Captain Audenried was ordered to report to him for duty as Aide-de-Camp; served as Aide-de-Camp from October 3d, 1863, being engaged in the march from Memphis, Tennessee, to Chattanooga, Tennessee, October 1st to November 20th, 1863, participating in the action at Colliersville, Mississippi, October 11th, 1863; battle of Missionary Ridge, November 24th and 25th, 1863; march to the relief of Knoxville, November 28th to December 2d, 1863, and return to Chattanooga, and thence to Vicksburg, Mississippi, December, 1863, to January, 1864. Expedition to Meridian, Mississippi, February 1st to February 25th, 1864; Atlanta campaign, May to September 1st, 1864, participating in the battle of Resaca, May 14th and 15th; New Hope Church, May 25th, 28th; Kenesaw Mountain, June 20th to July 2d; Atlanta, July 22d; Atlanta, again, July 28th; Jonesboro, September 1st; and siege and capture of Atlanta, July 22d to September 1st, 1864, for which he was brevetted, September 1st, 1864, Major in the regular army for gallant and meritorious services during the Atlanta campaign.

March from Atlanta to the sea, November 14th, 1864, terminating with the capture of Savannah, December 21st, 1864. Invasion of the Carolinas, January 15th to April 26th, 1865, participating in the battles of Averysboro, March 16th, and Bentonville, March 20th and 21st, 1865. Capture of Raleigh, April 13th, and surrender of General Joseph E. Johnson's Rebel army, at Durham station, April 26th, 1865, being brevetted, March 13th, 1865, Lieutenant Colonel in the regular army for gallant and meritorious services during the Rebellion. March to Richmond and Washington, D. C., April 28th to May 24th, 1865. Stationed at Head Quarters, Military Division of the Missouri, June 27th, 1865, to March, 1869.

In 1866, Major General Sherman having been appointed Lieutenant General, Captain Audenried was promoted to the rank of Lieutenant Colonel and Aide-de-Camp on the Staff.

July 1st, 1866, he was promoted in the regular army to the rank of Captain, Sixth United States Cavalry.

Lieutenant General Sherman, having been made General of the Army, March 4th, 1869, by General U. S. Grant being elected President of the United States, Lieutenant Colonel Audenried was promoted to the rank of Colonel and Aide-de-Camp to General W. T. Sherman, and with him changed his station to Washington, D. C., March 4th, 1869, where he remained until October, 1874, when General Sherman having at his own request removed the Head Quarters of the Army to St. Louis, Mo., Colonel Audenried is now stationed there.

JOHN STEWART, ESQ.

JOHN STEWART was born February 1st, 1807, in Adams county, Pa. In 1830, he removed to Loudon, Franklin county, Pa., where, in 1832, he was married to Mary C. Scott, daughter of Thomas Scott, of that place.

Leaving Loudon, he located himself in Waynesburg, in the same county, and engaged in merchandising and contracting. Here he connected himself with the Presbyterian Church in 1844. In 1845, he received from his fellow-citizens the compliment of an election to the Legislature. The duties of this office he discharged with fidelity, and to the satisfaction of his constituents, but declined a re-election in 1846.

In 1849, Mr. Stewart removed to Weaverton, Virginia, where he was ordained an elder in the Presbyterian Church of Harper's Ferry. At this place he acted in the capacity of a contractor on the railroad, and an event that occurred indicated the strong attachment felt to him by the men in his employment. On a certain occasion a mob of wild Irish laborers turned out upon the line. Some contractors had to flee for their lives, others were beaten and wounded. When the mob reached the works of Mr. Stewart, and threatened to attack his person, one hundred of his own men rallied for his defence, alleging that every one of them must be beaten before any violence should be done to *him*.

In 1855, Mr. Stewart settled in Altoona, Pa., and the next year in Pittsburgh, where he was Passenger and Ticket Agent of the Pennsylvania and the Western Railroads until 1864. Whilst active in this capacity, an incident occurred, illustrative of the truth that "A soft answer turneth away wrath." A traveler offered western money for a ticket, and when told by Mr. Stewart that he could not take anything but bankable money, the traveler became very angry, and said, "I think you are a mean fellow." Mr. Stewart quietly answered, "You don't think half as badly of me as I do of myself; we are only known by our own spirits and by our Maker." The incensed traveler, on a little reflection, came back, apologized, said he deserved the rebuke and would endeavour to profit by it.

In 1864, Mr. Stewart removed to Philadelphia, where he is engaged in the service of the United States. He is at present an acting elder in the Tenth Presbyterian Church, (Rev. Dr. H. A. Boardman's,) and is much esteemed by all who know him as an useful and exemplary member of the community. With but limited advantages of education and fortune to start with, he has, by his energy, wisdom and integrity, made for himself a highly creditable record.

HON. DAVID SPANGLER KAUFMAN.

DAVID SPANGLER KAUFMAN was born at Boiling Springs, in Cumberland county, December 18th, 1813. As a boy he undertook to prepare himself for mercantile pursuits, but his employer* perceiving by his thoughtful expression, disposition to study, and indifference to the sale of goods, that he had talents that would qualify him for a higher sphere, advised him to fit himself for one of the learned professions.

At a very early age he entered Dickinson College as a student, and afterwards graduated at Nassau Hall, Princeton, N. J. Having studied law, he located at Natchitoches, Louisiana, and commenced the practice of his profession in 1835. In 1841, he was married to Miss Jane Richardson. After Gen. Houston had obtained possession and established his right to Texas, about 1842, Mr. Kaufman had a meeting called at Natchitoches, offered the first resolution in favour of annexation, and delivered a strong speech in favour of that project. Houston, having been wounded at the battle of San Jacinto, came to New Orleans to recruit his health, and finding Kaufman's resolution and speech in the newspapers, he sent for him to come to that city, and on his arrival, made him his room-mate. Soon he prevailed on his young friend to return to Natchitoches, settle up his business, and go with him to Texas.

The government of Texas was soon established, and Kaufman was elected to the first Texas Legislature. Having served as Speaker of that body for three successive years, he was elected to the Senate of the state. During his career as Senator he was sent to New York to assist in arranging the code of laws for the state. About 1846 he was appointed minister to Washington, but when he arrived there the action of Congress upon the annexation resolutions had progressed so far that he could not be received in this character or capacity. These resolutions having passed, he returned to Texas, became a candidate for the United States Congress, and although he had six competitors, received more votes than all of them together. He took his seat in the House of Representatives in 1848, was re-elected in 1850, and again in 1852.

Soon after Mr. Kaufman had located in Texas, he was made a

---

*Maj. David Nevin, of Shippensburg.

Major in the army, and as the Indians were committing depredations along the border, it became necessary to drive them back. In an engagement of the forces which Major Kaufman commanded against nine hundred Indians, he received a wound which at first was supposed to be mortal. A ball entered his mouth and passed out near the left ear. About this time S. Rhodes Fisher, who was Secretary of the Navy, made a cruise at sea, and having committed some unlawful acts, was dismissed from office by the President. It required the concurrence of the Senate to effect his discharge. The Secretary employed Rusk, Lamar & Wharton, a legal firm of eminent ability, for his defence. The President (Houston) employed Major Kaufman on the part of the government, and in the earnest contest he was triumphant. A copy of his argument, published in the Texas *Chronicle* from which some interesting extracts might have been made, was sent to A. D. Kaufman, Esq., of Chambersburg, but unfortunately, it, with other correspondence from which other valuable historical details might have been gleaned, was consumed when that town was burned.

Major Kaufman was above medium size, and of prepossessing appearance and gentlemanly bearing. He was possessed of a very vigorous intellect and marked energy of character. His popularity in Texas was very great. As a token of respect a large and flourishing town in that state was named after him. The writer well remembers of being told by him in a confidential conversation in Washington, that he could easily have secured Gen. Houston's seat in the United States Senate, but could not think of doing so on account of his respect for the old General, and the friendly relations existing between them. A brilliant prospect seemed to open up before Major Kaufman, which was suddenly blasted by the dark shadow of death. Whilst occupying his seat in the National Hall of Representatives, in the full enjoyment of his usual health, he was taken suddenly ill, repaired at once to the hotel at which his family were boarding and expired in less than an hour. At his decease he had four children, two of whom are still living—a son and a daughter.

JOHN CUSTIS RICHARDS, M. D.

JOHN CUSTIS RICHARDS was born in Baltimore, Maryland, June 1st, 1812. His ancestry were of Welsh origin.

His grandfather was the Rev. Lewis Richards, of Glamorganshire, Wales, who was sent to this country about the latter part of the last century by Lady Huntington, as a missionary. He was married in Virginia to a Miss Custis; and from his maternal grandparent, the subject of this article derived his name. His father was John Custis Richards, an esteemed merchant of Baltimore, who died at an advanced age.

Dr. Richards was reared with all the advantages that superior social position could secure, and in the year 1825, when thirteen years old, was sent to the Academy at Belle Air, an institution of learning then with a reputation second to none, in charge of Rev. R. H. Davis, and was more extensively patronized and held a higher reputation than any other institution of its class in Maryland, the largest number of its students being from Baltimore. The discipline was rigidly strict; the course of instruction systematic, thorough and exacting in details; and it has been said "that the student who had passed with approval through his Greek, Latin and Mathematical studies under Reuben H. Davis, need have feared no other ordeal in those particular branches." After remaining at this institution nearly five years, he next entered a preparatory school at Burlington, N. J., where he remained six months prior to entering Yale College, where he matriculated in 1830, entering the Sophomore class. During his junior year, about eighteen months after his entrance, he was called home by the extreme illness of his mother and brother, who shortly after his return died. Being the only surviving member of a large family his father could not part with him again, and he entered at once upon the study of his chosen profession in the office of Dr. Samuel Baker, who was Professor of Anatomy in the Medical University of Maryland.

He graduated in medicine in the spring of 1834, receiving his degree from the Medical University of Maryland, one of the leading institutions in the country, the several chairs being filled by Professors Robley Dunglison, Elisha Geddings, Samuel Baker and other no less gifted and talented colleagues. Immediately after his graduation he opened an office in Baltimore for the practice of his profession and was successful to a marked degree, being connected with the hospitals there, and having served as Dispensary Physician for two years. But all his tastes and inclinations were opposed to the confining life of a city physician and he accepted the opening offered in Chambersburg, and he came there in June, 1837, much to the regret of all his friends in Maryland, but he never regretted his choice and the step he then took.

His personal accomplishments and professional skill soon won the regard of the community in which he settled, and he rapidly acquired an extensive and lucrative practice, which embraced a large portion of the affluent and influential families of the town and surrounding country. He was successful in an eminent degree and his reputation was most creditable and widespread, attracting to him from a distance the afflicted in great numbers. A gentleman of the old school, he was utterly incapable of a mean or dishonorable action. In every department of life he so comported himself as to win the esteem and confidence of all. Ever attentive, watchful and patient in his ministrations as a physician, he carried with him into the chamber of sickness an atmosphere of cheerfulness and sunshine that often robbed disease of half its terrors.

A self-reliant practitioner, deliberate, he was always careful in his diagnosis, and orthodox in his treatment, always prompt to the call of duty, a model of self-sacrificing devotion to his profession. In his consultations and intercourse with physicians, he was a careful observer of the ethics of the profession, conservative and scrupulous in the treatment of his medical friends, and never taking any advantage by word or act. And if at any time any unpleasant remarks were made in his presence, against any professional brother, if he was unable to make a defence he was never the man to condemn. He was held in no less esteem as a citizen and neighbour; he was always ready to extend a helping hand to the needy.

Dr. Richards was twice married, and left a widow, three daughters, and a son, to deplore his loss and revere his memory. As a husband and father he was kind, indulgent and loving to a degree that made his home happy and cheerful to all its inmates. His large and varied experience in life, and retentive memory, enabled him to draw upon a fund of reminiscence and anecdote which his rare conversational powers fitted him to delineate in a manner that rendered his companionship agreeable to all.

Dr. S. G. Lane, writing of him, says: "Dr. Richards was a notable man in many respects. He was remarkably handsome, his fine physique was developed and invigorated by athletic training in his youth, and by field sports which he enjoyed throughout his life; he was a splendid type of elastic strength. Added to his fine presence were rare graces of address and demeanour, courtesy, affability, refinement; all the pleasing traits which constitute the gentleman. His disposition was kind and affectionate; he was warmly attached to his friends; of a gentle, forbearing temperament, averse to contentions and controversies, yet compelling respect. Dr. Richards was a higher style of man still; he was a faithful Christian, a full member of the Falling Spring Presbyterian Church. In the public progress, and in the limited movements of the community about him, he took an active interest. During the rebellion his heart was loyal to the goverment, and his sympathies and anxieties were keenly enlisted in the cause of the Union and freedom."

The burning of Chambersburg, by the rebels, July 30th, 1864, swept from him the accumulation of many years of severe toil, but what he most regretted was the loss of a large and valuable library. He, with a number of other prominent citizens, was seized by the rebel commander and held as a hostage for the production of the immense sum demanded as a ransom, with threats to carry them to Richmond, and burn every house in the town if his demands were not acceded to; the demand being indignantly refused, the hostages were not released until after the town had been set on fire. When he reached his house it was already in flames, and everything in it destroyed. He was not able to secure even a memento, and only escaped from the burning town at the greatest personal peril.

Frequently during the war he rendered efficient service to the sick and wounded. He was the surgeon in charge of a hospital at Chambersburg for some time in the early part of the war, and received appointment upon the staff of the Surgeon General in 1863, as one of the Volunteer Aid Corps of Surgeons of Pennsylvania.

He was one of the organizers of the first Medical Society formed in Franklin county, about the year 1854, and was one of its most active and zealous workers. He was also one of the organizers of the present Medical Society, in whose deliberations he always took an active part, rarely being absent from its meetings, having acted as presiding officer and was always ready to advocate any measure for the advance of the medical profession.

Toward the close of his life, failing health and frequent disappointments, acting on a temperament extremely nervous, had rendered him somewhat reserved in general society. But those who knew him, knew that he had a warm heart, and that he loved to do good to all who came within the circle of his affections. He continued in active practice until the day he took his bed, but a few weeks before his death, which occurred June 11th, 1874.

At a meeting of the Medical Society of Franklin county, held July 7th, 1874, Dr. John Montgomery, who had long held most intimate personal and professional relations with Dr. Richards, was appointed to prepare a sketch of his life and character, to be read before the Society, and for publication in the transactions of the State Medical Society. This sketch we have great pleasure in transferring to our pages, presenting, as it does, a faithful record of the eminent and useful career of one whose memory will long be cherished with the warmest affection by those who had the privilege of enjoying his personal friendship, and with high esteem and great respect by all those who love the noble profession to which he belonged.

"Many of us," says Dr. Montgomery, at the conclusion of his sketch, "have been his pupils, and we long to pay a tribute of love and homage to the memory of our beloved preceptor. He was for many years one of us, and we take pride in transmitting to future members of the Society our keen appreciation of his manifold gifts and graces. His labours are closed, and his work among us is finished. How honourably he sustained the cares of life! When the summons comes to us, may our eyes close in death like his, and our dying pillow be as easy."

BREVET MAJOR GEN. WASHINGTON L. ELLIOTT, U. S. A.

THE subject of this sketch, son of Commodore Jesse D. Elliott, U. S. N., was born at Carlisle, Pa., March 31st, 1825. He was a student at Dickinson College until June, 1841, when he was appointed a cadet to the United States Military Academy. Commissioned Second Lieutenant of a mounted Rifle Regiment, May 27th, 1846, he served in Mexico during part of the war, and was promoted to a first Lietenancy, July 20th, 1847.

From May, 1849, until October, 1851, Lieutenant Elliott served at Fort Laramie on the Oregon Route. From February, 1852, until January, 1856, he was on duty in Texas, having been promoted Captain, July 20th, 1854, and from October, 1856, until November, 1860, he was on duty in New Mexico. During the past eleven years he has been engaged in service among the Indians, having had several skirmishes and fights with the Camanches, Kiowas, several tribes of Apaches and Navajoes.

In April, 1861, Captain Elliott was engaged in the muster into service of volunteers of the state of New York, at Elmira. From June to September, in the same year, he was on duty with the command of General Nathaniel Lyon, in southwest Missouri. In September, 1861, he was commissioned as Colonel of the Second Iowa Volunteer Cavalry, and in November of the same year, Major of the First United States Cavalry.

Major Elliott participated in the operations of General Pope's Army at New Madrid and Island No. 10, in March and April, 1862. In the following month he participated in the siege of Corinth, Miss., in command of Second Brigade, Cavalry Division, Army of the Mississippi, composed of Second Iowa and Second Michigan Cavalry; he made the first cavalry raid of the Rebellion, on the communications of General Beauregard, south of Corinth, near Booneville, Miss., destroying a large amount of Rebel property, and cutting off, for the use of our own army, a large number of locomotives and cars. June 11th, 1862, he was promoted Brigadier General of volunteers, and participated in the second battle of Bull Run, as Chief of Cavalry, Army of Virginia, in which battle he was slightly wounded. In September and October, 1862, he was assigned to the duty of organizing cavalry for protection of the frontiers of Nebraska and Dakota.

In March, 1863, General Elliott was assigned to the command of a Brigade in Shenandoah Valley, Virginia, and left at Maryland Heights to evacuate that place and remove property to Washington, D. C. On the completion of this work, he was assigned to the command of Third Division, Third Corps, Army of the Potomac. October, 1863, he was transferred to the Army of the Cumberland, commanded by Major General George H. Thomas, and assigned to the command of the cavalry of that army, consisting of four divisions. He participated in the operations in east Tennessee, for the relief of General Burnside, at Knoxville, during the winter of 1863-4; also in the campaign from May to September, 1864, resulting in the capture of Atlanta, December 2d, 1864. He was assigned to the command of Second Division, Fourth Army Corps, of the Army of the Cumberland, and participated in the battles of Nashville, December 15th and 16th, 1864, under command of General George H. Thomas, for which he was brevetted Major General.

August 31st, 1866, he was promoted Lieutenant Colonel, First United States Cavalry, and served in Oregon, Washington and Idaho Territories. During the Rebellion he served under the following Generals, from each of whom he received complimentary letters and recommendations to the War Department, viz: Majors General Pope, Rosecrans, Schenck, French, Thomas, together with endorsement of the latter by General W. T. Sherman. He is now in charge of Benicia Barracks, California.

Such is a succinct record of the public life of General Elliott. His steady advancement to higher positions is all the evidence that is needed that his career has been one eminently honourable to himself, gratifying to his friends, and creditable to his native valley.

COLONEL ALEXANDER KELLY McCLURE.

COLONEL A. K. McCLURE was born in Perry county, Pa., January 9th, 1828, of Scotch-Irish descent.
He is emphatically self educated. When fifteen years of age, he was apprenticed to the tanning trade. In three years, his term of indenture having expired, he commenced life as a journeyman, and, in the pursuit of his calling, during the year 1846, he traveled through Pennsylvania, New York, and New England, adding to his store of learning. The world was his teacher, and so apt was he to receive its lessons, that in the fall of the same year he removed to his native county, and boldly embarked in the avocation of a newspaper publisher. He established, at Mifflin, the *Juniata Sentinel*, and while devoting his mental abilities to its editorial management, he also practised and mastered the mysteries of the printer's art, and in one year became so conversant with the practical working of the composing room as to be able to turn out a paper, the work of his own brains and hands. Thus, before reaching his twentieth year, he had learned two practical trades, and was an editor well versed in local politics.

Upon his twenty-first birthday, Mr. McClure received a commission as aid from the then Governor, William F. Johnston, with the rank and title of Colonel. He was appointed in 1850, Deputy United States Marshal for Juniata county. In 1852, he became the proprietor and publisher of the *Chambersburg Repository*, which he enlarged and improved, greatly increasing its circulation and making it one of the most influential journals in the state. In 1853, being then but twenty-five years of age, he was nominated by the Whig party for the office of Auditor General, but was defeated. By Governor Pollock, in 1855, he was appointed Superintendent of Public Printing, but after holding the position for eight months, he resigned, and the same year was admitted to the bar, and commenced the practice of the law in Chambersburg, entering into partnership with his former preceptor, William McClelland.

In 1856, Col. McClure received from Governor Pollock the appointment of Superintendent of the Erie and Northeast Railroad, troubles in connection with this road having caused several riots and much mischief for a year previous, in the city of Erie. He directed his energies to the settlement of these difficulties, and finally succeeded in adjusting

affairs to the satisfaction of all concerned. The same year he served as a delegate to the National Republican Convention, and canvassed the state in behalf of its nominees, Fremont and Dayton. He was one of the few Republicans elected to the Legislature in 1857; the district which he represented had previously invariably given a majority against his party. As a representative, he was prominent, and exerted his influence in favour of the sale of the public works, and in aiding the construction of the Erie Railroad. He was re-elected in 1858; and in 1859, after a most exciting contest, he succeeded, as State Senator, an opponent who was deemed invulnerable. In 1860, he was appointed Chairman of the Republican State Central Committee, and arranged a complete organization in every county, township, and precinct in the state. At that time, he was prominently mentioned for United States Senator, but declined to be a candidate.

During the war, as Chairman of the Committee on Military Affairs, while in the State Senate, Col. McClure was most earnest in his support of the National and State Governments. From his place in the Senate house, he introduced war measures of substantial importance. In 1862, he was commissioned an Assistant Adjutant General of the United States Army, in order to qualify him for the military duty of enforcing the draft in Pennsylvania. After making the draft, thereby placing seventeen regiments in the field, he resigned his commission, This service he performed at the special request of President Lincoln and Secretary of War Stanton.

Col. McClure declined, in 1863, the Chairmanship of the Republican State Central Committee, but exerted his best efforts during the campaign to secure the re-election of Governor Curtin. A delegate to the Republican National Convention in 1864, he was formally tendered by three-fourths of the delegates the Chairmanship of the State Committee, but this he declined, in order to accept the nomination for the Legislature from a new and strongly Democratic district. He was elected by four hundred majority. In October of the same year, at the request of President Lincoln, he actively engaged in perfecting the political organization of the state for the following November's Presidential election. The July previous, the southern army under Lee, in its invasion of Pennsylvania, had entirely destroyed all his property near Chambersburg, inflicting a loss of $75,000.

The summer of 1867, for the benefit of the health of his wife and son, he spent in the Rocky Mountains. Upon his return he published in book form his impressions of the new territories. He then decided to reside permanently in Philadelphia, and resumed the practice of law.

He was Chairman of the Pennsylvania Delegation in the National Republican Convention that nominated General Grant for President, and strongly pressed the claims of Governor Curtin for the Vice Presidency. His labours in behalf of the Republican nominees were extensive and valuable during that campaign; he thoroughly canvassed the states of Pennsylvania, Connecticut, Rhode Island and Massachusetts. After the Presidential contest of 1868, in order to recruit both his health and finances, which had suffered much during his ten years of incessant political labour, he decided to withdraw from active participation in party affairs, and to devote his attention to his profession. In 1872, he was again called to the front as the candidate of the Independent Reform party, was elected to the State Senate from the Fourth District of Philadelphia. He was excluded from his seat by false returns, but he contested the matter with his usual energy and success, obtaining on March 27th a decision in his favour. He was Chairman of the Pennsylvania Delegation at the Cincinnati Convention which nominated Greeley and Brown, and was also Chairman of the Liberal Republican State Committee of Pennsylvania during the Presidential contest of 1872.

He was married February 10th, 1852, to Miss Matilda S. Grey. His record is indeed that of a busy life, in which the characteristics of the Scotch-Irish blood may be easily traced. Hard work, hard words or self sacrifices have never daunted him. An acknowledged leader, he has ever been found at the front. As a public speaker, lecturer, or legal advocate, he can at all times command the attention of an audience, and he is strong in his powers to convince. His prepared speeches, carefully digested, have always been remarkable for the soundness of their arguments, and the power of eloquence and earnestness with which they have been delivered. He is a ready and able debater, never failing to impress his hearers. Intimate with, and his valuable services acknowledged by, men high in power, he could have held many offices of great emolument had he sought them; but he has never permitted his name to be used in connection with any such position, his only desire in obtaining and retaining office seeming to be to secure the "greatest good for the greatest number." He is now the editor of *The Times*, a daily paper published in Philadelphia, and conducted with marked tact and ability.

RICHARD ALEXANDER F. PENROSE, M. D., LL. D.

THE subject of this sketch was born in Carlisle, Pennsylvania, March 24th, 1827, the second son of Hon. Charles B. and Valeria Fullerton Penrose. His father was distinguished for brilliancy of intellect, energy of character, and vivacity and urbanity of manner; his mother, for intelligence and great moral excellence.

Most of the early part of Richard's education was received at Dickinson College, where he graduated with the degree of A. B., in July, 1846. Soon after this he matriculated at the Medical Department of the University of Pennsylvania, where he attended lectures, graduating with distinction and receiving the degree of M. D., in March, 1849. In a little time he was elected Resident Physician of the Pennsylvania Hospital, which position he faithfully filled for three years. He began the practice of medicine in Philadelphia, in April, 1853. He rose rapidly to professional eminence, and very soon few practitioners had a more extended practice, or held a more enviable position among the most respected and wealthy families of the city. The wards of the Philadelphia Hospital (which had been closed for a number of years to the profession) were opened to medical instructions in 1854, mainly through his influence and energy, aided by several other energetic and rising medical men. About the same time, he was elected Consulting Physician to the institution, and commenced his clinical lectures on diseases of women and children. Here it was that Dr. Penrose first distinguished himself as a medical teacher, by his clear elucidation of truth. It was his custom to introduce numerous illustrative cases, selected from the wards he was instrumental in having opened, and he endeavoured to strengthen the effect of his description by the exhibition of the very patient before the student.

In 1856, Dr. Penrose was one of the founders of the Children's Hospital of Philadelphia, contributing to its success much of his time, energy, and pecuniary resources. He was for a number of years a very successful private teacher of medicine. His private course of lectures on Obstetrics was so concise and practical, that many young men about to enter into the profession, were attracted by the forcible way he had of putting things. He was even at this time a fluent and accurate speaker, and when under the impulse of high principle or strong feeling, was often really eloquent, attracting the fixed attention

of the students, and carrying their whole sympathy along with him. No
detailed account of the mode and spirit of his instruction could with
propriety here be given. Suffice it to say, that he always proposed to
the students a very high standard of medical attainment, warned them
against the dreadful evils of professional ignorance, pointed out with
paternal wisdom and kindness the temptations and perils which beset
the physician, and the snares into which so many are entrapped, and
especially medical men who are not firm in their moral convictions.
These, and kindred lessons, he instilled into the minds of his pupils,
not less by example than by precept. He was before them from year
to year, a model of the accomplishments, duties and responsibilities he
inculcated. In his social relations in the class-room with the students,
every one could see the beautiful harmony between his teachings and his
life, and learn how solicitous he was to make those under his tuition
not only able practitioners, but useful citizens, and good men. His
views on all the subjects which engaged his attention were clear, comprehensive, and of a salutary tendency, and in this mould he laboured
to fashion the character of the students under his care.

Appreciating his marked merit as a private teacher, the Trustees of
the University of Pennsylvania, in 1863, elected Dr. Penrose to the
Professorship of Obstetrics and Diseases of Women and Children,
lately made vacant by the resignation of the illustrious and beloved
Professor Hugh L. Hodge. As a lecturer, Dr. Penrose is dignified,
graceful and affectionate, but the pouring out unreservedly all that he
thinks and feels constitutes the chief charm of his professional instruction. His system of treatment in his peculiar branch is principally
original, and on this account his teaching mainly consists of vivid
pictures of his experience, in which the pupil is enabled to see the
very events as they pass, and to see them, too, with the trained eyes of
their Professor. His lectures become in fact to his pupils a sort of
experience of their own. Through them there frequently runs a vein
of good nature, enlivened with touches of humour, which adds much to
their attractiveness, and renders their impression more permanent.
Notwithstanding his busy life, he has contributed various medical
papers to the journals, all characteristic of his practical turn, and each
written with his usual gracefulness, facility, and extraordinary clearness and force.

Dr. Penrose is a gentleman of culture, strong convictions, and great
decision of character. He possesses powers of quick and accurate
observation, and a sound, cautious judgment. He is a faithful friend,
a man true to his calling, honourable in all things, conscientious and

upright in his profession. Towards the sick his deportment is most happy. The cheering smile with which he accosts his patients, his soothing kindness, his sympathy, his encouraging and confident manner while there is ground for hope, remain indelibly impressed on many grateful hearts in the city of his residence. He is scrupulously careful never to violate professional confidence.

By his professional brethren Dr. Penrose is regarded as notably skilful in diagnosis, and perhaps in no respect does he appear to greater advantage than in his relations with medical men. It is one of his maxims, that no physician can have a satisfactory professional standing, who disregards the good will and good opinion of his fellow-practitioners. Being himself in every sense a gentleman, he is strictly obedient to the code of medical ethics. He is often consulted by patients from great distances in obscure and difficult cases, and very often is called in consultation by other practitioners. He has none of those petty jealousies which would lead him to fear a rival in any person with whom he may be associated in attendance, nor of the arrogant self-esteem which owns no fallibility of judgment. Towards the junior members of the profession he always conducts himself in a manner calculated to win their affection as well as their respect. Instead of affecting or assuming any superiority, he takes them by the hand as young brothers, and is ever gratified with an opportunity of promoting their interests and aiding their professional advancement.

In 1875, Dickinson College conferred upon Dr. Penrose the degree of LL. D. This title reflects creditably on his professional status, and literary attainments. When we consider his character and ability, the important stations he *has* filled and *now* fills, the variety and magnitude of his labours, and the numerous powerful agencies he sets in motion by his sound instruction in the science of Obstetrics, it is not easy to measure the influence he exerts, and will exert upon the world. For many years he has been engaged in training and educating medical men. Many thousand doctors have been brought, for a longer or shorter period of time, under the joint instruction of himself and colleagues. To estimate aright the useful results of such a life, one must be able to gather up the results of *theirs*, to trace out the influence of this army of co-laborers in the medical profession, one by one, and then their influence again in all the forms in which influence radiates. Thus only can we estimate properly the great good of a sound, judicious, and practical teacher, whose experience and attainments are ever augmenting the stream of human happiness.

DAVID FLAVEL WOODS, M. D.

THE subject of this sketch, a son of Richard and Mary Jane (Sterrett) Woods, was born in Dickinson township, near Carlisle, Cumberland county, Pa.

When about twelve years of age, he was sent to board with his uncle, the Rev. David Sterrett, at McVeytown, Pa., where he might have the advantage of the academy as a preparation for entering college. In due course of time he entered the Sophomore Class in Dickinson College, Carlisle, and graduated at that institution in 1859.

Soon after leaving college, young Woods entered the banking house of Bell, Garrettson & Co., at Huntingdon. Not finding this business congenial to his taste, or furnishing a sufficiently large scope for his educational attainments, at his earnest solicitation his father sent him to Philadelphia to study medicine under Drs. Levis, Hunt and Penrose.

Having pursued his studies for three years, and attended the lectures at the University of Pennsylvania, he graduated at this celebrated school of medicine in 1862. Shortly after this, he was elected Resident Physician to Blockley Hospital, which position he filled for one year, when he was elected Resident Physician to the Episcopal Hospital for eighteen months.

In April, 1865, Dr. Woods opened an office for practice at 107 South Thirteenth Street. About the same time he was associated with Drs. Boardman and Black in the instruction of medical students in the different branches taught in connection with the University of Pennsylvania. He was a successful teacher and practitioner of medicine, and very soon acquired a large practice. In September, 1869, he removed from Thirteenth Street to 151 North Fifteenth Street. The following October he married Helen R. Stewart, daughter of B. D. Stewart, Esq., of Philadelphia. In 1872, he gave up the instruction of students, his practice having grown so large as to require most of his time.

Dr. Woods has been highly prospered in his profession. He was elected Surgeon to the Dispensary Staff of the Episcopal Hospital, and Visiting Physician to the Presbyterian Hospital in Philadelphia, and still continues to perform the duties connected with this latter institution. He is also a member of the College of Physicians of Philadelphia, and of the Pathological Society of the same city.

During his academical career, Dr. Woods connected himself with the Presbyterian Church at McVeytown, and has ever since honoured his profession of faith by a consistent life. He is yet in the prime of life, and apparently has a very bright future of usefulness and eminence before him. Though of a modest and retiring disposition, his sterling professional worth, instead of being concealed, grows rapidly in the public estimation. Dr. R. A. F. Penrose, his preceptor and personal friend, pays to him the following deserved tribute: "Dr. Woods possesses to a marked degree the peculiar qualities of his race, (Scotch-Irish Presbyterian,) energy, self-reliance and intelligence, controlled, as in him, by a religious conscientiousness as beautiful as it is rare. All these traits enter into and make his professional character, and the result has been, that no man in Philadelphia has risen more rapidly to professional eminence than he. An enthusiastic worker and learner in the arduous and ever advancing science of medicine, he brings to his patients not only knowledge and experience, but an unselfish devotion to their welfare which seldom is met with. Firm in his convictions, he holds them tenaciously and defends them with force and marked ability. In fine, we have in the character of Dr. Woods, honesty, truth, reliability. As a *man*, he is thoroughly *manly;* as a *physician*, learned, popular, successful; as a Christian, one who tries to resemble his Divine Master."

MAJOR JOHN M. POMEROY.

JOHN M. POMEROY was born in Shippensburg, Pennsylvania, on the 1st of April, 1823. The name and family are of Norman origin, Pomeroy, in French, signifying royal apple. For several generations his parentage has been Scotch-Irish, so that there is little of the Huguenot remaining except the name. His earliest ancestor, to whom his origin can be clearly traced, was a classical teacher in the family of a nobleman in Paris, who, being a Protestant or Huguenot, effected his escape from the French Capital, on the night of the massacre of St. Bartholomew. He was aided in effecting his escape by one of his pupils, the daughter of his patron, and he succeeded in getting on board a fishing vessel on the coast, and reaching Ireland in safety. This young lady soon afterwards joined him in Ireland, and they were married. A descendant of this couple, Thomas Pomeroy, a merchant of moderate means in Liverpool, England, immigrated when a young man to America, and located among the earliest settlers of Cumberland valley, about the year 1730, in Lurgan township, Cumberland, now Franklin, county. Some of his descendants have continued to reside there continuously until the present time, the late Judge Thomas Pomeroy, of Roxbury, having been a member of the fourth, and the subject of this sketch of the fifth generation, from the original settler.

Both the parents of Major Pomeroy having died in his childhood, his uncle, the late Honourable Joseph Pomeroy, took charge of him at Concord, Franklin county, where he grew to manhood. After acquiring a fair academic education, his uncle trained him to mercantile pursuits, and made him his partner in business at the age of nineteen. He was a young man of mark and influence in his own locality before he attained his majority, as was shown by the unusual event of his having been elected a school director before he was a voter, the citizens of his township being fully aware of his minority; by his having been made executor of an important estate while yet a minor; and by his having settled several cases of litigation by his skill and dexterity as a land surveyor. When twenty-two years of age he was elected to the Legislature from Franklin county, and was re-elected the following year. The position was then one of honour and distinction, the office seeking the man, rather than the man seeking the office.

In 1853, Major Pomeroy removed to Philadelphia, where he continued in mercantile pursuits until 1860.

In 1859, he represented the Tenth Ward of the city in Common Council. In 1860, he represented the Second Congressional District of Philadelphia in the National Republican Convention, at Chicago, Illinois, and supported the nomination of Abraham Lincoln for the Presidency. At the breaking out of the war, in 1861, President Lincoln appointed him a Paymaster in the army, which position he filled for two years with zeal and fidelity, when he resigned. He disbursed several millions of dollars in small sums to the soldiers, and at the settlement of his accounts with the government, there was found to be a balance due him of thirty-two dollars, which was an exceptional case with disbursing officers, although few, comparatively, proved to be defaulters.

In 1865, Major Pomeroy having acquired some property in Chester county, Pennsylvania, located upon it, and became identified with railroad enterprises in eastern Pennsylvania and Delaware. The Pennsylvania and Delaware Railroad, running from Pomeroy, (named after him,) on the Pennsylvania Railroad, to Delaware City, Delaware, was built mainly through his efforts. In August, 1874, he became the editor and proprietor of the Franklin Repository, at Chambersburg, Pennsylvania, which he is now conducting with much ability. He is warm in his attachments, earnest in his nature, active in his habits, and as a politician, exerts a marked influence upon public opinion, by his consistency, dignity, decision and unfaltering devotion to his principles.

A. H. SENSENY, M. D.

DR. ABRAHAM H. SENSENY is eminently entitled to mention among the remarkable men of the valley. For forty years he has been actively engaged in the practice of medicine at his native place, and has won a reputation for professional skill wide as the state.

The Doctor comes from a stock of noted physicians. His grandfather, Abraham Senseny, went to Chambersburg from New Holland, Lancaster county, in 1781, and practised in the former place until he was smitten to death by apoplexy, February, 1844, when he had nearly completed his eighty-third year. For a period of two years he was the only physician in the village. He was highly esteemed in the community for his abilities and his amiable disposition. In the year 1809, Dr. Jeremiah Senseny, son of Abraham, commenced the practice in his birthplace, and continued in the service until his death on the 6th of August, 1863, aged 75 years. He enjoyed a fine reputation, and did a larger business than any of his contemporaries. During the late war with England, he volunteered twice. He marched with Captain Reges' Company, on the way to the northern frontiers, as far as Meadville, when he was selected assistant to the Surgeon-in-Chief, but was obliged to resign soon after on account of ill health. In 1814, he re-enlisted and went to Baltimore in the company of Captain Finley. He was a man of vigorous constitution, strong mental powers and great kindness of heart.

Dr. Abraham H. Senseny, of whom we propose to furnish a brief sketch, is the son of Jeremiah, and was born in Chambersburg, February, 1811, and was brought up and educated there, receiving the usual classical education afforded in first rate country academies.

Graduating in Medicine at Jefferson Medical College in 1835, he began the active practice of his profession the same year. At once, he inherited an extensive business, which his splendid ability increased and has retained until the present day. We have no doubt that he has had a larger and more varied experience than any physician who has ever practised in his neighbourhood. For more than forty weary years, he has laboured with scarce a relaxation, practising all the branches of his profession, adding lustre to the family name, which, for almost one hundred years has been renowned in the medical annals of Franklin county.

Too busy in ministrations to the sick to give much time to composition, he has nevertheless contributed occasionally to medical periodicals, is an habitual reader of new medical publications, and somehow finds leisure hours for the perusal of leading works in literature, for which he has a decided taste. By a rare faculty of mental endosmosis—to borrow a word from the science—he absorbs the leading points in a book, which a singularly retentive and well trained memory presents for ready use. A record of the interesting forms of disease which have come under his observation would be a treasure to the profession, and would rank high as a treatise in clinical medicine. In every respect he is competent to the task, being a discriminating observer, a judicious therapeutist, and a clear and expressive writer.

The peculiar characteristics of Dr. Senseny are quickness and acuteness of perception, promptness of action, and unwearying energy. With intuition he perceives the nature of a disease, and with great rapidity brings his resources to bear upon its relief.

The Doctor is eminently a social personage, of strong attachments and prepossessions. In the care of the seriously sick, he is all gentleness and affection, but emphatic and positive to the querulous and intermeddling. No member of his community is more quoted for racy anecdotes, and quaint and pungent sayings. His great reputation fills his rooms with patients, takes him long journeys from home in consultations, and draws numbers of students to his office.

Three of his sons have entered the profession; the eldest, William D. Senseny, M. D., a youth of rare virtues, a few months after completing his course, died from a rapid illness, contracted from a too severe application to his studies; the remaining two, Dr. B. Rush and Edgar N., survive, and we hope will transmit the medical fame of their ancestry unsullied to future historians.

HON. ALEXANDER THOMSON.

AMONG the men who, by force of character and purity of life, have exerted a lasting influence upon the people and the prosperity of the Cumberland valley, we cannot omit to mention the Hon. Alexander Thomson. He was a descendant of one of the early settlers upon the Conococheague, in Franklin county, about five miles from Chambersburg. Alexander Thomson, his grandfather, emigrated from Scotland in 1771, embarking from Greenock with his wife and twelve children, and arriving in Boston in September of that year. He was a farmer, and his sturdy character may be gathered from the perusal of a long letter written by him in August, 1773, to a friend in Scotland, from his farm which he called "Corkerhill," after the name of his ancestral home. He states that he wished to settle two of his sons upon farms in Scotland, and that for five years he looked around for such as would answer their purpose. He says: "I traveled through the country for twenty miles around the place where I lived, but, though I found plenty of vacant farms, I told you before and I declare it again on the word of an honest man, that I could see no farm for which the laird did not ask more than double the rent it was worth, so that if I had meddled with any of them I saw well that my sons would not be able to pay the rent, and that in three or four years I would not have one shilling to rub upon another. After I had spent so much time and labour to no purpose I confess that at length I conceived a sort of distaste for the lairds."

The spirit and sentiments which actuated the Scotch emigrants of whom Alexander Thomson was a noble type, are best gathered by further extracts which we proceed to make from this letter. After having given an account of the selection of his farm and its improvements, he goes on to say: "This is the best poor man's country in the world, for the price of provisions is cheap and the price of labour is dear. * * * * The richest soil in all North America is on the rivers Ohio and Mississippi, and I intended to have gone and settled there at first but my wife did not incline to go so far back at that time, and that was the reason I made a purchase so soon and did not take Dr. Witherspoon's advice; but I made the purchase on the road that leads to the Ohio river, and, as I am told, I am just 150 miles from Fort Pitt; as soon as we have this plantation put into some order, I

Alex. Thomson

and one of my sons will go back and take up a large tract for the rest of my children. * * * * We are in no fear that any harm will be done us by the Indians. I have seen many of them, and by all that I can hear, they are a harmless people except they be offended or wronged. I hope we shall not have any bickerings with them, but it would not be a small number of enemies that would terrify us or even those about Fort Pitt, for besides a well trained militia we all have guns in our hands, for there is no disarming act or game act as with you. * * * * We have the privilege of choosing our ministers, schoolmasters, constables and all other parish officers, for laying and collecting all necessary assessments. In our law courts the poor are in no danger of being browbeaten and borne down by the rich. With respect to our laws, they are made by those who are not nominally only but really our representatives, for without any bribes or pensions they are chosen by ourselves, and every freeholder has a vote. * * * I might write to you at large about the religious liberty which is enjoyed in this province in the most extensive manner."

The daring enterprise, courage and self-reliance, the respect for the rights of the poor, and the reverence for law, the love of freedom, and the independent thought which are here revealed, are the characteristics of the Scotch and Scotch-Irish which have made so lasting an impress upon our republican government. These men and their descendants, it is perhaps not too much to say, had more to do than any other equal number of men, not only in moulding, but in sustaining both in the field and in the cabinet, and making successful, the American Republic.

It is not surprising that Alexander Thomson's "distaste for the lairds" should drive the sturdy Cameronian farmer from Scotland to America, and that the first man with whom he found himself in conference as to his future plans and prospects was Dr. John Witherspoon, at Princeton, the Presbyterian preacher, who a few years afterwards enrolled his name among the Signers of the Declaration of Independence. The letter from which we have quoted discloses a character which would be in full sympathy with one who, at that time, was helping to give form and direction to the growing sentiment in favour of freedom and self government.

They were both believers in that creed of which, in tracing its political influence, Bancroft has so happily said, that "it owned no king, but the King of Heaven; no aristocracy but of the redeemed; no bondage but the hopeless, infinite, and eternal bondage of sin;" that it "invoked intelligence against Satan, the great enemy of the human race, * * * * and nourished its college with corn and strings of wampum, and in every village built the free school."

Of the men who professed this creed, he further said, "they went forth in confidence that men who were kindling with the same exalted instincts would listen to their voice, and be effectively called into the brunt of battle by their side; and standing serenely amidst the crumbling fabrics of centuries of superstition, they had faith in one another." With these sentiments animating him, it was but natural that his sons should be found, as several of them were, in the American army, during the Revolutionary War.

It was from such an ancestry that Alexander Thomson, the subject of our sketch, descended. His father, Archibald Thomson, was one of the sons of the Scotch emigrant who served as soldiers in the Revolution.

Alexander, the subject of our sketch, was born in Franklin county, Pa., January 12, 1788. His parents both died young, leaving a family of five children, two sons and three daughters. At the age of fifteen Alexander was apprenticed to his uncle, Andrew Thomson, to learn the trade of a sickle maker. No statement that we could make would more strikingly suggest the rapid progress, and revolution in the industries of the Cumberland valley, than this one. Notwithstanding the immense crops which are annually gathered from its fertile fields, it is doubtful whether one sickle maker could find remunerative employment to-day, were he to have a monopoly of the business from the Susquehanna to the Tennessee.

While acquiring his trade he manifested his love of study, and by the time he was through his apprenticeship he had acquired a knowledge of Latin, and became well versed in the English poets. Milton was his favourite, and a retentive memory enabled him in his later years frequently to gratify his friends by reciting many of the most admired passages.

Among the Presbyterian ministers who, at that early day, made occasional visits into that part of the Cumberland valley, was the Rev. Mr. Grier, the father of the late Justice Grier, of the Supreme Court of the United States. The intelligence and studious habits of the young sickle maker attracted the attention of Mr. Grier, and he invited him to his home at Northumberland, where it was the expectation that he would pursue his own studies, and, while so engaged, instruct the sons of his friend in Greek and Latin. After three years spent in this occupation, his health broke down, and he went to Bedford to escape, as he believed, the injurious influences of the climate of the Susquehanna upon his system.

At Bedford he took charge of the academy, and studied law with Judge Riddle. He was admitted to the bar, and soon attained the confidence of the public both as a man and a lawyer. He was elected to the House of Representatives in the State Legislature, and afterwards represented the district in Congress, from 1824 to 1826. To the discharge of his public duties he brought the same untiring industry and scrupulous fidelity that were his characteristics through life.

He took a very warm interest in the welfare of the District of Columbia during his term in Congress, and so zealously and successfully did he labour in that behalf that his services were gratefully recognized by the citizens of Washington, who had his portrait painted and placed in the City Hall. About the end of his Congressional career he was appointed by the Governor to a Judgeship in the city of Lancaster. He occupied that position for a very brief time before he was appointed for life, President Judge of the Judicial District composed of the counties of Somerset, Bedford and Franklin, after which he removed from Bedford to Chambersburg. This position he filled until his term expired under the limited tenure of the amended Constitution of 1838. He was succeeded in this office by the Hon. Jeremiah S. Black, before whom he at once entered upon a laborious and successful practice in the district, attending the courts of all the counties and being engaged in many important cases. Among the first cases he tried before Judge Black, after his own retirement from the bench, was one which excited considerable interest in Franklin county—the case of Wilson against Bigger, reported in 7 Watts & Sergeant, involving the title to valuable lands near St. Thomas, and, as a question of law, the conclusiveness of decrees of the Orphans' Court. He was associated in this case with Hon. George Chambers, and opposed by Messrs. Bard and McLanahan. In cases of like importance throughout the district, and as the adversary or colleague of such lawyers as those already named, Thomas J. McCulloh, Frederick Smith, John F. Denny and Joseph Chambers, in Franklin county, James M. Russell, William Lyon, and Alexander King, in Bedford county, Joshua F. Cox and others, in Somerset county, he continued in the practice of his profession until his death, which occurred suddenly from paralysis, August 2d, 1848.

In addition to his professional labours in the courts, he also filled the Professorship in the Law School connected with Marshall College. In this capacity he had in his office a number of students, and in his attention to them he was most diligent. His classes were not large enough for formal lectures, but when not absent, attending the courts in the district, so devoted was he to his students that at least three times in each week, he had them assemble, and often for two hours in the early morning he would examine them, and give them the most valuable running commentaries upon the various branches of elementary law. The interest he took in his students and the paternal care he manifested for them, endeared him to them all, and it has been a source of gratification to his family that his memory has ever been cherished with feelings of gratitude as well as of affection by the numerous gentlemen who studied under his care. Among these were his nephew, Hon. Thomas A. Hendricks, late United States Senator, and now Governor of Indiana, Hon. John Scott, late United States Senator from Pennsylvania, and Hon. T. B. Kennedy, a prominent member of the Franklin county bar, and President of the Cumberland Valley Railroad Company.

Judge Thomson was not only a busy lawyer, but he took an active part in everything pertaining to the interests of the community in which he lived. He was an active member and a ruling elder in the Presbyterian Church of Chambersburg, a director of the bank, a trustee of the academy, and in all his relations he maintained an unsullied character and enjoyed the respect of his associates. As a judge he was laborious and conscientious in the examination of every case which came before him; he maintained the dignity of his high office, and his decisions were the result of a sound judgment guided by the highest learning of his profession. As a lawyer, he was esteemed, not only for his industry and courtesy, but for his legal and literary attainments. He commanded the confidence of the profession and the community by his moral and religious worth. The benevolence of his heart did not stop in wishing well to his fellows, and when the unfortunate claimed his aid his beneficence was limited only by his ability to do good and kind acts. We remember well how an unfortunate man who applied to him in his office for assistance feelingly and gratefully responded as he left the door, and how the Judge, looking after him, said, "*non ignara mali miseris succurrere disco.*" No one present ever forgot the incident or the quotation.

It was his delight to gather the young about him, and he was often seen the centre of a circle of the delighted students from the Female Seminary of Chambersburg, who had learned from his genial nature and cordial hospitality that his house always furnished a welcome second only to that of their own homes.

Judge Thomson was twice married, first to Miss Abbie Blythe, of Bedford, and after her death to Miss Jane Graham, of Stoystown, Somerset county, who still lives his widow. Of the children of his first marriage there now survive him Dr. Alexander Thomson, of Mt. Savage, Md., and Mrs. John Culbertson, of Springfield, Missouri. George Thomson, Dr. William Thomson, a Professor and eminent Oculist in Philadelphia, Frank Thomson, General Manager Pennsylvania Railroad, and two daughters, Mrs. James B. Dayton, of Camden, N. J., and Mrs. Elizabeth Lesley, widow of James Lesley, late Chief Clerk of the War Department, are children of his second marriage. Of these descendants four sons and two sons-in-law were actively engaged in the military service during the recent struggle for the preservation of the Government. It may here be added, that the degree of LL. D., was conferred on Judge Thomson, by Marshall College, in 1840.

No stronger encouragement can be given to the parents who bring up their children in the way in which they should go than the history of the numerous descendants of Alexander Thomson, of "Corkerhill." They number among them not only the subject of this sketch and his descendants and many others bearing his own name, but the Agnews, of New York, the Wylies, of Philadelphia, the Watsons, of Pittsburgh, the Hendrickses, of Indiana, many of whom have filled with honour positions alike in the high and the humbler walks of life.

WILLIAM THOMSON, M. D.

HON. ALEXANDER THOMSON, President Judge of the Sixteenth Judicial District, was one of the most eminent jurists of the Commonwealth. Before his elevation to the bench, he had served with celebrity in the halls of Congress. A close student and a cultivated scholar, he was an ardent friend of literature and a generous patron of education. All the advantages that culture could confer were bestowed upon his children, and the distinguished father has been amply repaid for his paternal solicitude by the reputation which his sons have added to the family name.

Of these sons, the eldest, Alexander Thomson, M. D., after being admitted to the bar of Franklin county, turned his attention to medicine, and for many years has been an honored and successful practitioner of the healing art in Maryland. During the war, he held prominent positions in the Medical Department, and discharged his duties with characteristic fidelity and modesty. The fifth and youngest son, Frank, became a practical engineer, won distinction as a railroad superintendent, and is now General Manager of the gigantic Pennsylvania road.

The subject of our sketch, Dr. William Thomson, was the fourth son of Judge Thomson. He was born in beautiful and historic Chambersburg, on the 28th day of January, 1833; was carefully educated, under his father's watchful eye, at the Chambersburg Academy, at that period one of the most noted seats of learning in the state, conducted by a brilliant preceptor, whose fame brought pupils from far and near to receive a training, in the classics especially, not inferior to the best of our colleges.

Drawn to the profession in which he was to acquire such high rank, he entered the office of the late Dr. John C. Richards, one of the most elegant gentlemen and ablest practitioners, and completed his pupilage under his accomplished brother, Alexander Thomson, of Mount Savage, Maryland. In 1855, he graduated at Jefferson Medical College, and began his successful career near Philadelphia. When the war broke out, in 1861, he relinquished a lucrative practice, was admitted, after an examination by the proper board, to the regular army, as Assistant Surgeon, before any volunteer troops were organized, and was assigned to duty with the Army of the Potomac, with which he served either in the field, or at its base at Washington, until the close of the war. Shortly before the battle of Bull Run, July, 1861, he was stationed at Alexandria, in the first General Hospital organized, and during the fall and winter succeeding, he had charge of more than three hundred beds. In May, 1862, he was ordered to a General Hospital, at Portsmouth, Va., where he remained until August, when he reported to Surgeon Letterman, the far-famed Medical Director of the army of the Potomac, (at Head Quarters, Harrison Landing,) who placed him in his office as his assistant, and in this capacity, he followed the army on the staff of McClellan. After the hotly-waged battle of South Mountain, at which he was present, he was ordered by the Medical Director "to take charge of all the hospitals," and had the care of the wounded at Middletown, until they were gathered into temporary hospitals and finally transported to Frederick. Rejoining the Head Quarters, after the battle of Antietam, he was placed in charge of the transportation of the wounded to the hospitals at Frederick and Baltimore. In the "Medical Recollections of the Army of the Potomac," by Surgeon Letterman, published by the Appletons, in 1866, the author thus refers to the services of Dr. Thomson: "As I anticipated, the wounded, under the supervision of Dr. Thomson, who labored with so much diligence and so much effect, were attended with great care and skill, and the hospitals soon placed in excellent order. This officer may feel well repaid for all the difficulties he encountered, by the complimentary manner in which the President, when on his way to the battle field of Antietam, spoke of the condition of the hospitals, and the great care of the wounded in them." Subsequently to the Maryland campaign, while the army was advancing into Virginia, Dr. Thomson remained on duty at Head Quarters, until he was sent to Washington to act as recorder of a Board convened to examine Medical Officers.

While serving as assistant to the Medical Director, he organized the system of "Brigade Supplies," which was issued through the order of the Commander in Chief, in the Circular of October 4th, 1862, entitled "Medical Supply Table for the Army of the Potomac for Field Service," and also the celebrated Division Hospital System, promulgated from the Medical Director's office of Army of Potomac, October 30th, 1862, by which, in the language of Surgeon Letterman, "The Department was better able than ever to discharge the duties devolving upon it;" and which not only saved the lives but the limbs, too, of many a gallant sufferer, as is well known to the writer of this sketch. These reforms were so favorably received and were so productive of good, that they were re-issued to all the armies by the War Department.

In February, 1863, Dr. Thomson was put in charge of Douglas Hospital, Washington, so called from its establishment partly in the commodious mansion of the illustrious Senator. This institution was thoroughly equipped, and was managed with such ability that it became one of the models of the hospital system. The Medical Inspector of United States Army reported to Surgeon General Hammond that he found it in "perfect condition in every particular part," and "had no suggestions to offer." Whereupon the Surgeon General added to the report, that "such a testimonial of attention to duty is received at this office with satisfaction."

The extraordinary fitness displayed by Dr. Thomson for hospital direction, so often manifested, was not overlooked by the head of the Medical Department, and he was elevated to the responsible position of the Medical Inspector of Department of Washington, which contained perhaps the largest number, certainly the most completely appointed hospitals ever established for wounded soldiers. The immense system placed under the supervision of the youthful inspector may be inferred from the fact that it contained over 23,000 beds; and that in the year 1864 it provided for *one hundred and thirteen thousand three hundred and fifty-seven patients!*

In this responsible and honourable position he remained with increasing credit, until the overthrow of the Rebellion and the general abandonment of the hospitals; when he was re-assigned for a few months to "Douglas," one of the last to remain open, and then returned to his duties as Inspector, rewarded by two brevets. In 1866, he took charge of a post hospital, established for the treatment of cholera, then epidemic. In 1867, having passed a second examination, and having been promoted, he was sent to Louisiana, and served there until 1868, when he resigned to engage in a wider and fuller and more distinguished field.

He has left his name enrolled among the most brilliant of the medical officers who were connected with the United States Army, as well as one of the most faithful and industrious. The splendid monument of American surgery, the Army Medical Museum at the nation's capital, in papers and specimens bears witness to his professional work; and he holds the proud distinction in its published catalogue of being its largest contributor.

After his resignation from the army he settled in Philadelphia, where he was welcomed by the eminent professional brotherhood in that centre of medical science. He was elected to all their societies: a Fellow of the College of Physicians, Member of Pathological Society, Academy of Natural Sciences, Biological Society, County Medical Society, Neurological Society of New York, and American Ophthalmological and Otological Society, etc., and was attending physician to the Hospital of the Protestant Episcopal Church, and Church Home for Children. The position in these hospitals he resigned to devote himself to the diseases of the eye and ear exclusively. In 1868, he was elected to the staff of the Wills' Hospital for Diseases of the Eye, and is now serving as one of its surgeons. In 1873, he was appointed Clinical Lecturer on Diseases of Eye and Ear, at Jefferson Medical College, where he gives practical instruction to the hundreds of pupils who crowd the gates of that famous temple of medical science.

Dr. Thomson stands in the front rank of Ophthalmic surgeons. He has contributed largely and given very valuable papers to the literature of his specialty, and has made important additions to its science and art. Professor Gross, when preparing the late edition of his "System of Surgery," the most comprehensive medical book produced in this country, placed the section on the Diseases and Injuries of the Eye in Dr. Thomson's hands for revision, and in the preface to the work, acknowledges his indebtedness exclusively to the Doctor "for his valuable remarks upon refraction and accommodation."

In many respects Dr. Thomson is a remarkable man. A more genial and brilliant conversationalist can scarcely be found; a better thinker and harder worker we need not seek to find. Music, art, and literature furnish him with recreation, but his study is the severe science of his vocation. As a lecturer he is said to be charming, his facility of explaining is striking and his wealth of expression unsurpassed. As an operator he is quick, sure and skilful; as an adviser, sagacious and authoritative. In general surgery he had acquired great experience, and had performed its most formidable operations; in the more delicate surgery of the eye and ear he is a recognized master.

FRANK THOMSON.

THE fifth and youngest son of Hon. Alexander Thomson, Judge of the Sixteenth Judicial District, Frank Thomson, was born at Chambersburg, on July 5th, 1841. His preliminary and classical education were obtained at the Chambersburg Academy which has given culture to so many men who have since reflected credit upon this excellent school. When seventeen years of age he determined to acquire a knowledge of the railway business, and for that purpose, entered the shops of the Pennsylvania Railroad, at Altoona. There he attracted the attention of Thomas A. Scott, then the General Manager of the line, who recognized his natural ability, and by valuable advice directed his practical studies towards the administration as well as to the construction and equipment of railroads and their machinery.

Upon the commencement of the Rebellion, Mr. Scott was summoned to the aid of the Government; and immediately after the memorable attack upon the soldiers in the streets of Baltimore, on the 19th of April, 1861, Mr. Thomson was detailed by Mr. Scott for duty in the military railway system, which was then just being organized—the efficiency of which contributed so essentially to the final success of the Government in the overthrow of the Rebellion.

At Alexandria, Va., early in 1861, previous to the battle of Bull Run, he was taking those practical lessons in restoring shops, machinery and rolling stock, disabled by the retreating southern forces; in re-building bridges, shoveling out cuts which had been filled, and constructing the roads and telegraph lines to keep pace with the advancing troops; in transporting men, munitions, wounded, and the various material requisite for an army, with no fixed organization or schedules; and in repairing the damages of sudden retreats or unexpected raids; and to such training he owes the self-confidence and fertility of resource which were used with such signal results in the great emergencies elsewhere before the close of the war. He was thus employed in the Department of the Potomac until July 1st, 1862, when he was sent to the west and assigned to duty with the military roads south of Nashville, which were used by Gen. Buell's army, operating on the line of Decatur, Huntsville and Stevenson. During this campaign, the military railroad played a conspicuous part, since it was requisite to accomplish the necessary concentration of troops, that the men, munitions of war, supplies, etc., from the various lines south of Nashville should be safely transported over three hundred miles of road in the enemy's country.

Having accompanied the army during its famous march through Kentucky, Mr. Thomson was directed to return to the Army of the Potomac, and took part in the railway achievements of the Antietam campaign. Afterwards he was appointed as Assistant Superintendent of the lines south of Acquia Creek, which were used for the supply of the Army of the Potomac, during the commandership of Burnside and Hooker, and the battles of Fredericksburg and Chancellorsville.

He was then recalled to the service of the Pennsylvania Railroad and assigned to a position which he held for one month only, being again honoured by a request from Col. Thomas A. Scott, then specially detailed by the Secretary of War, to aid him in the greatest transportation movement of the war—in the removal of two entire Corps, the Eleventh and Twelfth, with their full equipment of artillery, horses, wagons, camp utensils, tents, hospital supplies and baggage, from the front of the Army of the Potomac, near Washington, to the Army of the Cumberland, at Chattanooga. This difficult feat was deemed requisite for the salvation of the Army of the Cumberland, and was fully accomplished in the short space of fourteen days.

The battle of Rosecranz, at Chickamauga, the retiring of the army to Chattanooga, its environment by Bragg's army, the inadequacy of its line of supply, its desperate condition when General Grant was assigned to its command, are matters of history. It became necessary that the line of railroad, miserably constructed and equipped, running through a country thickly infested by guerillas, and subject to constant interruption from successful raids, should be rendered capable of transmitting re-inforcements and supplies enough to enable our army to advance. Mr. Thomson was placed in charge of these lines south of Nashville to accomplish this arduous task, in which he entirely succeeded, and thus contributed in an essential manner to those brilliant military movements which not only relieved our own army but enabled it to assume the aggressive with such splendid results.

At the request of the chief officers of the Pennsylvania Railroad Company, he then resigned from the military service and was appointed Superintendent of the Eastern Division of the Philadelphia and Erie Railroad, with his office at Williamsport, and assumed charge on June 1, 1864; in this position he remained until March, 1873, being detailed temporarily in 1865 to manage the Oil Creek Railroad, during the great oil excitement of that period.

In the autumn of 1871, the authorities of the Pennsylvania Railroad were requested by the Russian Government to designate a skilful officer to accompany the Grand Duke Alexis, and be responsible for his safety in an extended railway journey which he proposed to take through the country. Mr. Thomson was honored by their selection, and the details were left to his judgment. Under his direction *one special train*, fitted up with every convenience and comfort, was taken through the Eastern States and Canada, westward to Denver, thence south to New Orleans, and thence to Pensacola, run as a "special" over the various roads, an entire distance of six thousand miles, without any mishap or accident. In acknowledgment of their obligation to the Pennsylvania Railroad Company, the following letter was addressed to the President by the Russian Admiral:

PENSACOLA, *February 22d, 1872.*

SIR:—On arriving at the end of his journey, His Imperial Highness, the Grand Duke Alexis, begs me to assure you that he feels great pleasure in expressing his complete satisfaction with all the arrangements made by Mr. Frank Thomson. To conduct a large party over nearly six thousand miles of railway, belonging to many different companies, without the slightest misunderstanding or delay during the whole journey, requires an amount of intelligence, experience, foresight and energy, which we luckily found combined in the gentleman who had charge of the expedition. I may add that Mr. Thomson's gentlemanly manners made him no less agreeable as a companion, than his other qualities made him invaluable as a manager. As Mr. Frank Thomson has been so useful to the guest of the American Nation, I trust you will not regret having been for some time deprived of his services.

I am sir, your most obedient servant,

[SIGNED,] C. POSSIET.

To J. EDGAR THOMSON,
President Pennsylvania Railroad, Philadelphia.

Whilst Superintendent of the Eastern Division, Mr. Thomson initiated some valuable improvements in the construction of the roadway, and organized a system of track inspection, competitive in its nature which has been adopted on the entire road.

In March, 1873, he was promoted to the rank of Superintendent of Motive Power on the Pennsylvania Railroad, which placed under his charge all the various work shops of the entire line, and all of the rolling stock of all descriptions, together with over one thousand engines in active service.

On July 1st, 1874, he was appointed the General Manager of the Pennsylvania Railroad extending from New York to Pittsburgh with various lines, of the Philadelphia and Erie Road from Sunbury to

Erie, of the Northern Central Railroad, and Baltimore and Potomac Railroad, extending from Washington and Baltimore to Canandaigua, New York, and of the West Jersey Railroad, comprising a total under one control of twenty-three hundred miles; and these duties he is now successfully discharging.

Such a record deserves a place among any archives of men of our valley, and is an evidence that the descendants of our good stock possess those high traits which animated their grandsires a century ago, whilst they are fully alive to the demands of the progress of to-day. Although quick and incisive in manner in business, Frank Thomson is a genial, kindly gentleman, refined in all his tastes, an appreciative lover of music, fully alive to the charm of good art, and a friend of culture in all its branches.

MAJOR GENERAL S. W. CRAWFORD.

TAKING our Generals as a class, they presented some of the finest figures of men, such as a country might well be proud of. At the head of these stands the splendid Hooker and the "superb" Hancock; but alongside of them deserves to rank a Division Commander, who, for capable and faithful performance of duty certainly had no superior. That officer was Major General S. W. Crawford, now Colonel Second United States Infantry.

Tall, well-formed, in due proportion, strongly knit, erect, active and, as all well-made men are, graceful, he is worthy to be selected as a representative of our Volunteer superior officers.

Samuel Wylie Crawford is a Pennsylvanian by birth, born in Franklin county, a student of the State University, and a graduate of the class of 1846; a graduate of the Medical Department of that first class institution, in 1850, which, in 1867, conferred upon him the degree of LL. D. The same year he was examined by the United States Army Medical Board, and stood first in the class of 1850.

His first commission in the United States service as Assistant Surgeon, is dated 10th March, 1851, and he served in Texas from 1851 to 1853, and in New Mexico, from 1853 to 1856. Six years of frontier life! How were these employed? As in too many cases, wasted or worse? Not so! These six years were devoted to the practice of his profession and to scientific research.

Witness his paper, now in the Smithsonian Institute, upon the Flora and Fauna of the region near the headwaters of the Rio San Saba, published by order of Congress, and his collections of natural history, in the then wild and unexplored territory around El Paso del Norte.

In 1856, the War Department conceded permission for a tour through Mexico. Here again profit, and not pleasure, was the object of the young officer. In January, 1857, he was the first to carry a barometer to the summit of Popocatapetl, (the Volcan Grande de Mexico,) accomplishing the arduous task accompanied by a single guide. A Prussian scientific party, sent out under the auspices of their government to confirm the discoveries of Humboldt, having given out, the actual measurement of the American volunteer philosopher, was the one reported by the Prussian accredited agent. Not content with his first achievement, Crawford again ascended the volcano, remained all night in the crater, was let down by cords into its depths, and brought back valuable mineralogical specimens now in the collection at West Point. He next climbed to the snowy crown of "The White Woman," Iztuchihuatl, (the Sierra Nevada de Mexico,) and settled the vexed question, that this mountain was no volcano, demonstrating that no crater existed. For these explorations he was made a member of the Geographical Society of Mexico..

August, 1860, found him in Fort Moultrie, Charleston harbour. After crossing over on the memorable night of the 26th of December, with Anderson, to Fort Sumter, Crawford returned on the morning of the 27th, to Fort Moultrie, and removed thence the ammunition, &c., and hospital supplies. Thenceforward he discharged double duty, his own proper functions and those connected with the command of a battery, whose three guns were the first to open fire on Fort Moultrie in response to the Rebel bombardment which ushered in the Great American Conflict. In a letter, remarkable for the warmth as well as force of its expression, General Anderson recommended Crawford to the consideration of the War Department and asked that he be brevetted for his services.

Appointed Major 13th U. S. Infantry, upon the recommendation of General Scott, Crawford was sent to serve with Rosecrans in West Virginia. He made Crawford his Inspector General, and the subordinate justified the superior's selection. Had not "the stars in their courses fought against" him, Crawford would have accomplished the passage of the New river, on Floyd's flank—a severe test of skill and daring. That he failed was no fault of his; and such an estimate did Rosecrans put on the ability displayed by Crawford, that he recommended him for one of the two appointments as Brigadier General, whose nomination rested with him (Rosecrans.)

On the 28th of February, 1862, Crawford received his commission as Brigadier General. His first service was with Banks in the Shenandoah valley. His first active command was the First Brigade, First Division, Fifth Corps, with whom he led the advance into Virginia.

Crawford's first appearance on the battle field was at Cedar Mountain. This was on the 9th of August, 1862. On this occasion, he, with his little brigade on the extreme right, was ordered to charge across a wide opening into woods held by a large Confederate force. Nevertheless he drove the enemy from their strong positions; and had he been adequately supported, this would have been the decisive movement of the day. As it was, Crawford lost over half his effective force; and if our army did not win a victory, Crawford won the admiration of all cognizant of the facts, and demonstrated that he was eminently worthy of the star which the prescient intelligence of Rosecrans had deemed him worthy to receive. Throughout the Pope campaign—a campaign fought with surpassing constancy and courage—Crawford did his duty as a gallant and an able Brigadier.

His next appearance in action was as an agent in one of the most glorious feats of arms which illustrate the records of the Army of the Potomac, when he led in his West Virginia brigade to support that victorious assault in which the noble Reno fell, paying, although a Virginian, "the last full measure of devotion" to his country, in Fox, next Turner's Gap, of the South Mountain; on that bright battle Sabbath, not brighter than the scene and triumph, 14th September, 1862.

Three days later he succeeded to the command of (his) the First Division, after the fall of the good, devoted and intrepid Mansfield; and, after assisting to carry the blood-drenched corn field in front of the Dunker Church—that ebb and flow of slaughter on our right at Antietam—Crawford received a wound which consigned him to inaction for the ensuing nine months, and bids fair to cripple him for the rest of his life.

As soon as—nay, before—he was fully fit for active duty, on his own application for field service, at the special request of the Governor of Pennsylvania, Crawford was placed in command of the Divisiom comprising three Brigades from his native State, known as the "Pennsylvania Reserves."

Towards the close of the second day—the great day which determined that the decisive battle of the war at the east—perhaps the decisive battle of the whole war—should be fought at Gettysburg, and *fought out* THERE, Crawford arrived on the field just as the glorious old fighting Third Corps, sacrificed at Williamsburg, on the Peninsula, in the Pope campaign, amid the harvest of death at Chancellorsville, was being cut to pieces, not driven but pressed back from the position the maintenance of which had cost such hecatombs of its best and bravest, having been reduced from a strong Corps to a weak Division. Seizing the colours of his leading regiment as they fell from the wounded hand of the bearer, Crawford bore them aloft on his saddle, and, like the first Bonaparte at Arcola, the great Austrian Archduke at Aspern, and the Russian Bayard at the bridge of Licco, led on a charge which retrieved our desperate affairs on the left.

If the writer's many years' study of military history entitles his judgment to any respect, he would be false to his own convictions if he did not claim for Crawford all the honours due to a resultive "feat of intrepidity."

When the sublime charge of the enemy had resulted in glorious annihilation, Crawford was the first to assume the aggressive, which, had it been imitated, or, rather, had its imitation been permitted, the retreat of Lee from the field on which he made his mightiest and most desperate throw, would have been converted into a catastrophe, such as his allowed escape deferred until the hunt from Petersburg to Appomattox Court House.

In the ensuing "campaign of manœuvres;" in that blood bath from the Rapidan to the James; in that dreary series of operations dignified with the title of the "siege of Petersburg—Richmond," Crawford commanded his Division with dignity and ability.

The vastness of the field; the intensity of the labors; the sufferings and the fighting; the thousand accidents which smelted the actions of the different Divisions into an amalgam; which rendered the detection difficult of even the richest constituents; all this, as well as space, render it impossible to go into details of what Crawford did, and did well, at the head of the Third Division, Fifth Corps, from Lee's defeat at Gettysburg to his surrender at Clover Hill. At Williamsport, at Manasses Gap, in the battles of the Wilderness, at Spotsylvania, on the Fredericksburg road, at Alsop's farm, at Bethesda Church, Crawford was on hand with his "Pennsylvania Reserves." Their losses attested the fidelity of their service.

On the 31st May, 1864, the Reserves were mustered out of service, and Crawford was transferred to the command of a provisional Division—the Second Division of the Fifth Corps; and at Cold Harbor, all of the regiments (22) of the old First Corps were formed into a Division of three Brigades, and Crawford ordered to its command, as the Third Division. Before Petersburg, in the hard fight on the Weldon Railroad, and in the labyrinthine maze of Hatcher's run, Crawford did his best to support his comrades, his commander, and associate corps. Shortly after he was brevetted Major General of Volunteers.

In the second expedition to Hatcher's run, Crawford, judging from Lee's report, performed efficient service. As a demonstration of the estimation in which he was held, he was at this time offered the command of the Cavalry of the Army of the Potomac, by Major General Meade. Early in the war, in his reconnoissance to Luray, he had shown a marked capacity for the handling of this "arm of the moment." He declined the honour, preferring to remain with his

Division. This he led with marked ability at Gravelly Run, and at Five Forks, where he struck the rear of the enemy, and for his gallant behavior in the latter conflict, he was commended by Sheridan in his report, and subsequently brevetted Brigadier General in the United States Army, and afterwards Major General in the United States Army, for gallant and meritorious services during the war

Upon the reorganization of the Infantry of the Army, in the spring of 1869, when that arm of the service was reduced from forty-five to twenty-five regiments, Crawford was selected, although the *last* Colonel upon the list, and was promoted to command the Second Regiment of Infantry. On the 22d of February, 1869, he was promoted to the Colonelcy of the Sixteenth Infantry, and upon the reorganization of the Infantry, when the Sixteenth and Second Regiments were consolidated, in April, 1869, he was assigned to the command of the new Second Infantry.

General Crawford was retired from the United States Army, February 19th, 1873, by reason of disability, resulting from a wound received at the battle of Antietam, September 17th, 1872, with the rank of Brevet Major General. He visited Europe in the spring of 1873, and was handsomely received in the various counties through which he extended his tour. In the spring of 1875, he again visited Europe, as a delegate from the New York Geographical Society to the Geographical Congress then about to meet at Paris. He is a member of the Academy of Sciences, Historical Society, &c., and is at this time pursuing his foreign travels.

DR. ISAAC WAYNE SNOWDEN.

THE subject of this sketch, who for many years was one of the most prominent physicians, not only in the Cumberland valley but in the state, was born at Harrisburg on the 4th day of March, 1796. His father, the Rev. Nathaniel Randolph Snowden, was at that time pastor of the Presbyterian Churches at Harrisburg, Derry and Paxton. When Isaac was quite a youth his father returned to Philadelphia, where for four generations his family had resided.

Dr. Snowden was the eldest of six children, of whom four, including himself, studied and subsequently practised medicine. James Ross, his youngest brother, turned his attention to the law, and has since occupied many places of honour and trust. His only sister, Mary Parker Snowden, was married to the late distinguished Chief Justice Thompson, of the Supreme Court. Dr. Snowden received both his academical and medical education at the University of Pennsylvania. Shortly after leaving the University in the year 1816, he was appointed Assistant Surgeon in the United States Army, and ordered to report for duty at Sackett's Harbor. He remained for a brief period only at this post, when he was ordered to join the army under General Jackson then operating against the Seminole Indians in Florida. On his joining the army Dr. Snowden was assigned to duty at Head-Quarters, and became a member of Gen. Jackson's military family. From that period until the death of "Old Hickory," there existed between them the warmest personal friendship. So late as February 7th, 1844, Gen. Jackson, in writing to a gentleman in Pennsylvania, desired to be "especially remembered to his (my) old friend and companion, Dr. Snowden."

The limited space assigned for this sketch precludes the possibility of giving more than a passing glance at the services rendered by Dr. Snowden during the Florida campaign. He was in Fort Scott when it was besieged by the Indians, when the inmates were reduced to a pint of corn per day. And although his duties as Surgeon were special, yet his noble spirit would not permit him to remain an inactive spectator when so many of his brave companions were in deadly conflict with a relentless and bloody foe. He therefore joined heartily in the defence wherever his duties as Surgeon would permit. Whilst thus engaged he was severely wounded, which did not prevent him, however, from assisting in the defence until the Fort was relieved.

He participated in the subsequent campaign and was present with Jackson at the decisive battle of the Horseshoe, where the Indians were defeated after a long and desperate struggle.

In 1823, Dr. Snowden resigned from the army and resumed the practice of his profession in Mifflin county, Pa. In a brief period he acquired a large and lucrative practice, extending into the neighbouring counties. In 1832, he was united in marriage to Miss Margary B. Louden, youngest daughter of Archibald Louden, Esq., whose family were among the earliest settlers, and largest land owners in the Cumberland valley. Shortly after his marriage Dr. Snowden removed to Cumberland county, near the birth place of his wife, and there remained in active practice until his death, which occurred June 4th, 1850. Dr. Snowden was the type of a Christian gentleman, and died respected and beloved by all who knew him. He was an Elder in the Presbyterian Church, in which his ancestors for generations had been prominent as laymen and ministers. His father was one of four brothers who graduated at Princeton and all of whom were ministers in the same church.

Dr. Snowden had five children, two sons and three daughters. One of the latter still resides with her mother in the old homestead. The second son, Col. A. Louden Snowden, is now and has been for many years, an officer in the United States Mint at Philadelphia. He is also prominently identified with many of the most important interests of the city, and is justly esteemed one of her most valued citizens. He is a graduate of Jefferson College, Pa., and is a gentleman of fine literary culture, genial, popular manners, and growing influence.

GENERAL D. B. McKIBBIN.

JEREMIAH McKIBBIN, born in the county of Antrim, Ireland, at an early period settled upon the spot now occupied by the depot of the Cumberland Valley Railroad, at Newville. He was married to Mary Chambers, of Chambersburg.

Chambers McKibbin, his youngest son, and father of the subject of this sketch, alone survives him. He was born in 1798, at Newville, and married Jane Bell, of Shippensburg. Mrs. McKibbin was born in 1802, died in 1873, and was very highly and widely esteemed for her womanly and Christian virtues. Mr. McKibbin's life fully illustrates the cosmopolitan traits of the American character, having been farmer, financier and politician. He enjoyed the friendship and confidence of all the Democratic leaders of his time, and has been an active and influential citizen of Pennsylvania. He was Assistant Quarter Master at Pittsburg, under President Jackson, Postmaster in the same city, under President Polk, Naval Officer at Philadelphia, under President Buchanan, and Assistant Treasurer of the United States at the same city, under President Johnson, and at this time, in his 78th year, is a member of the Senate of Pennsylvania. His life has been a remarkable and unblemished one, and is now crowned with a 'green old age. Jeremiah, the eldest son of Mr. McKibbin, after spending several years in Mexico, settled in Philadelphia, became an active politician, was the nominee of the Democratic party for Sheriff, in 1864, and is now proprietor of the Girard House in that city. William, second son, died in Philadelphia in 1868, his death being greatly lamented by his numerous friends.

D. B. McKibbin, sixth child, was born in 1831. He served a campaign in the Mexican War when sixteen years of age. He was appointed Second Lieutenant, Ninth Infantry, on its organization, March 31st, 1855. The regiment was sent to the Pacific coast, and Company H, under the command of Lieutenant McKibbin, was in a desperate and successful Indian fight before the close of a year. He served continuously in Washington Territory against the Indians, and on the North Western Boundary Survey until 1861, when he was promoted to a First Lieutenantcy, and ordered, on the outbreak of the Rebellion, to Washington. He was appointed Captain Fourteenth U. S. Infantry, in May of that year, for gallant services against the

Indians. In February, 1862, he took the field with his regiment as second in command, having been appointed Assistant Field Officer, by General McClellan. He served with the Army of the Potomac through all the battles of the Peninsula until after the battle of Malvern Hill, when he took command of the Second Battalion of his regiment, which command he held until after the battle of Antietam, when sickness compelled him to leave the field for a short time.

In the following November, he took command of the One Hundred and Fifty-Eighth Pennsylvania Volunteers, a nine months' regiment, serving in Virginia and North Carolina. When this Volunteer Regiment was mustered out, he returned to the regular service in command of the Second Battalion, and remained with them in the Army of the Potomac until June 2d, 1864, when he was captured at Bethesda Church, Va., imprisoned in Libby, in Macon, Georgia, and in Charleston, S. C., in the last place, under the fire of our own guns during the bombardment. On his return from prison, he took command of the Eighth Union League (214th Pennsylvania Volunteer) Regiment, which command he retained until the end of the war. He was brevetted five times, viz: Major, Lieutenant Colonel, Colonel and Brev. Brigadier General of the Regular Army, and Brev. Brigadier General of Volunteers. He is now Major of Cavalry.

General McKibbin was highly and deservedly complimented by distinguished officers of the army. General Meade refers to him as "frequently distinguished for conspicuous gallantry in battle." Gen. Warren testifies to his "gallantry and noble disregard of personal danger." General Sykes says: "There was no more promising young officer in the Division of regulars, and no one that I would sooner have selected for any operation in which dash, energy and enterprise were required." And General Ayres, pronounced him "especially distinguished for gallantry and good conduct at the North Anna and Bethesda Church, at the latter of which he was captured." Several of General McKibbin's brothers deserve notice here for their valuable military services.

Joseph C. McKibbin, third son, was a lawyer by profession, emigrated to California in 1849, and served in the Senate of that State in 1852 and 1853. He was appointed Superintendent of Public Buildings in 1853, by President Pierce, elected to the Thirty-Fifth Congress in 1856. In 1861, he was appointed Colonel of Cavalry by President Lincoln, serving in the armies of the Southwest and Centre, was acting Inspector of the Army of the Cumberland under Major General Rosecrans and Major General George H. Thomas, from both of whom, officially and unofficially, he received most flattering notice for his "efficiency, gallantry and fearlessness in battle," as well as for his "distinguished integrity of purpose."

Robert P. McKibbin, eighth child, born in 1834, was a lawyer by profession. At the first call of the President for 75,000 three months' volunteers in 1861, he enlisted in a volunteer company in Philadelphia as private. He was elected Second Lieutenant, served until their discharge, when he was given a Second Lieutenant's commission in the Fourth United States Infantry for meritorious service. He served with his regiment in the Army of the Potomac throughout the war, and was repeatedly complimented in despatches for gallant conduct. He was twice very severely wounded, and brevetted three times, as Captain, Major and Lieutenant Colonel. He came out of the war as full Captain. During part of 1864, he served on the Staff of Major General Crittenden, who spoke of him as one of the most brilliant and daring officers he had met during the war.

Chambers McKibbin, thirteenth and youngest child, born in 1840, accompanied as a citizen his brother's regiment to the field. At the battle of Gaines' Mill, having volunteered his services to the Fourteenth Infantry, which were refused, he dressed himself in the uniform of a private soldier, and performed such acts of gallantry, that he was recommended by every officer present in the regiment for promotion to a commission, except by his brother, who disapproved of it, as the vacancies were left open for men who enlisted and distinguished themselves. At this battle Chambers was shot in the face, and before his wound had properly healed, he enlisted in the regiment, and was promoted to a Lieutenantcy for gallant conduct the following September. He continued with his regiment until the close of the war, having been severely wounded on three occasions. He was complimented for bravery in every battle in which he took part, was brevetted Captain, and afterwards, for gallant and meritorious services, was promoted to Captain in the Thirty-fifth Infantry. He is now Captain of the Fifteenth Infantry.

THOMAS B. KENNEDY, ESQ.

THOMAS B. KENNEDY was born in August, 1827, in Warren county, New Jersey.

His father, Hon. James J. Kennedy, removed, in 1839, to Chambersburg, Pa., in the academy of which town the son was fitted for college. He entered the Sophomore Class of Marshall College, at fourteen, and graduated with honours in 1844. He read law with the Hon. Alexander Thomson, of Chambersburg, and was admitted to the Franklin county bar in 1848. The next year he crossed the plains as the leader of a company bound for California. There he entered upon the practice of law, in Downieville. In 1851, he returned to Chambersburg, opened an office, and speedily grew into practice. He served one term as District Attorney with general approbation. He married Miss Arianna Riddle, granddaughter of the Hon. James Riddle, and spent a year in traveling in Europe.

On his return, Mr. Kennedy became the partner of the Hon. James Nill, one of the leading practitioners of that day. The business of the firm rapidly increased, so that upon the election of Judge Nill to the bench of the district, in 1862, his partner found himself in control of the largest and most lucrative practice at that bar, which he has steadily maintained ever since. Notwithstanding the incessant labours of his professional life, and the demands upon his time, arising from the care of his large private estate, he has been prominently identified with every movement tending to the advancement of the section of the country in which he resides. While aiding liberally in all local measures, as a Trustee of the Academy, one of the originators and founders of Wilson College, and one of the Board of Management, he has effectively aided the cause of education. The two railroads recently completed in Franklin county, owe their success in a great measure to his influence and public spirit. He has lately been elected President of the Cumberland Valley Railroad, and of the Southern Pennsylvania Road.

GENERAL CLEMENT A. FINLEY.

SAMUEL FINLEY, father of the subject of this sketch, was of Scotch-Irish descent, and was educated in the family of his uncle, the Rev. Dr. Samuel Finley, President of Princeton College. He was a Major in the Virginia line during the Revolutionary War, was taken prisoner at the battle of Long Island, and was confined in the Jersey Prison Ship. In the war of 1812, he commanded a regiment of Mounted Riflemen ordered to the frontier to protect the peaceable Indians, after Hull's surrender. He was also a receiver of public moneys, from the sale of public lands, during the administration of President Washington.

General Clement A. Finley was born in Newville, Cumberland county, Pa., in 1797, graduated at Washington College, in the same state, studied medicine in Chillicothe, Ohio, and received his diploma in the Medical Department of the University of Pennsylvania. Dr. Finley entered the army August 10th, 1818, as Surgeon's Mate of the First Regiment of Infantry, commanded by Colonel Daniel Bissell, then stationed at Baton Rouge, Louisiana. He subsequently filled the positions of Assistant Surgeon, and Surgeon, and was Medical Director in the field, with Generals Jessup, Scott, and Taylor, in the Black Hawk, Seminole, and Mexican Wars. He spent nearly eight years on the frontier of Arkansas, Louisiana and Florida, accompanied the commands that established Forts Leavenworth, Jefferson Barracks, and Gibson, and went with General Dodge on one of the earliest expeditions to the Rocky Mountains, in 1834. At these points, away from all the enjoyments of civilized society, the monotony of camp life found relief in the excitement of the chase, in company with such men as Colonel Bonneville, (whose "Expedition to the Rocky Mountains" was written from his notes by Washington Irving,) General Harney, and Captain Martin Scott, all famous hunters and gallant officers. It is a treat which General Finley's friends sometimes enjoy, to hear him relate his adventures among the Indians, and in the pursuit of the deer and buffalo.

In 1861, at the commencement of the Rebellion, he succeeded General Lawson, as Surgeon General of the United States Army. Having served his country honourably and acceptably forty-four years, he retired from active service upon his own application. The commission of Brevet Brigadier General was given him by the President, on his retirement, for long and faithful service.

Dr. Finley is a fine specimen of a Christian gentleman. His appearance is commanding and impressive. Though now advanced in years he retains the vigour of manhood, and the graceful bearing of the soldier. Modest and retiring, he yet is the centre of many strong friendships and attachments. He is by religious profession a Presbyterian, and his long and useful life has ever been adorned by Christian fidelity. His two brothers, James and John K., both entered the medical profession, and attained eminence. The former is now deceased, and the latter, who was once Professor of Chemistry in Dickinson College, now resides in Niles, Michigan. His sister, Martha, is the widow of the late distinguished Rev. William L. McCalla, of Philadelphia.

Dr. Finley married, in early life, Elizabeth, daughter of Dr. Samuel Moore, at that time Director of the United States Mint, and formerly a member of Congress from Bucks county, Pa.

COL. WILLIAM McFUNN PENROSE,

ELDEST son of the Hon. Charles B. Penrose, was born in Carlisle, Pa., March 29th, 1825. He graduated at Dickinson College in July, 1844, at once devoted himself to the study of law, and two years after he had received his degree of A. B., entered upon his chosen profession in his native place. He rapidly secured reputation and practice, and soon became a leader at a Bar celebrated for its learning and ability. In 1858, he was married to Valeria, daughter of General Charles Merchant of the United States Army.

At the breaking out of the Rebellion, Mr. Penrose joined the Pennsylvania Reserves, and was elected Colonel of the Sixth Regiment. His constitution, however, was entirely unfitted for the exposure of the camp, and he laid here the foundation of the indisposition which eventually cut short his life at an early age. After participating in the active campaign, and distinguishing himself at the battle of Drainsville, one of the first successes on our side in the War, he was obliged to resign on account of severe ill health from which he never entirely recovered.

In the community in which he lived, Colonel Penrose was universally beloved for his many noble qualities. Generous to a fault, and with a heart full of sympathy for the weaknesses and sufferings of others, his aid and counsel were sought by great numbers of people totally unable ever to remunerate him for his professional services. As a lawyer he was learned, quick in his perceptions, cogent in argument, highly gifted as a speaker, and very successful.

Col. Penrose died on Sept. 2d, 1872, after a short illness, but really from the effects of his military service during the War. His demise was greatly deplored. The entire bar assembled in the court room to pay a tribute to his memory. The Hon. James H. Graham, Judge Junkin, A. B. Sharpe, Esq., R. M. Henderson, M. C. Herman, Lemuel Todd, W. H. Miller, and C. E. Maglaughlin, Esq., eulogised in strongest terms the personal qualities, social virtues and professional ability of the lamented dead. Judge Graham referred to the deceased, as "the kind and amiable Penrose, removed in the prime of his life, in the midst of his usefulness, and in the enjoyment of a large and lucrative practice, well merited by a life of untiring labour and research in acquiring a knowledge of legal science surpassed by few of his age." And Judge Junkin said, "his astuteness, vigour of thought, and keenness of perception in grasping the result of a principle, and then wielding it with a steady hand, I have never seen surpassed."

The meeting, which subsequently, as a body, attended the funeral of their brother, unanimously expressed their opinion and feeling of his character and worth as follows:

"*Resolved*, That by indefatigable industry, unremitting devotion to the study of the law, united with a calm temper, aud uniform courtesy of manner, this able lawyer has left behind him a reputation which will long live in the recollections of the Bar and the community.

"*Resolved*, That we feel with deep sensibility the loss we have sustained by the death of Mr. Penrose, who has for a quarter of a century been actively engaged in his profession in our midst, for whose professional attainments we entertain the highest respect, and for whose estimable qualities as a man we have the most profound regard."

RIGHT REV. SAMUEL A. McCOSKRY.

THE REV. SAMUEL A. McCOSKRY, was born in Carlisle, November 4th, 1804, his father being an eminent physician of that place, and his mother a daughter of the Rev. Dr. Charles Nisbet, President of Dickinson College.

At the age of fifteen he was appointed a Cadet. As a student he had a good standing, ranking fourth in his class. He remained at the institution nearly two years.

The loss of Mr. McCoskry's brothers changed the direction of his life. He resigned, and became a student at Dickinson College. He entered the college near the close of the Freshman year, and graduated fourth in his class. He then studied law with Andrew Carothers, of Carlisle, and was admitted to the bar. After practising his profession one year. he was appointed Deputy Attorney General for Cumberland county, and held this office two years.

After practising law six years, Mr. McCoskry relinquished the Bar, and entered upon a course of Theological study under Bishop Onderdonk, of Pennsylvania. In one year he was called to be Rector of Christ (Protestant Episcopal) Church, Reading, Pa. After labouring a year in that charge, he was called to St. Paul's Church, Philadelphia. Here he remained two years, being consecrated, July 9th, 1836, Protestant Episcopal Bishop of Michigan.

Bishop McCoskry has presided over that diocese nearly forty years, and is now, by consecration, the oldest Bishop in the Anglican communion in the world, with one exception. His diocese grew to such an extent, that it was found necessary to divide it, and now there are two Protestant Episcopal Bishops in the State of Michigan. In Detroit there are ten parishes, and five missionary stations.

Bishop McCoskry is of tall, commanding figure, genial manners, cultivated tastes and decided character; he has ever enjoyed a large degree of popular favour. He is generally regarded as in sympathy with the "High Church" section of his denomination. He has done his work as Bishop well, and placed on the Church's register an excellent record.

WILLIAM T. SNODGRASS.

WILLIAM T. SNODGRASS, merchant, was born in Shippensburg, on September 17th, 1813. He was of Scotch-Irish descent. His father, William Snodgrass, was an extensive merchant in Cumberland county, and was a man of precision and sterling integrity.

At the age of thirteen he entered his father's store to be initiated into the routine of business, where he learned that systematic and prompt management of business matters which characterized him through life. At fifteen, he was left alone in Philadelphia, but, shunning evil associations, he spent his leisure time in study, and for five years it was his custom to devote three hours daily to mental culture. Starting with a capital of a few dollars, and refusing all aid from rich or poor relatives, by the power of his own industry, energy and merit, he rose to the highly creditable position which he occupied in the mercantile world. The fine building at the northwest corner of Ninth and Market Streets, Philadelphia, is a worthy monument to the ability of a man who carved out his own fortune, and educated to his business forty-nine young men. He never joined a club nor endorsed any paper outside of his business, which he made a life-time work, seeming fully determined to wear out rather than rust out.

Mr. Snodgrass was a member of the Board of Trade in the city in which he so long resided, and was a prominent and useful member of the West Arch Street Presbyterian Church.

Whilst Mr. Snodgrass was by birth, training and conviction, a Presbyterian, his religious sentiments were liberal, and he was strongly disposed to fraternize with and aid all evangelical Christians. Exacting as an employer, he placed every young man upon his own merit, but his active sympathy with all that concerned them drew them near to him and made them feel that in him they had more than a friend. To the world generally he was a pleasant, courteous and benevolent gentleman. He departed this life in the autumn of 1874, and his mortal remains now slumber in the beautiful cemetery of Laurel Hill.

INDEX.

	PAGE
HISTORICAL SKETCH	1-52
AGNEW, COLONEL JAMES	241
AGNEW, REV. DR. JOHN HOLMES	353
AGNEW, SAMUEL, M. D.	270
ALLEN, WILLIAM HENRY, M. D., LL. D.	394
ALLISON, REV. DR. PATRICK	312
ARMSTRONG, GEN. JOHN, SR.	75
ARMSTRONG, GEN. JOHN, JR.	84
ARMSTRONG, JAMES, M. D.	103
AUDENREID, COL. JOSEPH CRAIN, U. S. A.	397
BOGGS, JOHN, M. D.	215
BROWNSON, REV. DR. JAMES I.	391
BUCHANAN, HON. JAMES	231
BUCHANAN, REV. JAMES	300
CATHCART, REV. DR. ROBERT	98
CRAIGHEAD, REV. THOMAS	59
CRAIGHEAD, REV. JOHN	67
CRAIN, COL. RICHARD M.	96
CRAWFORD, EDWARD	239
CRAWFORD, MAJOR GENERAL SAMUEL WYLIE	436
CRAWFORD, REV. DR. SAMUEL WYLIE	160
CRAWFORD, WILLIAM, M. D.	107
CHAMBERS, GEORGE, LL. D.	139
CHAMBERS, BENJAMIN	53
CREIGH, REV. DR. THOMAS	281
CULBERTSON, SAMUEL DUNCAN, M. D.	288
CULBERTSON, REV. MATTHEW SIMPSON	371
DAVIDSON, REV. DR. ROBERT, SR.	112
DAVIDSON, REV. DR. ROBERT, JR.	341
DENNY, REV. DAVID	133
DENNY, MAJOR EBENEZER	92
DUFFIELD, REV. DR. GEORGE	87
DUNCAN, HON. THOMAS	204
DUNLOP, JAMES	373
ELLIOTT, DAVID, D. D., LL. D.	180
ELLIOTT, COM. JESSE DUNCAN, U. S. N.	219
ELLIOTT, MAJOR GENERAL WASHINGTON L., U. S. A.	408
FINDLAY, HON. WILLIAM	151
FINLEY, GENERAL CLEMENT A.	447
FISHER, REV. DR. SAMUEL R.	350
FOSTER, ALFRED, M. D.	257
FULLERTON, HON. DAVID	217
GIBSON, HON. JOHN BANNISTER, LL. D.	135
GRAHAM, HON. JAMES HUTCHINSON	327
GRIER, HON. ROBERT COOPER	325
GUSTINE, LEMUEL, M. D.	251
HAMILTON, HON. JAMES	213
HARBAUGH, REV. DR. HENRY	383
HERRON, REV. DR. FRANCIS	114
JOHNSTON, ROBERT, M. D.	177
JUNKIN, CAPTAIN JOHN	192
JUNKIN, JOSEPH	186
JUNKIN, GEORGE, D. D., LL. D.	195
KAUFMAN, HON. DAVID SPANGLER	402
KENNEDY, REV. ROBERT	167

INDEX.

	PAGE
KENNEDY, REV. JOHN H.	361
KENNEDY, THOMAS B.	446
KING, JOHN	178
KNOX, REV. DR. JOHN	254
KREBS, REV. DR. JOHN MICHAEL	358
LAIRD, REV. DR. FRANCIS	280
LANE, N. B., M. D.	297
LINN, REV. JOHN	276
McCARRELL, REV. DR. JOSEPH	235
McCLELLAND, HON. R. M.	328
McCLURE, COLONEL ALEXANDER KELLY	410
McCONAUGHY, D., D. D., LL. D.	120
McCOSKRY, RT. REV. SAMUEL A.	451
McCULLOH, HON. THOMAS GRUBB	310
McCULLOUGH, REV. DR. JOHN W.	320
McELROY, REV. DR. JOSEPH	209
McGILL, ALEXANDER TAGGART, D. D., LL. D	345
McGINLEY, REV. DR. AMOS A.	205
McKIBBIN, GENERAL D. B.	443
McKINLEY, REV. DR. DANIEL	330
McKNIGHT, REV. DR. JOHN	274
McLANAHAN, HON. JAMES X.	386
McPHERSON, HON. EDWARD	380
MOODEY, REV. JOHN	131
MOORE, REV. DR. THOMAS VERNER	375
NEVIN, MAJOR DAVID	284
NEVIN, JOHN WILLIAMSON, D. D., LL. D.	293
NISBET, REV. DR. CHARLES	108
PENROSE, HON. CHARLES BINGHAM	323
PENROSE, RICHARD ALEXANDER F., M. D., LL. D.	413
PENROSE, COL. WILLIAM McFUNN	449
POMEROY, JOSEPH	314
POMEROY, MAJOR JOHN M	418
RANKIN, WILLIAM, M. D.	333
RANKIN, DAVID NEVIN, M. D.	378
RAUCH, REV. DR. FREDERICK AUGUSTUS	338
REED, HON. JOHN, LL. D.	268
RICHARDS, JOHN CUSTIS, M. D.	404
RITNER, HON. JOSEPH	155
SANDERSON, HON. GEORGE	389
SCHNECK, REV. DR. BENJAMIN SHRODER	343
SCOTT, COLONEL THOMAS A.	369
SENSENY, A. H., M. D.	420
STEWART, JOHN	401
SHARP, REV. DR. ALEXANDER	229
SMITH, FREDERICK	278
SNODGRASS, WILLIAM T.	452
SNOWDEN, ISAAC WAYNE, M. D	441
SNOWDEN, JAMES ROSS, LL. D.	356
SPEER, REV. WILLIAM	202
STEEL, REV. JOHN	71
STEVENS, HON. THADDEUS	302
THOMPSON, REV. SAMUEL	62
THOMSON, HON. ALEXANDER, LL. D.	422
THOMSON, WILLIAM, M. D.	428
THOMSON, FRANK	432
WATTS, DAVID	94
WATTS, HON. FREDERICK	307
WATTS, HON. HENRY M.	315
WEIR, JAMES WALLACE	347
WILKINS, HON. WILLIAM	106
WILLIAMS, REV. DR JOSHUA	136
WILSON, REV. DR. HENRY R.	164
WILLIAMSON, HUGH, M. D, F. R. S.	80
WING, REV. DR. CONWAY PHELPS	366
WHITEHILL, ROBERT	65
WOODS, REV. DR. JAMES S.	261
WOODS, RICHARD	335
WOODS, DAVID FLAVEL, M. D	416
YOUNG, REV. DR. JOHN CLARKE	206

www.ingramcontent.com/pod-product-compliance
Lightning Source LLC
Chambersburg PA
CBHW060347080526
44583CB00012B/213